A. B. Ellis

A history of the Gold Coast of West Africa

A. B. Ellis

A history of the Gold Coast of West Africa

ISBN/EAN: 9783743318243

Manufactured in Europe, USA, Canada, Australia, Japa

Cover: Foto ©ninafisch / pixelio.de

Manufactured and distributed by brebook publishing software (www.brebook.com)

A. B. Ellis

A history of the Gold Coast of West Africa

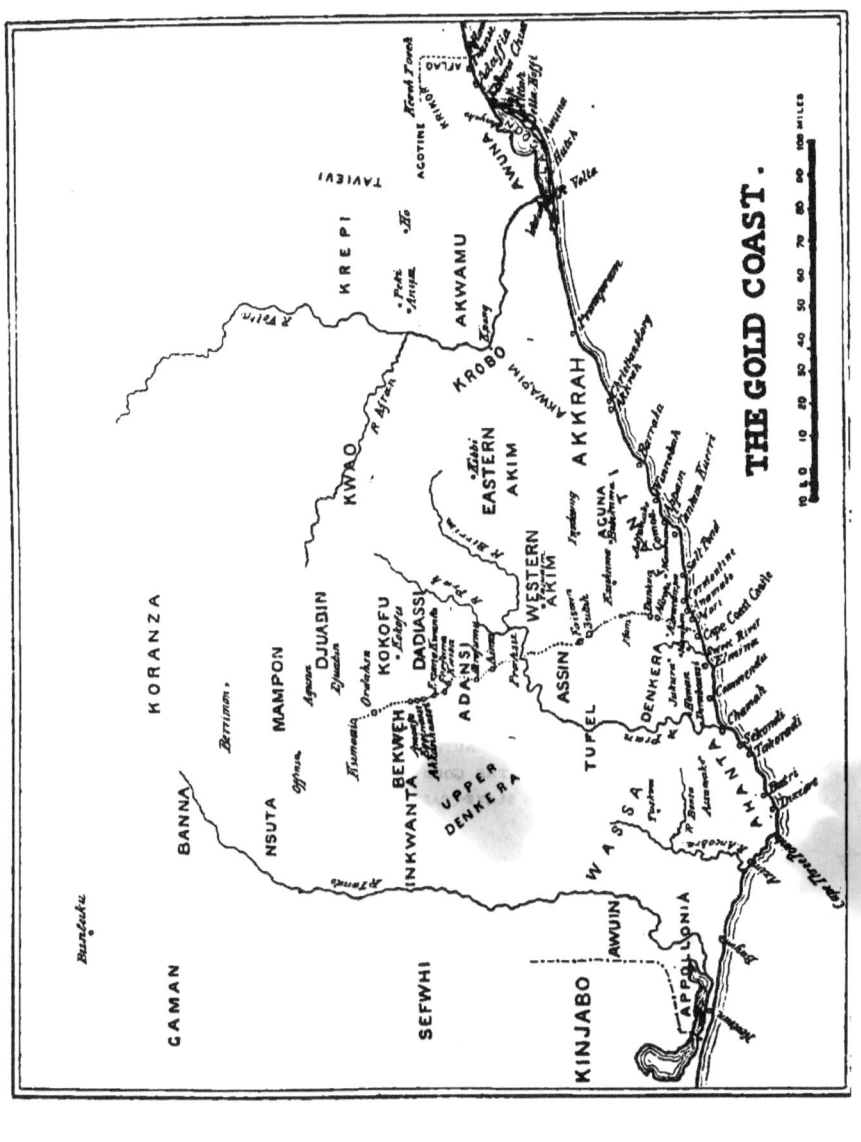

A History of the
Gold Coast of West Africa

BY

A. B. ELLIS,

Lieut.-Colonel 1st Battalion West India Regiment,

AUTHOR OF
"THE TSHI-SPEAKING PEOPLES OF THE GOLD COAST," "THE EWE-SPEAKING PEOPLES OF
THE SLAVE-COAST," ETC. ETC.

LONDON: CHAPMAN AND HALL, Ld.
1893.

[*All rights reserved.*]

CHARLES DICKENS AND EVANS,
CRYSTAL PALACE PRESS.

CONTENTS.

CHAPTER I.

West Africa as known to the ancients—Voyages of the Phœnicians—The Periplus of Hanno—Extent of his voyage—Expeditions of Eudoxus of Cyzicus—Traces of Phœnicians on the Gold Coast 1

CHAPTER II.

1393—1485.

The Portuguese discoveries in West Africa—Exploration of the coast—Formation of a settlement at Elmina—French claim of a priority of discovery 12

CHAPTER III.

1486—1594.

The Gold Coast under the Portuguese—Early English voyages—The voyages of Towrson—Adventures of a boat's crew—French trade on the Gold Coast—Reprisals of the Portuguese—Abandonment of the Gold Coast by the English and French adventurers—Native States on the Gold Coast at the close of the sixteenth century 24

CHAPTER IV.

1595—1642.

The Dutch commence to trade to the Gold Coast—They form settlements—Hostility of the Portuguese—Wars between the Dutch and Portuguese—Capture of St. George d'Elmina—Final expulsion of the Portuguese—Traces of their occupation . . 39

CHAPTER V.

1643—1668.

Return of the English to the Gold Coast—Growth of the slave trade—The English form settlements—Disputes between the English and Dutch—The Dutch seize Cape Coast Castle—Holmes's expedition to the Coast—De Ruyter's expedition—The treaty of Breda 48

CHAPTER VI.

1669—1700.

Formation of the Royal African Company—The Brandenburghers form settlements—Rebellion of the Elminas—Native wars—The voyage of Thomas Phillips—Capture of Christiansborg by the Akwamus—War between the Dutch and Kommendas—The English trade to Africa made open . . 62

CHAPTER VII.

1701.

Native States in 1701—European forts—*Personnel* of the Dutch establishments—Interlopers—Description of the Settlements—The trade in gold—Arms of the natives 74

CHAPTER VIII.

1701—1750.

Conquest of Denkera by Ashanti—The Elmina Note—Affairs in Ashanti to 1750—John Conny—Condition of the Royal African Company—The African Company of Merchants formed—The slave trade—Piracy on the Coast 85

CHAPTER IX.

1751—1804.

Affairs in Ashanti during the reign of Osai Kwadjo—First mention of Ashanti in the Records of Cape Coast Castle—War between England and Holland—Extraordinary affair at Mori—Reigns of Osai Kwamina and Osai Apoko II.—Accession of Tutu Kwamina—Position of Ashanti at the commencement of the nineteenth century 99

CONTENTS.

CHAPTER X.

1805—1807.

Disturbances in Assin—Condition of Fanti—First invasion of Fanti—Defence of Anamabo Fort—Torrane's convention—His dishonourable transactions—Continuation of the war—End of the invasion 107

CHAPTER XI.

1808—1818.

The Fantis attack Elmina—Message from the Ashanti King—Condition of the country—Rebellion of Akim and Akwapim—Second invasion of Fanti—Murder of Mr. Meredith at Winnebah—Third invasion of Fanti—The Fantis purchase a peace — End of the war—Embassy to Kumassi—Difficulty about the notes—Conclusion of a treaty—Gradual growth of British jurisdiction—The traffic in slaves 121

CHAPTER XII.

1819—1823.

New difficulty with Ashanti—Mr. Dupuis—His treaty—Skirmish at Mori—The Crown assumes the Government of the Gold Coast—Seizure of a sergeant at Anamabo—Expedition to Dunkwa—The Accras join the Government 137

CHAPTER XIII.

1823—1824.

The Ashanti invasion—Expedition to Essikuma—The Ashantis enter Wassaw—Sir C. Macarthy advances to meet them—Defeat and death of Sir Charles Macarthy at Assamako—Escape of Captain Ricketts — Movements of Major Chisholm's force — Sekondi burned — A camp formed on the Prah — Palaver with the Ashantis at Elmina—Release of Mr. Williams—His narrative . 151

CHAPTER XIV.

1824.

Effect of the Elmina palaver on the natives—Retreat from the Prah—Defeat at Dompim—A camp formed at Beulah—Action at Effutu—The Ashantis advance upon Cape Coast—Cape Coast attacked—Withdrawal of the Ashantis—Condition of the town—Outrage by the Elminas 167

CONTENTS.

CHAPTER XV.
1825—1829.

Major-General Turner—Advance of a second Ashanti army—Battle of Dodowah—Proceedings of Sir Neil Campbell—Peace negotiations—Blockade of Elmina—Further negotiations—The Home Government withdraws from the Gold Coast—A committee of merchants formed—Condition of the country . . . 179

CHAPTER XVI.
1830—1844.

Appointment of Mr. Maclean—Treaty with Ashanti—Expedition to Appollonia—L. E. L.—Her death—Charges made against her husband—Administration called in question—A commissioner sent out—The Crown resumes control—Domestic slavery—Missionary enterprise 195

CHAPTER XVII.
1844—1861.

Treaty with protected tribes—Death of Maclean—Expedition to Appollonia — Visit to Kumassi — Religious disturbances at Mankassim—A poll-tax agreed to—Formation of a local corps—Ashanti intrigues in Assin—Attempted invasion—Disturbances in the east—Siege of Christiansborg—The Krobo war . . 208

CHAPTER XVIII.
1862—1867.

Dispute with Ashanti—The Protectorate invaded—Engagements at Essikuma and Bobikuma—Military mismanagement—Native feeling—Mr. Pine's proposals—Expedition to the Prah—The Home Government puts an end to the operations—Effects of the campaign—Delusive proclamation—War with the Awunas—Ashanti intrigue in Awuna—Governor Blackall's treaty . 224

CHAPTER XIX.
1868—1869.

Exchange of territory with the Dutch—Native protests—Bombardment of Kommenda—The Fanti Confederation—Investment of Elmina—Fruitless negotiations—Condition of affairs in Ashanti—Palaver at Elmina—Dutch prisoners at Kommenda—Bombardment of Dixcove 243

CONTENTS.

CHAPTER XX.
1868—1869.

An Ashanti force sent to Elmina—Bloody march of Atjiempon—Affair at Elmina—Treaty with the Awunas—Ashanti invasion of Krepi—Mr. Simpson's adventure—Capture of German missionaries by the Ashantis—Hostages sent for their safety—Policy of the Government 256

CHAPTER XXI.
1870—1872.

Condition of affairs—Negotiations for the transfer of the Dutch possessions — Ashanti claim to Elmina—Affairs in Krepi—Negotiations for the release of the Europeans—Alleged renunciation of the Ashanti claim to Elmina—Further negotiations . 266

CHAPTER XXII.
1872.

Transfer of the Dutch forts—Mr. Hennessey's policy—Riot at Elmina—Question of a ransom for the Europeans—Palaver in Kumassi—War decided upon—Various messages—The captives sent to Fomana—Despatch of an Ashanti army—Causes of the war 275

CHAPTER XXIII.
1873.

Invasion of the Protectorate—Helpless condition of the Government—Defeat of the Assins—Actions at Dunkwa—Break-up of the allied force—Adu Boffo and Atjiempon—Distress of the Ashantis—Defeat at Jukwa—Arrival of Colonel Festing—Bombardment of Elmina—Action at Elmina—Condition of Cape Coast — Arrival of reinforcements — Unfortunate affair at Shamah—Cape Coast covered 285

CHAPTER XXIV.
1873.

Arrival of Sir Garnet Wolseley—Captain Glover's command—Sir Garnet's instructions—Palaver at Cape Coast—Expedition to the Elmina villages—The Ashantis break up their camps—Reconnaissances from Dunkwa—Defence of Arbrakampa—Amankwa Tia's retreat—Skirmish at Faisowa—Return of the army to Kumassi 299

CHAPTER XXV.

1873—1874.

Affairs in the West—Arrival of the European troops—Difficulties with the commissariat—The plan of operations—Captain Glover's proceedings—His trans-Volta campaign—Ultimatum sent to the King—Alarm in Kumassi—Release of the Europeans —Further correspondence with the King—Movements of the auxiliary columns 312

CHAPTER XXVI.

1874.

Battle of Amoafu—Attack of Kwaman and Fomana—Battle of Ordahsu—Kumassi entered—Incendiary fires—The King's palace—Messages from the King—Burning of Kumassi . . 325

CHAPTER XXVII.

1874.

Return march to the coast — Movements of Captain Glover's column—March of Captain Sartorius—Envoys from the King —The Treaty of Fomana—Adansi becomes independent—The trade in arms at Assini—The climate—Embassy from Kumassi —The Treaty signed—Treaty concluded with the Awunas—The Gold Coast made a colony—Abolition of slavery . . . 341

CHAPTER XXVIII.

1875—1881.

Affairs in Ashanti—Secession of Djuabin—Conquest of Djuabin by Ashanti—Fresh troubles in Awuna—Ashanti intrigues in Adansi—The Golden Axe—An invasion of Assin threatened— Protracted negotiations 354

CHAPTER XXIX.

1882—1886.

Gold Mining Companies in Wassaw—Human sacrifices in Kumassi —Quarrel between Ashanti and Gaman—Dethronement of Mensa—Rival factions in Ashanti—Election and death of Kwaku Dua II.—Renewed disturbances in Awuna—Disorganisation of Ashanti—War between Bekweh and Adansi— The Adansis driven across the Prah—Boundary Commissions . 370

CHAPTER XXX.

1886—1888.

Rival candidates for the stool of Ashanti—Raids made on Ashanti from the Protectorate—Effect of the unsettled condition of affairs upon British trade—War between Bekweh and Kokofu—The Colony intervenes to restore peace—Prempeh placed on the stool—Murder of Mr. Dalrymple in Tavievi—Expedition to Tavievi—Rebellion and defeat of Kokofu 386

A

HISTORY OF THE GOLD COAST OF WEST AFRICA.

CHAPTER I.

West Africa as known to the ancients—Voyages of the Phœnicians—The Periplus of Hanno—Extent of his voyage—Expeditions of Eudoxus of Cyzicus—Traces of Phœnicians on the Gold Coast.

It is a well-authenticated historical fact that frequent voyages were made from the Mediterranean along the Western Coast of Africa, both by the Phœnicians and the Egyptians, many hundred years before the Christian era; but considerable difference of opinion as to the extent of these voyages prevails, and it is not generally held that they were pushed as far south as the Gold Coast. There seems, however, fair ground for supposing that that part of Western Africa was not entirely unknown to the ancients, though it must be confessed the whole subject is involved in great obscurity. None of the writings of the Phœnicians, the greatest maritime people of antiquity, have been transmitted to us; but the numerous colonies which they established on the shores of the Mediterranean, and the Atlantic beyond the Straits of Gibraltar, attest the extent of their early voyages. Some of these colonies were founded between 1200 and 800 B.C., and it is morally certain that settlements would not be established at so great a distance from the parent state, until the seas had been frequently explored and become fairly well known. The accounts of the Phœnician discoveries furnished by other nations are very meagre, which may be accounted for by the fact that the Phœnicians, being jealous of foreigners participating in the advantages of their enterprises, were careful to keep them concealed. Everything relative to their navigation was not only a trade, but also a State secret; and Strabo records several instances of their anxiety to prevent other nations prying into their affairs. Hence most of these secrets perished with the downfall of the Phœnicians, and the conquest of Tyre by Alexander, and that of Carthage by Rome, was followed by a marked retrograde movement in the science of navigation.

The few facts that survived the destruction of these conquests have fortunately been preserved to our day. Thus Herodotus relates that the Carthaginians carried on a trade with an African people beyond the Straits of Gibraltar, with whom, however, they had no personal communication. On arriving at the territory of this people, they arranged their goods in a number of small heaps, and retired. The natives then came forward, placed opposite to these heaps the articles they were willing to offer in exchange, and then retired in their turn. If the Carthaginians were satisfied, they took away the offered commodities, and, if not, they carried away their own, and the trade was, for that voyage, at an end. This story has generally been regarded as incredible, yet Cada Mosto, who made a voyage to the West African coast in 1455 A.D., learned, at Cape Blanco, that just such a system of barter was carried on between the Moors of the kingdom of Melli, and a black people who lived in the neighbourhood of a great river; and Captain Richard Jobson, who made a voyage to the Gambia two hundred years later, mentions a similar system as existing some distance up that river. This would seem to show that the story of Herodotus was well founded.

Then there is the evidence concerning the circumnavigation

of Africa, which feat, according to Herodotus, the Phœnicians accomplished six hundred years before the Christian era. He says:* "Libya is everywhere encircled by the sea, except on that side where it joins Asia. Pharaoh Neco, king of Egypt, made this manifest. After he had desisted from his project of digging a canal from the Nile to the Arabian Gulf, he furnished a body of Phœnicians with ships, commanding them to enter the northern sea by the Pillars of Hercules and sail back by that route to Egypt. The Phœnicians, therefore, sailing from the Red Sea, navigated the southern ocean. At the end of autumn they anchored, and, going ashore, sowed the ground, as those who make a Libyan voyage always do, and stayed for the harvest. Having cut the corn, they sailed. Thus, two years having elapsed, they returned to Egypt, passing by the Pillars of Hercules; and they reported a circumstance which to me is not credible, though it may gain belief from others, that sailing round Libya they had the sun on the right."

The part of the narration considered by Herodotus incredible now furnishes the strongest presumption that Africa was really circumnavigated. At that time the existence of a southern hemisphere was considered impossible, and consequently the statement that the Phœnicians had, when rounding the southern portion of Africa, seen the sun to their right, that is to the north, was regarded as a mere invention; but it is exceedingly unlikely that the explorers would have invented a tale which was opposed to all the scientific knowledge of the age; and it is more reasonable to suppose that they did circumnavigate Africa, and reported a fact which they had observed.

The voyage of Sataspes, undertaken in the reign oi Xerxes, though it failed in its object, showed how confident the ancients were of the practicability of circumnavigating Africa. He, having been condemned to death by Xerxes, was reprieved on condition of making a voyage through the Straits of Gibraltar, and following the African coast until

* Melpomene, 42.

he returned by the way of the Red Sea. He sailed a considerable distance along the shores of Western Africa, and then returned home, where he suffered death. Indeed, the opinion that Africa was a peninsula, and that the Indian Ocean joined the Atlantic, appears to have been generally held by the Persians and the Egyptians; until, the science of navigation having declined, and the remembrance of former explorations having died out, Hipparchus, with his theory of seas separated into distinct basins, led the world into error, and caused the fragmentary accounts of the Phœnician discoveries to be regarded as mythical.

But of all the early attempts at maritime discovery of which we have any authentic accounts, the voyages of the two Carthaginians, Hanno and Himilco, along the coasts of Africa and Europe, are unquestionably the most important. These expeditions were undertaken when Carthage was at the height of its prosperity, and must therefore have taken place prior to the battle of Himera, which was fought in the year 480 B.C. Hanno was despatched by the Senate of Carthage to establish some colonies on the west coast of Africa. According to the Periplus, he had with him seventy-seven quinqueremes, together with a large number of women and children, and an ample supply of provisions and other necessaries. Passing the Straits of Gibraltar, he sailed two days to the southward, and anchored opposite a large plain, where he built a city called Thymisterium, on the banks of the River Marmora. Proceeding further to the south he built a temple, dedicated to Neptune, on a wooded promontory which he calls Soloeis, and which has been identified as Cape Cantin. Having doubled this cape, he built five other towns on the sea shore, at no great distance from each other. Continuing his southerly course, he passed along the shores of the Sahara, and, doubling Cape Blanco, colonised the island of Arguin, which he calls Cerne, and where the cisterns constructed by his colonists still attest to the enterprising spirit of the Carthaginians.

Still sailing to the southward, the expedition reached a river called by Hanno the Chretes. This they entered, and found that it opened into a wide harbour, containing several large islands. The hills in the neighbourhood were inhabited by black savages clothed in the skins of wild beasts, who drove away the voyagers with stones and other missiles. Not far from this was another great river, filled with crocodiles and hippopotami. Twelve days to the south of Cerne the Carthaginians came to a hilly country, covered with a variety of odoriferous trees and shrubs. The negroes of this coast were a timid race, and fled from the strangers. Seven days' further sail brought the expedition to a large bay, to which they gave the name of the Western Horn. In this bay was an island, on which they landed. During the day all was calm, but at night strange appearances presented themselves: the mountains seemed to be all on fire, and the sound oɩ drums and cymbals was mingled with strange cries. Terrified at these sights and sounds the explorers hastily embarked, and as they continued their course to the south, columns of flame still illumined the midnight sky. Sailing seven days along this coast they came to a bay, which they called the Southern Horn, and found within it an island with a lake, and in this lake another island, filled with savages of a peculiar description. The females were covered with hair and were called Gorillæ. The males fled across the precipices, and defended themselves with stones; but the Carthaginians captured three females. These, however, broke their bonds and fought so furiously that it was found necessary to kill them; but their skins were stuffed and brought to Carthage. The want of provisions prevented the explorers proceeding any further to the south.

The Periplus, which gives us the above account, is evidently an extract from or summary of some earlier account of the voyage, made by a Greek of apparently a much later age; and the imperfect manner in which the details of the voyage relating to time and distance have been transmitted to us, renders it extremely difficult to ascertain with precision how far it extended. Some geographers have confined it to the southern confines of Morocco; M. Gosselin determines

that Hanno never sailed further south than Cape Non, and
M. de Bougainville supposes the Western Horn to be Cape
Palmas, and the Southern Horn Cape Three Points. M.
D'Avezac limits the voyage to the River Ouro; while, on
the other hand, others have fixed the Cameroons Mountains
as the Southern Horn, Cameroons Peak as the Currus
Deorum, and Corisco, in the Bight of Benin, as the island
inhabited by gorillas. Most of these authorities, however,
had never visited the African coast, and were unacquainted
with the appearance of the various localities supposed to
have been reached; while many erred in applying the
word *keras* exclusively to promontories, whereas the Greeks
generally applied it to inlets of the sea.

Sir Richard Burton, whose intimate acquaintance with
the geography of West Africa entitles his opinion to respect,
appears to favour the supposition that the voyage extended
further than MM. Gosselin and D'Avezac suppose. Assuming the identification of Cerne with Arguin to be complete—
and the presence of Carthaginian remains in that island
supports that assumption—the first river met with to the
southward, the Chretes, would be the Senegal. There are
several islands in this river, which spreads out into a lagoon
inside the bar, notably the one on which the town of St.
Louis is built. There are hills in the neighbourhood, namely
those at Cape Verde. It is the first place at which, according to the Periplus, black people were met, and negroes
are not found north of the Senegal, which separates the
Djollof Negroes from the Moorish tribes. This seems to
fairly identify the Chretes with the Senegal, and the next
great river, filled with crocodiles and hippopotami, would
be the Gambia, which until very recently was remarkable
for the large numbers of those creatures which infested it.
From Cape Verde, north of the Gambia, to the peninsula of
Sierra Leone the entire coast is low, with the exception of
the Dubrika mountain; the mention therefore of mountains
in the vicinity of the large bay, to which the voyagers gave
the name of the Western Horn, seems to identify it with
Sierra Leone harbour, in the neighbourhood of which the

mountains of the Sierra Leone range attain in the Sugarloaf Peak a height of some 2,600 feet. The harbour, or bay, is the largest on the whole coast, and in the eastern branch of it, round Tagrene Point, there are several islands. The nocturnal fires observed by the voyagers were doubtless the bush fires, by means of which the negro inhabitants have been accustomed from time immemorial to clear the ground for cultivation. These bush fires are at times immense, and the country for miles round is seen illumined by advancing lines of flame, which well explains the sentence "fires continually issuing from the ground" in the Periplus. The sounds of drums and cymbals and the strange cries which so terrified the explorers, were no doubt caused by the nocturnal festivities to which the negroes are so addicted on moonlight nights.

So far this seems tolerably clear. The Senegal, the Gambia, and Sierra Leone are fairly well identified; but now the difficulties commence. Seven days from the Western Horn the voyagers arrived at the Southern Horn, where was the island inhabited by gorillæ. Now, there is no island on the whole coast between Sierra Leone and the Cameroons Mountains, except Sherbro Island, which, being only some forty miles from Sierra Leone harbour, cannot be supposed to be the one in question; and the voyage to Fernando Po, the island lying off the Cameroons Mountains, could not possibly have been accomplished in seven days. If then the voyage terminated at the Cameroons Mountains, many important details as to time and distance must have been omitted from the summary of the voyage which has descended to us.

The only attempt on the part of the Greeks to explore the West Coast of Africa was that made by Eudoxus of Cyzicus, who lived about 117 B.C. He was despatched by the successor of Ptolemy VII. on a voyage to India, and on his return, being driven by contrary winds to the East African coast, he there found on the shore, amongst other fragments of wreckage, the prow of a vessel, with the figure of a horse carved upon it. This relic, which he took with him as a curiosity, was exhibited in the market of Alexandria, and was there recognised by some pilots as belonging to a vessel from Cadiz. The smaller vessels belonging to that city, and which were employed in the fisheries along the West Coast of Africa as far as the River Lixus (Wadi al Khos), invariably had the figure of a horse carved upon the prow, and on this account were termed "horses."

The fact of the wreck of a vessel peculiar to Western Europe being found on the eastern coast of Africa, convinced Eudoxus of the possibility of sailing round the southern extremity of the African continent; and, proceeding to Cadiz, he equipped three vessels, one large and two of smaller size, and endeavoured to put his theory to the test. After sailing for some distance along the West African coast, the sailors, afraid of entering upon unknown seas, in spite of his remonstrances, forced him to beach his vessels. He soon contrived to reassert his authority, but it was found impossible to get the larger vessel afloat, and she became a total wreck. The cargo, however, was saved, and a third vessel, as large as a fifty-oared galley, having been constructed from the timbers of the wreck, the voyage was continued. Eudoxus at length reached a portion of the coast inhabited by negroes, Senegambia no doubt, and here, owing to the opposition of his crews, the voyage terminated, and he returned to Mauritania. Nothing daunted by this failure he shortly after fitted out another expedition, consisting of two vessels, and once more sailed to the south along the African shores. From this voyage he never returned.

The foregoing are all the accounts that have survived to our time of ancient exploration in Western Africa; from them it is fairly evident that Africa had been circumnavigated, but we have no direct evidence that any of the peoples of antiquity visited the Gold Coast. A variety of circumstances, however, lead us to suppose that the Phœnicians, or some other ancient nation, not only visited the Gold Coast but were accustomed to trade there, probably for the gold the country produced.

In Wassaw, one of the western districts of the Gold Coast, gold has been obtained in considerable quantities since the first occupation of the littoral by Europeans. The Portuguese built a fort at Axim to protect this trade, and the Dutch, who ousted the Portuguese, constructed for the same purpose two forts on the Ancobra river, which was the route to the gold-producing districts. The Dutch, towards the end of the last century, for some unknown reason, probably the hostility of the natives, abandoned these river forts and withdrew to the sea coast, with the result that the knowledge of the fact that extensive gold-fields existed in the interior gradually died out, or was only preserved in local traditions, which were regarded as half mythical. Some few years ago, however, the knowledge was accidentally revived, and the mineral wealth of the country having been ascertained by competent men, several mining companies were formed, and the country opened up in a way that had never been done before. Then it became apparent to the mining engineers that some other people had been there before them, in regions into which the Portuguese and Dutch had never penetrated. Many traces of ancient workings were found, in two cases at least consisting of tunnels, which had been driven into the bowels of the hills to follow up a gold-bearing vein. These were certainly not the work of the natives, who have never done more than dig pits for alluvial gold, and the discovery in one of these ancient workings of remains of antique bronze lamps, designed to hold a wick floating in oil, seems to point to some ancient nation as their author.

This supposition gains support from the fact that the aggry beads, the manufacture of which is a lost art, are only found in the western half of the Gold Coast, and chiefly in Wassaw. These beads, which were noticed in the possession of the natives by the earliest European explorers, are of two kinds, plain and variegated. "The plain aggry beads," says Bowdich,* who devoted some attention to the question of

---

* Mission to Coomassie, p. 218.

their origin, "are blue, yellow, green, or a dull red; the variegated consist of every colour and shade. . . . The variegated strata of the aggry beads are so firmly united and so imperceptibly blended, that the perfection seems superior to art. Some resemble mosaic work; the surfaces of others are covered with flowers and regular patterns, so very minute, and the shades so delicately softened one into the other and into the ground of the bead, that nothing but the finest touch of the pencil could equal them. The agatised parts disclose flowers and patterns, deep in the body of the bead, and thin shafts of opaque colours running from the centre to the surface. The colouring matter of the blue beads has been proved by experiment to be iron; that of the yellow, without doubt, is lead and antimony, with a trifling quantity of copper, though not essential to the production of the colour. The generality of these beads appear to be produced from clays coloured in thin layers, afterwards twisted together into a spiral form and then cut across, also from different coloured clays raked together without blending. How the flowers and delicate patterns, in the body and on the surface of the rarer beads, have been produced, cannot be so well explained."

As these beads are much valued by the negroes, various attempts have from time to time been made to imitate them, but without success. The natives regard them with a superstitious reverence, and declare that they dig them up; they have no tradition of whence they came, and the name "aggry" is an exotic word which no native can explain. Exactly similar beads have been found in ancient tombs in North Africa, in others in Thebes, and in parts of India; and when it is remembered that Sidon was famous for such work, it is not unreasonable to ascribe a Phœnician origin to them. It might well be that they were bartered by the Phœnicians with the natives for gold-dust, for they are only found in the gold-producing districts of the Gold Coast, and to this day the value of an aggry bead is always reckoned at its weight in gold-dust. What is certain is that the beads were introduced into the country from the sea, for, had they been brought overland, from Egypt for instance, some of them would certainly have been found in the far interior, which is not known to have ever been the case. And as the natives had these beads in their possession when the Portuguese first explored the Gold Coast, they must have been introduced there before the rediscovery of Western Africa by the nations of modern Europe.

CHAPTER II.

1393—1485.

The Portuguese discoveries in West Africa—Exploration of the coast—Formation of a settlement at Elmina—French claim of a priority of discovery.

IN the general relapse into barbarism which followed the downfall of the Roman Empire, the nations of modern Europe made but small progress in navigation, and voyages were undertaken merely along known coasts, and within sight of land. In the twelfth and thirteenth centuries discoveries were made in the far east, but principally by land, and it was not until the rediscovery of the Canary Islands, and the almost contemporary invention of the compass, that a fresh impulse was given to navigation.

Spain appears to have first taken the lead in the bolder spirit of enterprise which had now been awakened. In 1393 a Spaniard, named Almonaster, is said to have reached Lancerote in the Canaries; and, as a result of this voyage, about the year 1395, some adventurers of Andalusia, Biscay, and Guipuscoa visited the Canary Islands with a squadron of five ships, plundered all the populous districts, and carried off the King and Queen of Lancerote as captives, with about seventy of the inhabitants. In 1405, the dominion of the Canary Islands, together with the title of King, was granted by the King of Castile to a Norman Baron, Jehan de Betancourt, who in that year proceeded there, but met with little success in the conquest of the islands. It is worthy of note, however, that de Betancourt voyaged along the West African coast from Cape Cantin to the Rio d'Oro, beyond Cape Bojador, made some captives, gathered information respecting the harbours, and even projected the erection of a fort, to lay the country under contribution.

With the rediscovery of the Canary Islands the enterprises of the Spaniards, from some unknown cause, ceased, and the Portuguese came to the front. In 1412, John I. assembled a large armament at Lisbon, which was destined for an attack upon Morocco; and, while it was assembling, a few small vessels were despatched to sail along the West Coast of Africa to discover the unknown countries there. The Portuguese had, hitherto, although so near Africa, never ventured to sail beyond Cape Non, which promontory —the discoveries of Jehan de Betancourt being unknown— was considered an impassable boundary, and the limit of the navigable globe. The commanders of the vessels now despatched, more enterprising than their predecessors, doubled Cape Non, and coasted along the shore to Cape Bojador, 160 miles beyond it; but, fearing to pass that considerable headland, returned to Lisbon. Cape Non having thus been doubled, Cape Bojador became in its turn the fancied boundary of the globe; and a superstitious belief prevailed amongst mariners that whoever doubled it would never return.* They regarded with awe the rapid currents which swept round the cape, and the heavy surf which beats upon its arid coast.

Now, while the interior of northern and central Africa had thus been for many centuries a *terra incognita* to the nations of modern Europe, the successors of Mohammed had been rapidly extending their dominions over that continent. Although their knowledge of the actual western coast line probably did not at first extend beyond Cape Bojador, they had very early penetrated overland to the Niger; and, before the eleventh century, several states had been formed on the banks of that river, in which Moham-

---

* Mariana, Hist. Esp. lib. ii. cap. 22.

medans formed a numerous and the ruling part of the population. The principal of these states was that of Ghana, which has been identified with the modern Wangara; and next in importance was Tokrur, which appears to have been situated more to the east. To the south of these states lay the extensive forest country—then known as Niam-niam, or Lam-lam—on the outskirts of which the savage inhabitants were hunted by the Mohammedans of the Niger, and sold to the slave merchants of Barbary and Egypt. It has been observed that the Arabs have rarely been able to conquer except in countries in which cavalry can be used, and it was perhaps from this cause that the tribes on the seaboard, between the River Gambia and the Cameroons Mountains, secure in their vast and pathless forests, preserved their independence and their barbarism, while those on the plateaux of the interior, and in the territory now known as Senegambia, adopted the turban. The principal negroid state formed by these converts was Timbuktu, which was visited by the celebrated traveller, commonly called Ibn Batuta, in 1348, but whose foundation probably took place at least a century before that date.

In 1415 the town of Ceuta, on the African coast opposite to Gibraltar, was captured by the Portuguese, and Prince Henry of Portugal, the fourth son of John I., by Philippa of Lancaster, sister of Henry IV. of England, learned with astonishment from some Moorish prisoners who were there taken, that beyond the Sahara, to the south—beyond that supposed torrid zone or fiery belt, which offered an insurmountable barrier to communication between the peoples of the northern and southern hemispheres — there was a country rich in gold and ivory, fertile and populous. It was called by the Moors, who seem to have made special mention of the Djollofs of Senegambia, the "Land of the Blacks," and could be approached either by sea or land. To reach this country was now his sole waking thought. Immediately after his return from Morocco he retired to Sagres, near Cape St. Vincent, and, attended by the most advanced men of his nation, worked for the perfection of his scheme.

His first effort, made in 1418, was rewarded by the discovery of the rocky island of Porto Santo, one of the Madeiras; a ship which he had despatched, with orders to double Cape Bojador and sail on to the south, having been driven off the African coast by a storm and carried to that island. This success encouraged other commanders to venture boldly into the open sea, instead of as heretofore creeping along the coasts; but it was not until 1433 that Cape Bojador was doubled by a commander named Gilianez. On his return he reported that, contrary to the prevailing opinion, the sea beyond that cape was perfectly suitable for navigation, and the climate not inimical to man.

When, however, the explorers who followed Gilianez commenced to approach the torrid zone, the old fable of the Greeks and Romans that the heat there was so intense as to render life impossible, deterred their further progress for a time. Their own discoveries lent, in that age of ignorance, additional support to the old tradition. As they advanced to the south they observed men with black skins, which they considered to be the effect of the intense heat, and with short, crisp, woolly hair, which, to their minds, could only be due to the same cause. Even the furious surf, which they beheld increase in violence as they approached the equator, they attributed to the excessive heat of the torrid zone; which, they believed, made the very waves boil and seethe as they beat upon the shore. Returning, therefore, to Portugal, they represented to Prince Henry the impossibility of proceeding further into regions which the wisdom and experience of antiquity had pronounced to be unfit for the habitation of man, and in this opinion they were supported by the most learned men of their country.

But Prince Henry was not thus to be dissuaded from his cherished scheme, and in 1441 he sent Antonio Gonzales and Nuno Tristan to continue the exploration of the West African coast. The latter of these advanced as far as Cape Blanco, about three hundred and sixty miles beyond Cape Bojador, and kidnapped ten or twelve Moors. Some of these were persons of rank in their own country, and they promised liberal ransoms if allowed to return. In the following year, therefore, Gonzales was despatched to land the Moors at the spot whence they had been taken. As soon as the vessels arrived upon the coast, and it became known that the captives were on board, their friends assembled and paid the ransoms demanded. These were paid in gold-dust and negro slaves, and on this account Gonzales gave the name of Rio d'Oro to the arm of the sea in which the ship was anchored.

The negro slaves, about thirty in number, caused the greatest astonishment in Lisbon, and the gold-dust inflamed to a wonderful degree the spirit of adventure. In 1443, Tristan, encouraged by the reports of Gonzales, again sailed for the African coast, and discovered the island of Arguin; and, in 1444, the inhabitants of Lagos despatched six caravels, which are believed to have proceeded as far as the River Senegal; but, running short of provisions, were compelled to return, taking with them a number of unfortunate negroes whom they had kidnapped. In 1447 Prince Henry once more despatched Nuno Tristan, who advanced as far as the Rio Grande. Ascending this river in a boat, he was surrounded by some eighty natives in canoes, who, having probably heard of the kidnapping propensities of the white strangers, discharged several flights of arrows. Most of the Portuguese were killed, not one escaped unwounded, and Tristan died on board his ship from the effects of his wounds. Only four men were left in the ship, and these at last brought her home, after wandering about the sea for two months, for they did not know which way to steer. Alvan Fernandez, who prosecuted the next voyage, went forty leagues further than Tristan, when he also was attacked by the natives; but in the conflict the chief was slain, and the rest took to flight.

This hostility on the part of the natives, for which the Portuguese had only themselves to thank, rather damped the ardour of the discoverers, and it was not until 1462 that Sierra Leone was reached by Pedro de Cintra, who then pushed on to Cape Mesurado. The death of Prince Henry, in 1463, next checked all further progress for a time, and when, four or five years later, it was recommenced, the discoveries, instead of being a national work, became rather the business of private adventurers. Considerable importations of gold appear to have been made into Portugal by these men, and this raised such expectations from the African trade that, in 1469, the King was able to farm it to Fernando Gomez for a period of five years, in consideration of an annual rent of five hundred ducats, and an undertaking to extend the discoveries of the coast five hundred leagues to the south.

No detailed accounts remain of the several voyages that were made, but between the death of Prince Henry (1463) and that of Alphonso V. (1481) the Portuguese explored the whole Guinea Coast, including the Bights of Benin and Biafra. In 1470 Joao de Santarem and Pedro Escobar sailed past Cape Palmas, and proceeded as far south as the island of St. Thomas. On their return voyage they touched at a town on the Gold Coast, where they obtained such a quantity of gold that they named it La Mina (Elmina). Gold was also found at Shamah; and Fernando Gomez opened a gold mine at Approbi, near Little Commenda, called by the Portuguese Aldea des Terres.

On the accession of John II., in 1481, the exploration of the coast was resumed with fresh vigour. His revenues were largely derived from the importation of gold from Elmina and its vicinity, and one of his first cares was to improve and extend the Guinea trade. To effect this he gave orders for the construction of a fort and church at Elmina. All the necessary materials were shipped from Lisbon in a squadron of eight caravels and two transports, with five hundred soldiers and two hundred artificers and labourers. An experienced officer, Diego d'Azambuja, was placed in command of the expedition, and under him were Gonsalez de Fonseca, Ruy d'Oliveira, Juan Rodriques Gante, Juan Alfonso, Diego Rodriques Inglez, Bartholomew Diaz, Pedro d'Evera, and Gomez Aires, commanders of caravels.

All except the last-named were noblemen of the household of John II. Pedro de Cintra and Fernan d'Alfonso commanded the transports, and a small vessel attended the expedition as á despatch boat.

The squadron sailed on December 11th, 1481, and reached its destination on January 19th, 1482. At Elmina Diego d'Azambuja found a Portuguese named Juan Bernardo, who had come to the coast in search of gold, and as he knew the country and the language of the natives, he was despatched to the chief of the district to inform him of the arrival of the expedition and to arrange for a palaver. The name of this chief is given as Camarança, which, it seems probable, is a corruption of Kwamina Ansa. The Portuguese landed early in the morning of the day following their arrival, carrying their arms concealed upon their persons in case of treachery, and marched in great pomp to a large silk-cotton tree, near a native village, where a site had been selected for the intended fortress. This native village is, in the account left of the expedition, called Aldea; but that word simply means "village" in Portuguese, and there can be little doubt but that it was Oddena, the native town at Elmina. A flag bearing the Royal arms of Portugal was hoisted on the tree, an altar was built in its shade, Mass was celebrated, and prayers offered up for the success of the enterprise and the conversion of the natives. No sooner was this solemn farce concluded than Camarança was seen approaching with a numerous retinue, and Azambuja, who was sumptuously attired for the occasion and wore a rich gold collar, prepared to receive the chief in state, by seating himself on an elevated chair like a throne, and arranging his followers before him in two lines, between which the natives would have to pass.

The description given by De Faria of the latter is curious. They were naked to the waist, and wore round the middle monkey skins, or coverings made of palm-leaves. They were armed with spears, shields, bows and arrows, and wore a kind of helmet made of skin thickly studded with the teeth of sharks, which gave them a very warlike appearance. The legs and arms of the chief were covered with plates of gold, around his neck was a gold chain, and many small bells and tags of gold hung from his beard. He was preceded by a band playing upon rude instruments. The subordinate chiefs were distinguished by chains of gold hanging from their necks, and by the various gold ornaments worn upon the head and beard.

After the usual exchange of compliments and presents, Azambuja, through the medium of the interpreter, explained to Camarança the purpose of his expedition, using every argument to convince him of the power of the King of Portugal, and how necessary it was for him to seek his friendship, and consent to the meditated establishment at Elmina. He stated that the King's first desire was to instruct him in the Christian faith, but, says the Portuguese historian, De Faria, " I do not pretend to persuade the world our only design was to preach."

In reply, Camarança said he was fully sensible of the high honour done him by the King, and that he had always endeavoured to deserve his friendship by dealing justly with his people, and assisting them to obtain cargoes for their ships. The white men who had been there before had been poorly dressed and easily satisfied with the articles the natives had to give them, and so far from desiring to stop in the country, they had always been most anxious to get away as soon as possible ; but now there was a wonderful change. A number of richly-attired white men, persons of rank, "under the guidance of a commander who claims his descent from the God who created the day and the night," asked permission to build houses and remain in the country. But how could they live in such a poor place, where they would find none of those things to which they were accustomed? Moreover, disputes were certain to arise, therefore it would be better to remain on the same terms as before, by which their mutual interests would be preserved.

Camarança's diplomatic reply much perplexed the Portuguese commander, and it was only with great difficulty that he at last prevailed upon the chief to allow him to carry out his instructions without being obliged to resort to force. From the chief's fear of the possibility of disputes arising, it seems probable that some of the Portuguese adventurers who had previously visited Elmina had been guilty of excesses, which would well account for his disinclination to allow the white men to settle in his territory. In addition, the natives seemed to have held the belief that the Portuguese were a people, who, having no country of their own, were obliged to wander over the sea in ships, until they could dispossess some other people of their possessions. However, by promises, bribes, and an intimation that if permission were withheld it would be dispensed with, Camarança was ultimately led to acquiesce in the proposed settlement; the artificers and workmen were at once landed, and preparations made for the immediate commencement of the works.

Next morning, when the workmen were making preparations to lay the foundations of the intended fortress, they observed a large rock close at hand which would supply suitable stone for their work, and accordingly commenced to quarry it. It happened, however, that this rock was regarded by the natives as the sacred habitation of a local god, and, excited by the outrage, they attacked the workmen, wounding several, and driving them from their work. This commencement was not of very good augury, but the natives were finally appeased by presents and apologies, the workmen obtained building-stone from another source, and at length, after twenty days of constant labour, the fort began to assume a formidable appearance. On completion it was termed Sao Jorge da Mina, and in a chapel, consecrated within its walls, a solemn Mass was appointed to be celebrated annually in honour of Prince Henry, to whom the Portuguese owed their acquaintance with West Africa.

The fortress being completed, Diego d'Azambuja remained at Elmina with a garrison of sixty men, and sent back the fleet to Lisbon. He continued on the coast as Governor for two years and seven months, and then returned to Portugal.

At this point—namely, the first settlement of the Portuguese on the Gold Coast—it will be perhaps convenient to inquire into a claim, advanced by some French writers, of priority of discovery and settlement of the Gold Coast by France. It is said that in 1326 a French vessel, which was driven to the south of the Canary Islands in a storm, sighted the African coast, and that from this accidental discovery a regular trade was established between France and West Africa.

Villault, who made a voyage to the Gold Coast in 1666, appears to have been the first to put forward this claim. According to him, in the year 1364 the merchants of Dieppe made several voyages to Cape Verd, and as far south as a place which they named Sestro Paris, on the Grain Coast. In 1382 they, with other merchants of Rouen, sent three ships to make further discoveries along the coast, one of which, *La Vierge*, went as far as a town on the Gold Coast which, from the quantity of gold there obtained, the commander named La Mina. Next year they built a strong factory at this place, in which they left ten or twelve men; and as the trade increased they enlarged the factory and built a chapel. He says they remained in occupation of Elmina, or La Mina, until 1484, that is, till three years after the building of the fortress of Sao Jorge by the Portuguese; when, on account of the civil wars in France, their trade gradually declined, and they were ultimately forced to abandon all their settlements.

Villault also states that the French occupied Takoradi, Kommenda, Cape Coast, and Cormantine. He quotes no authority for this assertion, but, in support of it, says that the French names which he discovered on the Grain Coast, such as Petit Dieppe, prove that the French were the founders of those towns. This was, doubtless, true, but he was apparently ignorant of the fact that these settlements had been made on the Grain Coast by the Rouen Company about 1616, that is, fifty years before he wrote, and had afterwards been abandoned. The principal were Sestro Paris and Petit Dieppe; there is abundant evidence that they were founded after the year 1600, and the fact of the names being still retained in 1666 proves nothing with regard to the alleged French discoveries three centuries earlier. He also says that a battery in the Castle of St. George at Elmina was in his day called Bastion de France, which he considers as proof that the French built it; and that there was an inscription, illegible with the exception of the figures "13—," which he declares referred to the date 1383, when the French built a factory at Elmina.

These very slender grounds are those upon which the French claim was originally built, but several contemporary writers, for instance, Robbe and Ogilby, adopted Villault's views, and the latter repeated his story about the inscription and bastion at Elmina, almost *verbatim*. Barbot,* who in 1700 wrote his "Description of the Coasts of North and South Guinea," while noticing Villault's claim, is careful to say he places no credit in it; observing that it is strange no mention should be made of these facts by other French historians; and adding that such considerable undertakings, and so rich a trade, seemed to deserve a place in history, especially at a time when long voyages were regarded with dread, and as exceedingly perilous. He observes that Diego d'Azambuja saw no traces of previous occupation at Elmina in 1482, and he finally rejects Villault's testimony, and awards the honours of the first discoveries to the Portuguese.†

Notwithstanding this, Labat, in his "Nouvelle Relation de l'Afrique Occidentale," printed in Paris in 1728, revived the old French claim of priority of discovery, and supported it by what he called additional evidence. This was no other than an alleged Deed of Association, entered into between the merchants of Dieppe and Rouen in 1365, to carry on a trade with West Africa; but as this apocryphal document was said to have been destroyed, with all the archives of Dieppe, in the fire which consumed the Town Hall in 1694, it could not be produced; for, if it ever existed at all, it had ceased to exist thirty-four

* Agent General of the French African Company.
† Barbot, in vol. v. of Churchill's "Collection of Voyages," p. 10.

years before Labat wrote. It is worthy of note that among the archives destroyed in this fire was said to have been an account of a voyage, made by a native of Dieppe named Cousin, to the mouth of the River Amazon in 1488, or four years before Columbus discovered America. The French thus claim the honour of the discovery of the New World as well as that of the West Coast of Africa, and they must be regarded as peculiarly unfortunate in having lost at one blow the proofs of two such distinctions; for, in the absence of proof and of contemporary evidence, both stories can only be regarded as apocryphal.

The Portuguese indignantly deny the French claim, and point out that there were no traces of any former factory or fort at Elmina when Diego d'Azambuja founded the castle of Sao Jorge. On the other hand it has been argued that had he found any such traces, he would have carefully concealed the fact. But in that case, if the Portuguese had an interest in suppressing all proofs of a prior occupation, it seems incredible that, during the one hundred and fifty-six years in which they remained undisturbed in Elmina, they should have suffered to remain an inscription supposed to bear a date anterior to their own establishment there, and should have commemorated such a prior occupation by the retention of a former name of a portion of the fortifications. The Portuguese objections are sound, but perhaps the strongest proof of the mythical nature of the French claim is the silence of all French contemporary historians, and especially of De Serres and Mezeray, on the subject.

CHAPTER III.

1486—1594.

The Gold Coast under the Portuguese—Early English voyages—The voyages of Towrson—Adventures of a boat's crew—French trade on the Gold Coast—Reprisals of the Portuguese—Abandonment of the Gold Coast by the English and French adventurers—Native States on the Gold Coast at the close of the sixteenth century.

IN 1433, in order to secure the quiet possession of his African discoveries, Prince Henry obtained from the Pope, Eugene IV., a Papal bull, granting to Portugal all lands or islands which had been or might be discovered between Cape Bojador and the East Indies, with plenary indulgence to all who might lose their lives in prosecuting the discoveries. As these discoveries progressed, John II., impressed with the importance of his recent acquisitions of territory, added to his other titles that of "Lord of Guinea," and applied to the then Pope, Sixtus IV., for a confirmation of the grant that had been made to Prince Henry. The Pontiff readily complied, and in addition strictly prohibited all Christian powers from intruding within the limits which he had bestowed upon the Crown of Portugal.

In consequence of this prohibition, which gave to the Portuguese a positive monopoly of nearly half of the then discovered globe, but little is known of the proceedings of the Portuguese during the earlier years of their possession of the Gold Coast. The Papal prohibition was, it seems, scrupulously observed. In 1481, it being rumoured that two English merchant adventurers, John Tintam and William Fabian, were, at the instigation of the Duke of Medina Sidonia, preparing to make a voyage to Guinea, John sent Ruy de Sousa as an ambassador to Edward IV., to explain the Papal bull, and to call upon him to restrain his subjects from trading to the Portuguese possessions in Africa. As the authority of the Pope to dispose of kingdoms had not yet been called in question, the English King complied with the request, the projected voyage was prohibited, and the English were compelled for a time to abstain from profiting by the recent geographical discoveries.

In 1486, John II. bestowed upon the fortress of Sao Jorge de Mina all the privileges and immunities of a city, and a few years later he formed a Guinea Company, with the privilege of an exclusive trade to West Africa. This Company at first made a very considerable profit; it built a fort, named San Antonio, at Axim in 1515, and a small fort at Accra. A small depôt was also established at Shamah, at the mouth of the Rio San Juan, or Prah.* On the formation of the Company the King had reserved to himself the right of appointing a governor and other officers every three years, and it was by such appointments that he rewarded those who had served in arms against the Moors of Fez. Two fleets arrived on the Gold Coast from Lisbon each year, the first in April or May, and the second in September or October. They consisted, usually, of four or five vessels, which, after discharging their cargoes, remained a month or six weeks on the coast, refitting and taking in produce. The voyage out and back usually took from eight to nine months.

Of the dealings of the Portuguese with the natives in these earlier years we know nothing. It is said that they treated them with great cruelty; but as such stories were only related by the English, French, and Dutch, who were trying to oust the Portuguese from their possessions, they

---

* Prah, "The Sweeper."

must be received with great caution, and, as far as can be now ascertained, the natives appear to have been well able to take care of themselves. That the Portuguese had disputes with the natives is certain. Barbot mentions that, in the reign of King Emanuel, they erected a first fort at Axim, on a small headland near the native town, but were so harassed by the frequent attacks of the natives that they abandoned it and built Fort San Antonio, on a narrow, rocky peninsula, which was difficult of access. From this we may infer that the natives of the Gold Coast did not tamely submit to an appropriation of their territory by the Portuguese, and also that the latter were not sufficiently strong to extend their rule far from their fortified posts.

The Portuguese enjoyed the monopoly of the whole of West Africa until the Reformation entirely destroyed, in the eyes of those nations who had adopted the reformed religion, the validity of the Papal bull. The English were the first to avail themselves of the liberty thus obtained. In spite of the remonstrances and threats of Portugal, two ships, the *Primrose* and the *Lion*, manned with a crew of one hundred and forty men, and well armed, were despatched, under the command of Captain Thomas Windham, to trade on the Guinea Coast, in 1553. With Windham was associated a renegade Portuguese, named Antonio Anes Pinteado, who had taken service with the English, and this appointment of a colleague seems to have given umbrage to the English captain. He treated Pinteado with contempt, and because he recommended him to trade on the Gold Coast and to avoid the Bight of Benin, at once determined on going to the latter, where he and two-thirds of his crew died, scarcely forty men returning to England. The ships had, however, traded for a short time on the Gold Coast before proceeding to Benin, and had received gold to the weight of 150 lbs. in exchange for some of their wares, which so encouraged the English that the merchants of London despatched three vessels to Guinea, under Captain John Lok, in 1554. These vessels were the *Trinity* and *John Evangelist*, each of 140 tons, and the *Bartholomew*, of 90 tons. They met with no accident, traded along the coast, and returned with gold to the weight of 400 lbs., a quantity of "grains of Paradise,"* and two hundred and fifty elephants' tusks. Some negro slaves were also taken to England. The elephant seems most to have excited the curiosity of the English traders, and they brought home the skull of one, which, exclusive of the tusks and lower jaw, weighed over 200 lbs.

The towns visited on the Gold Coast in this voyage were Shamah, and Cape Korea or Cors (Cape Coast). At the latter was a native chief, who had been named Don John by the Portuguese, and with him the English established friendly relations. The adventurers found the natives sharp traders and great bargainers, and they advised all comers to treat them civilly, or otherwise they would not trade. Of the natives they say: "Their princes and noblemen pounce and raise their skins in diverse figures, like flowered damask. And though they go in a manner all naked, yet many of them, especially their women, are, as it were, laden with collars, bracelets, hoops, and chains, either of gold, copper, or ivory. . . . Some also wear on their legs great shackles of bright copper, which they think to be no less comely. They likewise make use of collars, bracelets, garlands, and girdles of certain blue stones, like beads. Some of their women wear on their bare arms certain fore-sleeves, made of plates of beaten gold; and on their fingers rings of gold wire, with a knot or wreath, like that which children make in rush rings."

The success of this voyage was so encouraging that a regular Guinea trade, carried on by private adventurers, was established, and continued without any remarkable event, although exposed to the continual hostility of the Portuguese. Of the voyages thus undertaken, the narratives of three, made by William Towrson, a merchant of London, in the years 1555, 1556, and 1557, give, perhaps, the best idea of the Gold Coast as it was at that time.

* Malaghetta.

The first voyage was made in the ships *Hart* and *Hind*, which, after trading on the Grain Coast for ivory and "grains of Paradise," proceeded to Cape Three Points, on the Gold Coast. They anchored off a native town, which appears to have been known to the English as St. John's Town, and they had at first some difficulty in establishing communication with the inhabitants, the Portuguese having the year before bombarded the town as a punishment for trading with the English; but eventually they succeeded in opening a trade. The English merchandise consisted chiefly of linen cloth and small basins, which they were able to exchange for gold-dust at a very profitable rate, since five basins were considered the equivalent of half an ounce of gold. The natives here wore caps of skin, and a cloth of native manufacture wrapped round the loins. This cloth, as well as their ropes and fishing-lines, was made, it is said, of the bark of certain trees, probably the palm. Their shields were also made of bark, very closely wrought; they were rectangular in shape, and sufficiently large to cover the whole body of a kneeling man. Their bows were short, "and pretty strong, it being as much as a man can do to draw them with one of his fingers." The bow-string was made of bark, flat, and about a quarter of an inch broad. The heads of their spears were made of iron, and Captain Towrson mentions that most of them carried great two-edged daggers of the same metal, exceedingly sharp, and bent "after the manner of Turkey blades." At this place the English learned that the Portuguese were in the habit of kidnapping natives, and keeping them in irons as slaves. There was said to be a garrison of sixty men in the castle of Elmina, and every year a large ship and a small caravel came from Portugal with supplies and reinforcements. From this it would appear that the Portuguese trade had already declined.

Hearing that Don John, the chief of Cape Coast, was at war with the Portuguese, Towrson proceeded thither, passing Elmina, where he saw the castle, and a white house, like a chapel, on the hill. Cape Coast then consisted, says Towrson, of about twenty houses only, and was enclosed by a wall, not above the height of a man, " made with reeds, or sedge, or some such thing." While the English were on shore trading here, they were attacked by a body of Portuguese. The natives had, it seems, warned them of the approach of the common enemy, but the warning had not been understood, and the Portuguese were almost upon them before they could reach their boat. They, however, succeeded in launching it under a fire from the Portuguese calivers, which injured no one; and after exchanging a few shots with their adversaries, returned in safety to the ships.

Next morning, finding that the Portuguese were still in the town, and that the natives dare not trade, they weighed anchor, and sailing about a mile further to the east, anchored off a town named De Viso Town, after its chief, John de Viso, who had been so named by the Portuguese. This town, probably that at Akwon Point, had only six houses standing, the remainder having been burned by the Portuguese. Proceeding again further to the east, they next anchored before a large town, which, from the description, appears to have been Cormantine. Here some of the English landed, but for a long time no natives came to them; then at last a chief came down, greeted them in a friendly manner, and endeavoured to engage their attention while a body of Portuguese approached in a hollow way. Fortunately the adventurers discovered this treachery before it was too late, and escaped to their boat, the Portuguese discharging, without effect, a piece of ordnance which they had brought up.

The natives of this town had formerly been friendly to the English, and had, in the previous year, offered Captain Lok land upon which to build a fort. Their hostility was now due to the fact that Gainsh, the captain of the *John Evangelist*, one of the vessels of Lok's adventure, had abused the trust of the natives by kidnapping four of the inhabitants of the town, one a son of the chief, and seizing the gold which they had brought on board his ship to trade with. After this misadventure the ships traded further to the eastward, taking large quantities of gold, and then returned to England. During the whole of their stay on the Gold Coast, a Portuguese brigantine had followed them from place to place, warning the natives to have no dealings with them. Nevertheless they appear to have obtained some 200 lbs. of gold, besides other commodities.

The second voyage was undertaken with the *Tyger*, 120 tons, and the *Hart*, 60 tons, both of London. They were accompanied by a pinnace of 16 tons, and took back with them the natives who had been kidnapped by Captain Gainsh. A little beyond the River de Sestos (Grand Sesters), they fell in with three French ships and two pinnaces. The two squadrons approached each other with sound of trumpet and with ensigns flying, and as the French ships had the weather of the English, the latter " waved to them to come under their lee and fight." But the French refused, and after some parley they decided to sail in company and defy the Portuguese, one of whose vessels, of about 200 tons, the French had already captured and burned.

Running down the coast the two squadrons passed the Portuguese fort of San Antonio, at Axim, and traded at a town named Hanta, beyond Cape Three Points, where they learned that there were five Portuguese ships and a pinnace at Elmina. Departing from this place they came to Shamma (Shamah), two leagues beyond, and went into the River Prah with five armed boats, expecting to find there some Portuguese. They landed here some natives of the place who had been kidnapped by Captain Gainsh, and were themselves very well received. The chief of Shamah appears to have been in some trepidation, fearing that the Portuguese would call him to account for having received the strangers, but the English promised to protect him, and to encourage him "ordered their boats to shoot off their bases and harquebuses. They likewise caused their men to land with their long-bows, and shoot before the captain (chief) and his people, who were much surprised, especially to see them shoot so far as they did, and assayed to draw their bows but could not. When it grew late they departed to their ships, for they looked every hour for the Portuguese."

They remained trading at Shamah for some days in the

following manner: "The twentieth, the English manned their five boats, and a great boat of the French, with their and the Admiral's men. Twelve of them had on their murrians and corslets, and the rest were all well armed. There were four trumpets, a drum, and a fife, and the boats were adorned with very fair silk streamers and pendants. In this order they went into the river and trafficed, their men-of-war lying off and on in the river to waft them, but they heard no more of the Portuguese."

On the seventh day of their stay at Shamah the natives warned the adventurers that the Portuguese ships had sailed from Elmina, and told them to be on their guard. The English said they were glad they were coming, and "to let them see they were serious, they sounded their trumpets, and shot off some guns." It took the Portuguese two days to beat up against the wind from Elmina, but on the afternoon of the second day five sail of the Portuguese were seen from the ships, which accordingly fired signal guns to call off their boats from the shore. By the time they had weighed anchor it was dark, but they lay close to the wind all night, and prepared for the fight. Next morning the Portuguese were seen riding at anchor off Shamah, and the combined adventurers bore up for them, the English all being furnished with white scarves so that the French might be able to distinguish them, if it came to boarding. However, the day passed without their being able to reach the enemy, and at nightfall they anchored within demi-culverin shot of them.

The following morning both parties weighed anchor together, and a running fight commenced. The Portuguese seem to have out-sailed and out-manœuvred both the English and the French, and their vessels, following in regular succession, riddled the largest French ship with shot; while the *Tyger* was unable to render any assistance, "because she was so weak in the side that she lay all her guns under water." The French commander, in trying to board the Portuguese, fell to the leeward; the other two Frenchmen would not close, the *Hart* was a long way astern, and the *Tyger* continued the fight alone. She followed the

Portuguese out to sea for two hours, when they tacked, and running down past the French commander's vessel, poured in each one its broadside, but dared not board because the *Tyger* was in close pursuit. As soon as the Portuguese had passed, the Frenchman crowded all sail and ran out to sea, where the other French and English vessels had already gone; but the *Tyger* continued the chase till nightfall, when she lost sight of the enemy.

The next morning the Portuguese were not to be seen; one of the French vessels had gone clear away, but the other two, with the *Hart*, remained. The French commander's ship had lost nearly half its men, and as they were afraid of remaining in that neighbourhood, the allies sailed further to the east along the coast. They traded at Mowra (Mori) and Lagoua (Leggu), but apparently with little success, and in consequence started to return to the west. But off Elmina they descried two large ships, one of 200 and one of 500 tons, which had just arrived from Portugal, and so put out to sea to escape. The Portuguese followed in chase for some time, but finally drew off, and the English ships then returned to the Grain Coast, and sailed to England, which they reached in safety, beating off a French ship that attacked them off the coast of Portugal.

The third voyage was undertaken with the *Tyger*, the *Minion*, the *Christopher*, and a pinnace named the *Unicorn*. They ran down the Grain Coast as before, and had commenced a trade on the Gold Coast at Hanta, when they met five sail of the Portuguese. A running fight ensued, and the English ships, standing out to sea, proceeded to Leggu, which is close to Tantamkwerri. There they learned that there were four French ships between Winnebah and Barraku, and, there being then war between France and England, they sailed to attack them. They surprised three French ships at anchor, two of which put out to sea and escaped; but the third, the *Mulet de Batuille*, a vessel of 120 tons, was captured, and in her 50 lbs. of gold was taken.

The English then traded at the various villages as far as Accra, when six men having died of fever, and a great many being sick, they returned to Cape Coast. There, however, the natives, formerly so friendly, refused to trade. They ran away into the woods, and the English returned to their ships, carrying off some goats and fowls. At Mori also they met with a hostile reception, and the natives stoned the men who attempted to land. Next day, to revenge this, the English returned in greater force, and, forcing a landing, killed and wounded several natives, burned the town, and destroyed all the canoes. There being nothing to be done on this part of the coast, the adventurers next proceeded to Shamah, where they hoped to revictual their ships, which were now short of provisions. But the chief of Shamah had come to terms with the Portuguese, and refused to trade or supply the ships; and the boats which were sent to Hanta for supplies came back equally empty. In revenge, the adventurers landed and burned Shamah, and then quitted the coast. Contrary winds at first carried them as far south as the Island of St. Thomas; but they eventually succeeded in reaching England in safety.

The high handed proceedings of the merchant adventurers in this last voyage were hardly calculated to cause the natives to regard the arrival of other English vessels with pleasure, and we find that the *Minion* and *Primrose*, which sailed for Guinea from Dartmouth, in February, 1562, were unable to trade at all upon the Gold Coast. Both at Cape Coast and at Mori the English were attacked by two Portuguese galleys from Elmina. At the second place the Portuguese were further assisted by a ship and a caravel, and the *Minion* was severely handled, her foremast being shot away. During the engagement a barrel of powder exploded, wounding most of the gunners of the *Minion*, and she was so disabled that she might have been easily captured; but the Portuguese drew off, and she and her consort at once ran out to sea and returned to the Grain Coast.

The following year, 1563, three more English ships, the *John Baptist*, *Rondel*, and *Merlin*, sailed for Guinea. This voyage is chiefly remarkable for the adventures of a boat's crew of nine men, who became separated from their vessels in a storm. The three ships were driven out to sea by a tornado, at a time when the boat was lying off a town on the Grain Coast, trading; and next day, when they beat back to the land, as they saw nothing of the boat, they concluded it was lost, and returned to England. The boat, however, had gone to the eastward, in which direction it was imagined the ships would be. For days the castaways followed the shore, exchanging here and there portions of their merchandise for food; but, generally, they found the coast "nothing but thick woods and deserts, full of wild beasts," especially elephants, which came down to the seashore in herds and frolicked in the water. At last, overcome with fatigue, and despairing of ever finding their ships, they decided to surrender themselves to the Portuguese, the prospect of being chained to the oars as galley-slaves at Elmina, being less appalling to them than the unknown evils they might experience at the hands of the natives. Neither alternative was pleasant; but necessity demanded a choice. For twenty days they had been cramped in an open boat, they had nearly lost the use of their legs, and "their joints were so swollen with the scurvy that they could scarce stand." By day they had been exposed to the burning rays of a tropical sun, and at night they had been drenched by frequent showers. They were, moreover, half-starved, and had frequently been without food for three days at a time.

They were making for Elmina in order to surrender, when they found themselves one morning off a fort, with a watch-house upon a rock, and a large black cross of wood standing near it. This was Fort San Antonio, at Axim, of whose existence they seem to have been ignorant. Some Portuguese showed themselves on shore, waving a white flag in sign of peace and signing to them to land;

and the castaways were pulling to the shore in response to this invitation, when they were suddenly saluted by a furious discharge from all the guns of the fort. The balls fell thickly about the boat, but fortunately none touched it, and the English rowed as fast as they could to the shore, shouting that they surrendered. When under the walls of the fort they were sheltered from the fire of the guns, which could not be depressed sufficiently to cover them; but showers of heavy stones were rained down into the boat from the battlements, and the natives came running down and discharged several flights of arrows, which wounded some of the English. The latter were naturally full of indignation at this perfidious conduct on the part of the Portuguese; and, burning to revenge themselves, they pushed off to a little distance from the shore, where they were still safe from the guns of the fort, and opened fire with their bows and harquebuses upon the natives and the Portuguese. After killing or wounding several, they rowed away, passing through another furious fusillade from the guns of the fort unscathed, and escaped out to sea.

The castaways now determined to place themselves in the hands of the natives, and eventually landed near Grand Bassam. There was still a considerable quantity of merchandise in the boat, and as they handed this over to the chief of the place they were well treated for a few days. Then, as the natives found there was no more profit to be made from them, they gradually neglected them, and the castaways were reduced to such extremities by hunger and exposure, that in a few weeks six out of the nine died. The three survivors dragged on a miserable existence for some time, and were at last rescued by a French ship.

The French soon followed the example of the English in breaking in upon the Portuguese monopoly of the trade to Guinea. Some writers, indeed, are of opinion that the French took the initiative, but all the evidence tends to show that they made no voyages to the Guinea coast till between 1554 and 1555; that is to say till a year or eighteen months after the English had commenced a Guinea trade. Even the voyages made in those and the succeeding years were few and far between, and it was not until the reign of Henry III. of France (1573-1589) that the French regularly frequented the West African coast.

The Portuguese, finding that their profitable trade was sadly crippled by the English and French adventurers, who offered their wares at a cheaper rate to the natives, did everything in their power to drive them from the coast. They forbade the natives to have any dealings with the adventurers, and, as we have seen from Towrson's voyages, they punished a neglect of this prohibition, whenever possible, by destroying the native towns and villages. As the ships of the adventurers were generally better armed and manned than the small vessels they themselves had on the Gold Coast, two large vessels were sent out from Portugal, for the purpose of capturing and destroying them, and several galleys were stationed at Elmina. With these they captured several ships, both French and English, and condemned the crews to perpetual servitude as galley-slaves. Amongst others thus taken was *La Esperance*, which was captured and sunk in 1582, a large number of the crew being barbarously put to death, and the survivors sent to Elmina in irons. A reward of one hundred crowns was promised for every English or French head, and many of both nations were treacherously invited to land by the natives, and then murdered.

These severe measures soon had the effect desired, and the adventurers gradually ceased to frequent the Gold Coast. At Accra the French met with some little success. The inhabitants of that place, provoked by the tyranny of the Portuguese, surprised their small fort in 1578, massacred the garrison, and invited the French to form a settlement. This they endeavoured to do, but the persistent hostility of the Portuguese rendered their ventures so profitless that they soon abandoned it, and before long entirely gave up any further trade with the Gold Coast. The English similarly found that the risks of a trade in the vicinity of the Portuguese establishments were too great to be lightly incurred; and finding it impossible to cope with the Portuguese, they abandoned the Gold Coast and turned their attention to the Sierra Leone coast and to Benin, where they could trade unmolested. To encourage commerce with Africa, Queen Elizabeth, in 1588, granted a patent to a company of merchants in Exeter to carry on a trade to Senegal and Gambia; and in 1592 a second patent was obtained granting a trade from the Rio Nunez to the south of the peninsula of Sierra Leone. These concessions had the effect of completely diverting the attention of the English merchant adventurers from the Gold Coast, and as the French had already ceased to frequent that portion of West Africa, for the next few years the Portuguese remained practically undisturbed.

At this point it will perhaps be convenient to enumerate the Native States on the littoral of the Gold Coast at the close of the sixteenth century, to several of which it will be necessary to refer when describing the steps taken by the Dutch to establish themselves in the vicinity of the Portuguese. There were then eleven States on the seaboard, which, commencing from the west, were as follows: Axim, Ante (Ahanta), Adom, Jabi, Commani (Kommenda), Fetu, Saboe, Fantyn (Fanti), Akron, Aguna, and Accra. Axim extended from the Ancobra River to the village of Akwidah, Ante (Ahanta) from the latter to Zaconde (Sekondi), Jabi from Zaconde to the mouth of the Prah, and Commani (Kommenda) from the Prah to the mouth of the River Beyah, at Elmina. The territory of Fetu lay between the Beyah and Queen Anne's Point, that of Saboe between the latter and the Iron Hills, and that of Fantyn (Fanti) between these and Salt Pond. Akron lay between Salt Pond and the Devil's Mount, the Monte de Diablo of the Portuguese, and Aguna between that eminence and the village of Barraku,* while the kingdom of Accra extended to the east from Barraku as far as Ningo. Of the inland States nothing appears at this time to have been known.

* Barraku is the name of a bird.

CHAPTER IV.

1595—1642.

The Dutch commence to trade to the Gold Coast—They form settlements—Hostility of the Portuguese—Wars between the Dutch and Portuguese—Capture of St. George d'Elmina—Final expulsion of the Portuguese—Traces of their occupation.

IT was not until the year 1595 that the Dutch began to make trading voyages to West Africa. It appears that their attention was first directed to the Guinea trade by a certain Bernard Ericks, or Erickson, who, having been captured at sea by the Portuguese, had been carried by them as a prisoner to Prince's Island, in the Bight of Biafra, where he learned many particulars concerning the Gold Coast. The reported richness of that part of the African continent in gold seems to have excited his imagination, and on returning to Holland he offered to attempt a voyage. Some merchants, influenced by his representations, furnished a ship and a suitable cargo, and in 1595 Erickson performed the voyage successfully, and returned in safety. This was the commencement of a regular trade to Guinea on the part of the Dutch, and which prospered in spite of the continued hostility of the Portuguese.

The Dutch, unlike the English and French, were not satisfied with a mere haphazard trade along the coast, and before long they sought to establish trading posts on the land. To this end they skilfully fomented quarrels between the natives and the Portuguese, and frequently allied themselves with the former. This was, indeed, no new feature in West African politics. The English had also encouraged the natives to rebel, promising them protection and assistance, and had then, after completing their cargoes, returned to England and left their allies to bear the whole brunt of the anger of the Portuguese. This conduct had naturally made the natives rather chary of entering into alliances with other Europeans against the Portuguese, and the Dutch seem at first to have met with little encouragement in their designs; but after some time they succeeded in inducing the King of Saboe to rebel, and as an earnest of their intention to continue to extend their protection to him, built, shortly before 1599, a small fortified trading "lodge" at Mori, in the kingdom of Saboe. Having thus obtained a footing on the coast, they rapidly extended their influence, and before long they succeeded in establishing other "lodges" at Butri and Cormantine.

This, of course, was not effected without opposition on the part of the Portuguese. They represented to the natives that the Dutch were mere slave-hunters, kidnappers of men, a trade in which, as we have seen, they were themselves adepts, and they offered a reward for every Dutch ship or Dutchman's head that might be taken. According to the Dutch, they aided and abetted the natives in every kind of treachery, and several Dutchmen were enticed ashore at various places and murdered. In 1596 they seized a Dutch vessel at Cape Coast, killed most of the crew, and sent the rest to the galleys, where all of them soon died. In 1598, assisted by the natives, they surprised and massacred the crew of a Dutch barque at the same place, and in 1599 they seized five Dutchmen from Mori, who were becalmed in a small boat off Elmina, struck off their heads and placed them on the castle walls as an example to others. In revenge for this last outrage the Dutch instigated the people of Commani (Kommenda) and Fetu to rise against the Portuguese. They assisted the natives with arms and ammunition, and it is said that the Portuguese lost some three hundred men in the war that ensued, but probably most of these were natives. The Portuguese succeeded in bringing the natives of Fetu to terms, but those of Commani achieved their independence, and as a result the Dutch formed a new "lodge" at Kommenda.

No doubt one reason why the Dutch succeeded where the English and French had failed was that the formation of trading posts satisfied the natives that they had no desertion to fear on the part of their allies; but the principal cause was that the Portuguese establishment on the Gold Coast had been much reduced, but for which it is doubtful if the Dutch would have succeeded in obtaining a footing. The decline of the Portuguese settlements dated from 1580, when, Portugal having become a province of Spain under Philip II., the African colonies were gradually neglected in favour of those of the New World; and they were still further reduced under the weak Philip IV., who came to the throne in 1621. By that time the Dutch trade had utterly ruined that of the Portuguese on the Gold Coast, for the former were able to sell goods on the coast cheaper than the latter could buy them in Lisbon; and the King, at whose expense the garrison and establishment at Elmina was kept up, finding that the trade now hardly covered his expenditure, reduced the garrison and limited the supplies. Not more than one or two ships a year sailed to Elmina from Portugal, the force on the coast was too small for the Portuguese to do more than maintain their authority in the towns under the guns of their forts, the Native States threw off their allegiance, and the whole trade was soon engrossed by the Dutch, who became virtually masters of the whole of the Gold Coast, except Elmina and Axim.

To strengthen their position, the Dutch, about 1620, commenced transforming their "lodge" at Mori into a fort. It was completed in the year 1624, and Adrian Jacobs was placed in command of it. The year following, the garrison of Elmina being reported to be much reduced by sickness, they made a bold attempt upon it with twelve hundred of their own men, and one hundred and fifty Saboe natives. The force, which was under the command of Jan Dirks Lamb, landed at Terra Pequena, or Ampeni, to the west of Elmina, in the kingdom of Commani; but before the troops had time to form up, they were furiously attacked, at sunset, by the natives of Elmina, and utterly defeated. The Dutch lost 373 soldiers, 66 seamen, most of their officers, and all the Saboe contingent. Lamb himself was wounded, and was only rescued with difficulty by the people of Little Kommenda. This repulse seems to have rather cooled the ardour of the Dutch, and no further attempt to oust the Portuguese was made for some years.

About 1631 the States General of Holland made over Fort Nassau at Mori, and their trading "lodges" at Butri and Kommenda, to the Dutch West India Company, and the latter appointed as their Director-General in Africa Nicholas Van Ypren, a man who proved most indefatigable in his endeavours to drive the Portuguese from the Gold Coast. By presents and promises he induced the Kings of the contiguous native kingdoms to enter into an agreement to assist the Dutch to capture Elmina, whenever a favourable opportunity presented itself; and, having thus paved the way for a fresh attempt upon the Portuguese stronghold, he suggested to the directors of the Company the advisability of sending a force to the coast. This suggestion was favourably received, and instructions were sent to Count Maurice, of Nassau, who, with a fleet of thirty-two sail, twelve of them men-of-war, carrying 2,700 soldiers, was then engaged in attacking the Portuguese in Brazil, to detach such ships as he could spare to the Gold Coast.

Count Maurice sent a fleet of nine sail under Colonel Hans Coine, which arrived at Cape Lahou, on the Ivory Coast, on June 25th, 1637. From this place Coine sent notice of his arrival to Van Ypren, and then proceeded to Assini. Van Ypren requested Coine to sail to Kommenda, the natives of which kingdom were the chief supporters of the Dutch, and on his arrival there met him with two hundred canoes full of native auxiliaries. Thence the flotilla proceeded towards Cape Coast, and on July 24th the force landed in a little creek about half a mile to the west of the Cape, which must have been the present salt-pond, or lagoon, at Cape Coast, though it is now separated from the sea by a ridge of sand. The army, which moved in three bodies, consisted of 800 soldiers and 500 seamen, carrying provisions for three days, and the native auxiliaries, who probably amounted to five or six thousand.

Advancing towards Elmina, they halted at the River Dana, or Dolce (Sweet River), to refresh; and Coine, who brought up the rear, being informed that a body of a thousand Elminas was posted at the foot of the hill of St. Jago, to prevent its capture—for it commanded the Castle —detached four companies of fusileers to beat them off. These four companies were cut to pieces by the Elminas, who struck off the heads of the slain and carried them in triumph into the town; but a second Dutch detachment, sent under Major Bon Garzon, fared better. Fording the River Dana while the majority of the enemy were still celebrating their victory in the town of Elmina, he dispersed the few natives who remained and carried the position with the loss of only four whites and ten native allies. The Elminas and Portuguese made two attempts to recover the position, but were on each occasion repulsed with loss, and on the remainder of the Dutch force coming up, the Portuguese retired into a small redoubt which they had built on the summit of the hill. The only path to this redoubt lay on the side of the hill opposite to the Castle, and was swept by its guns; but the Dutch rapidly cut paths through the thick bush on the northern slope, and the redoubt was soon carried. A mortar and two pieces of cannon were then brought up, and from that commanding position a fire was opened upon the Castle, while a detachment of Kommenda natives was sent to attack the western end of the town of Oddena. This latter body met with little success, and would indeed have been defeated, but for the skilful manner in which the Dutch officers kept the force covered by the River Beyah.

Next day the Dutch advanced to the assault of the town, from which the heavy fire of the guns of the Castle compelled them to retire; but the day following, at daybreak, Coine summoned the Castle to surrender, threatening to put the garrison to the sword if any further resistance were offered. The Portuguese Governor demanded three days' truce, ostensibly to consider the terms, but really to gain time; but Coine, who could not afford to wait, as he had only provisions for that day, refused this, and, drawing up his forces on St. Jago, continued the bombardment, though with but little effect. Next morning, being obliged to endeavour to take the place by assault or abandon the attempt, he ordered the grenadiers to advance, and the Portuguese at once beat the chamade, and sent out two persons to arrange the terms of capitulation. These were finally settled as follows:

1. The Governor, garrison, and all other Portuguese to march out that day, with their wives and children, but without swords, colours, or any weapons, each person being allowed but one suit of wearing apparel.

2. All the goods, gold, merchandise, and slaves to be handed over to the Dutch, with the exception of twelve slaves allowed to Portuguese officials.

3. The church furniture, which was not of gold or silver, to be allowed to be carried away.

4. The Portuguese and mulattos to be put on board the squadron, with their wives and children, and conveyed to the Island of St. Thomas.

Barbot says the Castle surrendered on August 29th, 1637; but this is probably a mistake for July 29th, as the Dutch force landed on July 24th. The Dutch found little gold or merchandise, but a large quantity of gunpowder, and thirty brass guns. At the time of the capture, the Portuguese establishment was very much reduced, which accounts for the easy surrender of a place considered so strong. It appears to have consisted of a Governor, a chaplain, a *viedor*, or chief factor, a King's *procurador*, or judge, the captain of the soldiers, and a chief clerk. The soldiers were criminals, who had been banished to Africa for life; their number did not exceed thirty, and a large proportion of them were sick. The defence of Elmina had chiefly been undertaken by the natives, some seven hundred of whom had been drilled and disciplined by the Portuguese, and it has been insinuated that the latter exhibited great want of spirit in surrendering so tamely. But what could the white garrison of thirty men, even supposing they were all fit for duty, have effected against Coine's force of thirteen hundred Europeans?

After the reduction of Elmina Van Ypren returned to Mori with his forces, leaving Captain Walraeven with a garrison of one hundred and forty men in the Castle of St. George. He sent a cartel to the commandant of Fort St. Anthony, at Axim, informing him of the fall of Elmina, and summoning him to surrender; but the latter replied that he would defend the place to the last extremity. It is not clear why the Dutch commanders did not take advantage of the presence of their large force on the coast to reduce this last stronghold of the Portuguese, which was in strength far inferior to St. George d'Elmina; but Coine returned to Brazil with his fleet, without making any attempt upon it, and it was not until January 9th, 1642, that Fort St. Anthony was captured by the Dutch.

After Coine's departure Van Ypren took up his residence at Elmina, which, henceforward, became the chief post of the Dutch upon the Gold Coast. They considerably enlarged and improved the Castle, and for its protection built Fort Conraadsburgh on the hill of St. Jago, on the site formerly occupied by the small redoubt of the Portuguese. The garrison of this new work consisted of an ensign and twenty-five men, who were relieved from St. George daily.

It has often been asserted that the Dutch attack on Elmina was unjustifiable, on the grounds that, in 1637, there was no war between the Netherlands and Portugal. This is, however, a mistaken view. There was no kingdom of

Portugal in existence in 1637, for, since 1580, when Philip II. laid violent hands upon it, Portugal had been a province of Spain, and Holland and Spain were the deadliest foes. The acknowledgment of the independence of the United Provinces, which the House of Nassau had succeeded in wringing from Philip III., was repudiated by Philip IV. when he renewed the war with Holland in 1621. On land the Spaniards, under Spinola, gained some advantages, for the Dutch soldiery could not stand against the veteran Spanish infantry, then the best in Europe; but at sea the Dutch were uniformly successful, and they wisely made use of their naval superiority to harass the Spaniards in every part of the world. In 1624 they defeated the Spanish fleet off Lima, and their expeditions to Brazil and to the Gold Coast can only be regarded as part of this policy, Portugal being then an integral portion of Spain. When the Portuguese, in 1640, taking advantage of the distracted condition of Spain, achieved their independence under the House of Braganza, war broke out between Portugal and Holland on the question of the possession of Brazil; and it was during the progress of these hostilities that the Dutch attacked and captured Fort St. Anthony, at Axim, and finally expelled the Portuguese from the Gold Coast. At the ensuing peace Portugal ceded all its possessions on the Gold Coast to the Dutch, the latter, in turn, renouncing all pretensions to sovereignty in Brazil.

The Portuguese occupation of the Gold Coast thus lasted from 1482 to 1642, a period of one hundred and sixty years, and traces of it may still be found in the languages of the negro tribes. From this we may infer that on the Gold Coast, as in Congo, Angola, and Cachao, the Portuguese mingled more with the natives than did their successors, whether Dutch or English. Among the words of Portuguese origin still used on the Gold Coast may be mentioned "palaver," from *palabra*; "caboceer," from *cabeceiro*; "piccaninny," from *picania*; "custom," from *costume*; and "fetish," from *feitiço*; while the familiar "dash me," *i.e.*, "give me," comes from the

Portuguese *das mc*, from which, naturally, the word "dash," meaning a "gift," is also derived. The existence of these words, nearly two centuries and a half after the Portuguese were driven from the coast, shows that they must have mixed with and influenced the natives to some considerable degree. Although the Dutch remained on the Gold Coast for two hundred and thirty-two years there are no similar traces of their occupation, nor are there even now many words derived from the English language in general use. Many of the names given by the Portuguese to places on the Gold Coast still remain, translated into English, but in the majority of cases their designations have been supplanted by the native ones. Amongst the former we have Cape Three Points (*Cabo de Tres Puntas*), Gold Coast (*Costa del Oro*), and Devil's Mount (*Monte de Diablo*); but the River Prah is now never spoken of as the Rio de San Juan, and no one would know Ampeni under the title of Terra Pequeña. A few Portuguese names exist in a corrupt form. The principal are Ancobra River (*Rio Cobre*), Elmina (*La Mina*), and Cape Coast (*Cabo Corso*).

CHAPTER V.

1643—1668.

Return of the English to the Gold Coast—Growth of the slave trade—The English form settlements—Disputes between the English and Dutch—The Dutch seize Cape Coast Castle—Holmes's expedition to the Coast—De Ruyter's expedition—The treaty of Breda.

THE success which attended the efforts of the Dutch to obtain a footing on the Gold Coast encouraged the English, some years before the capture of Elmina, to recommence a coasting trade, and several voyages were undertaken without any remarkable occurrence. The first record of any attempt made by England to establish a regular trade with the Gold Coast is in the charter granted by James I. in 1618, to Sir Robert Rich and some merchants of London, for raising a joint stock for a trade to Guinea. Under this charter vessels were despatched, but the profits of the undertaking not being found to answer expectation, the proprietors withdrew from the Company, and the charter was suffered to expire.

In 1631 Charles I. created a second Company for trade to Africa, granting by charter to Sir Richard Young, Sir Kenelm Digby, and other merchants, the exclusive trade to the Guinea Coast, between Cape Blanco and the Cape of Good Hope, together with the adjacent islands, for a period of thirty-one years. At this time the legitimate trade to West Africa had sunk into comparatively insignificant proportions beside a new trade that had arisen, namely the trade in slaves, in which all the western nations of Europe were now engaged. As early as 1452 slaves had been purchased at Elmina by the Portuguese and carried to Europe, and the traffic in slaves, such as it was, remained in the hands of that people until 1470, when the Spaniards established a mart and introduced negro slaves to Spain, the Canaries, and, subsequently, to the West Indies. As long as the wretched aborigines of the West Indies were sufficiently numerous to perform the labours demanded of them by the Spaniards, the negroes were considered very inferior workmen; and, in 1503, Ovando complained of their importation to Hispaniola, where they continually escaped to the woods and formed into predatory bands; but as the Indians succumbed to the cruelties of their hard task-masters, negro labourers became necessary to supply their place. In 1517 the traffic became firmly established under Papal authority, and it increased so rapidly that by 1539 the annual sales amounted to between ten and twelve thousand. Of all the nations of Europe, England was the last to embark in the slave trade, and the earliest attempt was made by Sir John Hawkins, as a private adventurer, in 1563. On his return to England, Elizabeth expressed her dissatisfaction that negroes should have been forcibly taken from their native land, but his subsequent successes against the Spaniards induced her to adopt other views, and in 1565 the British slave trade may be said to have been established.

At first the British trade in slaves was but small, but when England commenced the colonisation of the West Indies, and the Dutch West India Company, in 1627, introduced slavery to their colony of Manhattan, in North America, there became such a demand for negro slaves that the African Company of 1631 was induced to build forts and trading posts on the African coast for the protection of this commerce. Their charter granted them an exclusive trade to Guinea, but the trade practically remained open, for adventurers of other nations entirely disregarded their pretensions, and even English private adventurers continued to make voyages to the coast. Whenever the Company had reason to suppose that such a voyage was contemplated, they applied for the detention of the vessel. Thus we find that in 1637, upon an information laid by the directors, the ship *Talbot*, which had been equipped to trade upon the coasts of Guinea, Benin, and Angola, "to take nigers and carry them to foreign parts," was ordered to be stopped; but such detentions appear to have been of rare occurrence, for the English private adventurers kept their purpose carefully concealed until they were clear of English ports.

The Dutch could not have regarded the appearance of the English upon the Gold Coast with any great favour, but they do not appear to have offered any open opposition to the formation of establishments by the English Company. Their position on the Gold Coast was somewhat peculiar. The Portuguese, though they were established only at Elmina and Axim, had claimed, and for a time had certainly exercised, a sovereignty over the whole littoral of the Gold Coast; but the Dutch, though they had acquired all the privileges of the Portuguese by right of conquest, and, subsequent to the capture of Elmina, had built forts at Butri, Shamah, and Anamabo,* in order to control the natives, and engross the whole trade, exercised no such sovereignty. They claimed and exercised a jurisdiction over the native towns in the immediate vicinity of their forts and "lodges," but nowhere else; and the various petty kingdoms of the Gold Coast were regarded as entirely independent. No doubt the latter had contrived to regain something of their independence during the fifty years' struggle between the Dutch and the Portuguese, and at its conclusion were not inclined to resubmit to another yoke. The Dutch, then, could hardly resist the establishment of trading posts by the African Company so long as they were not formed at those places which were already in Dutch occupation. All that was necessary for the English to do was to obtain permission to build from the king of the state in which they

---

* Anama, "bird"; bo, "rock."

proposed to establish themselves, and the Dutch could only oppose them by diplomacy and intrigue.

The African Company proved a success until the outbreak of the Civil War in England, when the nation was so fully occupied at home that it had no time to spare in foreign adventures. The Dutch seized this opportunity of improving their position at the expense of the English; the Swedes also appeared and established themselves at Christiansborg, where they built a fort; and though in 1651 the grant to the African Company was renewed and confirmed by the Commonwealth, it is said to have suffered losses to the extent of three hundred thousand pounds. It is not known with certainty what forts or "lodges" the Company had built on the Gold Coast, but at all events it had a fort at Cormantine before 1651, for in that year the Council of State approved of a report upon the Guinea trade which had been drawn up by the Council of Trade, in which it was recommended that the African Company should have the exclusive trade for twenty leagues on each side of their two chief factories, namely, Fort Cormantine, on the Gold Coast, and the River Cerberro (Sherbro), near Sierra Leone. This exclusive trade was to last for fourteen years, and all the rest of the coast of Africa was to be free to all comers.

The Danes were the next nation to endeavour to obtain a share in the profitable business of exporting negroes to the New World. In 1657 they drove the Swedes out of Christiansborg, and shortly after built a small fortified factory on the summit of a hill about a quarter of a mile to the east of Cape Coast Castle, at a village called Mamfro, or Omanfo;* but they do not appear to have engrossed much of the trade, and the great rivalry was between the Dutch and the English.

The African Company had not succeeded in establishing itself on the Gold Coast without some molestation. In 1652 a frigate had to be sent out from England to protect its trade from the interference of the Dutch, and in 1653, the Swedes,

---

* Man, or Oman, "town"; fo, "people."

having encroached upon the Company and expelled some of its factors from places bought by it at Accra, Lord Ambassador Whitelock was instructed to represent the case to the Swedish Court and insist upon reparation being made; but it was not until 1660 that serious disputes arose between the English and Dutch. In that year the Dutch so encroached upon the trade of the African Company that the English Ambassador at the Hague formally remonstrated with the Dutch Government on the subject, but to no purpose. Indeed, instead of obtaining redress for the grievances complained of, his interference seems only to have produced fresh aggressions, and the Colonial State Papers for the years 1660, 1661, and 1662, are full of complaints, made by the agents of the English Company, of Dutch interference with their trade. In August, 1661, the English ship *Merchant's Delight* was seized by the Dutch and carried to "Castle de Myne," as Elmina was then called by the English, where the crew were imprisoned by the Dutch Director-General, Jasper Van Hewson. In November, 1662, further complaints were made of Dutch aggressions at "Comendo" (Kommenda) and "Cape Corso" (Cape Coast). At neither of these places, say the complainants, had the Dutch any factories, but they endeavoured to prevent the English trading, and the Dutch war vessel *Golden Lyon* fired at the boats of an English ship which attempted to land at Cape Coast.

Relations between the Dutch and English on the Gold Coast were in this strained condition when, towards the close of 1662, Charles II. granted to a new Company a charter of incorporation by the title of "Company of Royal Adventurers of England Trading to Africa." This Company engaged to supply the British West Indies with three thousand negro slaves annually, and it consisted of many persons of rank, amongst others the King's brother, James, Duke of York. According to the proposals for the settlement of this Company,* dated January, 1663, the posts on the Gold Coast were to be "Cape Corso, Anashan, Kommenda, Aga, and

---

* Dom. Chas. II., vol. lxvii., No. 162, Cal. p. 36.

Acra." Aga is evidently Egyah, a small village near Cormantine, and Anashan, or Anchiang, is another small village about two miles to the west of Anamabo, in the then State of Fanti. The Castle of Cape Corso (Cape Coast) was to be the head factory, and the residence of the agent for the whole Gold Coast. Two merchants, a gold taker, a warehouse keeper, two accountants, and three younger factors were to reside there, and the garrison was to consist of fifty English soldiers and thirty negro slaves, with a captain, and four sergeants or corporals. Anashan was to have a sergeant, ten English soldiers, and eight negroes, and the other factories two soldiers and two negroes each.

From the fact of no garrison being specified for Cormantine fort, we may infer that that post was to remain *in statu quo*, and that the posts now mentioned were either newly projected ones, or ones which were to be placed on a new footing. Anashan, Egyah, and Kommenda seem to have been new posts, but it is doubtful if Cape Coast was, for the "Castle of Cape Corso" is referred to as if it were a building already in existence. The question as to when Cape Coast Castle was built is involved in great obscurity. Smith, Surveyor of the Royal African Company, who visited the Gold Coast in 1727, says the Portuguese founded it in 1610; while Barbot (1687), says it was built by the Dutch shortly after the capture of Elmina. Neither of these gives any authority for his statement, and Barbot contradicts himself in two other places, saying in one that the Dutch "had a pretty good fort at Cape Coast, which they bought of the factor of one Carolof, who had built it for the Danish Company," and in the other that "Cape Coast is famous for the castle the English built there." In any case Smith is in error, for there is abundant evidence to show that the Portuguese had no fort at Cape Coast, and Barbot's statement that it was built by the Dutch is directly traversed by the complaint made by the African Company in November, 1662, in which it is said the Dutch had no factory at Cape Coast. There seems, therefore, but little doubt that Cape Coast Castle was built by the English, but at what date is uncertain. The probability is that it was built shortly before the formation of the Company of 1662, perhaps in 1662, for there is no mention made of it before January, 1663. It has been stated that one reason of Cape Coast being selected as the chief post of the new Company, was that it formed part of the marriage portion of Catherine of Braganza, whom Charles II. married in 1662; but this, if true, is certainly very peculiar, considering that the Portuguese had been expelled from the Gold Coast by force of arms twenty years before, and had since renounced all claim to their possessions in that part of the world in favour of the Dutch.

The formation of the new Company led to remonstrances from the Dutch Company, and on June 1st, 1663, John Valckenburgh, "Director General of the North Coast of Africa and the Island of St. Thome," on behalf of the States General, protested against the action of the English agents. He maintained that, by right of conquest from Portugal, the whole coast of Guinea now belonged to the Dutch, and complained that the English had set up a factory at Tacorary (Takoradi), "under the protection of Shamah, under which Tacorary, Saconde, and Abrary have always been tributary." He further complained that, in 1647, the English had encouraged the Dutch "vassals" at Cabo Corso to rebel, and had now, with their shipping, raised the blockade of the place.* From this it will be seen that the Dutch were now taking up a new position, and were disposed to claim a sovereignty over the whole Gold Coast, though such a claim ill accorded with the fact that the right of the English to Cormantine, where they had been established since before 1651, had never been called in question. However, in this protest they only made specific complaints of the action of the English in two places, and, as far as Takoradi was concerned, they were in the right, as they had had a fort there for some years. Their claim to Cape Coast does not seem to have rested upon any solid foundation.

* Col. Papers, vol. xvii., No. 34. Indorsed "The First Protest of ye Dutch."

But the Dutch did not limit themselves to mere protests. A few days after, they suddenly surprised and seized the English castle at Cape Coast, and gave large presents to the King of Fetu, "and his capeshiers" (caboceers), to induce him to exclude the English altogether from that place. They likewise bribed the "King of Fantyn and his capeshiers" to attack the English fort at Cormantine, and persuaded the King of Aguna to seize John Cabessa, "who was a great defence to Cormantine." "Had not Captain Stokes arrived, it is to be feared that the Flemish flag would be on Cormantine, as it is now on the Castle of Cape Corso."* Some of the aggressions of the Dutch seem to have preceded their protest, for the English agents complain that on May 28th the King of Aguna, instigated by the Dutch, had plundered their factory at Winnebah. However, the Dutch do not appear to have been uniformly successful in their endeavours to prejudice the natives against the English, for, from a letter from Captain Stokes, it seems that the latter succeeded in making a treaty with the King of Fanti, and had arranged to build a fort at the new post of Anashan.

In consequence of the complaints from the agents of the Company, and no doubt because the King himself had a pecuniary interest in its welfare, Sir George Downing, the Envoy to the States General, was instructed to demand full and speedy reparation for the Dutch aggressions. In the meantime the Dutch made a second protest, to the effect that Captain Stokes, "Commander in Chief of the English Forces upon the Coast of Africa," had erected a factory at Anashan, "upon the Stranel, under the jurisdiction of the country of Fantyn." They alleged that no person with a knowledge of the coast of Africa could be ignorant that the Portuguese, as the first discoverers, had maintained the Gold Coast against all comers, and that the Dutch Company, which had

* Col. Papers, vol. xvii., No. 60.

obtained it at the expense of much treasure and blood from the Portuguese, ought to be left undisturbed, especially in the neighbourhood of Anashan, as the "whole strand of Fantyn," with the traffic therein, had been made over, in March, 1629, to the States General and the Dutch West India Company.* This protest was handed to Captain Stokes on board the *Marmaduke*, by Huybert Van Gazeldoncq, Chief Factor, at the Fort Nassau Tot Moree.

Sir George Downing failed to obtain any satisfaction from the States General, and, influenced by the Duke of York, who, as Governor of the Company, took a strong interest in its progress, Charles II. despatched Captain Robert Holmes† to the West Coast of Africa, in the *Jersey*, with secret instructions to seize the Dutch fort at Goree, which was then considered to be the key of West Africa. This was done without any previous declaration of war against Holland being made, and Charles II. has on this account been blamed; but it must be remembered that the seizure of the Castle of Cape Coast by the Dutch could only be regarded as an act of war, and that consequently the Dutch must be considered to have been the first to commence hostilities. Neither must it be forgotten that notwithstanding this high-handed proceeding on the part of the Dutch, Charles II. did not take any measures of reprisal until after application to the States General for reparation had failed.

Holmes captured Goree, left a small garrison in the fort, and ran down to the Gold Coast. On April 9th, 1664, he arrived off Takoradi; the Dutch fort there, Fort Witsen, was taken by storm, and an English garrison left in it. On May 7th he retook the Castle of Cape Coast, placed in it a garrison of fifty men, with supplies and ammunition for six months, and left a number of workmen and a quantity

* Col. Papers, vol. xvii., No. 77.
† Afterwards Sir Robert Holmes, the barbarous destroyer of the open town of Brandaris on the Schelling, and who has been termed "the cursed beginner of the Dutch wars."

of materials for its repair. From Cape Coast he proceeded to Mori, where he reduced Fort Nassau, and then sailing to Anamabo, captured the fort and drove the Dutch out of Egyah.* Having thus taken all the Dutch posts on the Gold Coast, except Elmina and Axim, he returned to England. With the exception of Cape Coast Castle and Mori Fort, the places thus captured were rather fortified houses than regular fortifications; the garrisons of the two former barely numbered twenty men, while those of the smaller posts consisted of two or three men only; and as the Dutch were completely taken by surprise, Holmes' expedition was not such a glorious affair as has commonly been supposed.

The natural result of the action of Charles II. in despatching Holmes to the West Coast of Africa was the outbreak of war between England and Holland, during which, it may incidentally be remarked, a Dutch fleet ascended the Medway and destroyed our shipping; while to recover the lost possessions in West Africa, and to reduce the English forts and factories on the Gold Coast, Admiral de Ruyter was despatched with thirteen sail. De Ruyter arrived at Goree on October 11th, 1664, and as the breaches in the fortifications, made at the time of the capture by Holmes, had not yet been repaired, the place surrendered. He then ran down the coast, destroying the English factories at Sierra Leone, Cape Mount, Mountserrat (Mesurado), and Cœstus (Sesters), ard anchored at Elmina. On December 25th the Dutch attacked Takoradi with a small force, but being repulsed, returned with a body of a thousand natives and captured the place. The English were stripped naked, the town burnt, and the fort blown up, for it was only a small place, mounting seven or eight *patereroes*, and of great expense to maintain. The ruins of this fort, it may be remarked, were visible until quite recently.

The main object of De Ruyter's mission was the capture of the Castle of Cape Coast, and he next proceeded there,

---

* Dom. Chas. II., vol. cxiv., No. 19, Cal. 235.

but finding that the landing-place was swept by the guns of the Castle, and that the natives, whom the Dutch had tried to corrupt, were determined to assist the English, he abandoned the attempt, merely expressing his astonishment that the Dutch should have been so short-sighted as to allow the English to get a footing there. From Cape Coast he went on to Mori, and after retaking Fort Nassau, with the assistance of nine hundred natives from Elmina, returned to Elmina. Much disappointed at finding De Ruyter would not attempt the reduction of Cape Coast Castle, Valckenburgh, the Director-General, urged him to make an attempt upon Anamabo and Cormantine, which he represented as being very injurious to Dutch trade. De Ruyter complied, and sailing from Elmina on January 25th, 1665, passed on to Mori, where he took in the Dutch garrison, and early next morning attempted a landing at Anamabo, with 700 soldiers, black and white, and 1,000 Elminas. This attempt was repulsed with loss by the natives of Cormantine, under their chief, John Cabessa, aided by the fire of the small guns of the "lodge"; but the English had regarded its success as so certain that they had mined their "lodge" at Egyah, and had ignited the fuse so that the place might blow up when the Dutch occupied it, as they would have done during their advance from Anamabo to Cormantine. Owing to the failure of the attack this little plot fell through, and the mine exploded without injuring any one.

Finding things were not going on well, Valckenburgh himself came from Elmina to direct the operations. He entered into an agreement with the Fantis, and purchased their assistance for a combined attack by land and sea upon Cormantine; paying them, according to the English, fifty-thousand pieces of eight—an evident exaggeration—and according to Barbot, fifty-two marks of gold. On January 29th Valckenburgh landed his men without opposition at Egyah, and being joined by the Fanti auxiliaries, every man of whom wore a white handkerchief round his neck to distinguish him from the natives of Cormantine, marched with a total force of ten thousand men to attack Cormantine Fort by land, while three ships bombarded it from the sea. The natives, some three hundred in number, under John Cabessa, made a most obstinate resistance; the paths to the fort were choked with bodies, and the advance was checked for a long time; but by a flank movement of the Dutch main body, most of the English allies were cut off, and the remainder then retreated to the fort, which soon hung out a flag of truce. The English surrendered without terms, but the Dutch gave quarter, and only revenged themselves by blowing up John Cabessa's house. That chief, who had committed suicide to avoid capture, was, said the agents of the Company, truer to the English interest than any of the Englishmen who were there; the Dutch offered a large reward for his head, but the natives buried him at old Cormantine.* In this attack the Dutch lost forty-nine Europeans, and the Fanti contingent suffered heavily. They took in the fort a "tried lump of gold," of 105 lbs. weight, which was taken on board De Ruyter's ship. After the capture of Cormantine the three or four men in Anamabo "lodge" capitulated, and on January 30th De Ruyter and Valckenburgh returned to Elmina, leaving a garrison of eighty men in Cormantine Fort, which they now named Fort Amsterdam.

At the termination of De Ruyter's expedition the Company of Royal Adventurers had nothing left of their former forts and factories on the Gold Coast except the Castle of Cape Coast; and when the news of their losses reached England, they presented a petition to the King, in which they adopted a strange line of argument. They asserted that what De Ruyter had done had been done to revenge the losses inflicted by Holmes (Major Holmes they styled him); and they endeavoured to make it appear that they had not sanctioned Holmes's action, or taken any part in his engagements, or profited by them. Yet, as a matter of fact, all the Dutch forts and factories on the Gold Coast

* Col. Papers, vol. xix., No. 55. Indorsed "An Account of De Ruyter's barbarityes in Guinea in 1664."

that had been captured by Holmes, had been handed over to and occupied by the Company's servants, who, had matters afterwards turned out differently, would have hailed Holmes as their benefactor instead of denouncing him as their destroyer. They gave a brief narrative of their trade and late condition, showing that since their incorporation on January 20th, 1663, they had sent to the Coast goods to the value of £158,000; and, besides forts in the Gambia, at Sierra Leone, and on the Grain Coast, had, on the Gold Coast, built forts or factories at Anashan, Ahanta, Tantamkwerri, Cormantine, Cape Coast, Winnebah, Accra, Whydah, and Benin, from which they had exported £200,000 annually in gold, and £100,000 in slaves for the plantations. They had, besides, a trade at Old and New Calabar, and had engaged to supply the Spaniards with 3,500 negroes annually from those places. In consequence, then, of the loss of all this trade through the unjustifiable aggressions of Holmes, they begged that all the Dutch prizes which that commander had taken might be made over to them, to compensate them in some measure for their losses.* This strange request, owing probably to the influence of the Duke of York, appears in some respects to have been complied with, as the Dutch vessel, *Golden Lyon*, was, in April, 1666, handed over to the Company.

Very soon after De Ruyter's expedition the English must have taken steps to re-establish themselves at some of the places they had lost, for Villault, in the narrative of the voyage he made to the Gold Coast in 1666, says that they had at Anashan a small fort on an eminence, about six hundred paces from the sea. When he was at Cape Coast the King of Fanti had seized the Dutch commandant of Cormantine, who had gone on a visit to Anamabo, and had killed two men who were with him. The reason of this seizure, Villault was told, was that the Fanti King had promised the English to put them in possession of Cormantine again, and had given his son to them as a hostage

---

* Col. Papers, vol. xix., No. 5.

for the fulfilment of his promise. Afterwards, finding that he was unable to keep his word, he demanded his son, whom the English declined to give up till the conditions were complied with; and he thereupon seized the Dutch commandant and four others, intending to exchange them for his hostage. How this affair terminated we are not told. When Villault's vessel anchored off Cape Coast the Castle fired a shotted gun at it, upon which the governor of Fredericsburgh, the Danish fort at Omanfo, replied with a shotted gun at the Castle, which it commanded, to show that he took the ship under his protection.

By the treaty of Breda, in 1667, the Dutch retained possession of Cormantine and all the other posts they had captured from the English, and the right of the latter to Cape Coast Castle was acknowledged. The treaty does not, however, appear to have put an end to the differences between the two nations, for, in 1668, the Dutch demanded that the English should give up Egyah, which they had reoccupied, on the grounds that, being under the guns of Cormantine, it had been ceded to them with that fort. In July of the same year, too, the people of Kommenda plundered the Dutch factory at that place, and murdered the native servants of the Dutch Company; and as they were supposed to have been instigated by the people of Fetu, the Dutch declared a blockade of Kommenda and all the coast of Fetu, including Cape Coast, and called upon the English to cease trading at those places until they, the Dutch, had received satisfaction. Naturally, however, the English did not acknowledge a blockade of their own headquarters, and the consequence was that there was a good deal of bickering between them and the Dutch.

CHAPTER VI.

1669—1700.

Formation of the Royal African Company—The Brandenburghers form settlements—Rebellion of the Elminas—Native wars—The voyage of Thomas Phillips—Capture of Christiansborg by the Akwamus—War between the Dutch and Kommendas—The English trade to Africa made open.

In 1672 the "Company of Royal Adventurers trading to Africa" surrendered its charter to the Crown, and on September 27th a fourth exclusive company, entitled the "Royal African Company," was established. The King, the Duke of York, and many other persons of rank were among the promoters, and in nine months the whole capital of £111,000 was raised. Out of this sum the out-going Company was paid £34,000 for its three forts, viz., Cape Coast Castle, James Fort, in the River Gambia, and a fort on Bunce Island, in the Sierra Leone River. The new Company very shortly commenced to build new forts at Sekondi, Kommenda, Anamabo, Winnebah, and Accra, and much increased the trade. They exported annually English goods to the value of £70,000, and in 1673, 50,000 guineas, so called from the Guinea Coast, were coined from gold which they brought to England.

In 1679 the Danish commandant of Christiansborg John Ollricks, of Gluckstad, was treacherously murdered by the natives at the instigation of a Greek who was second in command; and who, after making himsel master of the Castle, sold it to Julian de Campo Baretto, a Portuguese who had formally been Governor of St. Thomas, for about £224. Baretto was supported by the Portuguese Government, which furnished him with a garrison, and, in spite of the remonstrances of the Danes, Christiansborg remained in Portuguese hands till 1683; when, the garrison having mutinied, and their affairs generally being in a wretched condition, the Portuguese permitted the Danes to redeem it by purchase.

In 1682* the Brandenburghers, or, to give them their present title, the Prussians, anxious if possible to obtain a share in the profitable slave trade, also commenced to form settlements on the Gold Coast. In that year the Elector of Brandenburgh sent out two frigates under Matthew de Vos and Peter Blanco, who, on arriving at Cape Three Points, landed their men at "Pokquefo," and set up the Brandenburgh flag on Manfro Hill. The chief of the district at first objected to this summary proceeding; but, eventually, he was induced to give them permission to build a fort. They landed some guns, built a few houses, surrounded the whole with a palisade, and leaving a small garrison in the place, returned to Hamburg. In the following year Blanco returned to assume command, with the title of Director-General for the Elector of Brandenburgh; and having built a fort, which mounted thirty-two guns, named it Great Fredericsburgh, in honour of his sovereign. The Brandenburghers subsequently built Fort Dorothea at Akwidah, and formed a "lodge" at Takrama. The Dutch drove them out of the former in 1690, and enlarged the fort, but restored it in 1698.

In 1687 the Dutch determined to build a fort at Kommenda, to endeavour to compete with the English, who had succeeded in engrossing the whole trade of that place. The natives, perhaps instigated by the latter, offered resistance to the Dutch occupation; but troops were collected from the other Dutch forts, and in the war which ensued the King of

---

* Bosman says 1674, but Barbot, who is more circumstantial, 1682.

Kommenda and several of the principal chiefs were killed, and the people entirely subjected. The Dutch fort was then commenced, about gun-shot distance from that of the English; it was completed in 1688, and named Fort Vrendenburgh.

The same year was remarkable for a rebellion of the natives of Elmina. The Portuguese had made the district of Elmina independent of the Kings of Commani (Kommenda) and Fetu, whose kingdoms were separated by the River Beyah at Elmina, and the natives had been governed, according to their own laws and customs, by three chiefs. This arrangement the Dutch now tried to upset, in order to bring the inhabitants under their direct control; but the Elminas resisted, and took up arms in defence of their ancient liberties. Twice they assaulted the Castle, being repulsed each time with great slaughter, although the Dutch lost only four men; and then finding they could not stand against the fire of the guns, they established, by land, a strict blockade of the Castle, and of Fort Conraadsburgh, permitting no one to enter or leave them. Affairs were in this condition when Barbot visited Elmina in 1688, and he saw three Elminas—who had been taken prisoners—in irons on the battery on the land side of the Castle. These men had been kept there for nine months, exposed to the heat of the sun and the inclemency of the weather, without any covering. The dispute was finally terminated by mutual concessions.

In 1688 the Royal African Company, and all other exclusive companies not authorised by Parliament, were, by the "Petition and Declaration of Right," on the accession of William and Mary, abolished. Notwithstanding this, however, the Company's officers on the coast still continued to seize the ships of private traders, and this gave rise to many disputes.

The year 1688 is also noticeable as having witnessed a attempt on the part of the French to obtain a footing c the Gold Coast. In that year, M. du Casse arrived on th Coast with four men-of-war from Rochefort, and establishe l a small factory at Kommenda; but the Dutch contrived to foment quarrels between the natives, and during the disturbances that ensued the French factory was pillaged, and its inmates compelled to fly to Cape Coast for safety. From that time forward the French abandoned all hope of gaining any footing on the Gold Coast, and their ships ceased to frequent it.

Between the years 1669 and 1692 two native wars of note took place. In the former year the Akwamus commenced hostilities against the Accras, and the struggle continued until 1680, when the latter were completely crushed, and large numbers of them migrated to Great and Little Popo, on the Slave Coast, the old kingdom of Accra thus ceasing to exist. The Akwamus completely depopulated the country, and the devastation was such that when Barbot visited Accra in 1682 the English and Dutch forts at Accra, and the Danish castle of Christiansborg had still to be supplied with food from the windward forts. Every plantation had been ravaged and destroyed, and maize sold for five pieces of eight per bushel. The other native war was between the kingdoms of Adom and Ahanta, that of Jabi subsequently joining the former against the latter. It broke out in 1690, lasted three or four years, and virtually destroyed for a time the kingdom of Ahanta.

In 1693 a Captain Thomas Phillips made a voyage to the Gold Coast, the narrative of which, published in the second volume of Astley's Collection, furnishes some curious particulars of the affairs of the coast and the manner of life of Europeans there at that time. After losing a number of men from fever on the Grain and Ivory Coasts, Phillips at length arrived at Axim, on the Gold Coast. He says there were more than a dozen "Interlopers"—*i.e.* private traders—trading on the coast, notwithstanding the exclusive grant of the trade possessed by the Dutch Company, and the power of the latter to seize and confiscate the ships and cargoes of interlopers. When such vessels were captured, the crews were confined in the dungeons at Elmina, and the commanders condemned to death. Yet Phillips saw

F

four or five interlopers together, lying off Elmina Castle for a week at a time, and trading in defiance of it. But these vessels were generally well armed and manned, and resisted capture to the last extremity.

At Axim the Dutch factor, Mr. Rawlison, came on board Phillips's ship, and was making merry, when the appearance in the distance of a twelve-hand canoe with a flag caused him to throw himself into a fishing canoe and hasten to the shore. Phillips was unable to account for the sudden flight of his guest; but he learned afterwards that he was afraid the canoe was bringing the Fiscal from Elmina, an officer whose duty it was to supervise all the Dutch establishments on the coast, and to see that the factors engaged in no private trade on their own account. "In discharging this trust," says Phillips, "he uses as much subtilty and rigour as the severest old searcher in the Port of London, and in case of a discovery, not only takes all the contraband goods away, but possibly seizing upon all the gold the factor has for the Company's use, carries his person to the Mina, where he is imprisoned; and the gentlest usage he meets with is to be well fined, and forced to carry a musket in the Castle as a common sentinel, another being put into his Government. It is the same likewise in case of any neglect or remissness in his duty as Governor, such as lying out, or letting black women in at night. The last of which, though it be a common practice in the English castles, yet the Dutch seldom or never do it, although they have black or mulatto wives as well as the English, which they change at pleasure. It is for these reasons that the Fiscal is so dreadful to them."

Leaving Axim, Phillips passed the Brandenburgh factory (Great Fredericsburgh), and anchored off Dikjes-chaft, or Dicky's Cove (Dixcove), where the English were building a fort—then half-finished. It had been commenced in 1691. From Dixcove he went to Tacoradi, and thence to Sekondi. Here he found Mr. Johnson—the English factor—in bed, raving mad, and his assistant—a young lad "who had been a Bluecoat Hospital boy"—in charge.

At Shamah the natives were afraid to trade, lest the Dutch should seize their goods; for, says Phillips, "the Dutch were very insolent upon this coast, especially since the Revolution, endeavouring by all manners to undermine and ruin the English commerce there; treating the Negroes with great severity, when they catched them trading with the English."

Passing Elmina Castle—which was saluted with seven guns—Phillips anchored off Cape Coast, where he remained twenty-nine days. He landed here thirty soldiers for the Company in as good health as when they left England; but in two months' time nearly half of them were dead. There was a curious fashion at that time of celebrating every social event with discharges of cannon or musketry. Phillips and his companions gave a dinner on shore in what he calls the "Castle garden," which appears to have been on Prospect Hill, to the officers of the Company; and he tells us that each of the captains brought six of his quarter-deck guns on shore, and that eleven were discharged at each toast.

While he was at Cape Coast the King of Saboe returned from a war he had been waging against the King of Fetu, in which the latter had been defeated, and compelled to seek protection at Elmina. A brother of the King had been placed on the "stool," and he came in to Cape Coast to "eat fetish" and swear to be true to the English interest. This war was caused by the Fetu people having molested the inhabitants of a small state called Akanna, which—from M. D'Anville's map of the Gold Coast, published in 1729—appears to have been situated where the present Assin is.* The Akanna people, called by the English Arkanis, had the purest gold, and traded exclusively with the English; and the Dutch, desirous of having a share in this profitable trade, instigated the King of Fetu to refuse the Akannas permission to pass through his territory, which intervened between Akanna and Cape Coast. The King of

---

* The dialect of the Tshi language spoken by the northern tribes of the Gold Coast is called Akan; and the name Akanna was probably applied to all who spoke it.

Fetu complied, and plundered some Akanna traders; whereupon the Akannas made war, and were assisted by the Company at Cape Coast with arms and ammunition, the King of Saboe and his people being also hired as allies. The Fetus were utterly defeated, a new King chosen, and a treaty drawn up in the name of the Royal African Company, and of the Kings of Fetu, Akanna, and Saboe, in which the new King swore to be friendly with the Akannas, and permit them a free passage through his territory.

On leaving Cape Coast, Phillips passed Mori and Anashan—at the latter of which the Company's establishment consisted of a thatched house—and anchored at Anamabo. Here the factors of Anamabo and Egyah came on board to dine with him, accompanied by two mulatto girls, their country wives. "This," says Phillips, "is a pleasant way of marrying; for they can turn their wives off, and take others at pleasure, which makes them very careful to humour their husbands, in washing their linen, cleaning their chambers, etc., and the charge of keeping them is little or nothing." At Winnebah, where a Mr. Nicholas Buckerige was factor, Phillips had an interview with the Queen, a corpulent woman of fifty. "She was free of her kisses to Mr. Buckerige, whom she seemed much to esteem, and truly he deserved respect from all who knew him, being an extraordinary good-humoured and ingenious gentleman, and understood this country and language very well." The factor lived here in a thatched house, without any defences, and was in constant fear of being attacked and plundered by the Akwamus.

Phillips found Christiansborg Castle in the hands of the Akwamus. It had been surprised by a number of natives secretly armed, who gained admission by pretending they had come to trade. While the assistant factor was showing them some goods, one of their number stabbed him, and his companions secured the other servants of the Company that were in the Castle, and ran to admit a body of armed natives who were lying in ambush outside. The Danish Director-General, hearing the tumult, came out of his room sword in hand, and was immediately attacked by two natives

He held his own against them for some time, but more natives coming up, he threw himself out of a window, and escaped to the Dutch fort at Accra. He had received several wounds, and by one of them his left arm was disabled. The Danish garrison, consisting of some twenty-five men only—for it had recently been much reduced by deaths—taken unawares, was soon overpowered, and the Akwamus became masters of the place.

The leader of this attack was, Bosman tells us, a man named Assammeni. He dressed himself in the clothes of the Danish Governor, caused himself to be addressed by that title, and saluted all the "Interlopers" with volleys of cannon. Assammeni invited Phillips and two of his companions to dine; an invitation which they accepted. He treated his guests well, and the food was very well dressed, for, says Phillips, he had formerly been a cook in one of the English factories, and now went very often to the kitchen to give the necessary orders. At dinner he sat in great state, having a negro boy, with a pistol, on each side of him, as a guard. He drank the King of England's, and the African Company's, and his guests' healths frequently, with volleys of cannon, of which he fired about two hundred during their visit. He had flying on the Castle a white flag, having on it a negro brandishing a scimetar.

Next day, two Danish vessels, each of twenty-six guns, arrived. They had been despatched from Denmark as soon as the capture of the Castle was known, and were empowered to treat. Assammeni at first made the most extravagant demands; but the Danes won over the King of Akwamu to their interest by a considerable present, and Assammeni eventually surrendered the Castle for fifty marks in gold, and an indemnity in writing for himself and followers. After accomplishing this service, the Danish vessels went on to St. Thomas, where they fell in with Avery, alias "Long Ben," a notorious pirate who had long infested the Coast, and were plundered and burnt by him.

In 1694 the people of Kommenda, who had only submitted by force to the Dutch occupation in 1687, once more took up arms; the immediate cause being as follows. In 1694 the Dutch sent out some miners from Holland to open up those hills in the neighbourhood of their forts which were thought to contain gold. It was known that the Portuguese had had a gold mine at Kommenda, which, according to tradition, had fallen in in the year 1622, and had since lain idle; a hill about half a mile from Fort Vrendenburgh was supposed to be identified with this, and the miners were there set to work. Now it so happened that this hill was believed by the natives to be the *habitat* of one of their local gods, and consequently sacred, and the Kommendas, resenting what they conceived to be a sacrilege, assaulted and beat the workmen, and carried them off as prisoners. After some negotiations the prisoners were released; but, as the Kommendas refused to make any reparation for the attack on them, the Dutch brought a force of mercenaries from Cape Coast and Elmina, at a cost of £5,000, and commenced hostilities. In the first general engagement which took place the Kommendas were completely victorious, and the greater number of the Dutch auxiliaries were killed or taken prisoners; but the Dutch succeeded by bribes in gaining over the brother of the King of Kommenda to their interest, and with a fresh force of auxiliaries essayed a second attempt. This, however, fared no better than the first, and the Dutch were driven back to their fort, which mounted twenty guns.

In 1695 the Kommendas attempted to dislodge their foes altogether, and made a determined onslaught upon the fort. Says the Dutch commander: "Our enemies attacked us by night. I had but a very sorry garrison—not full twenty men, half of which were not capable of service—and yet I forced them to retire with loss, after a fight of five hours. It was wonderful, and no small sign of divine protection, that we lost but two men in this action; for we had no doors to most of our gun-holes, and the Negroes poured small shot on us as thick as hail, insomuch that those few doors that were left to some gun-holes were become like a target which had been shot at for a mark; and the very staff which our flag was fastened on, though it took up so little room, did not escape shot-free. You may imagine what case we were in when one of them began to hack our very doors with an axe; but this undertaker being killed, the rest sheered off. The General, to whom I had represented my weak condition, advised two ships to anchor before our fort, in order to supply me with men and ammunition. Peter Heriken, the captain of one of these vessels, endeavouring to execute the General's order the day before I was attacked, sent his boat full of men with orders to come to me; but they were no sooner on land than the Negroes fell upon them so furiously, even under our cannon, that they killed several of them, which, though I saw, I could not prevent; for, attempting to fire upon the enemy with our cannon, I found them all nailed; of which piece of treacherous villany, according to all appearance, my own gunner was the actor, whom I therefore sent in chains to the General (at our chief place of residence), who swore that he would punish him exemplarily; but, instead of that, he soon after not only set him at liberty, but preferred him to a gunner's place of greater importance.

"For this reason I was forced to be an idle spectator of the miserable slaughter of our men, not being able to lend them the least assistance; and if the Negroes had at that instant stormed us, we were in no posture of resistance. But they going to eat, gave me time to prepare for the entertainment I gave them, as I have before told you. Here I cannot help relating a comical accident which happened: Going to visit the posts of our fort, to see whether everybody was at their duty, one of the soldiers, quitting his post, told me that the Negroes, well knowing he had but one hat in the world, had maliciously shot away the crown, which he would revenge if I would give him a few grenadoes. I had no sooner ordered him two than he called out to the Negroes from the breastwork in their own language, telling them he would present them with something to eat, and, kindling his grenadoes, immediately threw them down amongst them. They, observing them to burn, crowded about them, and were at first very agreeably diverted; but when they burst they so galled them that they had no great stomach to such another meal."*

The Dutch, after the failure of the attack on their fort, reopened negotiations, and peace would probably have been made had not the English, whose fort stood close to that of the Dutch, and who hoped to profit by the quarrel, instigated the King to demand satisfaction on the strength of his two victories. The Dutch soon, however, succeeded in fomenting discord amongst the Kommendas, and hiring more native allies, a desultory war, characterised by great barbarities, continued for some months, and at last died a natural death.

In 1698 the English trade to Africa, which had virtually been open since 1688, was expressly made so by Statutes IX. and X. of William and Mary, c. 26, which enacted "That for the preservation of the trade, and for the advantage of England and its colonies, it should be lawful for any of the subjects of His Majesty's realm of England, as well as for the Company, to trade from England and the plantations in America, to Africa, between Cape Mount and the Cape of Good Hope, upon paying for the aforesaid uses a duty of ten per cent., *ad valorem*, for the goods exported from England or the plantations, to be paid to the collector at the time of entry outwards, for the use of the Company." The duties so paid were to be applied to the maintenance of the forts, the purchase of munitions of war, and the pay of the soldiers. Persons paying these duties were to have the same protection from the forts, and the same freedom for trade, as the Company. This law was to continue in force for thirteen years, and both the Company and many private traders remonstrated against it without effect. In a few years the Company's trade declined to such an extent, that they were unable either to support their factories, or to pay the debts which they had already incurred. It may here be mentioned that this Act, which expired in 1712, was again renewed by Parliament.

* Bosman.

In 1698 the English fort at Sekondi was taken and burned by the Ahantas, and several of its occupants killed, amongst them the factor, Johnson, whom Phillips had found in bed mad. The whole place was plundered and gutted, only the outer walls being left standing. The English agents at Cape Coast charged the Dutch with having assisted the Ahantas, and sent a protest to the Director-General, John Van Sevenhuysen, who, however, denied complicity, and declared that the Dutch vessels that had been sent to Sekondi at the time of the occurrence had merely been in search of interlopers. It is not probable that there was any foundation for the charge, for, from the *Paris Gazette*, of November, 1694, it seems that Fort Orange, the Dutch fort at Sekondi, was also taken and plundered by the Ahantas in September of that year; and a small Dutch vessel that was at anchor was captured at the same time, and all the crew massacred. The Dutch, therefore, were not likely to be on friendly terms with the Ahantas.

CHAPTER VII.

1701.

Native States in 1701—European forts—*Personnel* of the Dutch establishments—Interlopers—Description of the Settlements—The trade in gold—Arms of the natives.

IN 1701 was written the "Description of Guinea," by William Bosman, Chief Factor of the Dutch West India Company at Elmina, a work which gives us a clear and succinct account of the Gold Coast at that time. The eleven Native States on the sea-board, already mentioned in Chapter III., still existed, with the exception of Accra, which was now replaced by Akwamu; but a few other changes are noticeable. Fetu had so declined as only to exist under the protection of Commani or Kommenda, and Accra was similarly under the protection of Fanti; while Ahanta, from being a powerful kingdom, had sunk to insignificance, owing to the protracted war between it and Adom and Jabi. We now for the first time hear of some of the inland States, and Bosman mentions Awuin and Eguira, to the north of Axim; Wassaw, north of Ahanta; Inkassa, north of Adom, and Jusser, north of Kommenda. North of these lay the kingdom of Denkera, then the most powerful State to the west of the Prah, and to which Awuin, Wassaw, Inkassa, and Jusser were subject. The last-named seems to have been the present Tshiforo, or Tufel. To the east of the Prah were Akanna (north of Fetu), Akim, and Akwamu. The last named extended from Aguna to the River Volta, and comprised the present Akwapim and

EUROPEAN FORTS.

Eastern Akim. Of the more remote inland tribes, Bosman expressly states, nothing was known except by report. He mentions Asiante (Ashanti) and Akim as the two principal, but neither of these peoples had as yet penetrated to the sea-coast.

The forts then occupied were as follows, commencing from the west:

			When built.
Axim	Fort St. Anthony	Dutch	1515.
Prince's River	Great Fredericsburgh	Brandenburgh	1682.
Akwidah	Fort Dorothea	Brandenburgh	1685.
Dixcove	Dixcove Fort	English	1691.
Butri	Fort Batenstein	Dutch	circa 1640.
Sekondi	Fort Orange	Dutch	circa 1640.
Shamah	Fort St. Sebastian	Dutch	circa 1640.
Kommenda	Fort Vrendenburgh	Dutch	1687.
	Kommenda Fort	English	circa 1673.
Elmina	Castle of St. George	Dutch	1482.
	Fort Conraadsburgh		1638.
Cape Coast	Cape Coast Castle	English	circa 1662.
	Fort Royal		circa 1659.
Mori	Fort Nassau	Dutch	1624.
Anamabo	Anamabo Fort	English	circa 1673.
Cormantine	Fort Amsterdam	Dutch	circa 1650.
Appam	Fort Leydfamheyd	Dutch	1697.
Winnebah	Winnebah Fort	English	1694.
Accra	James Fort	English	circa 1673.
	Fort Crevecœur	Dutch	circa 1650.
Christiansborg	Christiansborg Castle	Danish	circa 1645.

The Fort Royal above mentioned as being at Cape Coast was no other than the Danish fort of Fredericsburgh, at the suburb of Omanfo, which the English had purchased in 1685, and renamed. Notwithstanding all these fortified places, neither the English nor the Dutch were, according to Bosman, possessed of any real power, and trade was continually stopped by the natives, and the forts blockaded. As we have seen, the Ahantas had captured both the Dutch and English forts at Sekondi, and utterly destroyed the latter. He complained of the inefficient garrisons maintained, especially by the English.

Bosman's description of the *personnel* of the Dutch

establishments is curious. He commences with the soldiers
and their commanders, as being the lowest, for in those
days trade looked down upon arms as much as arms now
affects to do upon trade. He tells us that formerly those of
the soldiers who showed any aptitude for trade were promoted to be assistants, but that this had been now prohibited
for some years, so many of the men thus promoted proving
to be drunkards and utterly incapable. The assistant was
the lowest officer of the trading department, with pay and
allowances amounting to thirty-six guilders a month (£3 3s.),
and the Under-Commissary, or sub-factor, came next with
eight guilders a month more. From the oldest or best
qualified sub-factors were selected the factors for the forts,
who received sixty-six guilders a month (£5 13s.); and the
most experienced amongst them were appointed to Mori and
Cormantine, where they received fourteen guilders a month
more. These two places were considered so important that
the Company in Holland had retained in their own hands
the right of appointment to them, as well as to that of chief
factor of Elmina, who was the second person on the Coast,
with a salary of one hundred guilders a month. The
Governor, or Director-General, received three hundred
guilders a month (£26 5s.), and had beside a percentage on
the profits of the trade. The factors were held responsible
for the doings of the sub-factors, whose business it was to
receive the gold, and Bosman tells us that it was necessary
to watch them very closely. He mentions that one factor
had to make good between £800 and £900 lost or squandered
by his sub-factor, and says, that although a factor under such
circumstances had his remedy against the defaulter, yet as
the sub-factors rarely had either money or effects, this was not
of much avail, and the only satisfaction he could take was to
have the defaulter flogged. Any assistant might in course of
time, if he lived long enough, rise to become Director-General,
the only stipulation being that he should have previously
served as chief factor of Elmina for three years.

Besides these officers engaged in the trade, there was a
chief-fiscal, a bookkeeper-general, an accountant of the gar-

rison, and an under-fiscal. The chief-fiscal had a third of all gold or merchandise seized from interlopers, and of all fines or forfeitures of pay inflicted. The under-fiscal, whom Bosman stigmatises as an informer, received a tenth of all forfeitures or fines. In the spiritual department there was a minister with a salary of one hundred and ten guilders a month, and a clerk, with twenty guilders. All the officials of the Company were compelled to go to church every day, or forfeit twenty-five stivers, except on Sundays and Thursdays, when the fine was doubled.

The salaries paid by the Dutch Company seem ridiculously small, even when the great difference between the value of money in that day and this is taken into consideration, and it is a matter for wonder that Europeans should have been willing to exile themselves for years in such a pestilential climate for such miserable pittances; but, as Bosman says, no one ever came there who could live in Holland. The Director-General's annual salary was only £315, and that of a wretched assistant £37 16s., and out of this they had to feed and clothe themselves. The English officials seem to have been much better paid, for, according to Atkins (1721), the English Director-General received £2,000 a year, two factors, or merchants, £300 each, and a secretary £200. These four composed the Council for all the affairs of the Company on the Coast.

The Dutch and Brandenburgh Companies, though cordially disliking one another, were mutually agreed as to the seizing of those interlopers who trespassed upon their exclusive trade. These vessels, as already said, were commonly well armed, and did not surrender without a struggle, and Bosman mentions a case in which a Dutch interloper, the *Great Apollo*, was only taken after a determined resistance by the cruiser *Beschemer*, off Axim. However, the interlopers seem to have found the trade sufficiently profitable to run some risks, for Bosman says: "The negro inhabitants are very rich, driving a great trade with the Europeans for gold, which they chiefly vend to the English and Zealand interlopers, notwithstanding the severe penalty they incur thereby; for if we catch them, their so-bought goods are not only forfeited, but a heavy fine is laid upon them: not deterred, I say, by this, they all hope to escape; to effect which, they bribe our slaves (who are set as watches and spies over them) to let them pass by night; by which means we are hindered from having much above an hundredth part of the gold of this land." The trade of the three Companies was carried on inside their forts or lodges, to which the natives brought their gold and slaves; and Bosman expressly says that no goods were sent outside the walls for sale, and that no credit was ever given.

His description of the towns or villages in the neighbourhood of the forts, shows that they were in a condition almost identical with their present one. He describes the now entirely ruined and almost forgotten Brandenburgh fort, Great Fredericsburg, at Prince's River, as having four batteries, mounting in all forty-six pieces of ordnance. The gate of the fort was the most beautiful on the whole Coast. Sekondi, he says, was formerly one of the finest and richest villages on the Coast, but had recently been burned in the war between the Ahantas and Adoms. The former had resisted all attempts made by the English to rebuild the fort that had been destroyed in 1698. The town of Oddena, under the guns of St. George d'Elmina, he mentions as being built of stone, instead, as is usual, of swish. This was the disloyal quarter of Elmina, which we destroyed in 1873. Fifteen or twenty years before he wrote it had been very populous, and its inhabitants were dreaded by all the surrounding tribes; but it had been depopulated by smallpox and the wars with the Kommendas.

Of Cape Coast Castle he says: " The fort is strengthened with four very large batteries, besides a fifth, on which are planted thirteen pieces of heavy cannon, and these being pointed at the water passage can easily prevent any ships of their enemies' anchoring in that road; besides which a great rock lies just before the fort, so that it is impossible to shoot at it from the sea. The worst of all is that here is generally but a very weak garrison, one part of which (I mean the soldiers) consists of such miserable poor wretches that the very sight of them excites pity. They look as awkward and as wrisled as an old company of Spaniards; the reason of which is, partly, that they greedily entertain those who quit or desert our service, which they will never deliver over to us out of a mistaken mercy, thereby freeing them from their deserved punishment. And though by firm promises and mutual agreement we have frequently and interchangeably obliged ourselves not to countenance or entertain any deserters from each other, but, on the contrary, to send them home in irons, yet they have once more broken the articles; and notwithstanding that those who have run away from us are chiefly sottish wretches, yet they are very welcome to them, the English never being better pleased than when the soldier spends his money in drink, especially in punch, a liquor made of brandy, water, lime-juice, and sugar, which make together an unwholesome mixture. . . . It is incredible how many are consumed by this damnable liquor (pardon the expression), which is not only confined to the soldiery, but some of the principal people are so bigotted to it that I really believe for all the time I was on the coast that at least one of their agents, and factors innumerable, died yearly."

We might, perhaps, be disposed to regard this charge of intemperance brought against the English as unconsciously exaggerated by trade rivalry, but unfortunately it is only too well confirmed by the evidence both of Barbot and Atkins. The former of these two, however, disagrees with Bosman as to the inefficiency of the garrison maintained at Cape Coast Castle, for he says it consisted of one hundred white soldiers, and as many black, with officers, " all clothed in red."

The English Governor at Cape Coast was styled "Captain General of the English Settlements on the Gold Coast of Guinea." He required every ship that anchored in Cape Coast roads, no matter of what nationality, to salute the Castle by lowering the topsails to the tops; and fired shotted guns at all that omitted to pay this compliment. Barbot tells us that on his voyage there in a French vessel he saluted the Castle with seven guns, to which five were returned; and he was about to anchor when three shotted guns were fired at him. Thinking that war must have been declared between England and France, he hastened to quit the roads, and it was only afterwards that he learned the reason of this high-handed proceeding. According to Bosman, the English agents were but little acquainted with the affairs of the Coast, on account of the short stay they made; and they were guided in all matters concerning trade and the natives by a mulatto named Bartu, who lived opposite the Castle. Atkins, in his account of Cape Coast Castle, mentions "the spacious vault under the square or place of arms, cut out of the rock, and divided into several rooms, so as to contain a thousand slaves." The slaves were chained and confined in these dungeons—now used as stores—often for weeks at a time, till a ship came to carry them to the West Indies. They were all branded on the right breast with the letters "D. Y." (Duke of York)

Bosman also mentions the late Danish fort at the suburb of Omanfo, which the English had purchased. It used to mount six guns, but the English proposed enlarging and strengthening it. The summit of the hill was to be scarped and when finished it was to be the strongest position on the Coast. At the present day traces of the foundation of two or three buildings are visible on this hill, and there are a few small pieces of ordnance lying about. After lapse of one hundred and eighty years, the hill-top is still so steeply scarped that it can only be surmounted at one point, which is defended by a deep ditch.

At Mori, the chief station of the Dutch, while the Portuguese held Elmina, the majority of the inhabitants were in Bosman's time, as now, fishermen, and the toll of the fifth fish was exacted by the factor. "This sort of toll," says Bosman, "we yet reserve at three places besides, viz. at Axim, Shamah, and Elmina, by reason we have conquered those places, though I dare not affirm that of Mori. No other Europeans have this peculiar prerogative, nor do any of them exercise such a sovereign authority over their Negro subjects as we; which is indeed chiefly their own fault, and, by their means we have also lost some of our former power."

Of Anamabo, he says: "The English here are so horribly plagued by the Fantynean Negroes (Fantis), that they are sometimes even confined to their fort, not being permitted to stir out. And if the Negroes dislike the Governor of the fort, they usually send him in a canoa to Cabocors (Cape Coast); nor are the English able to oppose or prevent it, but are obliged to make their peace by a present. The town of Anamabo may very well pass for the strongest on the whole coast, affording as many armed men as the whole kingdom of Saboe or Commany; and yet in proportion but a fifth part of Fantyn."

The State of Aguna was ruled by a Queen, an unusual custom on the Gold Coast, but which had apparently been in force in Aguna from time immemorial. According to Barbot, the Queen was not allowed to marry, but could purchase male slaves as paramours. These were liable to be discarded and sold at any moment, and if they intrigued with any other women they lost their heads. The successor to the "stool" was the eldest daughter of the Queen, who, as soon as she arrived at puberty, was similarly entitled to purchase male slaves. Any male children of the Queen, or heiress apparent, were sold as slaves. It is probable that Aguna was the last surviving kingdom of a people who inhabited the Gold Coast before the tribes from the interior descended to the coast. These latter all spoke dialects of one language, the Tshi, but in the south of Aguna, even at the present day, a dialect of a totally distinct language still exists, although Tshi is the language of ordinary use; and there can be little doubt but that this distinct language is that of an older people. In none of the Tshi States on the littoral of the Gold Coast were women ever advanced to positions of power, and the existence of a Queen in Aguna seems to show that the pre-Tshi inhabitants had different customs.

The sanitary, or rather insanitary, condition of the native

towns appears to have undergone no change since Bosman wrote, and to it he attributes, no doubt correctly, much of the unhealthiness of the climate. In his day, however, the death-rate was probably increased by the "ignorant barbers," who were, he tells us, the only physicians. Added to this, medicines rapidly spoiled from the dampness of the atmosphere, and nothing was to be obtained to eat "besides fish and a dry lean hen." In the latter respect Europeans are not much better off at the present day.

The value of the gold annually exported Bosman calculates at 7,000 marks, reckoning three marks to one thousand guilders. This would be equivalent to rather more than £203,000. Of this he reckons that the Dutch West India Company obtained 1,500 marks, the English African Company 1,200 marks, and the Danes and Brandenburghers 1,000 marks; the remainder, 3,300 marks, being carried off by the interlopers. Even at that time the falsification of gold was largely practised by the natives, especially by those of Dixcove and Butri; and he mentions one instance in which the owner of two small English vessels received at the latter place dust which he imagined to be gold to the value of £1,700, but which afterwards proved to be quite valueless. In this case the goods were not recovered from the natives, nor did the unfortunate owner obtain any redress. The ordinary methods of fraud were to mix filings of a mixture of silver and copper with gold-dust, or to cast nuggets of copper or lead covered with a shell of gold; but where the traders were novices, the natives boldly palmed off brass filings upon them.

A large trade was done in fire-arms and gunpowder, which, says Bosman, the Dutch were compelled to adopt, because the English, Danes, and Brandenburghers would insist upon supplying them. The Portuguese had, it seems, wisely prohibited any trade in fire-arms, and probably the importation of such weapons had not long been carried on when Bosman wrote; or, at all events, not to any great extent, for he mentions, amongst the weapons used by the natives, swords, bows and arrows, spears, and shields.

All these have now disappeared from the Coast, except in the far interior, to the north of Ashanti. The swords, "shaped like hooks," were about "two or three hands broad at the extremity, and about one at the handle, and about three or four spans long at most." This shape, as well as that of the handle described by him, is still preserved in the state swords used by chiefs upon ceremonial occasions. Bows and arrows were, he tells us, not much in vogue amongst the natives of the seaboard, those of Akwamu excepted. The Awuins used poisoned arrows, but elsewhere this practice was not known. There were two kinds of spears—one for throwing, "about a Flemish ell in length," and the other for stabbing, about twice the size and weight of the former. The shields, about four or five feet long and three broad, were made of osiers covered with gilded leather, leopard and other skins. Some of them had plates of copper at the extremities and in the middle, to ward off arrows and javelins.

Elephants, which have now entirely disappeared from the forests of the Gold Coast, were then very commonly met with, even in the vicinity of the forts. In December, 1700, one walked along the shore of the River Beyah, under St. Jago Hill, and went into the Government Garden at Elmina, where he broke down the cocoa-nut palms. He was followed by a number of people, and above a hundred shots were fired at him, "which made him bleed to that degree, as if an ox had been killed. During all which he did not stir, but only set up his ears, and made the men apprehend that he would follow them. But this sport was accompanied with a tragical event; for a Negro, fancying himself able to deal with him, went softly behind him, and catched his tail in his hand, designing to cut a piece of it off; but the elephant, being used to wear a tail, would not permit it to be shortened in his lifetime: wherefore, after giving the Negro a stroke with his snout, he drew him to him, and trod upon him two or three times; and, as if that was not sufficient, he bored in his body two holes with his teeth, large enough for a man's double fist to enter. Then he let him lie, without making any further attempt on him; and stood still also whilst two Negroes fetched away the dead body, not offering to meddle with them in the least." After thus asserting himself, the elephant returned to the river, the crowd flying before him in every direction, but at last fell down through loss of blood, and was then hacked to pieces.

CHAPTER VIII.

1701—1750.

Conquest of Denkera by Ashanti—The Elmina Note—Affairs in Ashanti to 1750—John Conny—Condition of the Royal African Company—The African Company of Merchants formed—The slave trade—Piracy on the Coast.

At the close of the seventeenth century the most powerful native state on the Gold Coast known to Europeans was that of Denkera, which, embarking upon a career of conquest, had reduced most of the neighbouring tribes to the condition of feudatories, and was now, in the words of Bosman, accustomed "to lord it over all the neighbouring nations." Its latest conquest had been that of Awuin, which state, after some first reverses, when several thousand Denkeras fell victims to the poisoned arrows of the Awuins, it succeeded in overrunning and subjecting. It is in connection with Denkera that at this time we first hear of that nation which afterwards made such a mark in the history of the Gold Coast—the nation of Ashanti. The Ashanti King, as far as can be ascertained, then ruled over only a small extent of territory around Kumassi,* and a limited portion of Kwao, and the kingdom was considered of but little importance. Tradition, indeed, asserts that it was at this time tributary to Denkera, which seems probable enough, though the Ashantis now indignantly deny it, and assert that they have always maintained their independence.

* Kumassi, "under the Kum tree."

Early in the year 1701, Bosiante, King of Denkera, who had made his name celebrated all over the Coast for his valour, sent some of his wives, in accordance with native custom, on a complimentary visit to Osai Tutu, King of Ashanti, in token of esteem and friendship. The latter received his distinguished guests with all honour, treated them with due ceremony, and a month or so later returned the compliment by sending some of his wives to visit Bosiante. Now, it is a common artifice of native diplomacy for a chief to send some of his wives on a complimentary visit to another chief, after having instructed one or more of them to entangle their host in an intrigue, so that a reasonable pretext for a quarrel, by which conquest may be attempted or gold extorted, may be established. If this was Bosiante's intention in sending his wives to Osai Tutu, his scheme failed; but he himself fell a victim to the wiles of one of the wives of the Ashanti King, who, on her return to Kumassi, duly informed her husband of the fact. Osai Tutu professed to be outraged (perhaps he really was, though all the evidence now obtainable goes to show that Bosiante was entrapped) and declared his intention of washing out the insult in blood. In vain Bosiante offered gold and endeavoured in every way to pacify the injured husband; the latter rejected all offers of a peaceful settlement of the quarrel, and collected large supplies of muskets and gunpowder, which the Denkeras, most short-sightedly, allowed to pass through their territory.

In the midst of these warlike preparations Bosiante died, and his successor, Intim Dakari, sent to inform the Ashanti King of this event, and to renew proposals for peace. These proposals Osai Tutu contemptuously rejected, thus making it clear that he was meditating the conquest of Denkera, and that the insult offered by Bosiante was a mere pretext; for the quarrel between himself and the latter was entirely a personal one, and it could not be alleged that he had any grievance against the Denkeras as a nation. The Denkeras do not appear to have made any great preparations for war: Ashanti was then a small tribe, they had subjected several which were considered of equal or greater importance, and no doubt they imagined they would easily repulse and revenge the meditated aggression. They were entirely ignorant of the warlike spirit of the tribe they were about to meet, and of the system of military discipline which even then was characteristic of Ashanti.

Having completed his preparations, Osai Tutu suddenly swept into Denkera with a large army. The Denkeras were completely defeated in two great battles, and the Akims, who, alarmed at the unprecedented successes of Ashanti, came to the assistance of Denkera, were driven back to their own country with an alleged loss of thirty thousand men. The Ashantis overran and pillaged the whole of Denkera, and finally annexed the greater portion of it to Ashanti. Seventy thousand Denkeras are said to have fallen.

These events are commonly believed to have taken place in 1719, but this is evidently an error. The mistake may be traced to Dupuis, who in 1824 gave a short summary of Ashanti history, based on statements made to him by the Mohammedans, during his visit to Kumassi in 1822. His informants were unable to supply him with dates, but, believing that Bosman wrote in 1721, and knowing that he had referred to the conquest of Denkera as having taken place shortly before he wrote, Dupuis fixed that event in 1719, and later writers, following him, have perpetuated the error. It is probable that Dupuis saw a second edition of Bosman's "Description of Guinea," for the first edition was translated, and published in London, in 1705. However, the last letter in his series is dated January 2nd, 1702, and in an earlier letter he mentions the conquest of Denkera as having taken place "a few months back;" so that there can be little doubt but that it occurred in 1701. This is to a certain extent supported by Barbot, who says that Denkera was conquered in 1700 or 1701.

The King of Denkera had been so considerable a trader in slaves—prisoners of war taken in the subjection of Wassaw, Inkassa, and Awuin—that, on the eve of the Ashanti invasion, the Dutch Director-General at Elmina sent to his assistance two or three small pieces of ordnance and a few native gunners. History is silent as to what part, if any, these played in the two decisive engagements between the Ashantis and the Denkeras, but the cannon fell into the hands of the former, and were taken to Kumassi as trophies, where they might a few years ago still be seen in the open space known as Apprŭm m' (Cannon Place). But the Ashantis made a second capture, which was destined to bring about much more important results than the possession of a few cannon. This was a promissory note on the part of the Dutch, undertaking to pay a monthly sum to the King of Denkera. The view adopted by the Dutch authorities at Elmina in 1871 was that this monthly sum was paid to the King of Denkera as a sort of commission, to encourage him to supply slaves to the Dutch Company; but it really seems to have been a rent for the ground on which the Castle of St. George, or Fort Conraadsburgh, or both, stood. The "note" was first made payable to the chief of Elmina, but during the wars between the Elminas and Kommendas it passed into the hands of the latter, and thence came into the possession of the King of Denkera, who claimed, and regularly received, payment. The King of Ashanti now claimed that by virtue of his right of conquest the ground-rent should be paid to him, and the Dutch, caring little who received the money, readily complied. This compliance, of course, practically amounted to a recognition of the ownership by the King of Ashanti of the ground on which one or both of the Dutch forts at Elmina stood—a point which in aftêr years became of some importance.

The subjection of Denkera was the first of that long series of conquests which subsequently raised Ashanti to the position of paramount power upon the Gold Coast, and it will now be convenient to give some account of its early wars and successes. The dates here given, it may be observed, are those of Dupuis; but as they all seem to be based upon the original error that Denkera was conquered in 1719, it is probable that all are eighteen years too late.

After the conquest of Denkera, Osai Tutu turned his arms against Akim, to punish that people for the assistance lent to the Denkeras. The Akims were soon defeated, and, besides being compelled to pay a heavy fine, the King of Akim was reduced to the condition of a tributary. The chiefs of Akim, however, repudiated the terms forced upon their King, and the war being renewed, an Ashanti army again invaded the country. As Osai Tutu was on his way to join this army with a small escort, he and his followers were suddenly attacked by a strong body of the enemy, which, lying in ambush, fell upon them as they were crossing the Prah. The King was wounded in the side at the first fire; but he threw himself out of his hammock, and was rallying his men, when a second volley was discharged, and he fell dead upon his face in the river. This was in the year 1731.

Encouraged by this success, the Denkeras again took up arms and joined the Akims, as did the Assins, a nation then occupying the territory to the north of the Prah, between that river and Ashanti. The war was now prosecuted with greater fury than ever; the brother and successor of Osai Tutu, Osai Apoko, was successful on all sides, the Assins and Denkeras were thoroughly subdued, and the Akims crushed. A terrible example was made of Acromanti, the town in which the party of Akims who had slain Osai Tutu had halted on the night previous to their attack, every living creature found in it being put to death, and every house razed to the ground. To commemorate the death of their King, the oath *Akromanti Memereda* (Akromanti Saturday) was established by law as one of the most sacred oaths of Ashanti. From the Akims, Osai Apoko captured certain notes which undertook on the part of the issuers—English, Dutch, and Danish officials—to pay to certain chiefs of Accra and Christiansborg an annual sum as rent for the ground on which the English and Dutch forts at Accra, and the Danish castle of Christiansborg stood. These notes had, it is said, come into the possession of the Akims by the conquest of the chiefs of these sea-coast towns; and the Ashanti King now claimed payment by right of capture, just as he claimed payment of the Dutch note that he had captured from the Denkeras.

Osai Apoko, a few years after the conquest of Akim, invaded Gaman—a state to the north-west of Ashanti—defeated its King in a great battle, and reduced him to the condition of a feudatory. In the latter part of his reign he was obliged to fly from his capital before a dangerous conspiracy, caused by his attempting to curtail the power of the chiefs, and change the government by an aristocracy, which had hitherto prevailed, into a personal despotism. In his retirement, however, he collected together his adherents, and after endeavouring, unsuccessfully, to arrange a convention at Djuabin for the settlement of the quarrel, he attacked the rebellious chiefs, and finally defeated them. He died suddenly in 1742, and the chiefs, before raising his successor, Osai Akwasi, to the stool, were careful to stipulate that the old constitution should be restored.

The new King had not long been in power when the chiefs of Kwao and Western Akim, encouraged by promises of assistance from Dahomi, rebelled. Osai Akwasi unexpectedly fell upon them with a considerable army, completely crushed them, and then crossed the River Volta to call the King of Dahomi to account. Two days' journey beyond that river he met the Dahoman army, and a most sanguinary engagement ensued, which was only terminated by nightfall. Next morning the Ashantis were preparing to renew the contest, but were stopped by their priests, who declared that the omens were unfavourable. The Dahomans, mistaking this inactivity for want of resolution, advanced to the attack, and Osai Akwasi, without attempting any defence ordered a retreat to the Volta, which he hastily recrossed, losing the greater part of his army. The Moors of Kumassi who informed M. Dupuis of this event, ascribed the disaster solely to the superstitious fears of the Ashantis, they being persuaded that the resources of Ashanti were quite sufficient to have crushed Dahomi. This invasion of Dahomi is generally supposed to have taken place about 1750.

To return to the affairs on the littoral of the Gold Coast. The first event worthy of note is that the Governor of Elmina, in 1702, sent an expedition to endeavour to dislodge the French from Assini, just beyond the confines of the Gold Coast, where they had built a palisaded fort in the previous year; but the expedition failed in its object, and returned, after having lost some fifty men, who landed and fell into an ambush.

About 1720 the Brandenburghers abandoned their fort of Great Fredericsburgh, at Prince's River, for their trade there had gradually been declining for years, and they were on bad terms with the natives, who had murdered one of their directors by breaking all his limbs, and then throwing him into the sea. On their withdrawal, the fort was taken possession of by a local chief, who was known to Europeans as John Conny. In 1720 the Dutch determined to occupy this fort, and accordingly sent a bomb-vessel and two or three small craft to demand its surrender, on the grounds that they had purchased the building from the Brandenburghers. Suspecting that this was a mere pretext, John Conny astutely asked to see the deed of sale, which the Dutch were unable to produce, for the alleged purchase was a mere fiction; and, finding they could not obtain possession by fraud, they resorted to force. After bombarding the village and fort for some time, without producing much effect, they landed a body of men, who were, however, so warmly received that not one of them survived to return to the ships, which, thereupon, retired to Elmina. To celebrate his success, John Conny had a narrow path, leading from the outer gate of the fort to his apartment, paved with the skulls of the slain Dutch, reserving one of an unusual size to be lined with silver and used as a punch-bowl; and the tradition of these doings, considerably exaggerated, still lingers in the neighbourhood of Prince's River. Marchais says that 156 men were killed, and that the Dutch Director-General was wounded. He says that a French ship, *The Princess of Rochfort*, was at Prince's River at the time, and that, after the Dutch had sailed away, John Conny offered to give the fort to Morel, the French captain, for the purpose of forming a French settlement; but that Morel declined the offer. According to the Dutch accounts, a lieutenant and forty men were landed, and all killed.

After this success John Conny exercised sovereign rights in the district, and exacted one ounce of gold from each vessel that put into the place for the privilege of watering. In 1721 the British men-of-war, *Swallow* and *Weymouth*, neglected to pay this impost, and Conny seized the water-casks and carried off ten or twelve of the watering-party as prisoners. He, however, treated them well, saying that he knew it was not their fault, and the difficulty was finally settled by the payment of six ounces of gold and an anker of brandy by the British commander, Captain Chaloner Ogle. The native chief remained in possession of the fort until 1725, when the Dutch attacked the place with a large force, and forced him to fly for refuge to the Fantis.

The trade of the Royal African Company, which had commenced to decline with the passing of the Act of 1698, that declared the trade open, was now in a very wretched condition; the private traders, who had no establishments on the Coast to keep up, being able to sell their merchandise at a far cheaper rate than the Company could, while the payment of the ten per cent. *ad valorem* for the maintenance of the forts was generally evaded. In 1721 the Company found it necessary to raise a large sum by subscription; the salaries of the officials were cut down, and Surgeon Atkins, of the *Swallow*, who visited Cape Coast in that year, tells us that the Company's officers, with the exception of those of the first rank, were both wretchedly paid and badly used. They were liable to heavy fines for drunkenness, swearing, sleeping out of the Castle, neglect, and also for not going to church, and according to Atkins, these fines were so frequently inflicted that many of the subordinates found their whole pay swallowed up and themselves in debt to the Company, which in this way obtained a hold upon them, and prevented them from resigning their appointments. While he was there the captain of the Company's garrison at Cape Coast

Castle escaped by night to a brigantine which was leaving the Coast; but the escape was discovered, the brigantine was chased and overtaken by the *Weymouth*, her master fined seventy ounces and flogged, and the captain restored to the tender mercies of the Company. A Mr. Phipps was Director-General of the English Company at this time. He built a circular tower on a hill about half a mile to the north of the Castle, which it commanded; it was named, after him, Phipps's Tower, but in after years became known as Fort William. In the decay of their prosperity the Company was now compelled to give credit to the natives, in order to compete with the private traders, who were unable to do this, as they only remained a short time on the Coast. Atkins says that, to secure the payment, the Company's officials used to make persons asking for credit pawn themselves to the Company, with the liability of being eventually sold in default.

It was in consequence of the wretched condition of the affairs of the Company that on March 26th, 1730, the House of Commons resolved that the trade to Africa should be absolutely free, but that as it was necessary to keep up the forts on the Coast, Parliament should grant an allowance to the Company for that purpose. The trade had really been practically free since 1700, and all that this resolution effected was to transfer the cost of the maintenance of the forts to the English tax-payer, instead of making the private traders, who enjoyed their protection, contribute to their support; but it had been found impossible to collect the sums due from the latter under the old Act. In accordance with this resolution, £10,000 was voted annually till 1744, when, on account of the war with France and Spain, the amount was doubled. In 1745 the grant again fell to £10,000, but in the year 1747 nothing was granted. Relieved of the cost of keeping up the forts, the Royal African Company contrived to prolong its existence till 1750, when an Act, entitled "An Act for extending and improving the trade to Africa," was passed, and a fifth company, called the African Company of Merchants, was formed.

The slave trade had now increased to such an extent that

the Gold Coast alone was said to furnish annually ten thousand slaves for the West Indies. This impulse was chiefly due to the success which had attended the arms of Ashanti, and thousands of prisoners of war were sent by that people to the great slave mart of Mansu,* for sale to the native brokers. The Gold Coast negroes were termed Koromantees, or Koromantyns, in the jargon of the slave-traders, this name being a corruption of Cormantine, whence the English had first exported slaves. They were distinguished from all other slaves by their courage, firmness, and impatience of control; characteristics which caused numerous mutinies on board the slavers, and several rebellions in the West Indies. In fact every rebellion of slaves in Jamaica originated with, and was generally confined to, the Koromantees; and their independence of character became so generally recognised that at one time the Legislature of Jamaica proposed that a bill should be brought in for laying an additional duty upon the "Fantin, Akin, and Ashanti negroes, and all others, commonly called Koromantees," that should be imported. The superior physique of the Gold Coast negroes, however, rendered them very valuable as labourers, and this bill met with so much opposition that it was withdrawn; and, notwithstanding their dangerous character, large numbers continued to be introduced to the island. Bryan Edwards says : † "Even the children brought from the Gold Coast manifest an evident superiority, both in hardiness of frame and vigour of mind, over all the young people of the same age that are imported from other parts of Africa. The like firmness and intrepidity which are distinguishable in adults of this nation, are visible in their boys at an age which might be thought too tender to receive any lasting impression, either from precept or example. I have been myself an eye-witness to the truth of this remark, in the circumstance I am about to relate. A gentleman of my acquaintance, who had purchased at the same time ten

* Mansu (Water Town) is about thirty miles to the north of Cape Coast.
† "History of the West Indies."

Koromantyn and the like numbers of Ibos (the eldest of the whole apparently not more than thirteen years of age) caused them all to be collected and brought before him in my presence, to be marked on the breast. This operation is performed by heating a small silver brand, composed of one or two letters, in the flame of spirits of wine, and applying it to the skin, which is previously anointed with sweet oil. The application is instantaneous, and the pain momentary. Nevertheless, it may easily be supposed that the apparatus must have a frightful appearance to a child. Accordingly, when the first boy, who happened to be one of the Ibos, and the stoutest of the whole, was led forward to receive the mark, he screamed dreadfully, while his companions of the same nation manifested strong symptoms of sympathetic terror. The gentleman stopped his hand; but the Koromantyn boys, laughing aloud, and immediately coming forward of their own accord, offered their bosoms undauntedly to the brand, and receiving its impression without flinching in the least, snapped their fingers in exultation over the poor Ibos."

From the testimony of Phillips (1693) we find that Gold Coast slaves would always yield in the West Indies £3 or £4 a head more than those of Whydah, who were generally called Popo, or Pawpaw, negroes. These latter again were preferred to the Ibos, and the Awuna slaves were considered the worst of all. Snelgrave,* who made voyages to the Gold Coast in 1721 and 1722, confirms this, and says that the Koromantees were the most dangerous slaves to deal with. He gives particulars of two mutinies of slaves on board slave-ships, one at Anamabo, which were planned and carried out by Koromantees; and remarks that such slaves were "desperate fellows, who despised punishment, and even death itself." Some mutineers, when asked why they had mutinied, boldly told him that he was a great scoundrel to have bought them for the purpose of taking them away from their native country, and that they were resolved to obtain their liberty if they could.

* Astley's "Collection of Voyages."

The large majority of the slaves exported from the Gold Coast were prisoners of war, of both sexes, and of all ages; the residue being persons who were slaves in their own country, and those who under the customs of the country had become liable to enslavement for debt or crime. Many young men, it is said, were entrapped by the wives of men of rank, who, instructed by their husbands, formed intrigues with them, and then denounced them. By native law such an offence could only be expiated by the payment of a sum proportionate to the rank of the injured husband, with the alternative of slavery; and as the youths entrapped were commonly such as could not pay, numbers thus became enslaved and were sold out of the country.

The slaves, before being brought to market by their native owners, were close-shaven and anointed with palm-oil, so as to give the skin a glossy appearance, and it was no easy matter to distinguish a young from a middle-aged slave, except by the decay of the teeth. Various artifices were resorted to by native slave-dealers to give an appearance of youth and health to slaves of an inferior quality, and there was as much chicanery brought into play over the sale and purchase of slaves as there is at the present day in horse-dealing. Hence, all slaves bought for exportation were carefully examined by a surgeon, to see if they were sound in wind and limb, and were put through various performances. Such as passed the surgeon's examination were then branded on the breast or shoulder; the men were coupled together with irons, and all were consigned to the dungeons or slave-rooms of the various forts, till such time as a ship arrived to convey them to the West Indies.

The slaves so dreaded leaving their native country for an unknown fate in a strange land, that they often, unless most carefully watched and secured, leaped overboard from the canoe or ship, and kept under water till they were drowned; while others starved themselves to death. Death had for them no terrors; there was no uncertain future to be faced. There was simply a more or less prolonged struggle and then a change of residence to a spirit world similar in all respects to this, where they would continue the old life amongst their own people; and it is not surprising that they should prefer this to a life of unknown, and consequently dreaded, terrors in another sphere. The natives of the Gold Coast were so confident that after death they would rejoin their own people in their own spirit world, that during the suppression of every rebellion of slaves in Jamaica, numbers of Koromantees committed suicide; and dozens were sometimes found hanging to the branches of the silk-cotton trees. By some tribes it was held that dismemberment prevented this return, and it appears that the masters of some slave vessels, who had reason to anticipate wholesale suicides, did not hesitate to cut off the arms or legs of one or two slaves to terrify the rest.

On board the slave-ships, slaves were fed twice a day, and allowed in fair weather to be on deck from seven in the morning till sunset. The women and children were allowed to go about free; but the men were usually kept in irons, at all events till some days after the African coast had been left, and were invariably separated from the women. Every Monday they were allowed the luxury of pipes and tobacco. Although there were, no doubt, individual cases of cruelty here and there, yet, on the whole, it seems that this monstrous traffic was carried on with as much humanity as the circumstances and the system allowed. The traders had a pecuniary interest in the well-being of each human chattel, and therefore they did not ill-treat them, or so act as to cause their value to be lessened. The slave-ships were usually roomy and well found, and at this time, while the trade was lawful, not half the hardships were experienced that afterwards fell to the lot of slaves exported when the trade was declared to be illicit.

Any account of the Gold Coast at this time would be incomplete without some reference to the pirates who infested the whole West Coast of Africa. The breaking up of the haunts of the buccaneers in the West Indies had led those gentry to adopt a change of scene, and their vessels, two or three of which usually sailed in company, roamed up and down the whole African coast, and committed the greatest depredations. Some of the pirates made a business of waylaying slave-ships, transferring the human cargoes to their own vessels, and selling them in the West Indies; while others plundered and burned every peaceable merchantman they met. They were sufficiently formidable to capture some of the Royal African Company's forts. For instance, James Fort, in the River Gambia, was taken by Davis, the pirate, in 1719, and Bunce Island Fort, Sierra Leone, by Roberts, in 1720; and, as already mentioned, the two Danish men-of-war, each of 26 guns, sent out to recover Christiansborg from the natives, were taken by Avery in 1693. In one year Roberts destroyed over a hundred sail of ships along the coast, and at last commerce became so crippled that the English Government, in 1721 sent out the *Swallow* and *Weymouth*, men-of-war, to put an end to these depredations. The *Swallow* fell in with Roberts, with three pirate vessels, at Cape Lopez. In the action which ensued Roberts was killed, and the pirates some three hundred in number, nearly all Englishmen surrendered after a very feeble resistance. The prisoner were conveyed for trial to Cape Coast Castle, where fifty two of them were executed; and when Smith, surveyor o the Royal African Company, visited Cape Coast in 1727 the remains of several of these were still hanging in chains.

CHAPTER IX.

1751—1804.

Affairs in Ashanti during the reign of Osai Kwadjo—First mention of Ashanti in the Records of Cape Coast Castle—War between England and Holland—Extraordinary affair at Mori—Reigns of Osai Kwamina and Osai Apoko II.—Accession of Tutu Kwamina—Position of Ashanti at the commencement of the nineteenth century.

OSAI AKWASI, King of Ashanti, died in 1752, of a wound which he had received in an attack upon Banna. The natives of the Gold Coast, like the large majority of the uncivilised peoples of the earth, trace descent through the mother instead of through the father, and the crown now descended to a sister's son, Osai Kwadjo, the three preceding Kings having been brothers.

The new King no sooner succeeded to the stool than he demanded payment of tribute from the tributaries, who were some years in arrear. The Gamans, Denkeras, and Tshiforos, or Tufels, used this as a pretext for taking up arms, and, upon war breaking out, were joined by the Wassaws. Two invasions of Gaman by the Ashantis proved disastrous, principally because the people of that state were assisted by a large contingent from the Mohammedan state of Kong, armed with muskets; but a third invasion proved successful, and Osai Kwadjo returned to Kumassi with thousands of captives. Of these, the children were spared to recruit the army, which had suffered heavily, and the adults of both sexes were either sacrificed as thank-offerings to the gods, or sent to the great slave mart at Mansu to be sold into West Indian slavery. Gaman, Denkera, and Tshiforo having been reduced, Wassaw soon fell before the Ashanti army, and several large districts were entirely depopulated.

The defeat of Gaman and its allies laid open the Sarem country to the conqueror, and he might, had he chosen, have carried his victorious arms as far as Cape Palmas, but he satisfied himself with receiving the submission of the neighbouring Kings. Dahomi, alarmed at the rapid successes of Ashanti, and fearing that the King might be tempted to revenge the defeat which his predecessor had sustained, sent a friendly embassy to Kumassi, which was received in the most flattering manner, and an embassy sent to Dahomi in return, to cement the friendliness between the two monarchs.

Towards the end of his reign Osai Kwadjo was compelled by ill-health and the infirmities of age to confine himself to his palace, and his enemies circulated a report that he was dead. Assin, Akim, and Akwapim at once seized the opportunity to throw off the Ashanti yoke, and broke out in a fresh rebellion. Ambassadors sent by the King to recall them to obedience were murdered, and, as the rebels threatened to march upon Kumassi, the Ashantis at once prepared for war; but before the army could take the field Osai Kwadjo died. This was in 1781.

Cruickshank, the author of "Eighteen Years on the Gold Coast," who wrote in 1853, tells us that it was during the reign of this King that the first notice made of Ashanti was found in the Records of Cape Coast Castle which, it may be remarked, have long since disappeared On July 10th, 1765, the Council took into consideration the state of the country. It was represented that the Ashantis and Fantis having in conjunction destroyed Akim were on the point of commencing hostilities with each other; and the Council fearing that if the Fantis prevailed trade would be injured, and if the Ashantis were victorious the settlements would be endangered, determined to observe a strict neutrality in concert with the Dutch Governor. In 1767 the attitude of the Fantis and Ashantis was still hostile, and the Council stated that the Dutch were instigating the latter to conquer the country. They resolved to improve the fortifications, and applied to the Committee in London for ships of war to remain on the coast while this state of affairs lasted. In 1772 the Council were again anxious about an Ashanti invasion, and resolved to give all the assistance they could to the Fantis, but without leaving their forts or taking any active part in the struggle. The trade appears to have been greatly interrupted during the whole reign of Osai Kwadjo, who kept the Fantis in a state of continual alarm by threats of invasion.

On December 20th, 1780, England declared war against Holland, and in the following year an attack was made upon Elmina by a combined land and sea force. The former consisted of a few of the Company's soldiers and a body of some three hundred natives of Cape Coast, commanded by Robert Joseph McKenzie, captain of an independent company in the African service; and the latter of the fifty-gun ship *Leander*, Captain Shirley, and a sloop of war. There appears to have been a great want of cordial co-operation between the two commanders, and Captain Shirley cannot be acquitted of an exhibition of that jealousy of military commanders which unfortunately seems to have been then common, and which led Admiral Vernon, under somewhat similar circumstances, to passively regard the slaughter of General Wentworth's troops at Carthagena in 1741. Instead of attacking Elmina from the sea, in co-operation with the land forces, he waited until they were repulsed before commencing the bombardment; with the result that the Dutch, able to bestow their undivided attention upon him, beat him off also. Early in the following year (1782) Captain Shirley, reinforced by H.M.S. *Argo*, succeeded in taking the small Dutch forts of Mori, Cormantine, Appam, and Barraku, which were not in a position to offer any serious resistance; while Governor Mills, assisted by fifty men from the *Argo*, took Kommenda Fort. As a set-off to this, the Dutch captured the English fortified trading lodge at Sekondi.

These conquests were mutually restored at the peace of 1784, but while Mori was still in British hands, an affair took place there which will give some idea of the extraordinary events that sometimes occurred on the Gold Coast. From the "Annual Register" of 1784 we learn that, on December 10th of that year, Captain Robert Joseph McKenzie was tried in London for the murder of Kenneth Murray McKenzie, a soldier under his command, at Mori Fort, on August 14th, 1782. The murdered man, who had previously acted as adjutant, had, it seems, been placed in open arrest by his captain for some breach of discipline, and was not allowed to quit the fort; but one day he disobeyed this order and went out. On this coming to the knowledge of the captain, he sent out a sergeant and three men to bring him back; and it being supposed that the deserter had gone to join the Dutch at Elmina, the party went in that direction as far as they dared, and returned without having seen or heard anything of the fugitive. Captain McKenzie then concluded that the man must be in the native town of Mori, the inhabitants of which were all in the Dutch interest and covertly hostile to the English. It was probably on this account that instead of sending to demand his man, he opened fire upon the town, the inhabitants of which at once fled, but returned next morning and surrendered the deserter; who within an hour of his surrender was, by his captain's order blown from the muzzle of one of the guns. This act was committed without any trial having been held, and without the captain having either seen or spoken to his victim. The latter had declared to his comrades that he had no intention of deserting, and said that the reason of his not returning the same night was that he had been drunk, and had been detained by the natives. He had pleaded to be allowed to see his commander, and to defend himself, but

Captain McKenzie had refused to hold any communication with him. For the defence of Captain McKenzie it was shown that the murdered man was of bad character, he having, when a private in the 3rd Regiment of Foot Guards, been on three different occasions sentenced to death for robbery, but had each time been reprieved, and had finally been drafted as a convict into the African service. Since that time he had deserted twice, and evidence was called to show that he had on several occasions used mutinous language, and was plotting to murder his captain and surrender the fort to the Dutch. It was shown that the proportion of convicts to volunteers in the garrison was as sixteen to five, and it was urged that it was absolutely necessary to make some example in order to overawe the insubordinate soldiers. Judge Willes, in summing up, said that Captain McKenzie was not justified by martial law, and should have tried the soldier by court-martial, or at least have called upon him to make some defence. He left the question of justification to the jury, and the latter found the prisoner guilty, but recommended him to mercy. Captain McKenzie had previously distinguished himself at the defence of Jersey, and great efforts were made to obtain a reprieve. These were successful, for in the "Annual Register" for 1785 we find that he received His Majesty's pardon for the murder, but was detained in Newgate to be tried at the next Admiralty Sessions for piracy, in cutting out from under the guns of a Dutch fort on the Gold Coast a Portuguese ship with Dutch colours, of which complaint had been made by the Portuguese Ambassador. From the same source we learn that Government detained £11,000 worth of his gold-dust till he gave an account of the stores, etc., that had been in his charge. After this we hear no more of him.

To return to affairs in Ashanti. We left an Ashanti army about to take the field against the rebellious Assins, Akims, and Akwapims, when the death of Osai Kwadjo in 1781 delayed active operations for a time. Osai Kwamina, who succeeded to the stool, as soon as the ceremonies of his installation were completed, took an oath never to enter the walls of the palace, or visit his wives, till he had obtained the heads of the two principal rebels. He overran the revolted provinces with a large army, took the Akims by surprise by a forced march, and the rebellion was soon entirely crushed, while the skulls of the two rebel leaders found a place amongst similar trophies preserved in Kumassi.

Osai Kwamina also extended his conquests inland, and invaded Banna. Odrarsi, the King, opposed him for a while; but at last, perceiving that resistance was hopeless, he committed suicide, after having given orders that his head should be cut off and sewn up in the stomach of a dead woman, in order that it might not fall into the hands of the enemy. This order was obeyed, but the Ashantis discovered the head and carried it to Kumassi. Nsuta was also subjected in this reign, and Koransa became tributary after a struggle that lasted ten years and was carried on principally by Gaman auxiliaries.

The reputation of Ashanti was now so well established that, in 1792, the Danish Governor of Christiansborg applied to Osai Kwamina for a force to punish the people of Popo, on the Slave Coast, who had committed some outrages on Danish subjects. The request was granted, and a force was actually on its way to the coast, when the Governor, becoming alarmed at the approach of such dangerous allies, bought their return to their own country with two hundred and fifty ounces of gold-dust. On hearing of this proposed expedition, the Governor and Council at Cape Coast Castle had sent messengers to Kumassi to prevail upon the King not to send the force asked for, being naturally alarmed at the prospect of Ashanti interference in the affairs of the seaboard; but the mission was not attended with any success. This, it may be remarked, is the first time any direct communication took place between the English and the King of Ashanti.

In 1797 Osai Kwamina was deposed, he having given offence to the chiefs by prohibiting many festivals at which it was customary to offer human sacrifices. It was, more-

over, suspected that he was at heart a Mohammedan, and
was endeavouring to establish the law of the Koran in his
kingdom. He was succeeded by his brother, Osai Apoko II.
The chiefs of Gaman, instigated by the Mohammedans of
Kong, used the dethronement of Osai Kwamina as a pretext
for rebellion, and the King of Gaman transferred his tribute
to the King of Kong. The war that ensued lasted fifteen
months, during which the entire force of Kong, joined with
that of Gaman, crossed the Tando River and advanced into
Ashanti territory. The Ashanti King, whose force was only
a fourth of that of the enemy, acted for some months on
the defensive, till the arrival of the tributary forces from
Koransa, Banna, and Djuabin enabled him to act. He then
gave battle to the foe on the Tando, and after several days'
fighting routed them with great slaughter, returning to
Kumassi laden with spoil and captives, amongst whom were
upwards of five thousand Mohammedans.

A few months after his victory on the Tando, Apoko II.
died, after a lingering illness, which was attributed by the
natives to the magical practices of his deposed brother. His
brother, Tutu Kwamina, succeeded him in 1799, and shortly
after his elevation to the throne, commenced a war against
the Mohammedan kingdom of Ghofan, to the north-east of
Ashanti. The fortunes of war at first favoured the Mohammedans; but before long they were driven back, and finally
defeated in a sanguinary engagement near the Volta. Two
Kings fell alive into the hands of the Ashantis, and the King
of Ghofan was killed. By this victory the Ashantis acquired
a considerable increase of territory; but the war was scarcely
successfully terminated when a fresh rebellion in Gaman
occurred. This was rapidly suppressed, and for five years
peace ensued, till those disturbances commenced in Assin
which ultimately led to the first invasion of Fanti.

At this point it will be convenient to note the position of
Ashanti at the commencement of the nineteenth century.
Since the reign of Osai Tutu, Nsuta, Gaman, Koransa, and
Banna to the north; Denkera, Sefwhi, Tshiforo, Wassaw,
and Awuin to the west and south-west; Assin to the south;

and Akim, Akwapim, Kwao, and Akwamu to the east—had all been subjected; and the whole of the Gold Coast was now under Ashanti rule, with the exception of the states on the seaboard. But though the Ashantis could conquer they could not govern, and their authority over the tributary states was more nominal than real. It was their custom after subduing a kingdom to leave to the King a species of semi-independence, merely exacting a fixed annual sum as tribute, and military service in time of war. They established no garrisons in the conquered territories, appointed no governors or residents, and did not attempt in the least to blend with the people. Hence, whenever a tributary King conceived himself strong enough to throw off his allegiance to Ashanti he did so; and the Ashanti kingdom resembled a loosely united bundle of sticks, which any severe shock might cause to fall to pieces. Since their conquest, the Denkeras had rebelled twice; the Akims and the Gamans three times; and the Assins and the Akwapims once; and all this within about fifty years. The authority of the Ashanti King was in fact only maintained by repeated invasions of the tributary states, the people of which were not bound to their conquerors either by sentiment or interest.

CHAPTER X.

1805—1807.

Disturbances in Assin—Condition of Fanti—First invasion of Fanti—Defence of Anamabo Fort — Torrane's convention — His dishonourable transactions — Continuation of the war—End of the invasion.

IN 1805 Assin was divided into three chieftainships, under Tchibbu, Kwaku Aputeh, and Amu, the two former ruling over the western, and the latter over the eastern half. This division had been effected by Osai Kwamina, after the rebellion of Assin, in 1781. Towards the close of 1805 a dispute arose between Amu and Kwaku Aputeh, the origin of which was as follows. One of Amu's captains had died, and as he was a rich man, a considerable quantity of gold was, according to custom, deposited in the grave with the body. A follower of Kwaku Aputeh, who was present at the interment, rifled the grave and stole the treasure; but the theft was discovered, and Amu at once demanded redress, and the return of the gold, from Kwaku Aputeh and Tchibbu. Failing to obtain satisfaction from these, he laid his complaint before the Ashanti King, who summoned Aputeh and Tchibbu to Kumassi. The former obeyed the summons, the latter excusing himself on the ground of infirmity; but the case was heard, judgment was given in favour of Amu, and Aputeh was ordered to be detained in Kumassi till restitution was made. Shortly after this decision Aputeh contrived to escape from the capital, and as he set the King's decree at defiance, Amu took up arms to enforce it. He gained one battle, but Tchibbu having in the meantime joined Aputeh, he was severely defeated in a second engagement, and compelled to fall back upon the frontiers of Ashanti. The war was then continued for some months with varying success, until the Ashanti King called upon the combatants to refer their dispute to him. Amu obeyed this summons, and fell back upon the Adansi Hills, where he was directed to disband his force, and to repair to Kumassi, while Aputeh was ordered to refrain from molesting him; but that chief, so far from obeying, attacked and defeated Amu's force, put to death some Ashanti messengers who were in his camp, and seized their state swords, and the golden axe of Ashanti, as trophies. Upon this Tutu Kwamina at once raised a powerful army, and entered the Assin territory. Tchibbu and Aputeh attempted to make a stand at Ansa, but were defeated; a second attempt at Miassa, the capital of the old Assin kingdom, fared no better; and a retreat to the Prah was turned into a complete rout by the vigorous pursuit of the Ashantis. According to the popular Ashanti songs, thirty thousand Assins perished in these engagements, and a river of blood flowed from Miassa to the Prah.

Fanti was at this time no longer the insignificant state it had been a century earlier, when it extended in breadth merely from the Iron Hills to Saltpond, and had a depth of some twelve miles only. Since that time the Fantis had, by threats, promises, and force of arms, brought into subjection the two states of Acron and Aguna to the east, and those of Fetu and Sabi to the west, so that their territory now extended from the Sweet River to Barraku. The town of Cape Coast even fell under the influence of Fanti, and the people, as Meredith tells us, were obliged to submit to its laws and customs. In fact, Fanti had begun, in some respects, to emulate in the southern districts of the Gold Coast the career of Ashanti in the northern; and Meredith* complains of their ungovernable conduct,

* An Account of the Gold Coast.

which constantly kept the country in a turmoil. To the north-west of Fanti proper was the kingdom of Arbra, which was considered the leading state of Fanti; and to the north was the kingdom of Essikuma, which, though to some extent influenced by Fanti, still preserved a species of independence. The Government of Fanti appears to have been that of a federation. Besides the King of Arbra, there was a King at Mankassim,* and another at Anamabo, while several chiefs claimed to rule their own districts independently of all three.

Tchibbu, an old, infirm, and blind man, fled, with Kwaku Aputeh, to Essikuma, to the chief of which state the Ashanti King sent a present of twenty ounces of gold, asking for the surrender of the fugitives, and professing his friendship. It appears that the chief intended to comply, and the Assin fugitives, discovering his intentions, fled to Arbra, from whose King Osai Tutu Kwamina next demanded them. A council of Fanti chiefs assembled at Arbra to consider this demand, and as they refused to surrender the fugitives, the Ashanti King then sent to ask permission for his army to march through Fanti, to pursue the remnant of the Assin force; but this application was also rejected, and the Ashanti messengers were, it is said, barbarously murdered.

The Ashanti army, under its general, Appia Dunkwa, then advanced, and the Fantis, with the relics of Tchibbu's and Aputeh's army, were defeated in two engagements. Many prisoners were taken, and amongst them Attah, King of Arbra. The Arbras wished to ransom their King, and the Ashanti general expressed his willingness, provided that the state swords and the golden axe, which were now in the hands of the Arbras, were surrendered; but while the negotiations were going on, Akum, chief of Essikuma, in whose hands Attah had been placed for safe keeping, allowed him to escape. Aputeh then made offers of submission, which the King accepted, sending messengers with presents both

* Mankassim (Great Town), about fifteen miles north of Saltpond.

to him and Tchibbu; but the proposals had, it seems, only been made to gain time, for these Ashanti messengers were, like the former, inhumanly put to death. Enraged at this outrage, the King took his sacred oath never to sheath the sword or return to his capital till the heads of Tchibbu and Aputeh lay at his feet, and at once hastened to join his army. The utter extermination of the Fantis was determined upon, and orders were issued to spare none of either sex, or of any age. An engagement took place at Arbra which was most sanguinary. The Ashantis were at first repulsed with great slaughter; but a sudden attack in the flank and rear of the Fantis, made by the King in person, changed the fate of the day. Their retreat cut off, nearly the entire Fanti force was slaughtered, and only about one hundred men are said to have escaped from the fatal field. Arbrakampa was burned, and the inhabitants butchered or cast into the burning houses. The few survivors made their way to Anamabo, then perhaps the most important town on the sea-coast; but Tchibbu and Aputeh soon quitted that place for Cape Coast, where they received assurances of protection from Colonel Torrane, the Governor.

Akum, the chief of Essikuma, had, so far, taken no part in the hostilities, and had indeed supplied the Ashantis with provisions, on which account the King had overlooked his treachery in conniving at Attah's escape; but now, for some unknown reason, he suddenly committed an act of hostility, by seizing seven hundred carriers, who had been sent to him to procure food, and selling them as slaves. This action at such a time, when the Fantis had just suffered a crushing defeat, would appear incomprehensible, did we not know that the inhabitants of the Gold Coast, like most savages, are simply guided by the passion of the moment, and rarely consider the consequences of their acts. Appia Dunkwa at once moved against Akum, defeated his force, and scattered it in every direction. During this expedition the bulk of the Ashanti army, under the King, remained encamped at Arbrakampa, and Colonel Torrane, fearing for the safety of Cape Coast, on which the Ashantis might advance at any moment, purposed sending a flag of truce to them, but abandoned the design in consequence of the opposition of the Cape Coast chiefs. The fact was that the people of Cape Coast believed themselves fully able to cope with the Ashantis, of whom, it is but just to say, they had then had no experience.

The Ashanti force under Appia Dunkwa, after defeating Akum, moved leisurely down to the coast, destroying Mankassim and several other towns, and first gained sight of the sea in the neighbourhood of Cormantine. They destroyed the town, and Appia Dunkwa, after sending several calabashes full of salt water to the King, in proof of his victories, took up his quarters in Cormantine Fort, which the Dutch commandant surrendered without firing a shot.

The near approach of this force to Anamabo,* from which Cormantine is distant only some three miles, led Mr. White, the Commandant of Anamabo Fort, to send a flag of truce to the Ashanti general, asking what the King's motives in marching to the coast might be, and offering himself as mediator in any dispute the Ashantis might have with the Fantis. This appears to have been the first serious attempt made by the officials of the African Company of Merchants to open negotiations with the invading force, and their previous apathy is incomprehensible. Had offers of mediation been made earlier, no doubt much misery and bloodshed might have been avoided; but the time for such action was now past, and to expect the Ashantis to be moderate in their hour of triumph, when they had gained access to the much-coveted seaboard and were actually in possession of a European fort, was to show a lamentable ignorance of savage character. But the fact was, that the Company cared nothing for the natives. They exercised no control of any kind over any part of the country except those towns that lay under the guns of their forts, and as long as these were not directly threatened, they made no move. They were so short-sighted as to be unable to see

* Anamabo, "Bird Rock."

that if they quietly allowed the Northern Fantis to be crushed, a further advance of the Ashantis to the seaboard would be inevitable. Consequently they did nothing until the Ashanti army was at Cormantine; when, suddenly awakening to the fact that their forts were in peril, they commenced negotiations.

Appia Dunkwa sent messengers to Anamabo in reply to Mr. White's flag of truce, with a message that if the latter sent twenty barrels of gunpowder and one hundred muskets he would tell him what the King's designs were. The Commandant, in return, expressed to the messengers his regret that the general did not seem inclined for conciliation, and said that had he been told what offence the people of Anamabo had committed he would have obtained reparation for it, but that till he knew how they had offended, he would most certainly give them the protection of the fort, which would consequently fire upon the Ashantis should they attempt to advance upon the town. He ordered two or three guns to be fired, to give the messengers some idea of the destructive effects of artillery, and sent them back under escort to Cormantine. This last precaution was most necessary, to save them from being murdered by the Anamabos.

The town of Anamabo was then placed in a state of defence. Strong outposts were formed, and every approach to the town carefully guarded; while arrangements were made that on the first alarm the old men, women, and children should take refuge inside the fort, such as the fort could not contain keeping close to the walls under the shelter of the guns. As this was the first time the Ashantis had descended to the sea, Mr. White knew nothing of them, although he had been twenty-seven years on the coast. He thought they were like the tribes with which he was acquainted, and he was confident that a few discharges of cannon would suffice to put them to flight.

Nothing took place for a week, at the end of which time the Ashanti general unexpectedly made a forward movement and captured Egyah, a village on a cape about a mile to the east of Anamabo, from which the town could be conveniently watched. On the 14th of June, 1806, the Anamabos marched out to recover the village, and an action took place. The Ashantis, who appeared to be in small force, were driven out of the western end of Egyah; but retreating across a gully which intersects the village, and which the Anamabos did not seem inclined to cross, held the eastern end. The Anamabos were much elated by this partial success, which Appia Dunkwa had merely allowed them to gain for his own ends. In order to increase their force for the attack on Egyah, the Anamabos had withdrawn the posts covering the approaches to the town—a fact which was soon discovered by the Ashanti scouts and communicated to Appia Dunkwa; who, leaving a small body of men at Egyah to occupy the attention of the Anamabos, moved his force round to the north side of Anamabo and occupied the approaches without the least resistance. There he was joined in the evening by the main Ashanti army, which had moved down from Arbrakampa with the King.

Early on June 15th the Ashantis advanced to the attack of Anamabo, and every Fanti who could carry a musket took the field, while the old men, women, and children crowded into the fort, the gates of which, as soon as it was full, were closed and barricaded. For a time a continuous roar of musketry was heard all round the town, but the Anamabos were outnumbered, and the circle of fire gradually contracted as they were driven back. To intimidate the enemy, Mr. White ordered one or two guns to be fired over the town, but this did not produce the slightest effect, and by eleven o'clock the Ashanti bullets were whistling all about the fort. From all directions the Ashantis poured into the town, and the wretched Anamabos fled to the beach, hoping to be able to escape to sea in their canoes, but the enemy pursued too closely, and a terrible slaughter took place on the sands. The garrison of the fort did their best to check the pursuit. A 24-pounder that pointed to the west, along the sea-shore, swept down dozens of Ashantis with each discharge of grape, while a 3-pounder that flanked the eastern gate did great execution. But on this side the Ashantis pushed on over the heaps of dead, and actually seized and carried off the terrified and shrieking women who were standing close to the fort walls for protection. In the meantime others had been keeping up a very hot fire, by which White was shot in the mouth and left arm, and obliged to resign the command to Mr. Meredith, while one man was killed, and an officer and two men wounded.

The whole force of the Ashantis was now directed against the fort, which they imagined to contain a rich booty, and thousands of black warriors swarmed round it. The garrison consisted of twenty-nine men, including Mr. White, four officers of the Company (Messrs. H. Meredith, F. L. Swanzy, T. A. Smith, and Barnes), and four free mulattos. Of the remaining twenty, several were servants and workmen; but all fought with desperation, for they knew that if the place were stormed they could hope for no mercy. The Ashantis pressed on, but the walls were too high to be scaled, and the two gates—one on the east and one on the west—too strong and too well barricaded to be forced. Possessing neither ladders for scaling nor cannon for breaching, it is possible that the Ashantis might have been beaten off, but for one fatal defect in the construction of the fort. This was that the embrasures yawned to such an extent that the gunners were absolutely without cover; and, exposed to thousands of musket shots, so many were wounded that at last the guns had to be abandoned, and the defence carried on by musketry alone. Shortly after noon the garrison was reduced by casualties to eight, of whom four were officers, and as the fire of the defenders slackened the Ashantis strove to force the eastern gate. Twice they advanced to it, and twice had to retire, having lost heavily. The third time they brought fire, but the man who carried the firebrands was shot dead and extinguished them by falling upon them. Thus the afternoon passed in an incessant struggle, until, at 6 p.m. when darkness commenced to fall, the Ashantis drew off

The last glimpse of daylight was used by the garrison in repairing damages and making preparations for a night attack.

Day dawned upon a horrible scene of bloodshed and devastation. Eight thousand Fantis had perished, most of them in the vicinity of the fort; heaps of dead encumbered the beach in every direction, or were washed hither and thither in the surf, and the sands were red with blood. For a mile along the shore to the east nothing was to be seen but flaming houses, or the black and charred ruins of those that had already been devoured by fire. Some two thousand refugees were in the fort, and to a rock a few yards from shore, and surrounded by the sea, two hundred panic-stricken wretches were clinging. These were all the survivors of the populous town of Anamabo.

Soon after daybreak the Ashantis recommenced the attack of the fort. They came coolly up in masses to the very muzzles of the guns, and a perfect hail-storm of lead flew about the defenders. On the eastern side the garrison had been able to contrive some protection for the men working the guns, and two well-served 3-pounders that flanked the eastern gate swept away several of the foe at each discharge. The guns that flanked the western gate, however, were so exposed that it was found impossible to work them, and two of the officers, Messrs. Meredith and Swanzy, defended it with muskets alone. In keeping this gate clear they expended nearly three hundred rounds of ball-cartridge, and they fired till their shoulders were so bruised that they could no longer bear the recoil of their muskets. Not a round was wasted, and the enemy were so near and so crowded together that a ball frequently disabled two men.

So far the garrison had gallantly held their own, but surrender was inevitable unless they were speedily reinforced. Human endurance could not last much longer, and there were no provisions for the fugitives who crowded the courtyard, so that in another day famine would compel them to capitulate. Added to this, the bodies of the thousands slain on the previous day were already beginning to putrefy under the burning rays of the tropical sun, and a sickening stench arose on all sides. Fortunately the Ashantis had also had nearly enough. They had lost over two thousand men round the fort, and began to despair of ever taking it; but neither side wished to be the first to make overtures.

About 4 p.m. (June 16th) two vessels from Cape Coast Castle anchored in the roadstead opposite the fort, and a small force of three officers and twelve men was landed without any interruption from the Ashantis. On receiving this accession to their strength the garrison wished to continue the struggle; but the reinforcement brought orders from Colonel Torrane to show a flag of truce, and a white flag and a Union Jack were accordingly lowered over the fort walls with two men. These were received by the Ashantis with exultation, and they crowded so closely round the bearers of the flags that the King's officers had some difficulty in penetrating the mass to conduct the two soldiers to his presence. The Ashantis observed the truce except that some of them made an attempt to reach the rock upon which the fugitives were still clinging, but a musket shot or two from the fort brought them back About 7 p.m. the flag of truce returned from the King who had given the two soldiers a present of a sheep Several Ashanti captains accompanied the flag back to the fort, and waited upon Mr. White. They entered into a long account of the invasion, so that Colonel Torrane might be able to understand the merits of the case. They disclaimed on the part of the King any intention of making war upon the white men, and attributed the attack on the fort to the English themselves, who had first fired upon the Ashantis. It was agreed that a report of the King's views should be made to Colonel Torrane, and the Ashanti captains returned to their camp.

Colonel Torrane, delighted to find the King disposed to be friendly, sent him a considerable present, and invited him to Cape Coast Castle to settle their differences, an invitation which was declined. Eventually, Torrane, finding that the King would not come to him and that nothing could be definitely settled by his messengers, decided to go to Anamabo, and, in order to ensure a favourable reception, determined to surrender to the King the two Assin chiefs Tchibbu and Kwaku Aputeh. The chiefs of Cape Coast were indignant at this breach of faith, and resolutely declared that they would never surrender those whom they had promised to protect; but Torrane sent an armed force unexpectedly to the houses occupied by the Assin chiefs, where Tchibbu was seized, not without resistance, while Aputeh beat off his assailants and escaped. The unfortunate Tchibbu was at once sent to the Ashanti camp, where he was put to death with the most exquisite tortures, and his jawbone was affixed as a trophy to the King's death horn.

Some difficulty arose as to the place of meeting at Anamabo, for the King would not consent to go to the fort, and the Governor refused to go to the Ashanti camp; but at last a neutral spot was fixed upon behind the ruins of the town. The meeting took place on June 23rd, and was devoted to ceremony and courtly speeches. The King spoke of the losses he had sustained from the fire of the fort, which he estimated at nearly three thousand men, complimented the garrison on their gallantry, and expressed his regrets at Mr. White's wounds. In subsequent interviews Colonel Torrane concluded some kind of convention with the King, but as it was never reduced to writing it is difficult to say positively what took place. The general opinion was that Torrane acknowledged that, by right of conquest, Fanti, including Cape Coast and every other town in Fanti, belonged to Ashanti. He reserved a judicial authority for the Company over the towns under the forts; but paid arrears on the "notes" for ground-rent for Anamabo Fort and Cape Coast Castle, which the King now claimed. Osai Tutu Kwamina was much pleased with Colonel Torrane. He said to M. Dupuis in 1821: "From the hour Governor Torrane delivered up Tchibbu, I took the English for my friends, because I saw their object was trade only, and they did not care for the people. Torrane was a man of sense, and he pleased me much."

Among the chiefs of the Ashanti army present in Anamabo was a Moor who had been to Tunis and Mecca. He was said to be a native of a place called Kassina, supposed to be to the south-east of Timbuktu, and commanded a body of men a part of whom were armed with bows and arrows. His presence with the army attracted some attention, for this was the first time any Mohammedan had been seen on the littoral of the Gold Coast.

The disposal of the Fanti refugees in the fort was found to be one of the most difficult matters to settle. The King claimed them as prisoners, which claim was resisted by Torrane; but the King remained obdurate, declaring that no peace with the English would be concluded unless his right to these people was acknowledged. In the meantime the poor wretches were dying of starvation at the rate of five or six a day, and at last a middle course was adopted. The King, in consideration of Torrane's services in seizing Tchibbu, agreed to be satisfied with one half of the fugitives leaving the other half at Torrane's disposal. This partition was immediately made, and the fort relieved of their presence.

The number of these unfortunates is variously stated. Mr. Meredith estimates it at two thousand, but Colonel Torrane in his letter to the Committee states it to have been thirteen hundred. Of those who fell to the share of the Ashantis many were sacrificed, and the remainder sold to the traders; for during this invasion the Ashantis maintained a friendly intercourse with Elmina and Accra, and carried on with them a steady traffic in slaves. Those who fell into Torrane's hands fared no better. After the King had received his share of the refugees, the remainder were carried to Cape Coast Castle, divided into lots for the Governor and members of Council, and sold to the slave vessels. To his eternal honour, Mr. John Swanzy, one of the members of Council, refused to be a party to this monstrous transaction. He was Commandant of Accra Fort at the time, but as soon as he heard of the proceedings of the Governor and his colleagues, he rose from a sick bed and went to Cape Coast Castle by canoe to lodge an indignant protest. His threats of exposure probably had more weight with the members of Council than his appeals to their honour and humanity; they began to be alarmed, and promised to undo what could yet be undone. A large number of the refugees had already been sold and carried off the coast, but some still remained in the dungeons of the Castle, and these were now released. Having accomplished this, Mr. Swanzy returned to Accra, where he fell a victim to the fatigue and exposure he had undergone.

Colonel Torrane died in 1808, and a letter written by Mr. White shortly after that event, and which was preserved amongst the archives of Cape Coast Castle as late as 1850, discloses another iniquity committed by him. On February 10th, 1808, Mr. White informed the Committee that Torrane died in debt to the people of Cape Coast to the value of forty slaves, "Assins whom they seized at the time the Governor captured Tchibbu, and whom he sold off the coast." It appears that, in order to purchase the co-operation of some of the people of Cape Coast in seizing Tchibbu and Aputeh, he promised that they should be allowed to enslave as many of their followers as they could capture; and then, to save them the trouble of finding buyers, kindly took them off their hands himself, and sold them with the other captives who fell to his own share. Thus, after having promised an asylum at Cape Coast to the Assin chiefs and their followers, he surrendered one chief to a cruel death, sold forty of their followers for the supposed benefit of his native accomplices, and kept the money himself.

The convention with Colonel Torrane did not put an end to the war, for the peace that had been concluded was only with the English, and the natives, except those of the town of Cape Coast, were not included in it. Kwaku Aputeh was still at large, and Akum, of Essikuma, who had succeeded in getting together a considerable force, was advancing to meet the Ashantis. The King hastened to leave Anamabo, where his army was beginning to suffer severely from the bad supply of water and the pestilential effluvia arising from the putrid bodies of the still unburied slain; and on July 3rd, 1807, he broke up his camp and went to meet Akum. Two days later he came upon the Fanti army a little to the east of Cormantine. A great battle took place, which was witnessed by Torrane; the Fantis soon gave way on all sides, leaving the beach covered with heaps of dead, and Akum and the remnant of his army would have been entirely destroyed had they not escaped across the Oki River, which lay in their rear, and with the fords of which the Ashantis were unacquainted.

After this defeat the Fantis were never able to take the field in force, but a guerilla warfare was kept up, during which the stragglers of the Ashanti army were cut off, and several insignificant skirmishes took place, while the Ashantis moved leisurely through Fanti towards Accra, leaving famine and desolation in their train. They were encamped for some time in the neighbourhood of Winnebah, which town they destroyed in October, 1807. Then small-pox broke out amongst them, and committed such frightful ravages that towards the end of the year the King returned to Kumassi without having returned to Anamabo, as he had promised Torrane to do, for the purpose of entering into a definite treaty. Ashanti detachments were left at Accra to collect prisoners, and dispose of such as they did not wish to carry back to Ashanti.

CHAPTER XI.

1808—1818.

The Fantis attack Elmina—Message from the Ashanti King—Condition of the country—Rebellion of Akim and Akwapim—Second invasion of Fanti—Murder of Mr. Meredith at Winnebah—Third invasion of Fanti—The Fantis purchase a peace—End of the war—Embassy to Kumassi—Difficulty about the notes—Conclusion of a treaty—Gradual growth of British jurisdiction—The traffic in slaves.

By the return of the Ashanti army to Kumassi the Fantis were for a time relieved from actual warfare; but as no treaty of peace had been made, they still preserved a defensive attitude and formed a camp at Arbrakampa. They even pretended that they had driven the Ashantis from the country, although it was well known that the departure of the Ashanti army was solely due to sickness and the scarcity of provisions. In the early part of the year 1809 the Ashanti chief who had been left at Accra, instructed by the King, communicated with Mr. White, who was now Governor, with a view to concluding a peace with the Fantis; but the latter, now that their foe was at a distance, rejected all advances. The real object of their encampment at Arbrakampa was to concert measures to revenge themselves upon those who had not assisted them to resist the invasion, and they even threatened to attack Cape Coast, simply because it had not suffered during the war. Their anger however was chiefly directed against Elmina, whose inhabitants had barbarously ill-treated and sold numbers of Fantis who had sought refuge in the town; and a Mr. Neizer, a coloured gentleman of Elmina, was accused of having suggested the invasion to the Ashanti King.

The Fantis and Wassaws now formed an alliance against Elmina, which the people of Cape Coast soon joined, in spite of the advice and remonstrances of Mr. White; and towards the close of 1809 the confederated tribes formed a camp behind Elmina and made several attacks upon the town, all of which failed through the assistance lent to the inhabitants by the guns of Fort Conraadsburgh. Finding it impossible to capture and plunder the town, the allies closely invested it, and the inhabitants were reduced to great straits; but, as there was a free communication on the sea-front there was no absolute want of supplies. The Elmina applied to Kumassi for assistance, and the King, anxious to relieve his friends, renewed his overtures of peace with the Fantis, through the Governor, in July, 1810, with the result that, after several communications, messengers arrived at Accra from Kumassi, and were conveyed to Cape Coast Castle by sea, it being unsafe for them to journey by land. These messengers declared on the part of the King that he wished to remain on friendly terms with the white men, whom he considered his masters; that his invasion of Fanti had been undertaken solely to punish the fugitive Assins; that he was about to send another army for the same purpose; and that he would wage war with all, white or black, who gave them protection. The Governor caused this message to be conveyed to the camp of the allies behind Elmina; but they treated it with contempt, and maintained the blockade until 1811, when, weary of non-success, they broke up their camps.

In 1808, it should be observed, another body of Fantis had attacked the Accras, in revenge for the assistance given by that people to the Ashantis; but they were repulsed with such loss that they did not venture to make a second attempt. From the close of the Ashanti invasion till 1811, the whole country was in the most distracted state, and the authority of the Dutch and English was entirely disregarded. The

Elminas murdered Hogenboom, the Dutch Governor, in 1808, and the entreaties, remonstrances, and threats of Governor De Veer and Governor White during the blockade of Elmina, were alike treated with contempt. The greatest lawlessness prevailed in every district, and murder, kidnapping, and pillage were daily occurrences. No language can convey an adequate idea of the misery and suffering endured in these three years upon the Gold Coast.

On the return of the messengers to Kumassi with the intelligence that the Fantis rejected all overtures of peace, the King at once made preparations for a second invasion, and, in 1811, Appia Dunkwa was sent with a force of four thousand men to protect Elmina, while another general, Apoko, was despatched with twenty-five thousand men to destroy the Fantis of Winnebah and Barraku, as a punishment for their attack on Accra. To swell the latter force he sent to his tributary, Attah, King of Akim, a present of gold and gunpowder, and directed him to join Apoko with the Akim contingent. This chief had accompanied the King in his former invasion, and had indeed done good service at Anamabo, but he now proved refractory. He recapitulated the wrongs Akim had suffered at the hands of Ashanti, declared that he would not be always at the King's call when he wanted to go to war, and informed the messenger who had brought the gold and ammunition that he would employ them against the King. The latter, upon this being reported to him, sent another messenger to know if he had been rightly informed, not wishing, perhaps, to proceed hastily against a powerful tributary; but before there was time to learn the result of this second embassy, Attah committed an overt act of hostility which precluded all possibility of a peaceful arrangement. Learning that one of the King's captains, who had been collecting tribute at Christiansborg, was on his way to Kumassi with a large amount of gold, he intercepted him and killed the whole party except one man, whom he spared to convey his defiance to the King and inform him of what had been done.

The army under Apoko had not yet crossed the Prah

when the news of this outrage reached Kumassi, and the general received immediate orders to march into Akim and subdue the rebellion there. Attah had induced Kwow Saffatchi, King of Akwapim, to throw off the Ashanti yoke and join him, and the combined forces attacked Apoko as soon as he entered Akim. The battle was long and obstinate, and was only put a stop to by nightfall. Neither party could claim the victory, but the Ashantis had suffered so severely that Apoko could not venture to renew the contest without additional aid; and he therefore sent an order to the Accras to join him, which they did in such force as to make resistance vain, and the Akims and Akwapims retreated, the former to the west towards Fanti, and the latter to the east towards Addah, on the Volta. Apoko went in pursuit of the Akwapims, but being unable to bring them to an action or capture Kwow Saffatchi, he made a prisoner of Mr. Lindt, the Danish Commandant of Addah Fort, whom he charged with conniving at Kwow Saffatchi's escape. Mr. Lindt was detained five months in the Ashanti camp, but was not illtreated, and was finally ransomed by his government for one hundred ounces of gold. Towards the close of 1811 Apoko was recalled to Kumassi without having effected the capture of Kwow Saffatchi, who, as soon as the Ashantis quitted Akwapim, returned to it and resumed his independent position.

In the meantime the force under Appia Dunkwa entered Fanti early in 1811, fought several small skirmishes with the Fantis, in which the Ashantis were always victorious, and marched through Insabang and Aguna to the coast, which they reached near Winnebah. The Fantis of Anamabo, Adjumako,* Appam,† Mumford,‡ Winnebah, and Gomóa had formed a camp near Mumford, and the opposing forces met near Appam, where a severely contested engagement took place, resulting in a victory for the Ashantis. Mr. Smith, the Commandant of Tantamkwerri Fort, opened

---

* Adjuma, or Adyuma—work, labour.
† Appam—alliance.
‡ Mumford is a corruption of the native Man-fo, "Town's people."

communications with the Ashanti general, but could learn nothing of his intentions, beyond that he intended to proceed to Elmina to protect it from the Fantis, a design, however, which Attah, King of Akim, frustrated. Attah, after parting company with the Akwapims, had, as already stated, retreated towards Fanti; and now, with a force of some three thousand men, he advanced with the greatest rapidity to attack the Ashantis, who, since their victory over the Fantis, had been encamped near Tantamkwerri Fort. The original force of four thousand men with which Appia Dunkwa had entered the country was now much reduced, heavy losses having been sustained in the last battle; and fully appreciating the difference between the warlike Akims and the Fantis, the Ashanti general thought it prudent to retreat; but Attah followed him up, engaged and routed him, and finally drove the Ashantis from Fanti. Attah then formed an alliance with the Fantis, and was projecting a combined attack upon Apoko, in Akwapim, by which he might have cut off his retreat from Kumassi, when he died, in October, 1811, of small-pox.

Some of Attah's proceedings had caused considerable alarm both to the Dutch and the English. Before his attack upon the Ashantis at Tantamkwerri he entered the Dutch Fort at Appam, threw all the guns over the walls, and released a number of Cape Coast prisoners whom he found there, and who had been panyarred, or forcibly seized, by the Dutch, to be sold as slaves. He likewise visited the English fort at Tantamkwerri, where, though he showed less violence, he helped himself to everything that took his fancy, and treated the Commandant roughly.

Attah was succeeded by his brother, but as the new King seemed inclined to submit to Ashanti, the Akim chiefs in secret council decided to depose him and put him to death. Not being willing, however, to have his blood upon their hands, they communicated their decision to him, and commanded him to commit suicide, which, after a week passed in performing his own funeral obsequies, he did. Kwadjo Kuma, who was next placed on the stool of Akim, seems to have inherited some of Attah's spirit, for he kept the Ashantis shut up in their own country during the whole of the years 1812 and 1813. It should be observed, however, that the Ashantis did not make any very serious attempt to break out. During these two years of freedom from invasion the eastern Fantis again attempted to revenge themselves upon the Accras, and, in 1812, in conjunction with Kwow Saffatchi, of Akwapim, they attacked Accra, but after a severe contest were signally repulsed.

In the month of February, 1812, Mr. Meredith, the gallant defender of Anamabo Fort, now Commandant of Winnebah, was done to death by the natives of that place, who had for some time enjoyed an unenviable notoriety for violence and rapacity. One day, while walking in the garden of the fort, he was suddenly seized by a number of natives, who dragged him away into the bush, and there charged him with detaining a quantity of gold, the property of a native. This gold, they asserted, a sergeant of the Company's soldiers had delivered to him for safe keeping at the time when the Ashantis were in the neighbourhood, and they declared they would not set him at liberty until he gave it up. It appeared that the sergeant, to whom the gold really had been committed, upon being asked for it by the owner, had evaded payment by declaring that he had forgotten to whose care he had entrusted it. The owner then consulted the great god of the Fanti country at Mankassim, and was told by the oracle that Mr. Meredith had it, hence his seizure. It was in vain that the unfortunate Commandant declared that he knew nothing of the gold, for the dictum of the oracle was conclusive and final to the minds of the natives, it being impossible that the god could be mistaken. They treated their captive with the greatest barbarity. Not satisfied with making him walk several miles bareheaded in the heat of the sun, they set fire to the dry grass, and taking off his boots, forced him to walk over it barefooted. He was frequently beaten, and his arms were stretched out horizontally at full length, and fastened to a long pole which pressed upon his throat, and caused him much pain.

The news of this outrage soon reached Mr. Smith at

Tantamkwerri Fort, and he at once proceeded to Winnebah, where he had no sooner landed than he also was seized by a number of natives and hurried into the bush. Being brought before a meeting of chiefs and headmen, he remonstrated with them upon their conduct, and urged them to produce Mr. Meredith, which after some discussion they did; but refused to give him up, and Mr. Smith was obliged to leave him in their hands, where he died from exhaustion and exposure before any effectual means could be taken for his release. It may here be added that Mr. James, his successor at Winnebah, was blockaded in the fort for three months by the natives, in consequence of which H.M.S. *Amelia*, Captain Irby, brought him away after blowing up the fort, and the place was abandoned by the Company. For many years afterwards English vessels passing Winnebah were in the habit of pouring a broadside into the town, to give the natives some idea of the severe vengeance that would always be exacted for the murder of a European.

In 1814 the King of Ashanti determined to make a supreme effort for the subjection of Akim and Akwapim, which had now been in rebellion for three years. With this object he despatched an army of twenty thousand men, under a new general, Amankwa, to attack Akim in front; while in order to prevent Kwadjo Kuma from escaping to the west into Fanti, as his predecessor had done, he sent Appia Dunkwa with a smaller force in the direction of Winnebah. The Akims retired before the advancing Ashantis, and Amankwa was within a day's march of Akwapim before any engagement took place. Then one of his foraging parties was cut off by Kwadjo Kuma, and the next day the Akims and Akwapims gave battle to the Ashanti army at Egwah-arru. The struggle lasted for six hours, and ended in the total defeat of the allies. Amankwa announced his victory by sending a jawbone and a slave to each of the Accra towns, and then proceeded with his army to Accra. He remained in that neighbourhood for nearly a year, levying contributions throughout the country, to the great discontent of the Accras, who had hitherto been staunch allies of Ashanti, but who now found that even the most valuable services rendered did not protect them from extortion and tyranny. He afterwards returned to Akwapim, where he received a message from the King, forbidding his return to Kumassi without the heads of Kwadjo Kuma and Kwow Saffatchi.

In the meantime the force under Appia Dunkwa had encountered the eastern Fantis on several occasions. The Adjumakos and Agunas were defeated with great loss, the towns of Winnebah and Barraku plundered and burnt, and the natives generally subjected to the most cruel impositions Appia Dunkwa then retired to New Assin, south of the Prah where he died, and was succeeded in the command by Appia Nanu. This general incurred the King's displeasure by remaining inactive, and Amankwa was ordered to move from Akwapim and unite the two forces. They met at Essikuma and advanced through Adjumako, the Fantis flying before them without daring to offer any resistance. They then moved into Arbra, where a large body of Fantis, who had been assembled to give them battle, fled at the first onset and the Ashantis encamped on the ground.

Crowds of fugitives now flocked to the forts for protection and four thousand men, women, and children are said to have sought refuge in the Castle of Cape Coast alone. The Governor, Mr. J. Hope Smith, who had been appointed in 1814, sent a flag of truce to the Ashanti general, to learn his intentions; but in the meanwhile the Ashantis approached nearer and nearer. On March 13th, 1816, a large body of them appeared near Mori, while another party, principally Assins, under the command of Kwasi Amankwa, showed themselves at the salt pond, quite close to Cape Coast town, and had a slight skirmish with the inhabitants.

On March 16th messengers arrived from the Ashanti camp at Arbrakampa to bring a reply to the flag of truce. They stated that the army had come to Fanti in pursuit of Kwadjo Kuma and Kwow Saffatchi, and to punish all who harboured them. Three Fanti chiefs, Kwow Aggri, Painti, and Amissa, who had, they said, stood in arms against the Ashantis for the defence of these men, were now required, and it was thought they might be in Cape Coast. The Governor offered his mediation to settle the palaver, and Director-General Daendels, the Governor of Elmina, offered to co-operate. A meeting was therefore held in the palaver hall of the Castle on the 21st, a deputation of Dutch officers from Elmina being present. Upon the headmen of Cape Coast taking a sacred oath that Kwadjo Kuma and Kwow Saffatchi were not in the town, the Ashanti messengers declared that they were satisfied upon that point; but they demanded that the three Fanti chiefs should be delivered to them, to go to the camp, as they had been in arms against the King. The chiefs consented to go, provided that the messengers guaranteed their safety; but it was finally agreed that the demand for their surrender should be waived upon payment of one hundred ounces of gold by the people of Cape Coast and the Fantis, to purchase peace. The money was advanced by Governor Hope Smith, and the messengers and Fanti chiefs then took a sacred oath to abstain from all further hostilities.

Shortly after this the Ashantis broke up their camp at Arbrakampa and moved to the east in search of the two proscribed Kings. The Fantis offered no resistance to their march, and the Ashantis, considering the country conquered, exacted heavy contributions. Their men were spread over the whole country in small detachments, making active search for the two rebels, and inflicting incalculable misery on the inhabitants, whom they deprived of everything. Kwadjo Kuma was at last surrounded by a party of Appia Nanu's force at Inkum, and, being unable to escape, committed suicide. Soon afterwards Kwow Saffatchi was betrayed by his brother, Adu Dunkwa, on condition that he should be raised to the stool of Akwapim in his stead; and a party of Ashantis was conducted to his hiding-place, where he was killed. The object of the Ashanti invasion was now accomplished. The heads of the two rebel Kings had been taken, Akim and Akwapim had again been reduced to the position of tributary states, and the King's authority had, moreover, been established throughout Fanti; Amankwa therefore returned to Kumassi with the bulk of the army, leaving Ashanti Residents in charge of the principal districts of Fanti to keep the Fantis in subjection and collect the King's tribute.

The repeated invasions of Fanti had produced such a feeling of alarm and insecurity that Mr. Hope Smith requested the committee of the Company in London to authorise and equip an embassy to Kumassi, with a view to the conciliation of the Ashanti King and the negotiation of a treaty of commerce. An additional reason given was that there were good grounds for believing that the Dutch Governor, Daendels, was intriguing with the King, and doing his utmost to bring the English into disrepute and involve them in difficulties. The committee regarded Mr. Hope Smith's proposal with favour; presents for the King were sent out from England, and on April 22nd, 1817, Mr. James, Commandant of Accra Fort, Mr. T. E. Bowdich, writer in the Company's service and nephew of the Governor, Mr. Hutchinson, and Surgeon Beresford Tedlie set out from Cape Coast Castle on a mission to Kumassi. Part of its object was to establish a British residency or consulate at Kumassi, and it was intended, if all went well, to leave Mr. Hutchinson as Resident at the King's court. In passing through Fanti and Assin the members of the embassy were much struck with the desolation the Ashantis had everywhere left behind them. Scarcely a vestige of cultivation was to be seen, ruined and deserted villages met the eye on every side, and long tracts of country were traversed without a single human being being met with. Of the populous slave mart of Mansu only a few sheds remained and the few natives seen were gaunt with famine.

On the 15th of May the embassy entered Kumassi This was the first time that Europeans had visited the capital, and they were honoured with a public reception attended by a display of barbaric pomp and wealth to impress them with the greatness of the King. They were met at the entrance of the town by upwards of five thousand warriors, who, keeping up an incessant discharge of musketry led them slowly through the crowded streets to the marketplace, where the King was waiting in state, surrounded by his chiefs and the officers of his court. The ambassadors, accustomed only to the petty kings of the coast, were astonished at the wealth and magnificence exhibited. Bands of barbarous music played, hundreds of immense umbrella canopies made of gorgeous silks were flaunted, flags and banners were waved, and gold was displayed in profusion; but Mr. Bowdich's description* must be read to form any adequate conception of the scene. The Europeans estimated the number of soldiers present at 30,000.

The embassy was very favourably received by Osai Tutu Kwamina, but at an early stage of the negotiations a difficulty arose concerning the payment of the notes for Cape Coast Castle and Anamabo Fort. As we have already seen, the King had long been in the habit of receiving rents for the Dutch fort at Elmina, and for the English, Dutch, and Danish forts at Accra. The actual notes for these were in his hands, but it seems that when Colonel Torrane paid the King the arrears due on the notes for Cape Coast Castle and Anamabo Fort, the King had not obtained possession of the documents for these two. Some time after 1814, the Kings of Anamabo and Mankassim, who still retained these notes, had persuaded Mr. Hope Smith to write others, engaging to pay the Ashanti King four ackis† per month for the two forts, and reserving to themselves the remainder of the rent of four ounces per fort, specified in the original notes, which they kept. This was certainly a very curious transaction, and the King charged the Governor with having combined with the Fantis to defraud him, and demanded an explanation from the embassy. Mr. James by his answers confirmed the suspicions of the King, who broke into an uncontrollable fit of rage. His captains were equally furious, and swore that they would set out that night to take the heads of the Fanti chiefs. There was such a tumult that the lives of the Europeans were in some danger. Mr. James,

---

* Mission from Cape Coast Castle to Ashanti.
† An acki is, roughly speaking, gold to the value of one dollar.

who seems to have entirely lost his presence of mind, volunteered no explanation, and the assembly was breaking up in the greatest confusion, when Mr. Bowdich asked to be heard. He assured the King that the Governor would do what was right, and proposed that messengers should be sent down to Cape Coast to receive his explanation of the affair. His evident earnestness much impressed the King, who suffered himself to be appeased, and adopted Mr. Bowdich's proposal.

The result of this appeal to the Governor was that Mr. James was recalled, Mr. Bowdich placed at the head of the embassy in his stead, and the demands of the King, with regard to the notes, complied with. Mr. Hope Smith declared that he had been deceived by the two Fanti Kings, and sent the King two new notes, promising to pay four ounces of gold per month for each of the two forts. According to his version of the affair, the arrangement of the two notes had been made between the King's messengers and the Fanti Kings in the Ashanti camp at Arbrakampa, after peace had been concluded at Cape Coast Castle; and he declared that he had only issued the notes for four ackis on the understanding that he had nothing to do with the arrangement, and that it was made with the mutual consent of the Ashanti King and the Fanti chiefs. Another difficulty which now arose was the conduct of the Kommendas in a quarrel between themselves and the Elminas. This was finally disposed of by the Kommendas acknowledging their fealty to the King, and paying one hundred and twenty ounces of gold dust, an arrangement which was only effected after a great deal of negotiation, the first demand made on the Kommendas being for two thousand ounces.

All differences being thus settled, a treaty of peace was concluded on September 7th, 1817. It consisted of the following articles:

1. There shall be perpetual peace and harmony between the British subjects in this country and the subjects of the Kings of Ashanti and Djuabin.

2. The same shall exist between the subjects of the Kings of Ashanti and Djuabin and all nations of Africa

residing under the protection of the Company's forts and settlements on the Gold Coast, and it is hereby agreed that there are no palavers now existing, and that neither party has any claim upon the other.

3. The King of Ashanti guarantees the security of the people of Cape Coast from the hostilities threatened by the people of Elmina.

4. In order to avert the horrors of war, it is agreed, that in any case of aggression on the part of the natives under British protection, the King shall complain thereof to the Governor-in-Chief, to obtain redress, and that he will in no instance resort to hostilities, even against the other towns of the Fanti territory, without endeavouring as much as possible to effect an amicable arrangement, affording the Governor the opportunity of propitiating it as far as he may with discretion.

5. The King of Ashanti agrees to permit a British officer to reside constantly at his capital for the purpose of instituting and preserving a regular communication with the Governor-in-Chief at Cape Coast Castle.

6. The Kings of Ashanti and Djuabin pledge themselves to countenance, promote, and encourage the trade of their subjects with Cape Coast Castle and its dependencies to the extent of their power.

7. The Governors of the respective forts shall, at all times, afford every protection in their power to the persons and property of the people of Ashanti who may resort to the water-side.

8. The Governor-in-Chief reserves to himself the right of punishing any subject of Ashanti or Djuabin guilty of secondary offences; but, in case of any crime of magnitude, he will send the offender to the King to be dealt with according to the laws of his country.

9. The Kings agree to commit their children to the care of the Governor-in-Chief, for education at Cape Coast Castle, in the full confidence of the good intentions of the British Government and of the benefits to be derived therefrom.

By virtue of this treaty Mr. Hutchinson was left as British Resident at the court of Ashanti, and Mr. Bowdich returned to Cape Coast Castle.

At this point—the first recognition by treaty of the right of the British to exercise protection and control over the natives residing in the towns under the guns of the forts—it will be convenient to trace the gradual growth of British jurisdiction on the Gold Coast prior to this date. The officials of the former trading companies had not attempted to assert any territorial jurisdiction, or any interference in native affairs, beyond the exercise of a kind of mediatory influence, to prevent the interruption of trade by native quarrels. The jurisdiction of the director-generals of the companies extended only over the officers and slaves of the companies, and the right of the natives to the soil on which the forts were built was acknowledged by the payment of notes for ground rent. The first record of any treaty with native Kings is found in the treaty of 1693, between the Royal African Company and the Kings of Akanna, Saboe, and Fetu; and in 1754 we find the governor of the African Company of Merchants placing a King of Fetu on the stool. But at the same time we have evidence of how little authority the Company possessed, from the fact that the people of Cape Coast, about the same period, prevented the Company's slaves from cutting firewood in the bush, upon the grounds that no rent had been paid to them for the use of the wood. Under Governor Archibald Dalzel (1802) some attempts to control the natives were made, and the first material point gained was in 1803. Prior to that date complaints against natives, other than the Company's servants, had to be made before the corrupt native tribunals, where redress could never be obtained without a bribe to the chiefs who tried the case, and not even then if it involved the curtailment of any custom by which the chiefs profited; but in that year the Governor, at the instigation of Mr. John Swanzy, imprisoned one of the headmen of Cape Coast for passing false gold. The natives took up arms; it became necessary to defend the Castle, and a fire was opened on the town by which a number of houses were destroyed and the natives forced to submit to the innovation. In 1805 this jurisdiction was further extended, when some canoemen of Accra, who had stolen gunpowder to the value of £100 from the Commandant, were brought to trial and punished at Cape Coast Castle. Thus, before the first invasion of Fanti, it had come to be recognised that the native inhabitants of the towns under the guns of the forts were amenable to British laws for offences committed against the Company or its servants. The invasion and destruction of Fanti by the Ashantis materially assisted the British in bringing the natives of these towns more under control, and the years immediately preceding Mr. Bowdich's treaty show a gradually increasing influence. It was British mediation that caused Cape Coast to be spared in 1807; and there can be little doubt but that it was through fear or respect for the British that that town was allowed to be redeemed on such moderate terms in 1816. They were now (1817) the means of preserving the Kommendas from destruction, and the advantage of their protection, inadequate as it was to secure great results, was felt and acknowledged. But it must be carefully borne in mind that this protection and control was limited to the towns under the guns of the fort. The rest of Fanti was entirely independent; and even the mediatory influence, which, under the treaty of 1817, the British could now exercise in its behalf, was a new departure.

The abolition of the slave trade had not by any means put a stop to the traffic in slaves on the Gold Coast, which, through being declared illegal, was now attended with greater violence and injustice than before. Spaniards were chiefly engaged in the trade, and its abolition by Spain had no effect in checking it, as the fast-sailing Spanish vessels could easily elude the men-of-war. In February, 1818, no less than seven large slave ships were seen taking in cargoes near Cape Coast Castle. Great encouragement was given to the slave trade by Governor Daendels and the Elminas; and panyarring, or the forcible seizing of peaceable traders—a crime which had been little heard of when the trade was legal—was now very common. Mr. Hope Smith did his utmost to suppress the traffic, and on several occasions acted with energy. He sent an expedition against the people of Leggu, who had seized some Cape Coast canoemen, and compelled them to give them up and pay a heavy fine. He also banished from Cape Coast a coloured man named Brew, who had been detected in intrigues with Ashanti for the purpose of upholding the slave trade. About this time, too, a first attempt was made to put a stop to human sacrifices and torture. On the death of a chief of Cape Coast one of the headmen was accused of having procured it by witchcraft, and was sentenced to death by torture; but Mr. Hope Smith was able to rescue him from this fate, though he was obliged to send him to Sierra Leone for safety.

CHAPTER XII.

1819—1823.

New difficulty with Ashanti—Mr. Dupuis—His treaty—Skirmish at Mori—The Crown assumes the Government of the Gold Coast—Seizure of a sergeant at Anamabo—Expedition to Dunkwa—The Accras join the Government.

A FEW months after the departure of Mr. Bowdich's embassy from Kumassi a rebellion broke out in Gaman which engaged the whole attention of the Ashantis, and as the King did not appear to wish Mr. Hutchinson to remain in the capital, fearing probably that he might witness some reverse, it was thought advisable to recall him. The King then invaded Gaman territory with a large army, all Ashantis being withdrawn from Fanti country and the paths closed in order that he might prosecute the war unobserved; and during its progress the British authorities remained in a state of complete ignorance as to its probable result. At the close of 1818 a few Ashanti stragglers reached the coast in a miserable plight; but they would not, or could not, give any information about the state of affairs in the interior; and this, coupled with the King's long silence, gave rise to rumours that the Ashantis had been defeated. The people of Cape Coast gladly believed these reports, and openly exulted over the Ashanti resident in that town; while Mr. Hope Smith, not sorry perhaps to see the people of Cape Coast inclined to free themselves from Ashanti domination at a favourable opportunity, did not restrain or discourage them.

But while the Fantis were thus indulging their fancies with reports of the King's disasters, messengers suddenly arrived from Kumassi to demand satisfaction, under Article 4 of Mr. Bowdich's treaty, for an alleged insult offered to the King by the people of Kommenda. The rumoured defeats of the Ashantis had been altogether without foundation. The Gamans had been totally defeated, their King slain, and their capital, Buntuku, burned; while, as a punishment for the rebellion, Gaman itself had been reduced from the rank of a tributary state to that of a province of Ashanti

The offence of the Kommendas was as follows: The King had sent messengers to Kommenda to announce the subjection of Gaman, and to demand from them a contribution of gunpowder and rum to the value of one hundred ounces of gold, to enable him to make a great "custom" at Kumassi. The extreme poverty of the inhabitants of Kommenda—a small place—rendered any compliance with this demand almost impossible; and with that sturdy independence which has generally characterised them, they met the Ashanti envoys outside their town, which they declined to allow them to enter, at the same time positively refusing to submit to any extortion. The Ashanti messengers then proceeded to Cape Coast, whence one of them returned to Kumassi to report the failure of their mission, the other remaining at Cape Coast, on the plea that he could not convey to his master the insult which had been offered him, but really to watch the course of events and keep the King informed of all that transpired.

In a few days a message arrived from the King to the effect that if the people of Cape Coast did not give him immediate satisfaction for the insult offered him by the Kommendas, whom he termed their dependents, he would send down an army to destroy their town. At the palaver which was held in the hall of the Castle, the envoy, in the name of the King, demanded redress from the Governor by virtue of the treaty, which he produced. He handed it to Mr. Hope Smith, desiring that it might be publicly read, and he added that he had the King's instructions to leave it with the Governor, if the latter should refuse to abide by its provisions, as the King could not retain it and go to war. The treaty was then read, and when the fourth article was reached the envoy rose and demanded satisfaction under its provisions.

Mr. Hope Smith had not endeavoured to persuade the Kommendas to comply with the King's extortionate demand, and for this he has been considered to blame; but on a more careful consideration of the question it will be seen that he acted wisely. The fourth article of Mr. Bowdich's treaty was framed with the object of settling, if possible, in a peaceable manner, through the mediation of the Governor, any differences that might arise between the Ashantis and the inhabitants of the towns under the guns of the forts; the presumption, of course, being that the Ashantis should have a *bonâ fide* cause of complaint. But this case was quite different. The Kommendas had committed no offence beyond refusing compliance with an unwarrantable demand that had suddenly been made upon them; and for the Governor to have used his authority and influence to induce them to submit to it would, besides being a gross injustice, have been highly impolitic, and would only have led to the local Government being regarded as responsible for the acceptance and fulfilment by the protected natives of all future demands, however unreasonable, that Ashanti might choose to make upon them. No doubt the King wished to construe Article 4 as meaning that the Governor was to act as his collector of fines, and that he was in all cases, whether just or unjust, to do his best to make the people submit to all exactions. But it could never be so interpreted by the British; the local Government could never acknowledge that they were bound by treaty to back up and enforce the exactions of an irresponsible King. Mr. Hope Smith therefore declined to bring any pressure to bear upon the Kommendas or to act in any way in support of the King's unjustifiable demand.

There was present at the palaver a Mr. Dupuis, whom the Home Government, anxious to cultivate a friendly intercourse with Ashanti, had sent out as Consul for Kumassi. He had arrived on the coast in the beginning of 1819, but the constant misunderstandings between himself and the local Government, and the unsettled state of the country, had delayed his journey to the capital. Mr. Dupuis had denied the right of the Governor to give him any instructions, and the latter naturally regarded with some jealousy his independent position. The appointment of Mr. Dupuis was very unwise, for it greatly impaired the Governor's authority in the eyes of the Ashantis, and also caused a conflict of authority which destroyed the unity of action that was so necessary. Mr. Dupuis's views of the politics of the country were diametrically opposed to those of Mr. Hope Smith. He appears to have regarded the Ashantis as the personification of barbarous honour and honesty, and his policy was to maintain and uphold the authority of the King over the coast tribes. His bias in favour of Ashanti is so marked that it seriously impairs the value of the account he has left of these transactions, which is written in a strong spirit of partisanship, and is contradicted in the most important particulars by Major Ricketts and others.

While the Ashanti envoy was urging his demands upon the Governor, Mr. Dupuis desired that he might be informed of the nature of his appointment. When this was done the envoy seemed to think that so unexpected a circumstance as the arrival of an agent direct from England might alter the King's views, and he therefore, after a little consideration, resolved to retain possession of the treaty for the present, and to apply to the King for fresh instructions. Mr. Hope Smith, on his part, declared that the people of Cape Coast could not in any way be held responsible for the refusal of the Kommendas to pay the sum demanded from them, and that if the King endeavoured to put in force his threat to destroy the town, every assistance and protection should be afforded the inhabitants.

On January 5th, 1820, a nephew of the King, with a

retinue of 1,200 armed attendants, arrived at Cape Coast, making his entry with the greatest pomp and state. He brought a fresh demand—namely, that the people of Cape Coast should pay a fine of sixteen hundred ounces for having, as he asserted, abetted the Kommendas in their refusal; and that the Governor should pay a similar fine for having, as he alleged, broken the fourth article of the treaty by not obtaining satisfaction for the King from the Kommendas. The King thus arrogated to himself the privileges both of plaintiff and judge, and Mr. Hope Smith naturally declined to submit to any such extortion. It is probable that the whole of this difficulty had been got up by the King designedly. He knew very well that the Kommendas could not pay the sum asked for, and the whole affair was possibly contrived in order to obtain pretexts for making demands upon the Government.

Every attempt at negotiation having failed, it was at length resolved to send Mr. Dupuis to Kumassi. He left Cape Coast Castle on February 9th, 1820, leaving behind, with a protest, the instructions which the Governor had given him, and arrived at Kumassi on the 28th. The Fanti and Assin villages along the route were still found uninhabited and in ruins. In fact, Mr. Dupuis estimated that the Fanti and Assin population had, from between three and four millions, been reduced to as many hundred thousands; but this was the merest conjecture.

At the audiences which ensued, Osai Tutu Kwamina complained of the conduct of the Cape Coast people, whom he accused of wishing to set him at defiance. An offer from the Governor to compromise the demand made upon Cape Coast, by paying one hundred ounces of gold dust, caused a violent display of anger; and the King finally dismissed Mr. Dupuis from the capital, saying that the palaver must be settled at Cape Coast. It is a pity that this offer was made, for it undoubtedly weakened the Governor's just contention that the King had no reasonable grounds for making any demand upon Cape Coast; but it was doubtless made in the interests of peace.

Mr. Dupuis reached Cape Coast Castle on April 5th, and laid before Mr. Hope Smith what purported to be a treaty which he had concluded with the Ashanti King. The stipulations were to the following effect: That the King should acknowledge Mr. Dupuis as Consul; that he should, when called upon, march his armies to any part of the country to support the interests of Great Britain; that he abandoned the claim of sixteen hundred ounces from Cape Coast; that he should encourage trade; that the British Government acknowledged the Fanti territories to be a part of the kingdom of Ashanti, but that those natives residing under the forts should have the benefit of English law, and any complaint brought against the inhabitants of the towns under the forts was to be submitted to the consul for settlement. Al former treaties between the British and Ashanti, particularly the treaty of 1817, were declared null and void. To these were added four supplementary articles, of which three were of little importance; but by the remaining article, the second in order, it was stipulated that the natives of Cape Coast were excluded from participating in the advantages of th treaty, "as the King is resolved to eradicate from his do minions the seeds of disobedience and insubordination" and the King reserved to himself the right to adopt an measures he thought fit to bring those people under subjection but promised not to destroy the town of Cape Coast. Th claim of sixteen hundred ounces from that town was also declared not to be abandoned.

This was the extraordinary document which Mr. Dupu s produced, and he seems strangely to have misunderstood h s position. He had been sent to Kumassi to settle, if possibl , the dispute with the people of Cape Coast, and to explain ɔ the King the Governor's views of what might reasonably l e asked· of him under Article 4 of Mr. Bowdich's treaty, ar d for no other purpose. With other matters he had nothing o do, and the treaty of 1817 was beyond his sphere of actiоɪ ; yet he took upon himself to declare that treaty null and voi l, and to draw up and sign another, under which the princiɼ ɪl matter it had been his business to settle was left unsettle l.

In the treaty of 1817 the sovereignty of the King of Ashanti over Fanti was not specially acknowledged; but Mr. Dupuis went out of his way to have it recognised; and, further, exempted the people of Cape Coast from the protection they had hitherto enjoyed. It was a complete surrender. He seems to have regarded himself as a plenipotentiary entirely independent of the Governor and the local officials, whom he speaks of as "the servants of a mercantile board." One of the stipulations of his treaty was that his successor should be appointed by himself. He appears to have been morbidly jealous of Mr. Bowdich, and the numerous attacks upon that gentleman which his book contains do him little credit. Naturally, Mr. Hope Smith declined to ratify a treaty by which the inhabitants of Cape Coast, who had committed no offence, were to be left to the tender mercies of the King. In this he was supported by the Home Government, and Mr. Dupuis, after a succession of altercations, finally embarked for England on April 15th, having considerably aggravated matters by his visit.

The Ashanti King received the news of the repudiation of Mr. Dupuis's treaty with an outburst of passion, and one can imagine that he was annoyed to find that an engagement which granted everything he asked was to be abandoned. The Ashanti envoy, however, still remained at Cape Coast, and the Governor endeavoured to bring matters to a settlement. His position was, that Mr. Dupuis's treaty not having been ratified, the treaty of 1817 was still valid. The position of the Ashanti King appeared to be that he had made a treaty with Mr. Dupuis, and that the Government had broken it. In order to remove all grounds of complaint, Mr. Hope Smith used his best endeavours to induce the inhabitants of Cape Coast to pay the sixteen hundred ounces demanded. The demand was unwarrantable and unjust, but a refusal to comply might only bring greater ills in its train. These endeavours were successful, and by June, 1820, the people of Cape Coast, assisted by a considerable contribution from the Castle, paid to the Ashanti envoy the sum demanded.

It was now expected that the envoy would leave Cape

Coast and return to Kumassi, he having no further business to transact; but he did not do so. The insidious policy of the Ashanti King was to keep in existence small matters of dispute with the people of Cape Coast, and by keeping up a continual friction goad them into committing actions which would serve as pretexts for further extortion. Such a pretext was already made to hand. A Fanti chief named Paintri, who had been placed by the Ashantis upon the stool of Arbra, had, some twelve months before this date, sent an armed party against an outlying village of Cape Coast which had been destroyed, and the inhabitants carried off and sold.' Nine months after this outrage the sub-chief, who had headed the attack against the village, came to Cape Coast where he and several of his followers were seized by the owner of the village, conveyed to a house in the town, and blown up with gunpowder. This matter had been almost forgotten under the pressure of weightier affairs; but now the Ashanti envoy declared that he had the King's order to inquire into it. He summoned Paintri to appear at Cape Coast during the investigation, and announced that he would require one hundred peredwins of gold (£1,000) from the person who was adjudged to be in the wrong. Paintri, asserting that his life would be in danger if he came to Cape Coast, declined to comply with the summons, but in order to show that he submitted to the authority of the envoy, went to the village of Mori. This was early in April, 1821.

On the 9th of the same month intelligence was received at Cape Coast that a native of that place had been barbarously murdered at Mori. The greatest excitement prevailed, the town companies turned out, and accompanied by eighty-five men of the garrison of the Castle, under Mr. Colliver, marched to the scene of the crime. On arriving there, some two thousand men, consisting of the inhabitants of Mori, Paintri's followers, and a party of Ashantis, were found assembled in arms, and the headless body of the murdered man was discovered outside the village. As soon as the Company's soldiers entered the place fire was opened on them from the houses, but as they advanced the natives retired. In the meantime, another body of Ashantis, who had been encamped in the neighbourhood of Cape Coast, took up a position to cut off the retreat of the party, but being threatened by another force from Cape Coast, retired. In this affair the Ashantis and Fantis lost some fifty men killed, and amongst them Paintri himself. The loss on the part of the Cape Coast force was two killed and a few slightly wounded.

Trade with Ashanti, and with the rest of Fanti, which had now thrown in its lot with the former, at once altogether ceased. Cape Coast was completely isolated, and it was not safe to venture beyond the outskirts of the town, except in large parties. To ensure the place against a sudden attack, the people built a loop-holed wall of mud from the sea-beach on the east of the town, across the hills in a semicircle to the sea-beach on the west, and the Government hastily erected a tower* on a hill to the west of Phipps's Tower, which was armed with guns landed from H.M.S. *Tartar*. Several messages were exchanged between the King of Ashanti and the Governor, and in August a final message was received from Kumassi, to the effect that the King acknowledged that the affair at Mori had been misrepresented to him, and had given orders for the roads to Cape Coast to be opened. Trade, however, was not renewed, and matters were in this state, when the Home Government decided to assume the control of the settlements on the Gold Coast.

The reason assigned for this step was that the local authorities connived at the maintenance of the slave trade, and that the annual grant which they had received from Parliament had always been expended with the intention of keeping others from participating in legitimate trade, which was, in fact, monopolised by the local agents. A Bill was accordingly passed in the Parliament of 1821 for abolishing the African Company of Merchants, and for transferring to the Crown all the Company's forts and possessions on the Gold Coast, which were to be placed under the government of Sierra Leone. The forts were eight in number, namely, those of Cape Coast, Anamabo, Accra, Kommenda, Dixcove,

* Afterwards called Fort Victoria.

Sekondi, Prampram, and Tantamkwerri. At the time of the transfer the white establishment consisted of forty-five persons, and the number of black and coloured people in the Company's pay was four hundred and fifty.

On March 28th, 1822, Sir Charles Macarthy, Governor of Sierra Leone, arrived at Cape Coast Castle in H.M.S. *Iphigenia*, and assumed the government of the Gold Coast. The new Governor, a stranger to the Gold Coast and its politics, had no ordinary difficulties to contend with, for the servants of the late Company, almost to a man, refused to take office under him. They also withdrew themselves from all participation in native affairs, and Sir Charles Macarthy was left to grope in the dark, without a single responsible or reliable adviser. In order to reopen friendly relations with Kumassi, he despatched messengers to the King, announcing his assumption of office, and bearing the customary presents: while to provide for the defence of the forts he formed the native troops in the service of the late Company into a colonial corps, composed of three companies, and entitled the Royal African Colonial Corps of Light Infantry. Having thus set matters in train, he departed for Sierra Leone early in May, leaving Captain Chisholm and Lieutenant Laing, of the 2nd West India Regiment—the latter destined to afterwards become celebrated as an African traveller—to organise the new force. Sir Charles Macarthy seems to have had no idea of the critical condition of affairs, and apparently thought that everything would go on smoothly.

Affairs continued quiet until the month of November when a mulatto sergeant of the new corps was kidnapped by Ashantis at Anamabo, where he was stationed on duty and taken as a prisoner to Dunkwa, where he was put "in log," *i.e.*, secured to a heavy log of wood by an iron staple which is the native mode of securing prisoners. This outrage was attributed to a quarrel that had taken place between the sergeant and an Ashanti trader at Anamabo in the preceding May, but which had been investigated and definitely settled at the time by the commandant of the fort. Demands for the restoration of the sergeant and the punishment of those concerned in his seizure met with no reply; and early in January, 1823, a nephew of the Ashanti King was sent to Dunkwa with one of the state executioners, to put the sergeant to death, and to convey the skull, jawbone, and one of the arms of the victim to Kumassi. This murder was committed on February 1st, 1823.

In the early part of December, 1822, Sir C. Macarthy had returned to Cape Coast from Sierra Leone, bringing with him a company of the 2nd West India Regiment, and he now determined to punish the perpetrators of this crime. He proceeded to Anamabo to inquire personally into the circumstances under which the sergeant had been carried off, and on his return to Cape Coast was received with a perfect ovation. The streets and hills were crowded with spectators, volleys of musketry were discharged, and the natives exhibited the greatest enthusiasm at the return of him who, they were now informed, was prepared to deliver them from Ashanti oppression. The reputation which Sir Charles Macarthy had gained, both at the Gambia and at Sierra Leone, for extreme benevolence and justice tempered with mercy, had doubtless preceded him; but it was as the person who was to protect them from the exactions and tyranny of Ashanti, that the people of Cape Coast and Anamabo looked up to him. Their enthusiasm was, no doubt, increased by the knowledge that they were now cut adrift from the rest of the Fantis, who seemed to have thoroughly accepted the position of subjects of Ashanti; and that, unless their cause was strenuously adopted by the Government, they could look for nothing but destruction.

In the middle of February it was ascertained that Aduku, King of Mankassim, had, with the principal Fanti chiefs, left Dunkwa and returned to their homes, leaving at that place the Ashanti prince and a few of his followers who had been present at the murder of the sergeant. These did not amount to more than three hundred men, and an expedition against them was at once formed with the greatest secrecy. At six p.m. on the 21st, the Cape Coast volunteers, a new corps formed by the Governor, and a body of natives, were called into the Castle, ammunition was served out to them and to the garrison, and before seven o'clock the force marched. Through the treachery or imbecility of the guides, the expedition, which ought to have reached Dunkwa before daybreak next morning, took the wrong road, and long after sunrise was suddenly fired upon by a numerous force of Ashantis and Fantis, who were ambushed in dense bush on both sides of a narrow and rugged path. The advanced guard, consisting of a company of the 2nd West India Regiment, drove the enemy from their position, but the object of the expedition, the surprise of the Ashantis at Dunkwa, having failed, it was deemed advisable to fall back upon Anamabo. In this affair six men were killed, and Lieutenant Swanzy, of the Royal African Colonial Corps, and thirty-eight men wounded. This expedition to the bush, though it proved unsuccessful, created the greatest sensation. It was an entirely new departure, for never before had a British force quitted the forts to engage in any operations; and the natives began to see that the Government was in earnest.

In April Sir C. Macarthy proceeded to Accra to endeavour if possible to detach the Accras from the Ashanti alliance That people had suffered so much injustice at the hands o Amankwa when the Ashanti army was quartered at Accra in 1814, that the Governor found no difficulty in entering into an agreement with them, made with the concurrence o Mr. Richter, the Commandant of Christiansborg, to stop supplying the Ashantis with munitions of war. Having effected this, and formed the nucleus of a volunteer militia o the most intelligent natives, as he had already done at Cap Coast and Anamabo, he returned to the former place.

He had scarcely left Accra when the good faith of th Accras was put to the test. A party of Ashantis arrived a Christiansborg to purchase gunpowder, and were at onc attacked and dispersed by the garrison of James Fort an the newly-formed militia. A day or two later a second bod of Ashantis arrived for the same purpose, and being refuse gunpowder by the inhabitants of Christiansborg, deliberate murdered a mulatto and four other natives. The whole town rose in arms to revenge this outrage; fourteen Ashantis were killed and the remainder driven into the bush, where a few days later they were again attacked and forty killed. Henceforward the whole of that part of the sea-coast was closed to the Ashantis, who lost in the Accras one of the most active and serviceable of their allies.

While these occurrences had been taking place a message had arrived from Kumassi to the Dutch Governor of Elmina, in which the King thanked him for his past friendship, informed him that Sir Charles Macarthy was "wrong in his palaver," and advised that Cape Coast Castle should be enlarged, as he intended to drive the English into the sea. He also recommended that the latter should arm all the fish in the sea, for all would be of no avail against the army he intended sending against them. Nothing, however, immediately took place, and in the middle of May Sir Charles Macarthy sailed for the Gambia, where he had, six years before, founded the colony of Bathurst on the Island of St. Mary.

When the Government assumed the control of the forts on the Gold Coast, the only regular troops in West Africa were five companies of the 2nd West India Regiment, which were divided between Sierra Leone, the Isles de Los, and the Gambia. There had formerly been serving in West Africa a regiment denominated the Royal African Corps, consisting of six companies of white troops and three of black, and which was a disciplinary corps as far as the whites were concerned; that is to say, the men were all of bad character, and had been sent to serve in its ranks as a punishment. The habits of these men were not such as to enable them to resist the attacks of the climate; in one year half the European troops in Sierra Leone died, and this dreadful mortality induced the Government in 1819, when Goree and Senegal were restored to France, and a reduction of the West African garrison could be effected, to withdraw all the European soldiers from the coast. The white companies of the Royal African Corps were sent to the Cape of Good Hope, the black companies were disbanded, and the left wing of the 2nd West India Regiment was brought from Jamaica to garrison the West Coast settlements. So long as these consisted only of Sierra Leone and the Gambia this force was sufficient; but when the control of the Gold Coast was assumed, a larger force became necessary. Sir C. Macarthy had, as we have seen, formed the soldiers of the late African Company of Merchants into a black corps of three companies, but these men were chiefly natives of the Gold Coast, and in view of the threatened hostilities with Ashanti, he asked that the Europeans of the late Royal African Corps might be sent back from the Cape of Good Hope to join the Royal African Colonial Corps of Light Infantry, and that recruiting might be carried on in England to raise that corps to a strength of one thousand men. The Government seem to have acquiesced in this complete reversal of their declared intention *not* to employ white troops in the pestilential West African climate, without hesitation; and, in April, 1823, two companies of white soldiers arrived from South Africa. Thus on the eve of the outbreak of hostilities, the force on the Gold Coast consisted of one company of the 2nd West India Regiment, which Sir C. Macarthy had brought down with him from Sierra Leone, and five companies (two white and three black) of the Royal African Colonial Corps, the whole amounting to not more than five hundred men.

CHAPTER XIII.

1823—1824.

The Ashanti invasion—Expedition to Essikuma—The Ashantis enter Wassaw—Sir C. Macarthy advances to meet them—Defeat and death of Sir Charles Macarthy at Assamako—Escape of Captain Ricketts—Movements of Major Chisholm's force—Sekondi burned—A camp formed on the Prah—Palaver with the Ashantis at Elmina—Release of Mr. Williams—His narrative.

IN June, 1823, the long-threatened invasion took place, a force of three thousand Ashantis crossing the Prah at Prahsu* on the 4th of that month. Major Chisholm, who was administering the Government, at once sent Captain Laing with the whole of the troops, and a large native contingent from Cape Coast and Anamabo, to meet them, and at the approach of this force the Ashantis retired. The movement of this large body of men seems to have convinced the chiefs of Fanti that the Government seriously intended to resist the Ashanti advance; and Appia, chief of Adjumako, first, and subsequently most of the other Fanti chiefs, renounced their allegiance to Ashanti, and sent offers of assistance to Major Chisholm. Kwasi Amankwa, chief of Essikuma, refused, however, to join the English, and Captain Laing destroyed his town, after which he returned to Cape Coast.

On July 28th a second Ashanti force crossed the Prah, and it being reported that it had orders to make its way to Elmina, Captain Laing marched to Yankumassi Fanti,†

---

* Prahsu—Prah water.
† Yankumassi—"Joined to Kumassi."

twenty-four miles from Cape Coast, to dispute its progress. Here he remained encamped for some time, and, no enemy appearing, then withdrew to Dunkwa.

In the middle of August, Kwasi Amankwa, who, with the assistance of the Ashantis, had reoccupied Essikuma, was attacked by the Fanti allies, and again driven away. A few days later, however, he again advanced, strongly reinforced by a body of Ashantis, and attacked the allies. As soon as the news of this reached him, Captain Laing marched from Dunkwa to the assistance of the Fantis, and, after a long and fatiguing march, reached Adjumako on the 20th. Next morning he marched to Essikuma and arrived there just as the Ashantis had succeeded in taking it after a sharp engagement. The appearance of the troops on the scene caused the Ashantis to abandon the place in great disorder and without any resistance, but not without massacring all the prisoners who had fallen into their hands, whose bodies were found still warm. The approach of evening prevented the troops from following in pursuit, but early next morning they moved against the Ashanti camp, which was taken by surprise, and abandoned by the enemy in such haste, that they left their dinners cooking on their fires, and the ground covered with arms and baggage. Instead of following up the retreating enemy, as they were directed to do, the Fantis stayed to plunder the camp, so that the Ashantis retired unmolested. Touch of them was completely lost, and after a few days, during which several unsuccessful efforts to discover their whereabouts had been made, Captain Laing returned to Cape Coast with the regular troops, leaving a force of Anamabo volunteer militia and Fanti levies at Mansu, and another, composed of Cape Coast volunteer militia and levies, at Jukwa. This latter post, situated about eighteen miles to the north-west of Cape Coast, was designed to prevent the Ashantis from obtaining arms and ammunition from Elmina.

On November 28th, 1823, Sir Charles Macarthy returned to the Gold Coast, bringing with him a third white company of the Royal African Colonial Corps, that had been raised in England. A few days after his arrival he inspected the camp at Jukwa, and in the following month visited Anamabo, where Appia, chief of Adjumako, and other chiefs came down to meet him. From Anamabo he proceeded to the camp at Mansu, where he entered into an offensive and defensive alliance with the King of Mankassim, and engaged that no peace should be made with Ashanti without the concurrence of the Fanti chiefs; a stipulation which the latter, having in mind Colonel Torrane's cowardly surrender of Tchibbu in order to obtain favourable terms for the Company, now exacted for self-protection.

Towards the end of December, it having been ascertained that a third, and much larger, Ashanti army had crossed the Pràh, and was rapidly advancing to the coast in twelve divisions, Captain Laing was ordered to march to Assin with the Fanti levies, and the Governor with the regular troops proceeded to Jukwa, where a body of some two thousand men was concentrated by January 4th, 1824. On the 6th, Sir Charles Macarthy sent Major Chisholm with the regulars, and a proportion of the native levies, to form a camp at Ampensasu, a village on the Prah some eighteen miles north of Jukwa; and when, on the 8th, news was received at Jukwa that the Ashantis had entered western Wassaw, Sir C. Macarthy decided to go to Wassaw with the force that still remained with him, and to leave Major Chisholm at Ampensasu to await further orders. This decision was strongly but vainly combated by the King of Jukwa and the Cape Coast chiefs, and on the morning of the 9th, the Governor, with less than half his available force, made a first march to Bansu,* a village seventeen miles from Jukwa, where, owing to the difficulty experienced in obtaining carriers for the supplies, they did not arrive till evening. Sir Charles Macarthy committed the too common mistake of underrating his enemy. He had with him a Fanti company of the Royal African Colonial Corps, only eighty strong, under Ensign Erskine; one hundred and

* Ban—fence, or boundary; Su—water.

seventy Cape Coast Volunteer Militia, a corps but recently embodied, and officered by merchants of Cape Coast; and two hundred and forty undisciplined natives under their own chiefs; yet with this force of less than five hundred men he intended to oppose the advance of an unknown number of Ashantis, inured to fighting and flushed with victory. He was accompanied by Captain Ricketts, 2nd West India Regiment, who acted as his brigade major; Ensign Wetherell of the same corps, who was his private secretary; Mr. Williams, Colonial Secretary; Surgeon Beresford Tedlie, and two West India soldiers, his orderlies.

The force remained halted at Bansu during January 10th, and on the 11th marched to Himan,* a village on the Prah. The carriers who had been brought from Jukwa having deserted, the greatest difficulty was found in transporting the munitions and supplies. The women of the villages passed through on the march were impressed for this service but numbers of them, when they had the opportunity, threw down their loads in the bush and ran off. On the morning of the 12th the troops started for Deraboassi, a village seventeen miles lower down the Prah. The road was extremely bad, being in some places rendered almost impassable by swamps three or four feet deep, while in others there were steep ascents to be climbed. Deraboassi was reached late in the day, and early next morning the force commenced crossing the Prah in eight small canoes, only sufficiently large to contain two persons beside the canoe man. The Fanti company of the Royal African Colonial Corps having first crossed, the Governor advanced with it over an exceedingly bad road, to the village of Guah, leaving the remainder of his men to follow; and next day the advance was continued to Assamako, where by three in the afternoon the whole body was assembled. It remained halted here to enable the natives of the neighbourhood to come in, and on the 17th an order was sent to Major Chisholm to join with the force from Ampensasu. The

* Himan—Chief's Town.

letter conveying this order was unfortunately entrusted to a native who was unacquainted with the country, and it was so delayed as not to arrive at its destination till the 22nd.

The Denkeras, who, after having remained quiet since 1752, had now joined the allies, were, with the Wassaws, in full retreat before the advancing Ashantis, and Mr. Williams was sent to rally them, and announce that the Governor was at hand with reinforcements. They were found completely disorganised, and it was only with the greatest difficulty that they could be persuaded to halt and form a camp on the banks of the Adamansu, a small stream some twenty miles from Assamako. Captain Ricketts reached this spot on the morning of the 20th, with the company of the Royal African Colonial Corps and the militia, after a night spent in the bush under heavy rain. During the afternoon of the same day an alarm was given that the Ashantis were advancing, and the troops remained under arms for five hours exposed to torrents of rain; but at nightfall, no enemy having appeared, and it being well known that the Ashantis did not make night attacks, they returned to their quarters. Early next morning Sir C. Macarthy arrived with a body-guard of two hundred men, who had been sent by Appia, chief of Adjumako. Kwasi Yako, chief of Assamako, an infirm old man who had to be carried on the heads of his slaves in a basket litter, also accompanied him with his followers; while two hundred Kommendas, and the carriers with the ammunition, were reported to be close behind.

The Governor seems to have been of opinion that there was but a small force of Ashantis at hand, and that the main body was at the distance of two or three days' march; and although the native allies and scouts asserted that the entire army was in front of him, he did not credit them, believing that they had invented the report in order to induce him to retire beyond the Prah, as the chiefs had already asked him to do. However, as some hostile body, large or small, was close at hand, the natives were told off for the positions they were to occupy in case of attack, but with such a force it was almost impossible to ensure orders being carried out. In fact the body-guard which had been furnished by Appia, and whose sole duty was to protect the person of the Governor, at once left the spot where they had been posted, and took up a position on the extreme left, which they refused to quit, saying that they understood bush fighting and had now got a place that they liked.

About two p.m. on February 21st, the Ashantis, who are said to have exceeded ten thousand in number, and who were all concentrated instead of being dispersed, as Sir C. Macarthy believed, advanced to within half a mile of the position on the Adamansu, blowing their horns and beating their drums. The Governor then ordered the band of the Royal African Colonial Corps, which had accompanied him, to play "God save the King," and the bugles to sound, for he had been so misinformed as to entertain the extraordinary belief that the greater part of the Ashantis only wanted an opportunity to desert their own people and come over to him. The Ashantis played in return, and this musical defiance was kept up for some time, after which a dead silence ensued. This was before long interrupted by the fire of the allied native upon the enemy, who had advanced and lined the opposite bank of the river, here about sixty feet wide. This movement was executed with the greatest regularity, the Ashantis advancing in a number of different divisions under their respective leaders, whose horns sounded their calls; and upon hearing them, a native who had been in Kumassi was able to name nearly every Ashanti chief with the army.

The action now commenced on both sides with great vigour, and for about an hour neither side could claim any advantage. But about four o'clock it began to be rumoured that the allied natives had expended all their ammunition. The ordnance storekeeper, Mr. Brandon, who arrived about this time, was at once applied to for more, but the reserve ammunition had not yet come up. He had left Assamako with forty natives carrying ammunition, but on hearing the firing had unwisely hurried on, leaving them to follow; and the carriers, who had been obtained almost by force, seeing the Wassaws making off from the field, hastened to follow their example. A barrel of powder and one of ball, which were all that remained, were at once issued, but the Ashantis, perceiving that the fire slackened, commenced to cross the river, which though swollen from the recent rains was still fordable. At the same time, in pursuance of their usual tactics, they despatched a considerable body of men to outflank the allied force and threaten its line of retreat; and soon they closed in from all directions. The Wassaws had abandoned the field already, and Sir C. Macarthy, who had himself been wounded, seeing that all was lost, retired to where Kwadjo Tchibbu, King of Denkera, was still fighting bravely, surrounded by his people.

On joining the King of Denkera Sir Charles wished to sound a retreat, but not a bugler could be found, every man of the Royal African Corps having joined his company in the action. It was impossible to see far in the dense bush, and only a few wounded men were got together. A small brass field-piece, which had arrived during the battle, and had been flung down still lashed to the poles on which it had been carried, was untied, some powder was obtained from the King of Denkera, and the piece, loaded with musket-balls, fired towards the enemy, to check, if possible, their advance; but it only served to draw them in that direction, and they immediately rushed forward and killed the two West India soldiers.

The Governor now left the King of Denkera, and Captain Ricketts, suddenly missing him, was about to follow, when a general discharge of musketry was poured in from the bush close at hand, and he was swept away in the rush of fugitives. Despairing of joining the Governor, Captain Ricketts, followed by Mr. De Graft, lieutenant in the militia, and some wounded men, endeavoured to force a way through the bush to where the King of Denkera, though retreating, was still keeping up a fire and presenting a front to the victorious Ashantis. At this moment a Wassaw man who was running by was seized by a militia sergeant, and offered a reward if he would guide the party through the bush. A silver whistle and chain were given him by Mr.

De Graft, and he led the way, one of the party holding him fast. He led them up a small stream, and then some distance along its banks, the enemy all the time scouring the bush so closely that they were several times obliged to halt and hide themselves. At last, it having become so dark that they could scarcely see each other, the guide ordered a halt, saying that it was impossible to proceed till the moon rose. The exulting shouts and cries of the Ashantis, and their attempts to sound the musical instruments they had captured, were distinctly heard at a distance of a few hundred yards; and the fugitives cowered in the darkness of the bush, momentarily expecting discovery and death.

At about midnight the moon rose, and the small party directed by their guide, commenced cutting a path through the bush. With the exception of a short interval between the setting of the moon and the rising of the sun, they continued this work until three o'clock in the next afternoon when they hit upon a path leading to Assamako. They had proceeded some little distance along this when they perceived a party of Ashantis in front. They at once hastened back, and, the guide having fled, turned up a narrow path to their right. A short distance along this they fell in with a party of some fifty Wassaws, who reported that there were some Ashantis further on, and that they themselves had turned back in the hope, now that the Ashantis were plundering in every direction, of being able to recover some of their women and children, who had been carried off from their villages. Captain Ricketts's party joined these men, and about nightfall the whole penetrated some way into the bush, and halted on a small island in the midst of a swamp, in crossing which Captain Ricketts lost one of his shoes. In the middle of the night two Ashantis thinking it was a party of their own people, came into their midst; and the Wassaws, after extracting from them all the information they could give, immediately cut their throats. At dawn they struck into a path that led toward the Prah, and after a slight skirmish with a small party of Ashantis, reached at nightfall a deserted village on the banks of that river. At this place they were obliged to halt for the night, there being only one small broken canoe, that would scarcely float, with which to cross the river. During the day's march the Wassaws had found several of their women and children in hiding in the bush. Several children were also found with their brains dashed out, and others in a dying condition where they had been cast away; for the Ashantis had compelled the women to throw away their infants, in order that they might the more easily carry their plunder.

Next morning at daybreak, the whole party crossed the Prah, on the bank of which two European soldiers of the Royal African Colonial Corps met Captain Ricketts, and informed him that they belonged to the advanced guard of Major Chisholm's force, which was marching to join the Governor. Fainting from hunger and exhaustion, and with his feet torn and bleeding, Captain Ricketts was unable to proceed further; but the two men constructed a litter of the branches of trees and carried him to a small village, where before long Major Chisholm arrived. Thus terminated the disastrous expedition into the Wassaw country, which was one of the rashest and most ill-conceived schemes imaginable. Sir C. Macarthy was crushed by overwhelming numbers, and the failure of ammunition at a critical moment turned defeat into disaster. The engagement is generally known as the battle of Assamako, though, as a matter of fact, the struggle took place on the banks of the Adumansu,* some twenty miles from that town.

As has already been stated, the letter sent by Sir C. Macarthy to Major Chisholm on January 17th did not reach him until the 22nd; a second letter, written on the 21st, and containing the most pressing orders for him to join with his whole force immediately, actually arriving two hours earlier. The whole of the 23rd, however, was occupied in crossing the Prah, five miles from Ampensasu, only one canoe being available, and at nightfall the force was still at a village on

* Adu-man-su—the water, or river, of Adu's town.

the river. Here Major Chisholm heard that an engagement had taken place, but could not learn the result, and next day was pushing on with all haste, when he met Captain Ricketts and learned the full extent of the disaster. Sir Charles Macarthy's force being entirely dispersed or destroyed, and his own being inadequate to cope with the victorious enemy, who, he imagined, would advance upon Cape Coast by rapid marches, Major Chisholm, on the 25th, commenced to retreat thither. An hour after the march had begun, Captain L'Estrange, of the Royal African Colonial Corps, dropped dead from fatigue and exposure. The troops halted for the night at a deserted village, marched through Effutu shortly after noon next day, and arrived at Cape Coast in the evening. In Cape Coast was found Captain Laing, who, agreeably with his instructions, had advanced some thirty miles into Assin; but hearing of the defeat of Assamako, prudently retired, bringing back in safety the whole of his force.

Contrary to expectation, the Ashantis had made no attempt to follow up their success, and had not even crossed the Prah. In fact, such is not the Ashanti mode of waging war. After a victory they usually remain halted for some weeks, overrunning and plundering the surrounding country and destroying the villages and plantations; and when they do finally advance, it is in a very leisurely manner. Every exertion was now made to assemble a force sufficient to oppose the enemy; but the effect of the defeat of Assamako was soon visible in the excuses made by the different chiefs to avoid taking the field, most of them bitterly regretting that they had been induced to take up arms at all. However, on February 5th, Captain Laing marched from Cape Coast to Jukwa with a detachment of the Royal African Colonial Corps, and a small party of Fantis—in all some four hundred men; and being joined in the course of the week by some six hundred more natives, he was ordered to move to Kommenda, where Major Chisholm himself proceeded on the 15th.

The object of this movement was to punish the inhabitant

of Dutch Sekondi for an attack made, on January 25th, on Captain Woolcomb and some officers of H.M.S. *Owen Glendower*, who had landed to gain intelligence concerning the battle. Two marines and a Kruman had been killed and several wounded on that occasion, and the Dutch Sekondis had also murdered several wounded men who had escaped from the field of Assamako. On February 16th the force was embarked on board H.M. ships *Bann* and *Owen Glendower*, but owing to contrary winds and a strong current, did not reach Dutch Sekondi till the following afternoon. It was at once disembarked, the town, which was immediately abandoned by the inhabitants and a party of some four hundred Ashantis, was set on fire and destroyed, and the force returned to Kommenda the same night.

The Ashantis, who were now ascertained to be some fifteen thousand in number, were still at Assamako, but it was reported that they intended advancing on March 1st. The Accra Militia, under Captains Hansen and Bannerman, having joined Captain Laing at Kommenda, and thereby brought his force up to a total strength of six thousand men, he was ordered to take up a position on the Prah, in order to dispute the expected passage of the enemy; but before this movement could be effected, Captain Laing was invalided to England, and the command of the native force devolved upon Captain Ricketts. That officer posted the detachment of the 2nd West India Regiment, under Lieutenant Macarthy, at Deraboassi, on the direct route from Assamako to Kommenda, distributed some of the native levies in other villages along the Prah, and proceeded with the bulk of his force to the mouth of that river, where he encamped. The 1st of March passed without the enemy making any appearance, and the continued inaction was beginning to affect the morale of the native levies, whose chiefs were urgent in their entreaties to be allowed to cross the river and attack the enemy, saying that their men would lose their courage if they waited much longer. A forward movement, however, formed no part of the present plan of operations, and the chiefs were informed that they must wait. On March 10th, Major Chisholm being seriously ill, Captain Ricketts, the second in command, was recalled to Cape Coast, and Captain Blencarne, of the Royal African Colonial Corps, took command of the force distributed along the Prah.

While affairs were in this condition, the Ashantis plundering Wassaw, and the allied natives losing heart in enforced idleness awaiting the expected attack, Governor Last, the Dutch Director-General, who had recently arrived at Elmina from Holland, wrote to inform Major Chisholm that some Ashanti messengers had arrived at Elmina, and that they wished to hold a palaver with the English. Captain Ricketts was accordingly sent from Cape Coast, and had a meeting with the Ashanti messengers, and with Atjiempon, their resident ambassador at Elmina. In the course of the conference which took place, the messengers declared that they were authorised to say that the King had not sent his army to fight against the white men, but to capture Kwadjo Tchibbu, King of Denkera, Awusucu, chief of Tshiforo, or Tufel, and Annimelli, King of Western Wassaw, who had made war against him, their sovereign. They added that if these three men were delivered up, the Ashanti army would immediately return home, but that they had special orders from the King to take Kwadjo Tchibbu, even should he be locked up in Cape Coast Castle.

The reason the capture of the King of Denkera was so insisted upon was as follows: The Ashanti King, suspecting that he was meditating a rebellion, had inveigled him to Kumassi, where he was kept a prisoner for some time, until, being informed privately that it was intended to put him to death he contrived to bribe some Ashanti captains and escape On returning to Denkera, he at once proclaimed war against Ashanti, in which he was joined by his neighbours the King of Tufel and Western Wassaw; and having taken prisoner some Ashantis who were working in the Denkera gold mine, he sent them to Kumassi with a message to the King that h captains were not very trustworthy persons, since for gol they had allowed him to escape. This charge created great excitement in the capital, and the whole of the assembled Ashanti captains, after denying the accusation, swore by the King's head, a most sacred oath, that they would follow and bring back to the capital their accuser, even should he seek protection within the walls of Cape Coast. It was the army despatched with this object that had entered Wassaw and defeated Sir C. Macarthy.

The reply of Captain Ricketts to the Ashanti messengers was unfortunately ambiguous. Instead of at once declaring that the British Government would never treacherously surrender chiefs who had stood by it in the hour of need, he contented himself with affirming that it was not the wish of the King of England to make war upon any of the natives of Africa, and that if the Ashantis wished for peace it could be at once effected, provided that properly accredited ambassadors were sent for that purpose. The Ashanti messengers interpreted this speech as meaning that no difficulty would be made about surrendering the three chiefs, so on their part they promised that their army should remain stationary until ambassadors could arrive at Elmina to arrange a peace, and asked that orders might be given to the troops and allied natives not to attack the Ashantis. To this Captain Ricketts agreed, and the meeting broke up. As a proof of their friendly intentions, the Ashantis now surrendered Mr. Williams, the Colonial Secretary, who had been captured by them at Assamako; but unable to deny themselves the satisfaction of a triumphant procession before the inhabitants of Elmina, they led him naked through the streets, with his hands tied behind him, before giving him up to Governor Last.

From Mr. Williams's account it appeared that he had left the battlefield with Sir Charles Macarthy, Mr. Buckle, and Ensign Wetherell, and after proceeding a short distance along the path to Assamako, had been suddenly attacked by a party of the enemy. At the first fire one of Sir C. Macarthy's arms was broken, and almost immediately afterwards he received a wound in the breast and fell. At the same time Mr. Williams received a ball in the thigh and fell fainting, the last thing he remembered seeing being Ensign Wetherell, who was lying wounded close to the Governor, cutting with his sword at the enemy as they were tearing off Sir Charles's clothes. When he recovered his senses he found that some Ashantis were trying to cut off his head, and had already inflicted one gash on the back of his neck. Fortunately, at this moment an Ashanti trader, to whom Mr. Williams had been able to show some kindness at Cape Coast, came up, and, recognising the prisoner, ordered his life to be spared. Close at hand were the headless trunks of Sir C. Macarthy, Mr. Buckle, and Ensign Wetherell.

Mr. Williams was marched as a prisoner to Assamako, where the Ashanti army was encamped. During the day he was kept under a thatched shed, and every night he was locked up in a small room with the heads of the Governor, Mr. Buckle, and Ensign Wetherell, which, owing to some peculiar process, were in a perfect state of preservation. The Governor's head in particular presented nearly the same appearance as when he was alive. The only sustenance allowed the prisoner during his captivity was as much snail soup every morning and evening as he could hold in the palm of his hand; and, with a refinement of cruelty, the Ashantis, whenever they beheaded any of their prisoners, compelled him to sit on one side of their large war drum while the heads were struck off on the other. The Ashantis had intended sending Mr. Williams to Kumassi, and as he was not able to walk, on account of the musket-ball in his thigh, they endeavoured to force it out by tying strings tightly round the leg, above and below the wound. This treatment, while it caused the prisoner the most excruciating pain, entirely failed in its object, and Mr. Williams was in daily expectation of being put to death, when he received the welcome news that they were going to send him to Elmina. During his captivity he learned that Mr. Jones, a merchant and captain of militia, who had fallen into their hands, had been sacrificed to one of their gods, because he had received five wounds. Mr. Raydon, captain in the militia, had also been brutally murdered because, when stripped naked and deprived of his boots, he had been unable to keep up with his captors.

The losses sustained by the regulars and militia engaged in the battle of Assamako, were now ascertained to have been as under:

KILLED.

Officers.

Brigadier-General Sir Charles Macarthy.
Ensign Wetherell } 2nd West India Regiment.
Surgeon Beresford Tedlie }
J. S. Buckle, Esq., Colonial Engineer.
Captain Heddle }
Captain Jones } Merchants holding Commissions in the Cape Coast Militia.
Captain Raydon }
Captain Robertson, Cape Coast Volunteer Company.
Mr. Brandon, Ordnance Store-keeper.

Men.

2nd West India Regiment...	2
Royal African Colonial Corps	41
Royal Cape Coast Militia	81
Royal Volunteer Company	54
	178

WOUNDED.

Officers.

Captain Ricketts, 2nd West India Regiment.
Ensign Erskine, Royal African Colonial Corps.
Mr. Williams, Colonial Secretary.

Men.

Royal African Colonial Corps	17
Royal Cape Coast Militia	58
Royal Volunteer Company	14
	89

The brunt of the day had been borne by the regulars and militia, who in consequence had suffered severely. The

Royal African Corps had 58 killed and wounded out of a total of 80, the Cape Coast Militia 139 out of 170, and the Volunteer Company 68 out of 76. The loss sustained by the native levies was never ascertained, but it was probably not very heavy, as the whole of them, except the Denkeras under Kwadjo Tchibbu, quitted the field early in the day. The Denkeras fought bravely and suffered a considerable loss.

CHAPTER XIV.

1824.

Effect of the Elmina palaver on the natives—Retreat from the Prah—Defeat at Dompim—A camp formed at Beulah—Action at Effutu—The Ashantis advance upon Cape Coast—Cape Coast attacked—Withdrawal of the Ashantis—Condition of the town—Outrage by the Elminas.

THE ambiguous language used by Captain Ricketts to the Ashanti messengers at Elmina soon produced its natural results, for the palaver had been conducted openly, and the matter discussed was of such vital importance to the native allies, that everything that had been said was soon known and commented upon. It soon became commonly believed that the Government intended purchasing a shameful peace by delivering to their barbarous foes Kwadjo Tchibbu and the two other chiefs who had been demanded, and unfortunately the recollection of a former disgraceful surrender only tended to confirm the natives in their belief. This belief was further strengthened by the fact that Captain Blencarne, who had at last yielded to the importunities of the chiefs, and had fixed a day for crossing the Prah and attacking the enemy, was now obliged to cancel this order, in consequence of the engagement to abstain from hostilities made by Captain Ricketts with the Ashanti messengers.

The native chiefs, conceiving themselves about to be abandoned by the English, now decided to attack the Ashantis by themselves, and it was in vain that Captain

Blencarne strove to dissuade them. On the morning of March 24th, they crossed the river about seven thousand strong, leaving Captain Blencarne with only the regulars, militia, and a party of Accras, and commenced cutting paths towards the enemy's camp. The Ashantis, of course, regarded this advance as a breach of the engagement to suspend hostilities, and moving from Assamako, appeared in force on the banks of the Prah opposite Deraboassi. As they appeared to be preparing to cross at this point, the regulars and militia were moved there, and an exchange of shots across the river took place daily. By a chance shot fired in this way, Ensign Erskine was one morning wounded in the thigh and completely disabled, while sitting in a hut near the river bank.

For eight days the native levies who had crossed the river continued cutting paths through the bush towards the Ashanti camp, and though Captain Hutchinson, of the Anamabo militia, was specially sent by Major Chisholm to assure them that the English would never consent to make peace by surrendering the three chiefs, they persevered in their design. On the night of the ninth day, however, their courage failed them. The Wassaws, who were on the extreme left, deserted their post in the darkness, and swam across the river; and this being discovered at daybreak, the whole native force, seized with a disgraceful panic, fled across the Prah with such precipitation that two thousand muskets and nearly all the ammunition were lost, and several men drowned. As they landed on the left bank they dispersed in every direction, making their way to their homes, and the native force ceased to exist.

The Ashantis, who had been alarmed by the noise made by the panic-stricken natives in their flight, no sooner ascertained what had taken place than they prepared to follow in pursuit; and Captain Blencarne, being left with a mere handful of men, retired on April 2nd through Effutu to Cape Coast. On the way he met Kwadjo Tchibbu, at the village of Bansu, and it was only with the utmost difficulty, and after giving the most solemn pledges that neither he nor any of his family would be surrendered to the Ashantis, that he could persuade the chief to accompany him to Cape Coast.

On April 10th, Major Chisholm ordered Captain Blencarne to move out and form a camp at Effutu. He was followed by the King of Denkera and Appia, chief of Adjumako, with their people, and these chiefs, at the request of Captain Blencarne, took up a position near the village of Dompim,* some twelve miles beyond Effutu, and close to a stream from which the enemy, who had now moved from the Prah, obtained their water. The two loyal chiefs fired on several Ashantis who came down to the stream, upon which some of the enemy shouted from the dense bush that "they would soon see who was master," and on the morning of the 25th the Denkeras and Adjumakos were attacked in force. The allies fought well, and, when the centre of the Ashanti line fell back, they conceived that they had won the day. But it was only a stratagem of savage warfare, for as the allies pushed after the retreating centre, the Ashanti flanks wheeled in upon them, and, attacking them on both sides, threw them into confusion. The slaughter was immense, and only a small proportion of the allies escaped from the field. Appia, who had become separated from his men, was missing for several days, but at last, when all hope had been nearly abandoned, he was found in a starving condition in the bush. He was carried to Cape Coast, where small-pox was raging, and there this brave and loyal chief unfortunately fell a victim to that disease. Captain Blencarne at Effutu, having heard the firing, had marched to the assistance of the allies, but finding them defeated and dispersed, and the Ashantis busily engaged in cutting paths towards Effutu, ordered a retreat to Cape Coast. The Ashantis followed with unusual alacrity, and actually entered Effutu at one end as the troops were leaving it at the other, making prisoners of two European soldiers, and nearly capturing Ensign Mackenzie, who had just time to leap out of the window of a house and escape.

* Dompim—Place of bones.

A few days later, the Ashantis having made no further advance, the troops were again ordered out and directed to encamp in the Government garden at the village of Beulah, about six miles from Cape Coast and three from Effutu, where the enemy had now fixed their quarters. After much difficulty in getting natives to the camp, a force of about six thousand men, including regulars and militia, was collected; and it being reported that the King of Ashanti was advancing in person with ten thousand men to reinforce his army at Effutu, Major Chisholm ordered the allies to cross the Kakum, or Sweet River, which runs close to the garden, and attack the enemy before the junction was effected. Several days were wasted in a dispute between the allies as to who was to take the right during the projected attack. The Fantis insisted upon occupying that position, and the Denkeras and others, knowing their cowardice, strongly opposed such an arrangement, for the route to Fanti country lay to the right, and there was every probability that the Fantis would retreat there during the action; while, if they were placed on the left, they would be unable to run away, as the Elminas, the allies of Ashanti, would be behind them. The Fantis, however, would not yield, and succeeded in carrying their point by saying that if they were not allowed to take the right they would return home without fighting. This being settled, the force was told off to its various positions, and each body commenced cutting its way through the thick bush to the enemy, now about two miles off.

On May 18th, Lieutenant-Colonel Sutherland, of the 2nd West India Regiment, arrived from Sierra Leone, bringing with him forty men of his corps, which was all that could be spared from the garrison of Sierra Leone. He assumed the government of the Gold Coast, and on the 19th proceeded to the camp at Beulah; but finding the paths to the enemy's position were almost completed, and not wishing to deprive Major Chisholm of the honour of the command in the action he had planned and which was about to take place, he returned to Cape Coast to forward some necessary supplies. On the morning of the 21st every available man from the garrison of Cape Coast was despatched to Beulah, the marines from the men-of-war in the roadstead being landed to garrison the Castle and towers, and at one in the afternoon the battle commenced. The Ashanti position was on a hill covered with dense wood, the front of which had been cleared of bush for some considerable distance, so that they had a full view of the troops and native allies as they advanced to the attack. The enemy fought bravely, keeping up a heavy fire from the thick bush, and making several attempts to turn the flanks of the allies; but finding themselves baffled at all points, after five hours' fighting, they retired from the position with great loss in killed and wounded. The Denkeras behaved with their usual gallantry, and pursued the enemy into Effutu.*

The fruits of this engagement, the first since the beginning of the war in which the Ashantis had suffered any material reverse, were lost through the cowardice of the Fantis. As had been expected, at the very commencement of the battle, the whole Fanti contingent, three thousand strong, had fled without firing a shot. Nor was this the worst, for meeting in their flight the carriers from Cape Coast bringing up supplies and ammunition, they swept them back with them, reporting that the English were defeated; and in consequence the troops and native allies found themselves at nightfall short of ammunition and without supplies. They were also much distressed for want of water, which was to have been sent to them, and there being no stream nearer than the Sweet River, they were

---

* The British force engaged consisted of 2 officers and 99 men of the 2nd West India Regiment, 3 officers and 136 men of the Royal African Corps, and 470 militia of all ranks. The native auxiliary force consisted of 77 chiefs and some 5,000 men. The losses were as follows :

	Killed.	Wounded.
Regulars	9	20
Militia	83	54
Native Levies... ...	84	603
	176	677

constrained to fall back to Beulah. Although Major Chisholm announced that he intended to advance next day and renew the engagement, this retrograde movement so disheartened the natives, that during the night the whole of them, with the exception of the Denkeras and a few men from Cape Coast, dispersed; and Lieutenant-Colonel Sutherland then ordered the troops to return to the Castle, a party of observation, under Lieutenant Rogers, of the Royal African Colonial Corps, being left at Beulah.

Two days after the action the Ashantis, who had been joined by a strong body of Elminas, returned to their camp at Effutu, where on the 28th they were reinforced by the army from Kumassi under Osai Okoto, for Osai Tutu Kwamina had died on January 21st, the very day on which Sir Charles Macarthy had lost his life. Osai Okoto sent to Colonel Sutherland to say that the walls of the Castle were not high enough and should be made higher, and that he ought to land all the guns from the men-of-war, as he intended throwing every stone of the Castle into the sea; but notwithstanding this bombast he did nothing for three weeks, during which time many of his foraging parties were cut off by the native allies, who were readier at lying in ambush and firing volleys upon small bodies of unsuspecting stragglers than at fighting pitched battles.

At last, on June 21st, the Ashanti army advanced from Effutu to within five miles of Cape Coast, driving in before it Lieutenant Rogers's party of observation. Next day the enemy moved considerably nearer, taking up a position which the smoke of their camp fires showed to be about three miles in extent; and on the day following they advanced so near that they were distinctly seen in great force on the hills behind Forts William and Victoria. An attack was considered imminent, and the whole of the male population of the town was ordered out to repel it, while the women and children of Cape Coast, together with those who had fled into the town from the surrounding villages, rushed to the Castle for protection. The crush at the gate, the wicket only of which had, through some mismanagement, been left open, was terrible; several women were squeezed to death in the crowd, and the cries of the terrified people struggling for an entrance were pitiful beyond expression. To add to the terrors of the moment a vast conflagration now broke out, and soon involved the whole town in destruction. In past years the natives had been suffered to encroach upon the open space in front of the Castle, and had built thereon several houses which actually overlooked and commanded the Castle ramparts. Colonel Sutherland had given orders for these to be pulled down, but the owners had neglected to comply, and when the near approach of the enemy was signalled from Fort William, there being no time for anything else to be done, he ordered four of them to be set on fire. The strong sea breeze caused the conflagration to spread, and the flames, springing from one thatched roof to another, soon destroyed the roofs and all the woodwork of nearly every house in the town. The mud walls, of course, could not be seriously damaged, and fortunately nearly all goods of value had already been moved into the Castle for safety; but still the destruction of property, especially that of the poorer people who could not easily replace it, was very great.

After all, the enemy made no attack on that day, but after advancing to within less than a mile of the Castle, halted, and without any apparent cause retired early next morning, the 24th, to Beulah. Many years afterwards the Ashantis explained this movement by saying that the conflagration of the town dismayed them. They seem to have thought that the people had destroyed it in a frenzy of despair and were preparing to perish in its ruins, and that therefore it would be wiser to postpone the attack for another time. They remained stationary at Beulah until the end of the month, detaching strong parties to lay waste the country and destroy the neighbouring villages, which work they effected without molestation, for the garrison of Cape Coast consisted of less than four hundred men, one-third of whom were in hospital, and no dependence could be placed upon the native levies.

On July 4th a welcome reinforcement of one hundred and one officers and men of the Royal African Colonial Corps arrived in H.M.S. *Thetis* from England; and two days later the garrison of Cape Coast was further increased by a reinforcement of some five thousand natives, who had been raised from Accra and the sea-coast towns to the eastward as far as the Volta. This contingent had been got together by Major de Richelieu, the Danish Governor at Christiansborg, who had recently arrived on the Gold Coast, and who throughout exhibited the greatest friendliness to the British. He sent a Danish officer, Captain Peloson, in command of the force, and announced that he was assembling another strong force to advance through Akim, commanded by himself, and create a diversion by threatening an invasion of Ashanti territory. Unfortunately the reinforcement brought no munitions of war with them, and the troops were already so badly supplied with lead that all the waterpipes from the Castle, the lead from the roofs of the merchants' houses, and every pewter vessel that could be procured, had been taken for the casting of bullets and slugs.

On July 7th the enemy again approached the town, and were seen defiling over a hill by several paths in great force and moving towards a line of heights, where they took up a position. Near to the left of this position, at a spot where the bush had been cleared, the King pitched his tent, and the Ashantis were so near that their movements could be easily observed from the town. Some of them were wearing the uniforms of the officers and men who had been killed at Assamako, and they displayed English, Dutch, and Danish flags, together with others designed by themselves. The allied natives were now ordered out to take up a position on a line of hills opposite to those occupied by the Ashanti, and several skirmishes took place with small bodies of the latter, who were busily engaged in cutting paths towards the town. On Sunday, the 11th, the enemy were seen descending the hills in large masses soon after daylight, and forming long lines in the valley that lay between the two opposing positions. Shortly after noon they made a further advance, and, being fired upon by some skirmishers, a general engagement ensued, and continued till dark, when the enemy retired. During the action two of their camps were plundered and burnt by some of the native levies, who, although it had been necessary hitherto to drive them daily to their posts at the point of the bayonet, fought well this day for four hours, especially those stationed on the right, at Prospect and Connor's Hills, where the enemy, who showed the greatest courage, made the most determined efforts.*

Next day the enemy again formed up in the valley as if to renew the engagement, and being fired at by a few skirmishers who had crept through the bush to reconnoitre, opened a heavy fire in return, which they kept up for half an hour. They then remained quiet until about two in the afternoon, when, on a few random shots being fired into the bush from a field-piece, they returned to their former position. Next morning they were again observed in motion, descending in single file from the line of hills by several paths towards the valley. A renewal of the engagement was momentarily expected and everything was held in readiness, but throughout the whole day, and until darkness set in, they still continued marching down the hills. During the night hundreds of fires gleamed in the valley, but when daylight appeared not an enemy was to be seen, and it was soon ascertained that the entire army had decamped. In order to enable their wounded, carriers, and prisoners to retire unmolested, they had marched men down the hills in full view of the English, taken them by hidden paths through the bush to the back of the hills, and then again marched them down in full view. The reason of

---

* The allied force engaged on the 11th was as follows:

	Officers.	Men.
Royal Marine Artillery	1	2
2nd West India Regiment	1	90
Royal African Corps	15	193
Militia	2	118
Native Levies	—	4650
	19	5053

The loss was one officer (Lieutenant Swanzy, Royal African Corps) and 103 men killed, and 448 men wounded.

this abandonment of the attack on Cape Coast was that the army had suffered terribly from small-pox and dysentery, as well as from want of food, they having, with very little foresight, destroyed all the plantations for miles round. Discontent was the natural result, and on the night of the 11th the entire Assin contingent had deserted, saying that they could not fight when hungry. From native prisoners who escaped from the Ashantis it was now learned that the principal Ashanti chiefs had divided and eaten the heart of Sir Charles Macarthy, in the belief, common to most savages, that they would thereby acquire some portion of the courage that had animated it. It was further said that his flesh had been dried, and divided amongst all the chiefs and captains in the army, as charms to inspire bravery.

The Ashanti army retired in the direction of Elmina, Beulah, and Effutu, and though every effort was made to induce the allies to follow and harass it, it was without effect. On June 19th a reconnoitring party from Cape Coast reported that the enemy had retreated in the direction of Anamabo, in the vicinity of which town they remained, destroying villages and plantations, till the report of the advance through Akim of the force raised by Major de Richelieu caused them to retire to Kumassi. When they withdrew they left behind three or four hundred sick and wounded, all of whom fell into the hands of the Fantis, and were murdered.

The wanton destruction of the plantations and provision-grounds, which had necessitated the withdrawal of the Ashanti army, was now the cause of a famine that devastated Cape Coast and Anamabo. These two towns were filled to overflowing with the fugitives from the inland towns and villages, for whom there was absolutely no food. The officers and soldiers of the garrison were themselves very short of provision, having neither meat nor flour, and five or six Europeans died daily. The natives perished by hundreds from mere starvation, and an epidemic of small-pox and dysentery carried off scores of others. Dozens of dead and dying were seen lying about the streets of Cape Coast, and the Castle yard was so crowded with women and children in the last stage of exhaustion, that it was impossible to pass from one side of it to the other without treading on them. The stench was horrible, and the frequent showers of rain which washed into the cisterns the filth naturally accumulated under these conditions, aggravated the situation by causing the water to become polluted. Providentially a vessel with a supply of provisions arrived from Sierra Leone, and as soon as the dreadful condition of Cape Coast was known, several ships laden with rice were despatched from England. These supplies preserved the life of the garrison and the remaining inhabitants, for the country could produce nothing in the way of food till fresh crops were sown and had grown up, a process which would require some months.

Scarcely had the Ashanti army retired into its own territory than the Elminas gave a fresh proof of their hostility to the natives allied to the British. When it was ascertained that the enemy had really crossed the Prah, some of the inhabitants of the deserted villages returned to their former homes, to rebuild their houses and resume their avocations, amongst them being the Kommendas. The majority of the Kommendas returned home by sea, but a number of women and children who sought to proceed by land, were seized as they were passing through the town of Elmina, and murdered by the inhabitants. The Governor, Colonel Grant, of the Royal African Corps, for Colonel Sutherland had been invalided to England towards the end of July, at once wrote to Governor Last at Elmina to demand that the perpetrators of this crime should be punished; but the latter replied that he had no sufficient force to control the people, much less to compel them to surrender some of their number to condign punishment. Colonel Grant then offered to send the troops from Cape Coast, and Governor Last at first accepted this offer, but changed his mind at the eleventh hour, when every arrangement for their conveyance had been made and the hour of landing fixed. Further remonstrances failed to produce any effect, and none of the Elminas were ever brought to justice for their crime.

The mortality among the officers and European troops during this campaign had been terrible. The account is contained in an old letter-book in the Military Hospital at Cape Coast, and a part of it is given here in detail to show what the climate of the Gold Coast really is; for the Colonial Government, probably not wishing to terrify its European officials, has never published any death statistics. Out of the first two companies of white soldiers, who arrived at Cape Coast from the Cape of Good Hope in April, 1823, only one man remained alive in December, 1824. Out of a second detachment that had arrived in November, 1823, from England, only eight remained alive; the greater part of a third detachment which disembarked at Cape Coast on 12th March, 1824 died within three months of landing; only six men remained alive of a fourth detachment that arrived on 20th March; and out of the one hundred and one men who landed from H.M.S *Thetis* on July 4th, forty-five died within a week of arrival. The deaths of fifteen officers are recorded within the same period, viz., between April, 1823, and December, 1824. As if it were not sufficiently bad to send men to serve in such climate, the Government actually sent out the soldiers' wives and children. Forty-two women and sixty-seven children arrived at Cape Coast in October, 1823, and by December, 1824, twenty-nine women and forty-one children were dead, sacrificed to official ignorance, and twenty-seven women and children had been sent to England to save their lives. Well might Assistant-Surgeon Bell, of the Royal African Colonial Corps, who compiled this record, say: "The destruction of life that has taken place ought to prevent any more European women and children being sent out. . . . I sincerely hope I will never rewitness the many trying sights I have done this year, in beholding the father and four or five fine children, laid up with fever in a small hovel of a place, totally helpless to each other, and gradually dying, without my being able to mitigate their sufferings even in a small degree."

CHAPTER XV.

1825—1829.

Major-General Turner—Advance of a second Ashanti army—Battle of Dodowah—Proceedings of Sir Neil Campbell—Peace negotiations—Blockade of Elmina—Further negotiations—The Home Government withdraws from the Gold Coast—A committee of merchants formed—Condition of the country.

COLONEL GRANT was soon succeeded in the government by Major Chisholm, and nothing worthy of note occurred till the death of the latter, which took place on October 17th, 1824. His loss was much regretted, for he possessed an intimate acquaintance with native affairs, having served in West Africa in various capacities since 1809. At the end of March, 1825, Major-General Turner, who had been appointed Governor-in-Chief of the British Settlements in West Africa, arrived at Cape Coast with three transports, containing seven hundred European soldiers of the Royal African Colonial Corps from England, and the 2nd West India Regiment from Sierra Leone. Finding that there was no hostile body of Ashantis south of Prahsu, he issued a proclamation, charging the Ashanti King with having, with the assistance of the Elminas, waged a cruel and unjust war against the English and their native allies, and stating that he would not enter into any treaty with Ashanti until the King abandoned all claim to tribute from, and authority over, the tribes on the sea-coast. He also announced

that Elmina was only suffered to exist because of the
friendship between the Dutch and English Governments.
This proclamation was, under the circumstances, rather
bombastic, considering that the Ashantis had not asked for
a treaty, and were not likely, having been the victors in the
late war, to do so. From January to June, a period of six
months, they had held possession of Wassaw, Denkera, and
Fanti, which they had depopulated and pillaged. They had
defeated and slain an English Governor, and had compelled
the troops to keep under the protection of the forts, only
ultimately retiring on account of sickness and the scarcity
of food. In Africa, as in Europe, it is the vanquished and
not the victors who sue for peace; and it was therefore,
to say the least, curious for the Governor to announce
that he would not conclude a treaty except on his own
terms. But this flourish deceived nobody, and on April 14th
he returned to Sierra Leone, taking with him nearly all the
Europeans of the Royal African Colonial Corps, and sending
the 2nd West India Regiment to the West Indies.

Major-General Turner died at Sierra Leone on March 7th
1826, after a residence in West Africa of fourteen months
and news having been received in England that another
Ashanti army was advancing to the coast, Major-General
Sir Neil Campbell was appointed his successor, and was
ordered to proceed to Africa at once. This new army of
invasion, which had left Kumassi in the beginning of the
year, had been overrunning eastern Fanti and destroying the
towns and villages, particularly Essikuma, the chief of which
Kwasi Amankwa, had, after the withdrawal of the former
army in 1825, reconsidered his position and decided to join
the British. It remained thus occupied, without meeting
with the least resistance till August, 1826, when the King
concentrated his whole force to the north of Accra, he being
determined to punish the Accras for joining the allies. A
considerable force of natives was hastily got together to
meet the expected attack, and Lieutenant-Colonel Purdon,
who was administering the government, joined it with the
Royal African Colonial Corps, and the militia of Cape Coast

and Anamabo, under Messrs. Jackson and Hutchinson respectively.

On August 7th the Ashanti army moved to the village of Dodowah, which lies inland nearly due north from Ningo, and it being Monday, a day considered propitious by the Ashantis, an attack was expected. The allied force accordingly took up a position to await it, and formed up in a line, which extended about four miles east and west, four miles south of Dodowah, and twenty miles north-east of Accra. The country here was open, and consisted of a rolling, grass-covered plain, dotted here and there with clumps of trees and underwood. The centre of the allied force was composed of the Cape Coast Militia (Mr. Jackson), the Anamabo Militia (Mr. Hutchinson), the Accra Militia (Mr. Bannerman), and the Christiansborg Militia (Mr. Richter); the Royal African Colonial Corps, sixty strong, being drawn up in rear as a reserve. The Akwamus were on the extreme right, and the Denkeras and Akims on the left. This disposition had not been effected without difficulty, all three tribes demanding to be posted on the right, where it was expected the Ashanti King would lead in person; but in the end they were all equally disappointed, for, learning that there were white men in the centre, the King selected that post for himself in order to gain more honour. The allies were distinguished from the enemy by white strips of calico hung from the barrels of their muskets, and by large seashells, which they wore suspended from the neck in front and behind.

At about half-past nine o'clock the attack commenced from right to left. For some time the centre was not engaged, and several natives from the flanks came and taunted the militia with cowardice, with the result that they became impatient and began to get out of hand. This being reported to Colonel Purdon, he directed the centre to advance about four hundred yards, and the movement had just commenced, when a heavy and destructive fire was opened on it; but the advance being steadily continued the enemy slowly and stubbornly fell back. A hand to hand conflict now raged for some little time, men seizing and dragging each other from the opposing ranks, and fortunate were they who were at once put out of their misery, for, in spite of the orders and entreaties of the officers of the militia, numbers of the Ashantis were ripped up or horribly mutilated, and left writhing on the ground. The fighting was so close, that when an Ashanti captain ignited a barrel of gunpowder and blew himself up, some of the Europeans were nearly involved in his destruction.

As the Ashantis gave way, a large quantity of spoil fell into the hands of the militia, who, instead of pressing their advantage, broke their ranks and ran hither and thither collecting it, and would not listen to orders and continue the attack; but while they were so engaged a cry arose that the Ashantis had pierced the line to the left of the centre, and the imminent danger recalled them to their duty. The fact was that a body of men from Dutch Accra had given way, and the Ashantis had pushed forward into their place; the whole of the Danish natives from Christiansborg had also fled, and the swallow-tailed banners of Denmark were now seen flying far in the rear. At this moment a vigorous attack was made upon the centre, which, still disorganised by its eagerness for plunder, was compelled to fall back, closely followed by masses of the enemy. At the same time a galling fire was opened on the flank, and Captain Rogers, o the Royal African Corps, who was bringing up a piece o artillery, was nearly captured. This was the critical momen of the battle. The retreat of the centre was fast becoming a flight, which, although the natives on the extreme right and left were still holding their own, would soon have involved them also, when Colonel Purdon ordered the reserve to advance, and opened fire with Congreve rockets. It was the first time that these missiles had been used against the Ashantis, and their effect was prodigious. Terrified at the screaming sound and the trail of fire streaming behind and astonished at the explosion and the frightful wound they inflicted, the Ashantis, imagining that the English wer fighting with actual thunder and lightning, first wavered, and then broke and fled in irretrievable disorder, and the day was won.

On the left old Kwadjo Tchibbu, King of Denkera, had well sustained his former reputation. The Winnebahs, who were next to him, had fled almost at the first fire, but a few rounds of grape fired over the heads of the allies had checked the Ashanti advance in that quarter, and Tchibbu gallantly led on his followers to drive them back. The issue of the conflict on the right had not been doubtful for a moment. The King of Akwamu had driven all before him, and penetrating to the Ashanti camp had taken the enemy in flank. His advance was marked by a dense column of smoke, the dry grass having taken fire, and by loud explosions, followed by columns of white smoke shooting up above the trees, as the Ashanti captains blew themselves up in despair. The shouts and groans of the combatants, many of them writhing and struggling in the midst of the burning grass, the roar of the musketry and the savage yells of the victors, completed a scene which can be better imagined than described.

About one o'clock the allies began to bring in the heads of the Ashanti chiefs who had fallen, and several of them were recognised as those of noted captains and princes of the blood royal, to whom, even in the heat of the battle, human sacrifices had been made by the King's order, as their deaths were reported. Among the trophies thus brought in was a head taken by the King of Akwapim, and subsequently sent to England by Colonel Purdon, in the belief that it was Sir Charles Macarthy's. The skull was enveloped in paper covered with Arabic characters, and wrapped in a silk handkerchief, while over all was a leopard skin, the emblem of royalty. It was said that the Ashanti King regarded it as a powerful talisman, and had offered a libation to it on the morning of the battle, invoking it to cause the heads of all the white men in the field to lie beside it. It was afterwards discovered to be the head of the late King, Tutu Kwamina.

The whole Ashanti camp fell into the hands of the allies, with great quantities of baggage and gold. The amount of the latter was said to have been exceeding large, but it was never known with certainty how much the natives obtained. The Christiansborg contingent, which, as has been said, fled almost at the first onset, reaped the greatest harvest of spoil; for directly they saw that the enemy was repulsed, they returned and took possession of immense quantities of plunder, with which they deliberately walked off the field. On being charged with cowardice, they excused themselves by saying that it was "against their fetish" to fight on a Monday, a circumstance which, if true, they should have remembered before the battle began. Towards the end of the day the natives, satiated with slaughter, took a great many prisoners, and until it was dark, parties kept coming in encumbered with booty and driving captives before them.

The troops lay on their arms all night, not knowing but that the King might make a desperate effort to retrieve his fallen fortunes, and under cover of the darkness attack with the remainder of his force. At intervals throughout the night the drums of the different allied chiefs were sounded, accompanied by the usual recitative of voices. Each time, the sounds were repeated all along the line, until they died away in the distance; and the hollow beat of the drums, mingled with the weird notes of the singers, suggestive of devilish and mysterious rites and human sacrifices, caused many of the Europeans to shudder. These melancholy sounds were generally followed by answering wails and lamentations from the clumps of trees and bushes in front, where the unhappy Ashanti women were searching for their relatives amongst the heaps of slain, and whose voices rose out of the intense blackness of the night like the cries of despairing spirits. It was a veritable night of horror.

Next morning the allied chiefs were urged to follow in pursuit of the fugitive King, but every argument was exhausted in vain, and the whole of the allies returned to Accra laden with booty. There was so little cohesion between the various bodies that composed the allied force, and the chiefs were so mutually jealous of each other, that, probably, had the Ashantis delayed their attack for a few days, the whole coalition against them would have fallen to pieces, and the enemy would have been able to enter Accra almost unopposed. The total force engaged at Dodowah has been estimated as follows:

Royal African Corps	60
Militia of Cape Coast, Anamabo, English and Danish Accra	500
Native allies	10,820
	11,380

The regulars suffered no loss, but the combined loss of the militia and native levies was stated to be 800 killed and 1,000 wounded. It has been commonly supposed that there was a body of some five or six hundred Europeans engaged, and to them has been attributed the success of the day; but although the use of rockets and grape turned the scale at a critical moment, the above figures show that the whites had numerically very little to do with the contest, which was really a struggle between natives.

But few chiefs of importance were lost on the side of the allies. Mr. Richter was wounded in the thigh early in the action, and the Akwamu and Akim generals, with Kwasi Amankwa, chief of Essikuma, were killed. The latter, having been accused by the natives of intended treachery, had determined to prove his loyalty during the battle, and had made a bold attempt to seize the Ashanti King. He had actually reached the royal basket litter, and had put his hand on it to pull it down, when he was shot in the neck and secured. The King, charging him with having deserted his cause, directed him to follow him, and, on his refusing to do so, ordered his head to be struck off. A party of Tchibbu's Denkeras made a bold effort to rescue him, but they reached the spot too late, and his head was carried off as a trophy. The Ashantis, who were supposed to have been 10,000 strong, left about half their number on the field. Twenty-four powerful chiefs were killed, the King himself was wounded, and several women and children of the royal blood were taken prisoners.

On August 21st, fourteen days after the battle, Sir Neil

Campbell arrived at Cape Coast, and Colonel Purdon returned to England. Beyond holding a meeting of the chiefs of Cape Coast, to congratulate them on the victory that had been won, the Governor did nothing until the end of September, when he held a palaver, to which were summoned the Kings of Denkera and Tufel, the King of Mankassim, and the two principal chiefs of Anamabo. The chiefs and headmen of Cape Coast were also present. Sir Neil Campbell thanked the several chiefs for their gallantry at Dodowah, and suggested that now, while the King of Ashanti was suffering from his terrible reverse, would be a good time to send messengers to him to make peace. This was the exact opposite of Major-General Turner's policy, and although to a European mind the generosity of holding out the olive branch to a vanquished foe might commend itself, to the native mind it appeared utter folly. The native view was and is that overtures for peace should emanate from the party that has been worsted in the struggle; and the chief assured the Governor that any such application as he contemplated would be regarded, not only by the Ashantis, but by all the neighbouring tribes, as an act of submission. To this the Governor replied that peace would only be made on conditions that the Ashanti King furnished securities for it continuance; that the object of going to war was to obtain peace; and that although a proposal for peace might be construed as an act of submission if made after a defeat, such could not be the case if made after a victory. Barbarous peoples, however, do not reason in this way, and the chief, not wishing to destroy the effect of their success by commencing peace negotiations, and desirous, on the other hand, of avoiding any rupture with the British, adopted the middle course of asking for a delay of twelve months; stating, as the sequel proved with truth, that the Ashantis would with in that time themselves ask for peace. To this Sir Neil Campbell refused to consent, and the chiefs then asked that at least, before any irretrievable step was taken, those who were so materially interested in the question as the Queen of Akim and the Kings of Akwamu and Akwapim, might be consulted. To this the Governor also objected, on the ground that there was not time to send for them ; and he finally peremptorily told the chiefs that he had orders to make peace at once, and that he would do so, without any stipulation in their favour, if they would not consent to send representatives to the King of Ashanti.

The Kings and chiefs, much dissatisfied with the result of this palaver, were still in Cape Coast when Sir Neil Campbell resolved to send presents on the part of the Government to Kumassi. The chief of Cape Coast was directed to select three men to form an embassy and convey these presents ; and the Kings of Denkera, Tufel, Wassaw, and Mankassim were ordered to furnish an escort for the party. This they all positively refused to do, and the Governor thereupon summoned the King of Denkera to appear in the Castle and answer for his conduct. Being afraid that he would be made a prisoner, and then delivered up to the Ashantis in order that a peace might be concluded, Kwadjo Tchibbu disobeyed this summons, and, in consequence, was ordered, with the King of Tufel, to leave the town at an hour's notice, with his followers. Thus this old man, who had fought gallantly beside the British in every battle since the commencement of the war, was driven from the town which he had so materially assisted to defend. The projected mission to Kumassi was fortunately now abandoned ; but these occurrences had produced the worst possible effect upon all the native tribes, and when, on October 10th, the Governor proceeded to Accra to hold a palaver with the chiefs of that place and the surrounding districts, they declined to assemble and meet him ; and on November 15th, disgusted by his want of success, Sir Neil Campbell sailed for Sierra Leone, leaving Major Ricketts to administer the government of the Gold Coast. During his short stay of less than three months he had, through his blind adherence to instructions and his ignorance of native character, awakened all the old feelings of distrust of the British Government, and virtually shattered that union of the English and the coast tribes which had been cemented by the victory of Dodowah.

About the middle of January, 1827, the Ashantis began to feel their way towards commencing peace negotiations, and engaged the services of the King of Adansi as an intermediary. The Adansis, it may be noted, were really those Assins who had remained north of the Prah in 1806, when the bulk of that tribe had fled southward, and this is the first time they appear under their new designation. The King of Adansi wished to act as arbitrator between the British and the Ashantis, and have the palaver held in his capital; but Major Ricketts would not consent to this, and after most protracted negotiations an Ashanti embassy crossed the Prah at the end of August. It was delayed by the allied chiefs —who had assembled to deliberate as to what their line of conduct should be—for a considerable time at Yan Kumassi Assin, but finally reached Cape Coast on October 23rd.

The palaver was conducted by Lieut.-Colonel Lumley, who had arrived on October 11th. The Ashanti ambassador declared that he was authorised to say that the King was sorry for what he had done, and hoped that the English would pardon him; that he found there was no use in fighting against white men, and therefore wished to be under their control. In token of submission he laid his cap at the Governor's feet. Colonel Lumley wisely decided to enter into no engagement without first consulting the chiefs who had been in arms against Ashanti, and these being sent for, a palaver was held on December 12th, at which the Kings of Wassaw, Denkera, Tufel, and Assin, the chiefs of Cape Coast, Anamabo, and Fanti, and others of minor note, were present; and the following terms were agreed upon as those on which peace should be granted to the Ashantis: That the King should lodge four thousand ounces of gold in the Castle of Cape Coast, to be appropriated in purchasing arms and ammunition for the use of the allied tribes, in case Ashanti should again commence hostilities; and that two of the royal family of Ashanti should be sent to Cape Coast as hostages. The King of Akwamu, the Queen of Akim, the King of Akwapim, and the people of Accra were not present at the meeting, but messengers from each arrived a few days later, and on the terms on which peace had been offered being explained to them they signified their approval. It was, of course, understood that all the tribes allied with the British were henceforward to be independent of Ashanti rule; and after a short delay the Ashanti embassy returned to Kumassi, accompanied by messengers from most of the allied chiefs and two natives of Cape Coast who could read and write.

When matters thus seemed fairly in train for the final conclusion of a peace a new difficulty arose. The allied tribes, seeing the Ashantis humbled and suing for peace, considered this a good opportunity for demanding reparation for the injuries they had received at the hands of the Elminas. The seizure and sale by that people of fugitives from Fanti during the invasion of 1807, and the wanton murder of the Kommenda women in 1824, had never been revenged; and, in addition to these barbarities, the Elminas had fought beside the Ashantis against the British and allied natives at Effutu, Beulah, and Cape Coast. Moreover, ever since the withdrawal of the Ashanti army from before Cape Coast in 1824, they had, in spite of the efforts of the Dutch Governor, continued to supply the Ashantis with gunpowder, which they obtained by night from American vessels. Having now nothing to fear from the Ashantis, the allied tribes demanded a moderate sum from the Elminas in reparation for these injuries, and this being haughtily refused, they encamped in considerable numbers round Elmina, and closely blockaded it.

During the stay of the Ashanti embassy at Cape Coast, it had been ascertained that there was in Kumassi a white man who had been captured at Effutu, and a mulatto of Cape Coast who had been taken at Assamako, and the surrender of these prisoners having been insisted upon as one of the preliminaries to peace, they were sent down shortly after the embassy returned to Kumassi with a message from the King that he surrendered them at once in accordance with the Governor's request, to show his sincerity in wishing for peace. The surrender of the two captives, however, was not made without an equivalent being expected in return, for the King asked that some of the members of his family, particularly his head wife, who had been captured at Dodowah, might be sent back to him, and also that Atjiempon and his followers, who were at Elmina, might be permitted to return. This request, which was reasonable enough, unfortunately could not be complied with, as his wife was in the hands of the chief of Christiansborg who had captured her, and the natives under Danish rule being dissatisfied with the terms of peace that had been arranged, determined to keep her, in the hope that through her influence they might be able to make separate and more favourable terms for themselves. The allied tribes who were blockading Elmina likewise refused to allow Atjiempon or any Ashanti to quit that town till the King had lodged the securities according to the conditions agreed upon. Although a mutual restoration of prisoners at the conclusion of a peace seems the natural corollary of such an act, it is probable that the natives understood their own interests and the Ashanti character better than did the Government. The two persons the King had surrendered were of no importance to him, and if he could have succeeded in obtaining his wife and the other members of his family in exchange, it is possible that he might have adopted quite another tone, and have shown no anxiety to be on friendly terms with the coast tribes.

The two prisoners from Kumassi had been well treated during their captivity. The European, who had been there for nearly four years, proved to be Patrick Riley, a private of the Royal African Corps, who had been taken at Effutu on April 25th, 1824. From his account, when the troops evacuated Effutu on that date, he and two other soldiers stayed behind to discuss some ration rum of which they had obtained possession, and while so employed had been surprised in a house by the Ashantis. One of the men fixed his bayonet and offered resistance, and was immediately shot down and decapitated, but Riley and the other, who were too drunk to resist, were spared. They were stripped of their uniforms, attired in native cloths, and sent at once to Kumassi, where twelve months later Riley's companion died.

In the meantime the blockade of Elmina was continued, and all the neighbouring plantations having been destroyed, the Elminas were obliged to cultivate the ground within the range of the guns of Fort Conraadsburgh, and of some small blockhouses which the Dutch had built for the protection of the town. The Ashanti King, who was fully informed of what was taking place, protested against the action of the allied tribes, saying he had understood that the conditions of peace were meant to include all his subjects, amongst whom were the Elminas, and asking therefore that the blockade should be raised. He also objected to the amount of the security to be lodged, and offered four hundred ounces in lieu of the four thousand demanded. The letter treating of these matters was received at the latter end of April, 1828, by Captain Hingston, of the Royal African Colonial Corps, who was administering the government, both Colonel Lumley and Major Ricketts having proceeded to Sierra Leone in January. Captain Hingston had received strict injunctions not to permit any alteration of the terms offered to the Ashantis, so he wrote, under date of May 1st, that no other terms could be acceded to than those originally proposed, and that a dispute between the Fantis and the Elminas could not be allowed to interfere with the more important question between the British and the Ashantis. If the King was not disposed to comply with the terms, he was to send back the messengers from the allied tribes within twenty days from the receipt of the letter.

No reply was made to this letter, in which the King's contention that the Elminas were equally his subjects with the inhabitants of Ashanti proper, seems to have been overlooked or ignored; and matters were in this state, nothing further having been heard from Kumassi, when Major Ricketts returned to administer the government on June 5th. A few days later he wrote to the King, saying he was sorry to find on his return to Cape Coast that peace had not yet been made, and pointing out that six months had now elapsed since the Ashanti embassy had returned to Kumassi. To this letter four letters were received in reply, from which it appeared that the King had no intention of making peace till the blockade of Elmina was raised. He also complained that though he had given up Riley and the mulatto, the captive members of his family had not been restored to him. In order to remove the chief obstacle to the conclusion of peace, Major Ricketts used every means in his power to induce the allies to break up their camp near Elmina. He went to Elmina, interviewed the chief of that town, and strove to induce them to make peace with the Fantis, and engage to act with them against the Ashantis, should the latter again invade Fanti; but the Elminas would not hear of breaking with the Ashantis, and the Fantis refused to have any alliance with the Elminas, so that his attempts at a settlement were fruitless.

This was the last act of importance in which Major Ricketts was concerned. The Home Government, weary of the perpetual disturbances, failures, and disgraces connected with the administration of the Gold Coast, came to the resolution of altogether abandoning the settlements; which, as the defeat of Assamako had been avenged by the victory of Dodowah, they could now do without incurring the imputation of a cowardly abandonment. A vessel of war was sent out to remove the merchants and their property, and Major Ricketts received instructions to abandon and destroy the forts. This decision was palatable neither to the merchants nor to the natives; the former could not possibly abandon their business without incurring great loss, perhaps ruin, and the natives were terrified at the prospect of being left without protection. They accordingly made representations to the Home Government, which, supported by Major Ricketts, and the merchants in England connected with the African trade, caused a middle course to be adopted. The government of the Gold Coast was to be transferred to the merchants, who were to receive £4,000 per annum for the maintenance of Cape Coast Castle and James Fort, Accra ; and the Home Government was to be relieved of all responsibility. A code of regulations for the government was drawn up with the approval of the Colonial Office, and the settlements on the Gold Coast were still to be considered as dependencies of Sierra Leone. A committee of three London merchants, with a secretary, was to be entrusted with the direction of the affairs of the country and the appointment of the local officials, who were to consist of a Governor, his secretary, a surgeon, an officer of a guard of one hundred men, and a commandant for James Fort. A council of local merchants, presided over by the Governor, was to be appointed to assist the latter in the administration.

As soon as this decision was known, the merchants of Cape Coast formed themselves into a council of government, pending the arrival of a Governor, Mr. John Jackson, the oldest merchant, being chosen president ; and on September 20th, 1828, Major Ricketts, having transferred to the new government such of the garrison as were willing to take service under it, embarked for Sierra Leone, taking with him the remainder of the troops, and leaving Mr. Jackson in charge. Throughout his long service on the Coast he had, with the solitary exception of the palaver at Elmina in 1824, displayed considerable ability and knowledge of native character. He had much improved the town of Cape Coast by opening up some streets among what had previously been a maze of houses traversed by devious and narrow passages, and had also cleared a space round the Castle, and removed those houses that had commanded it.

During these protracted differences with Ashanti the condition of the country was so insecure that the natives dared not live in detached villages. The agricultural populations had been compelled to congregate in the towns for mutual protection, and these were shut off from each other by vast tracts of forest without the vestige of a single human habitation. By the close of 1828, however, the general tranquillity which prevailed led to a gradual restoration of confidence, and huts and hamlets were then beginning to spring up on every side.

CHAPTER XVI.

1830—1844.

Appointment of Mr. Maclean—Treaty with Ashanti—Expedition to Appollonia—L. E. L.—Her death—Charges made against her husband—Administration called in question—A commissioner sent out—The Crown resumes control—Domestic slavery—Missionary enterprise.

THE committee of merchants in London offered to confirm Mr. Jackson in the appointment of Governor, but he agreed with the other local merchants in thinking it would be better to have at the head of the government an officer who was altogether unconnected with trade; and they asked that Mr. George Maclean, an officer of the Royal African Colonial Corps, who had accompanied Colonel Lumley to the Gold Coast in 1826 in the capacity of military secretary, and whose abilities had then recommended him to the notice of the merchants, might be appointed. Mr. Maclean, being willing to accept the appointment, proceeded to the Gold Coast in 1830. Just before his arrival the allied tribes had made an attack upon Elmina, in which they had been assisted by a body of Cape Coast militia in the pay of the Government, who had joined their countrymen in open defiance of orders. The attempt, ill-concerted and badly carried out, had proved, however, perfectly abortive; for the allies, after making a feeble attack, had been repulsed on all sides, and the retreat was changed to a rout by the guns of Fort Conraadsburgh.

Mr. Maclean found the condition of affairs anything but hopeful. The Ashantis were indeed quiet, but they had entirely stopped all communication with the coast, and their whole trade now went to Assini. The blockade of Elmina was at an end, but open hostilities were still going on between the Elminas and the Fantis, and British authority was so little regarded as scarcely to be any protection to the oppressed. But the new Governor was no ordinary man. Endowed with great moral courage and perseverance, he was exactly the man required for the occasion. His attention was first directed to the relations between the allied tribes and Ashanti, for until there was some security for the continuance of peace, no permanent improvement in the condition of affairs could be expected. Both the allies and the Ashantis fortunately wished for peace, and the Governor managed to assemble a congress of deputies from Ashanti and from the allied chiefs to discuss terms at Accra. It was however, found to be no easy matter to reconcile the different demands made. The Ashantis, though smarting under the crushing defeat at Dodowah, and weakened by the defection of Denkera, Akim, and Accra, could hardly be brought to submit to have terms dictated to them. Their pride was hurt at the idea of treating with the allied tribes of Fanti on equal terms, and their interest demanded that such an extensive field for plunder and extortion should not be closed to them. On the other hand, the coast tribes, believing themselves to be now more than a match for Ashanti, and exasperated by the memory of countless wrongs, demanded compensation for the past as well as security for the future. By skilful management, however, Mr. Maclean contrived to induce both parties to moderate their pretensions, and the fact of the members of the royal family still being in the hands of the allies enabled him to bring pressure to bear upon the King, so that after much trouble a treaty was finally concluded upon the following terms:

1. The King of Ashanti having deposited six hundred ounces of gold in Cape Coast Castle, and having delivered into the hands of the Governor two princes of the blood

royal as security that he would keep the peace, peace was accordingly declared between the King of Ashanti and the British and their allies. The securities to remain in Cape Coast Castle for six years.

2. In order to prevent all future quarrels which might lead to an infraction of the treaty, the following rules and regulations were agreed upon :

(*a*) The paths to be perfectly open and free to all persons engaged in lawful commerce, and persons molesting traders in any way to be liable to punishment.

(*b*) Panyarring to be rigorously punished, and no chief or master to be held responsible for the crimes of his servants, unless committed with his sanction or by his orders.

(*c*) The King of Ashanti renounces all title or right to any homage or tribute from the Kings of Denkera, Assin, and others formerly his subjects.

The treaty was signed by the Governor, the Ashanti messengers, the chiefs of Cape Coast, Mankassim, Anamabo, Essikuma, and Adjumako, and the Kings of Denkera, Wassaw, Tufel, Assin, Arbra, and Appollonia. It did not explicitly state that all the native signatories were to be held as being henceforward perfectly independent of Ashanti, but it was well understood that such was to be the case, and it was implied under regulation (*c*). It was arranged that the Denkeras under Kwadjo Tchibbu should leave Denkera and settle on a small extent of territory around Jukwa, about twelve miles to the north of Elmina. The two Ashanti princes sent as hostages were Ansa Awusu and Kwanta Bisa, the former the son of Tutu Kwamina, the latter of Okoto, his brother. They were granted pensions of one hundred pounds per annum, and sent to England to be educated, where they remained till 1841. Kwanta Bisa died at Cape Coast soon after his return, but we shall hear more of Ansa.

The conclusion of this treaty, which was signed on April 27th, 1831, marks another stage in the growth of British jurisdiction, for by it the chiefs acknowledged the control of the British, and bound themselves to conform to certain rules and regulations. In return it was tacitly understood that they could claim British protection against Ashanti aggression. There was no longer any question of the payment of "notes" for the British forts. These notes having passed from the possession of the original owners—the lords of the soil on which the forts were built—into the hands of the Ashanti King by virtue of conquest, now, by virtue of the victory of Dodowah, similarly passed into the hands of the government, which thus became, for the first time, the owner of the ground on which the forts stood.

The outstanding difficulty with Ashanti now being settled Maclean next turned his attention to the condition of the protected tribes. He ruled with a strong hand, firmly suppressed outrages, and did much to put down human sacrifices. If any chief refused to obey his commands, instead of wasting time in negotiations, he sent a few soldiers to arrest him, confined him in the Castle till he was repentant, and made him pay an indemnity. This kind of rule is one that appeals directly to the sympathies of uncivilised peoples; and the natives not only feared the Governor, but respected and admired him for his strength of purpose. His authority was so well established that only on one occasion had he to resort to anything like armed force, which was in 1835, when he undertook an expedition to Appollonia.

The King of Appollonia, Kwaku Akka, had for some time been committing a variety of offences, robbing and insulting the masters of ships which went there to trade, and committing the most shocking barbarities upon the natives of other tribes. Several letters of remonstrance sent by the Governor, were treated with contempt, and the bearer of the last letter was shown the bodies of twelve Wassaw traders who had been murdered, with the remark that this was the King's answer. In consequence of this outrage a deputation from Wassaw went to Cape Coast asking for redress, and it being necessary to take strong measures to save the government from falling into absolute discredit, Maclean decided to organise an expedition against the recalcitrant King. He withdrew from the Castle such soldiers as could be spared, and with the Cape Coast Militia and a small detachment of Dutch troops under an officer lent by the Dutch Governor, proceeded to Appollonia. His whole force only amounted to one hundred and eighty men, with two officers, viz., Mr. F. Swanzy, Commandant of Dixcove Fort, and Mr. Bartels, the Dutch officer. Upon the first appearance of danger the Cape Coast Militia fled in a body, and Maclean found himself compelled to retreat upon the Dutch fort at Axim; but he soon contrived to capture the deserters, and H.M.S. *Britomart* fortunately arriving, he again took the field. The Appollonians were driven along the beach during a skirmish which lasted a whole day, and the King's town being taken, Kwaku Akka was compelled to pay the expenses of the expedition, and to deposit a large sum of gold as security for future good behaviour. The manner in which this affair was brought to a conclusion well exemplifies Maclean's great moral and physical courage. Although Kwaku Akka had offered a reward of two hundred ounces of gold for his head, he went, accompanied only by a corporal's guard, to meet the King in the midst of his followers, at a distance of some miles from his own small force, and under these circumstances imposed upon him the treaty. Had his life been sacrificed he would doubtless have been charged with foolhardiness; but he understood native character well, and recognised that when dealing with natives, conduct which at first sight seems rash is often well advised.

About the end of 1837, Maclean proceeded to England for the benefit of his health, and there made the acquaintance of Miss Letitia Elizabeth Landon, a young poetess better known as L. E. L. Before meeting Maclean she had had lent to her by a friend his MS. describing the expedition to Appollonia. His manly narrative had made a great impression upon her romantic mind, and she was apparently predisposed to fall in love with the author. In any case, they were married, and, to the astonishment of every one, the popular favourite accompanied her husband to Cape Coast, where she landed on August 15th, 1838.

On October 15th of the same year, Mr. and Mrs. Maclean entertained at dinner Mr. Cruickshank, Commandant of Anamabo Fort, and author of "Eighteen Years on the Gold Coast." The Governor was in ill-health, but Mrs. Maclean was in good spirits, and talked gaily to Mr. Cruickshank till after eleven o'clock, when he went home. He was at breakfast next morning about nine, when a servant came and said he was required at the Castle, as Mr. Maclean was dead. He hurried off, grieved, but not surprised, for the Governor had been ill for some time; when, on arriving at the Castle gate, he learned to his astonishment that it was Mrs. Maclean, and not her husband, who was dead. It appeared that she had left her bedroom about 7 a.m., and had gone to her dressing-room, which was up a short flight of stairs in the tower now known as L. E. L.'s Tower. There she occupied herself for an hour and a half in writing letters and then, calling her servant, a Mrs. Bailey, sent her to the storeroom for some article. Mrs. Bailey was absent only a few minutes, but when she returned found great difficulty in opening the door, some heavy object pressing against it, which, on forcing an entrance, she discovered to be the body of her mistress, who was lying senseless against the door. She immediately called the Governor, and the surgeon, Dr. Cobbold, was sent for; but from the first moment of discovery of the body life was extinct. A phial containing a preparation of prussic acid was seen upon the toilet-table, and, upon being asked whence it came, the servant said she had found it in the hand of her mistress, who it was known was in the habit of using this drug as a remedy for the violent spasms to which she was subject. Her husband had been greatly averse to her using so dangerous a medicine, and had asked her to throw it away, but she had entreated him to let her keep it, saying that without it she would die. Dr. Cobbold was requested to make a post-mortem examination, but did not consider it necessary to do so, as he felt convinced she died from prussic acid. He believed he could detect its smell about her, and the appearance of the eyes confirmed him in the opinion that she had died from it. An inquest was held, and the jury found that Mrs. Maclean died from an overdose of Scheele's preparation of prussic acid, taken inadvertently. She was buried the same evening in the courtyard of the Castle, where her resting-place is still marked by a flat slab bearing the letters L. E. L.

The news of the death of Mrs. Maclean was received in England with dismay. It is difficult at the present day to estimate the exact position she held in the affections of the public, but there can be no doubt that she was a very popular authoress, and the public, robbed of its idol, looked for some one on whom to vent its anger. All kinds of outrageous reports about her husband were circulated and eagerly believed. It was currently reported that there was a dark and secluded portion of the Castle to which Mrs. Maclean was never admitted, and where her husband gave himself up to frightful debaucheries. Maclean was asserted to have quarrelled with his wife, to have ill-treated her, and neglected her for a native woman. Mrs. Bailey, on her return to England, with a view to gaining notoriety made a number of flagrantly false statements, and Maclean became regarded as a monster of iniquity. It was said that L. E. L. had been driven to commit suicide, and others went so far as to say that the poison had been forced upon her by the alleged native woman, who was believed to have been an inmate of the Castle.

There was not, however, the smallest foundation for these accusations. From the testimony of all the Europeans of Cape Coast, Mr. and Mrs. Maclean were on the most affectionate terms, and the precarious condition of the health of the former, who had been confined to the Castle through sickness nearly the whole time his wife was on the Coast, effectually disposed of the supposed debaucheries, and of a charge afterwards made that he neglected her nightly for orgies in the town. Nor could the suggestion of suicide be maintained, for upon the table at which she had been writing lay an unfinished letter to a lady friend in England, written in a most cheerful strain, and recommending to her notice Mr. Cruickshank, who was about to leave for England that day. Mr. Cruickshank himself, who gives a most circumstantial account of the whole tragedy, was of opinion that she died of heart disease, he having learned, on his return to England, that she had before her marriage nearly succumbed to that ailment. No unprejudiced person can, after reading Cruickshank's narrative, avoid acquitting Maclean of all responsibility for his wife's death, and it is much to be regretted that at the time of the Ashanti War of 1873-4, when public attention was directed to the Gold Coast, the charges against him should have been reiterated, with numerous additions, by persons who plainly had not taken the trouble to make themselves in the slightest degree acquainted with the facts of the case.

The rumours against Mr. Maclean were, as has been said, eagerly received and believed in England, while he himself, crushed under the unexpected calamity that had befallen him, was at a distance, unable to contradict the aspersions, and even ignorant of their existence till they had been current for months. His reputation thus became so evil that nothing was too bad to be imputed to him, and every act of his was keenly scrutinised, to bring him, if possible, to disgrace. He had, very shortly after assuming the government, announced his intention of putting an end to the practice of offering human sacrifices at the decease of natives of rank, and, amongst the Fantis, had generally succeeded in so doing. Shortly after L. E. L.'s death the mother of Kwadjo Tchibbu, King of Denkera, died at Jukwa, and the King sent to Maclean to inform him of the event, and to assure him that he would observe his law and abstain from human sacrifices. This announcement was received with great satisfaction, but the Governor, knowing the kind of saturnalia the natives held on these occasions, sent a soldier back with the messenger to watch their proceedings. At the same time he sent a present to Kwadjo Tchibbu, to encourage him to persevere in his good intentions, but threatened him with punishment if he broke his word. Probably the chief found it difficult to act counter to the prejudices and superstitions of his people, for human sacrifices were made privately, yet not so secretly but that the Governor heard of them. Kwadjo Tchibbu was therefore summoned to Cape Coast and heavily fined, and a Fanti chief, who was proved to have sent him a slave to be sacrificed, was similarly punished. In the general clamour against Maclean these measures were magnified into acts of tyrannical oppression, and representations were made to the Home Government of the Governor's severity. The position the English held in the country did not authorise them, it was affirmed, to interfere with native customs. The natives were not subject to the laws of England, and therefore could not be punished for adhering to their own time-honoured customs. But while this outcry was raised against Maclean for interfering with the horrible custom of human sacrifices, his opponents, with the most extraordinary inconsistency, found fault with him for not interfering with the equally time-honoured but less barbarous native institution of domestic slavery. They seemed to think it was wrong for the Governor to prevent and punish murders committed under the plea of human sacrifices, and yet that it was equally wrong not to prevent domestic slavery. Public opinion, however, was very strong in England at this time on the subject of slavery, and where that subject was concerned the people cared nothing for logic. There was an idea that the Gold Coast was a British colony in which the Governor encouraged, or at all events permitted slavery, and it was even alleged that the export trade was connived at by the local authorities, though it was a notorious fact that it had been entirely suppressed along the whole line of coast, not a single slave being known to have been shipped during the whole period of Maclean's administration. Finding it impossible to obtain slaves even by stealth, the slave-ships had entirely ceased to frequent the Gold Coast, though only a few years before Maclean's administration they had been so numerous that we find a Governor reporting that seven slavers were taking in cargoes within sight of Cape Coast Castle; and it was a well-known fact that numbers of the Ashanti prisoners taken at Dodowah had been shipped as slaves at Accra and the ports to the eastward.

The Secretary of State for the Colonies, seemingly understanding nothing of the nature of the British position on the Gold Coast, and taking a narrow official view, disapproved of Maclean's action in fining Kwadjo Tchibbu. His view was that the chief was either a British subject or an independent chief. In the former case he considered him worthy of death in the latter he held that the Governor was wrong in fining him. This view was, however, quite a mistaken one. The King of Denkera was neither a British subject nor independent. He was one of several chiefs who had, in return for British protection, surrendered a portion of their independence and submitted to British control. This control had for years been exercised for the suppression of inhuman customs, and Mr. Maclean was only following out a policy that had been continuous since 1817.

The reports of the encouragement given to slavery by the Local Government were so assiduously propagated that at last the Home Government, in deference to the popular clamour considered it necessary to send out a commissioner, Dr Madden, to inquire into and report upon the condition of the settlements. Dr. Madden paid a very short visit to Cape Coast Castle, where the state of his health did not permit him to acquire the information necessary for a reliable report. This, however, did not prevent him from sending in a report which, because he found that domestic slavery was an institution of the country, and that justice was administered according to a compromise effected between English and native law, was most unfavourable to the Local Government. He does not appear to have in the least understood in what relation the natives stood to the British Government.

On Dr. Madden's return to England a select committee of the House of Commons was appointed to report to Parliament upon the state of the settlements; and after a very prolonged inquiry they, in 1842, agreed upon a report which entirely relieved the Governor and the merchants of the imputations cast upon them. At the same time they considered it desirable, in order to give greater confidence in the character and impartiality of the government, that it should be rendered completely independent of all connection with commerce, and that the Crown should resume control. Of Mr. Maclean's government they said : "We fully admit the merits of that administration, whether we look to the officer employed, Captain Maclean, or to the committee under whom he has acted, which, with the miserable pittance of between £3,500 and £4,000 a year, has exercised from the four ill-provided forts of Dixcove, Cape Coast, Anamabo, and British Accra, manned by a few ill-paid black soldiers, a very wholesome influence over a coast not much less than one hundred and fifty miles in extent, and to a considerable distance inland; preventing within that range external slave trade, maintaining peace and security, and exercising a useful though irregular jurisdiction among the neighbouring tribes, and much mitigating, and in some cases extinguishing, some of the most atrocious practices which had prevailed among them unchecked before."

In consequence of the recommendation of the committee, the Colonial Office, in 1843, resumed the direct management of the affairs of the Gold Coast, the settlements, as before, being placed under the control of the Governor of Sierra Leone, from which place a company of a West India Regiment was detached as a garrison. In 1844, Commander Hill, R.N., was appointed Governor, and Mr. Maclean's long and eminent but ill-appreciated services were rewarded by the appointment of judicial assessor. He was to administer justice amongst the natives, and to try, in concert with native chiefs, cases in which natives alone were concerned, according to native law, as far as it could be applied in harmony with the principles of justice. It was, in fact, a continuance of that kind of jurisdiction which he had himself originated, which had been so much cavilled at, and was now approved of and legalised by an Act of Parliament.

The question of domestic slavery, over which such an outcry had been made, was also dealt with. Slavery within the

British possessions on the Gold Coast was abolished by the Statute 3 and 4 William IV. c. 73, but the actual British possessions were undefined, there having been in fact none till 1828, when by the victory of Dodowah the payment of notes for the ground rent of the forts ceased. According to some, however, British territory extended to the limit of the range of the guns of the forts, so that it was expansible, and increased in area as artillery became improved; but this idea was clearly untenable, so slavery within the protected area was considered not to be affected by the statute of William IV. and no attempt was made on the part of the British Government to uproot it. In fact, Lord John Russell in a despatch dated July 14th, 1841, had said : " If the laws or usages of those countries tolerate slavery, we have no right to set aside those laws or usages except by persuasion, negotiation, and other peaceful means." This position was still maintained now that the Crown had resumed control, but the judicial assessor was instructed to use his influence to mitigate the harsher usages of slavery.

It was during Mr. Maclean's administration that a first attempt was made by England to introduce Christianity amongst the natives of the Gold Coast. There had been for years previous a chaplain in the Castle at Cape Coast, whose ministrations were confined to the soldiers of the garrison and the few European officials; but in 1835 the Wesleyan Society sent out a first missionary to Cape Coast. An attempt to establish a mission at Christiansborg had been made by the Germans a little earlier, but it met with much opposition, several of the missionaries died, and the sole survivor returned to Europe about 1833. The members of the new mission at Cape Coast succumbed to the deadly climate with terrible rapidity. The first missionary, Mr. Durnwell, died six months after his arrival, and was succeeded by a Mr. Wrigley, who came with his wife in September, 1836. She died in the following January, and he in November, 1837. A Mr. Freeman next came in January, 1838. He was also accompanied by his wife, who died a few weeks after arrival, but he, after several serious attacks of fever, managed to exist. Mr. Maclean gave the greatest possible encouragement to missionary enterprise and, furnished with a letter from him to the Ashanti King, Mr. Freeman visited Kumassi in 1839, to try and establish a mission there. This new proposal was the cause of much perturbation in the mind of the King, who thought that it concealed some sinister design; and Mr. Freeman was, by his order, detained at Kwisa for six weeks, so apprehensive was he of the intentions of the "white fetish-man." His conduct was closely watched during this detention, and it was only when he threatened to return to Cape Coast that he was permitted to proceed to Kumassi, the King thinking it was a lesser evil to admit him to the capital than to incur his wrath by a refusal. He was received with the ceremonies usually accorded to a visitor of distinction, but was regarded with the greatest suspicion, as a man possessed of unknown powers, and at last had to leave Kumassi without having obtained any concession.

CHAPTER XVII.

1844—1861.

Treaty with protected tribes—Death of Maclean—Expedition to Appolonia—Visit to Kumassi—Religious disturbances at Mankassim—poll-tax agreed to—Formation of a local corps—Ashanti intrigues in Assin—Attempted invasion—Disturbances in the east—Siege of Christiansborg—The Krobo war.

ONE of the first acts of Commander Hill was to enter into a treaty with the chiefs of some of the protected tribes to define their position and bring them more under control. This treaty, which is dated March 6th, 1844, runs as follows:

"1. Whereas power and jurisdiction have been exercised for and on behalf of Her Majesty the Queen of Great Britain and Ireland, within divers countries and places adjacent to Her Majesty's Forts and Settlements on the Gold Coast, we, chiefs of countries and places so referred to, adjacent to the said Forts and Settlements, do hereby acknowledge that power and jurisdiction, and declare that the first objects of law are the protection of individuals and property.

"2. Human sacrifices, and other barbarous customs, such as panyarring, are abominations and contrary to law.

"3. Murders, robberies, and other crimes and offences will be tried and inquired of before the Queen's judicial officers and the chiefs of the district, moulding the customs of the country to the general principles of British law."

It was signed by the Kings of Denkera, Assin, and Arbra, and by the chiefs of Cape Coast, Anamabo, Donadi, and

Donomassi, and defined and sanctioned that jurisdiction which since 1803 had been exercised over the towns under the guns of the forts, and which Mr. Maclean had extended to the rest of the Protectorate.

Shortly after Commander Hill's appointment, an Ashanti was murdered in Assin, and the King took advantage of this occurrence to try what could be done with the new Governor, sending down executioners to demand the murderer's head, and requesting the Governor to withdraw his protection from the Assins, so that he might punish them. These attempts at encroachment were, however, firmly resisted, and the messengers returned to Kumassi convinced that the Governor was not to be imposed upon.

Peace being now firmly established, and the export slave trade at an end, there was no longer any reason for keeping up so many forts, and those of Appollonia, Sekondi, Kommenda, Tantamkwerri, and Prampram were abandoned by the Government. The Dutch also, for the same reason, abandoned their forts at Sekondi, Kommenda, Mori, Cormantine, and Barraku, retaining only Axim, Butri, Shamah, Elmina, Appam, and Accra.

In 1847 Mr. Maclean died. He was held in such honour by the people of Cape Coast that for fourteen days all business was suspended, and the discharges of musketry, fired in accordance with native custom at the decease of a man of rank, were incessant. As the news of his death reached the chiefs of the inland towns, they despatched bodies of armed men to pay him this last honour, who, on arriving at Cape Coast, took up a position before the gate of the Castle and continued firing for hours. Even for months after, any chief from the interior, who had not visited Cape Coast since the event, considered it necessary on arriving there, and before attending to any other business, to pay this last mark of respect to the old Governor. It was not only the natives over whom he had exercised jurisdiction that thus paid tribute to his memory; the Ashantis equally deplored his loss, for the terror of his name had amply guaranteed the safety of all Ashanti traders visiting the coast, and they had never failed to obtain redress for any injury inflicted on them by the protected tribes. He was buried in the court-yard of Cape Coast Castle, next to the grave of "L. E. L.," and a flat slab, bearing the initials "G. M.," still marks the spot.

Commander Hill soon resigned his appointment, and was succeeded by Commander Winniett, R.N., who had scarcely assumed the duties of Governor when he found himself compelled to undertake an expedition against Kwaku Akka, King of Appollonia. For a little time after Mr. Maclean's expedition this chief had remained quiet, but before long had recommenced his former conduct, and had thereby forfeited the gold he had deposited in Cape Coast Castle as security for good behaviour. Maclean had been anxious to lead another expedition against him, but the Government would not sanction it; and an attack projected by Governor Hill had to be abandoned because the senior naval officer on the station refused to co-operate. Governor Winniett soon after his arrival had tried to open communications with the insubordinate chief, but he imprisoned the messengers, and openly set the local authorities at defiance. A little later he committed a variety of outrages that brought matters to a crisis, for he waylaid and murdered the French commandant of Assin, struck off the heads of a party of Wassaw traders, forcibly seized and carried off some Dutch natives from Axim, and incited his followers to hunt down and murder every stranger by offering two ounces of gold for each head brought to him. The French and the Dutch, as well as the natives, looked to the British for redress, and it was imperative for the Governor to take some action. Kwaku Akka was known to have some two thousand well-armed followers, and as the Governor had only at his disposal one company of the 1st West India Regiment and some thirty armed policemen, he called upon the chiefs of the protected tribes for assistance. These furnished some four or five thousand men; indeed five times that number were forthcoming, and the only difficulty was to refuse their services without creating inter-tribal jealousies.

On March 24th, 1848, the expedition left Cape Coast, and after a march of over a hundred miles the whole force was concentrated at Axim on April 3rd, and entered Appollonia on the 6th. The Appollonians defended the passage of the Ancobra River on that day, and that of the Abmussa River on the day following, but being driven from each point they abandoned all further resistance, and, to make terms with the Governor, surrendered their King, who had been hiding in the bush with a few faithful followers. On April 18th Kwaku Akka was removed to Cape Coast Castle, and being tried by the allied chiefs, presided over by the Governor, was sentenced to death; but the sentence was commuted into imprisonment for life in the Castle, where he died early in 1852. The Appollonians elected to the vacant stool an old captain named Bahini, who was made responsible to the Local Government for the tranquillity of the district.

Although this expedition was absolutely necessary, and materially strengthened the position of the British in the country, by showing with what ease a force could be raised to support order and good government, it was regarded with marked disfavour by the Secretary of State for the Colonies. In fact at first Governor Winniett was severely blamed for undertaking it, and it was only its satisfactory termination that at last extorted a reluctant approval. Although the matter had been so urgent that it was impossible to delay action for the three months necessary to communicate with and receive a reply from England, the Home Government had even threatened to charge the Governor with the cost of the expedition, should it fail, thus making him personally responsible for a line of conduct forced upon him by circumstances. His government would have most justly been regarded with contempt alike by natives and Europeans, had he not taken some steps to suppress the barbarities of Kwaku Akka; and other chiefs, seeing the impunity with which the Local Government might be defied, would have been tempted to set it at defiance also.

Governor Winniett had received instructions to use every

means in his power to put an end to human sacrifices beyond the Protectorate, and on September 28th, 1848, he left Cape Coast with an escort of the 1st West India Regiment to proceed to Kumassi and endeavour to accomplish this object. He was accompanied by Mr. Freeman, the Wesleyan missionary, and was well received in Kumassi, where he remained till October 26th; but he entirely failed to attain his object, and the visit itself had on the whole a bad effect. The protected tribes thought it derogatory for a Governor to visit the Ashanti King, considering it to be an acknowledgment of inferiority; and the Ashantis themselves claimed it to be so, in which contention they were supported by the rules of native etiquette.

The year 1849 was marked by a series of events which narrowly escaped culminating in a religious war. The missionary movement inaugurated by the Wesleyan Society had rapidly spread, for the natives imagined that by adopting the religion of the white men they would arrive at positions of equal wealth and distinction, and a number of schools and chapels were established in the towns near the sea-coast. Later on chapels were established further inland, and amongst others, one at a small village near Mankassim.* Now, Mankassim might be regarded as the religious head quarters of Fanti, since in a gloomy hollow in the adjoining forest was the shrine of the god Brahfo, who was generally regarded as the chief deity of that part of the Gold Coast. This god had a large train of priests who drove a very lucrative business, for the oracle of Brahfo was celebrated far and wide, and was constantly being inquired at by persons in search of advice and assistance. The near approach of a hostile religion could not therefore be regarded with unconcern by those who profited by the existing state of affairs, and the priests strongly resented the intrusion; but, fearing perhaps to bring themselves into conflict with the Government, under whose protection they imagined the native Christians in some measure to be, they abstained from using

* Man-Kassim—Great Town.

the power they undoubtedly possessed, and driving away the intruders. The native Christians themselves, unfortunately, did not exhibit the same moderation. Either mistaking the inaction of the priests for fear, or believing that they could best display zeal for their recently adopted faith by outraging their fellow-countrymen who still believed in the gods of their fathers, they continually insulted the priests and derided the worshippers.

As a rule the pagan natives of the Gold Coast are exceedingly tolerant. They do not wish to force their own particular views upon any one, and there is no attempt to establish conformity of ideas; but tolerance has a limit, and when some of the native Christians designedly violated the shrine of Brahfo by cutting down trees in his sacred hollow, the priests were roused to action, and urged upon the Fanti chiefs the necessity of avenging the insult to their god. The chiefs, however, declined to take any such steps, explaining that their interference was unnecessary, since Brahfo was well able to avenge himself; and a few weeks passed without anything being done, till the Christians, encouraged by their previous immunity, shot, in the sacred hollow itself, an antelope that was dedicated to the god; and this was considered such an unheard-of act of sacrilege, that the priests at last prevailed upon the chiefs to take the matter into serious consideration. A council was held at which it was agreed that the chiefs should mutually combine to punish the next individuals who might insult their deity, and Adu, chief of Mankassim, was, because he resided on the spot, appointed by the council the immediate guardian of Brahfo's honour. Shortly after this meeting, three of the native Christians, actuated by the same spirit of intolerance, cut down some more trees in the sacred hollow; and Adu, being called upon by the priests to punish them, collected his men and proceeded to the village of the Christians by night, where he burned their houses, and seizing ten of their number, carried them to Mankassim as prisoners.

When the news of this affair reached Cape Coast, a

soldier of the garrison was sent to Mankassim to demand the liberation of the prisoners, and to summon Adu to appear at the Castle and account for his conduct. To this latter demand Adu demurred, but he promised not to injure he prisoners, and as he had the support of all the Fanti chiefs, a compromise was arrived at, by which he consented to go to Anamabo to have the whole matter inquired into. The judicial assessor accordingly proceeded to Anamabo on the appointed day, and was much astonished to find that the whole of the Fanti chiefs, with upwards of three thousand followers, were assembled to watch the proceedings. On investigating the case he found that the Christian converts had intentionally insulted the worshippers of Brahfo, and that their conduct had been calculated to provoke disturbances ; he therefore sentenced them to pay a fine of twenty pounds to the Fanti chiefs. Adu, who did not deny his act, which he and the other chiefs justified as a duty which he owed the god, was fined forty pounds for his contempt of law and the authority of the Government, and further ordered to pay to the Christians the value of the property destroyed, which was assessed at fifty-six pounds. To this compensation for losses the chiefs strenuously objected. They acknowledged the justice of the 'decision with regard both to the sum to be paid to them, and to the fine imposed on them for the violation of the law ; but they could not entertain the idea of compensating the Christians for losses which were, they held, an altogether inadequate punishment for the insults offered to the god. They declared that they could not compromise the dignity of the great Brahfo by consenting to a payment which would greatly offend him. These arguments were maintained for a considerable time, but at last, finding that the judicial assessor was inflexible, the chiefs professed to submit to his decision, Anfu Otu, King of Arbra, and Amunu, chief of Anamabo, becoming responsible for the payment.

The followers of the chiefs had not been admitted to the court during the hearing of the case, but as soon as they learned the result they seized their arms, and Adu was carried defiantly through the town, surrounded by more than a thousand men chanting hymns in honour of Brahfo. Some kegs of powder were borne before the chief, as a sign that he was prepared to fight in defence of his gods, and cries were raised to kill and exterminate the Christians. Anfu Otu and Amunu were reviled as traitors to their religion, and Adu returned with his people to Mankassim, honoured and applauded by the inhabitants of every town and village through which he passed.

Adu, who was supported by the majority of the Fanti chiefs, and had the sympathies of the populace entirely with him, now prepared to resist the Government, if necessary, and maintained himself in an attitude of armed defiance for four months, during which all trade was interrupted. Anfu Otu and Amunu were willing to pay the sums for which they had made themselves responsible, but this mode of escape from the difficulty was considered unsatisfactory, and the Governor at last decided to send an expedition against Adu. Following the precedent set by the Appollonia expedition, the head-men of Cape Coast were asked to furnish a contingent, but this case was very different to the former one; this was a religious war, and the head-men declared that they could not fight against their god, or engage in a struggle against the religious feelings of the whole people. They, however, offered to send a deputation to Adu to persuade him to submit, and begged the Governor to postpone his hostile intentions for a week. This offer was gladly accepted, but in the meantime the garrison were daily exercised with field-guns and rockets, and these demonstrations, coupled with the arguments of the Cape Coast deputation, had the desired effect, for Adu, attended by most of the Fanti chiefs, and with a very large following of armed men, came to Cape Coast, which presented a scene of extraordinary excitement, every street being crowded with people. The chiefs had hoped by the display of force to deter the Governor from compelling Adu to submit to the decision of the judicial assessor; but any act of violence they might have contemplated was baffled by the measures taken. A party of gunners was stationed in Fort William, ready to open fire upon a preconcerted signal, the garrison was under arms, the gates of the Castle closed, and only a small wicket left open for the admission of the chiefs and principal men. Fully six hundred of the chief men of the country were assembled in the Palaver Hall, and before them Adu formally made submission, and acknowledged his error. He did not, he said, regard the question as his own, but rather as that of the whole Fanti nation, by the chiefs of which he had been appointed guardian of the honour of the god. He still protested against the sentence of the assessor, but expressed his willingness to abide by the decision of the Governor. The latter upheld the former judgment, and the amount being at once paid, this troublesome affair, which had threatened to involve the whole of Fanti in insurrection, and had been caused simply by the unseemly acts of a few fanatical converts, was happily settled.

About 1850 the King of Denmark became desirous of disposing of his possessions on the Gold Coast, and made overtures to the British Government for their purchase. These possessions consisted of Christiansborg Castle, and three small forts at Ningo, Addah, and Kittah,* of which Kittah Fort was the only one habitable. After some negotiations they were purchased for £10,000, and handed over in 1851, the natives making no difficulty about transferring their allegiance. The purchase of these forts was considered a favourable opportunity for imposing customs duties on certain imported goods in order to create a revenue to defray the expenses of the Government, and negotiations were opened with the Dutch to induce them to adopt a similar course. They, however, declined to enter into any fiscal arrangements, and their possessions being so interspersed amongst those of the British that it

* Commonly spelt "Quittah," but always pronounced "Kittah." It means "Sand-hill."

would be impossible to collect duties in the latter if the former were free, it became necessary to abandon the project.

Governor Winniett died at the end of 1851, and was succeeded in the government by Major S. Hill, during whose administration an important change took place. The Home Government considered that the natives ought to contribute either directly or indirectly towards the cost of the Government that protected them, and it having being found impracticable to raise a revenue by import duties, a poll-tax was now proposed, on the recommendation of Lord Grey. The protected tribes, well understanding the advantages they derived from British protection, raised no objection, and in 1852 a meeting of all the chiefs of the Protectorate was held to discuss the matter. The meeting first resolved itself into a legislative assembly, with power to enact laws; and then, "having taken into consideration the advantage of British protection, considered it reasonable that the natives should contribute to the support of the Government," and agreed to a poll-tax. The ordinance at once received the sanction of the Home Government, and by it the natives acquired a positive and definite recognition of their right to protection. They had undertaken to pay a tax in consideration of that protection, and the obligations of the Government were no longer doubtful. The treaty concluded by Mr. Bowdich in 1817 having been cancelled by the one made by Governor Maclean in 1831, that document, with the treaty of 1844 and this new ordinance, now defined the position of the British Government, Ashanti, and the Protected Tribes. The latter had consented to submit to British control, to modify their laws, and to contribute to the support of the Government, which on its part was bound to preserve order, to protect from aggression, and to guarantee their independence of Ashanti.

The Gold Coast, since the resumption of the government by the Crown, had been garrisoned by one company of the 1st West India Regiment, but this force being altogether inadequate, and the imposition of the poll-tax having placed the Government in a better financial position, it was now decided to raise a local corps to garrison the forts, and to dispense with the services of the imperial troops. This new force, which was to consist of natives trained as gunners, was to be termed the Gold Coast Corps. Its formation nearly caused a serious disturbance. The Governors of the Gold Coast had been instructed not to deliver to their owners runaway slaves, who were considered to have recovered their freedom as soon as they entered a British fort; and by a diplomatic fiction no slavery was supposed to exist within the British jurisdiction. There was no authority for thus withholding slaves from their owners, and to do so was a violation of implied engagements; but the instructions had been issued in deference to the clamour of the anti-slavery party in England. As a rule, slaves had not taken advantage of the asylum offered by the British forts, for unless they could obtain employment they would starve; but now the formation of the new corps offered an opportunity for obtaining both freedom and the means of existence. The corps was to consist of three hundred men, and numbers of slaves presented themselves at Cape Coast Castle for enlistment, whom Major Hill, in accordance with his instructions, refused to deliver to their masters. These slaves, it may be remarked, were not native-born, for such slaves rarely, if ever, sought to leave their owners, they being considered a part of the family, and inheriting, in default of other heirs, the family property. They were generally Odonkos, men of a tribe living to the north of Ashanti, a regular trade in whom had existed for a long time past between the Ashantis and the protected tribes, and from which tribe the present Houssa Constabulary was at one time largely recruited. The property of the well-to-do natives consisted largely, if not chiefly, of slaves, and no reasoning could convince them that this forcible detention of their property was not an act of robbery. The greatest excitement prevailed, and several of the principal chiefs adopted an almost hostile attitude.

They appeared determined to defend their rights, and had the Governor persisted in acting up to his instructions, an outbreak would certainly have taken place; but he prudently effected a compromise. The chiefs promised to procure the required number of men, provided they were paid for; and the Governor allowed the recruits to arrange to pay their late masters a small sum monthly, until the sum of eight pounds, the price of an Odonko slave, was paid. Under this arrangement the new corps became completed about the middle of 1852, and the company of the 1st West India Regiment, which had been reduced by deaths to only fifty rank and file, proceeded to Sierra Leone early in 1853.

Ashanti, which had for a long time abstained from meddling with the affairs of the Protectorate, now recommenced its old policy, and bribed Kwadjo Tchibbu, a chief of Assin who had defied the authority of the Government, and committed a number of offences, to bring his people under Ashanti rule. For this Tchibbu was arrested and brought to Cape Coast, where he was tried before a native court under the presidency of the Governor, convicted, sentenced to imprisonment for life, and confined in the Castle. There was at this time a strong war-party in Ashanti, whose people could not forget the former sway they had exercised over the coast tribes, and the large revenue they had extorted from them; and it was only the peaceful disposition of Osai Kwaku Dua, who had succeeded to the stool at the death of Osai Okoto in 1838, that prevented an immediate collision. At the urgent request of the chiefs, Governor Hill after a time liberated Kwadjo Tchibbu, but before so doing he exacted hostages from all the Assin chiefs for their future good behaviour, and required that all the Assins still remaining north of the Prah should cross over to the south side and live under British rule. He also stipulated that the Assins and Fantis should at once make a military road from Cape Coast to Prahsu, a stipulation which was unfortunately never enforced. But by accepting bribes from the Ashanti King, Kwadjo Tchibbu had, according to native custom brought himself under Ashanti rule, and early in 1853 the Ashantis crossed the Prah to seize him and another chief. He was accordingly brought to Cape Coast for safety, and troops were moved into the Assin country, while the protected tribes were called out and camps formed at Mansu and Dunkwa. The King made various excuses for the invasion, but the chief in command of the small body of men who had crossed the frontier acknowledged that his orders were to seize Kwadjo Tchibbu and the other chief. This first force having failed to effect its object, a larger body was soon despatched from Kumassi, to meet which a small detachment was sent to Prahsu under Ensign Brownell, of the Gold Coast Corps, with orders not to fire a shot except in self-defence, and to do all in his power to induce the Ashantis to retire peaceably. He succeeded so well in this that the Ashantis, seven thousand in number, returned to Kumassi, promising to preserve the peace; but Governor Hill still feared their return, and stated in his despatches that he could place no reliance upon their promises.

At the close of 1853 disturbances arose amongst those nations near Christiansborg who had formerly been under Danish rule, and the disaffection soon spread as far as the Volta. The outbreak was partly due to the enforcement of some new laws governing the sale and transfer of slaves, and partly to the suppression of human sacrifices, which the Danish authorities had been much too weak to interfere with. By the end of December a body of some four thousand natives from the sea-coast villages to the east of Christiansborg was in arms, but they made no attack, and Governor Hill, who arrived from Sierra Leone early in January, 1854, thinking it probable that if left to itself the force would melt away, made no movement against it. The result fully justified his expectations, for by January 19th the force dispersed, and the leaders, who asked for pardon, were punished by the infliction of a small fine.

Though this outbreak had died a natural death, great dissatisfaction still prevailed in the eastern districts, and difficulties were thrown in the way of the collection of the poll-tax. The natives of this portion of the Gold Coast, of a different race to those of the western districts, were by nature unruly, and they would have declared themselves independent of the Government had they been able to do without its protection from Ashanti. In August, 1854, they again rose in arms and blockaded Christiansborg Castle, in consequence of which their villages were bombarded and destroyed by H.M.S. *Scourge*. The immediate cause of the outbreak on this occasion was the seizure by Captain Bird, Gold Coast Corps, of some rum which had been smuggled into Christiansborg; when an excited mob had attacked and severely beaten the men, and stoned a party of soldiers under Lieutenant Brownell. On August 13th the *Scourge* bombarded Labaddi, the head-quarters of disaffection, and the town of Christiansborg was reduced to ruins by the guns of the Castle; but the natives kept up so hot a fire that the men at the guns suffered heavily, three men being killed, and Captain Bird and twenty-three men wounded, out of the garrison of one hundred and thirty-one. After the destruction of Christiansborg town the natives remained in occupation of the ruins, whence they kept up a desultory fire upon the Castle, particularly at night; and the siege being still pressed and an attack on James Fort, Accra, threatened, reinforcements were asked for from Sierra Leone. They arrived on October 27th, and the blockading force thereupon retired some miles into the interior, where it gradually dispersed; and the chiefs, abandoned by their followers, were compelled to ask for terms.

The disaffection in the eastern districts slumbered until August, 1858, when a rebellion broke out in Krobo. The country of Krobo consists of a vast undulating plain, traversed by several isolated ranges of abrupt and rocky heights of small extent, one of which, known as the Krobo Mountain, can be distinguished from the sea at a distance of forty miles. This mountain, which is almost perpendicular on the east and south-east, and is everywhere inaccessible, except at one point on the northern side, where a narrow, steep path leads to the summit, is regarded as the cradle of the Krobo tribe, and was the stronghold to which the women and children were sent in time of war, and where the men retired when defeated. All Krobos were, and still are, buried on the mountain, on which a yearly mourning custom for the dead is held. Under another custom, called Otofo, all Krobo girls of respectable parents are sent to the mountain at nine or ten years of age, and remain there for about six years, under the care of the priestesses, performing certain ceremonies; and no girl is considered really eligible for marriage unless she has gone through this period of tutelage and instruction. During the Ashanti invasion of 1814, the whole Krobo tribe had withdrawn to this mountain fastness, and had beaten off every assault of the enemy by rolling down masses of granite upon them. At the present time there are twelve villages on its summit, but in 1858 there were only two, situated on almost inaccessible crags about one mile apart.

The leader of the outbreak was Ologo Patu, chief of Southwestern Krobo, aud the whole district was so unsettled that Major Bird, who was administering the government, determined to take prompt measures and stamp out the rebellion before it had time to assume more serious proportions. The Gold Coast Corps was accordingly concentrated at Accra, and strong contingents having been furnished from Accra, Akwapim, Akwamu, and Eastern Krobo, the whole force moved to Prampram early in September. On the 11th it advanced from Prampram, and on the 13th encamped under the Krobo Mountain without meeting with any opposition, but on the previous night the whole Akwapim contingent had deserted. On the 18th a small party under Captain Brownell, which attempted to occupy a height commanding the town, was driven back, and in the afternoon the Krobos made a vigorous onslaught on the camp, which was only repulsed after two hours' fighting, and then with so much difficulty that it was thought advisable to withdraw the expeditionary force to

Assabi, and await additional native levies. The operations then dragged wearily, and it was not until October 19th that sufficient reinforcements had come in to justify a fresh advance; but on that day nearly fifteen thousand men were concentrated at Saddle Hill, about a mile and a half to the south of the Krobo Mountain, and Ologo Patu, convinced that further resistance was hopeless, surrendered.

CHAPTER XVIII.

1862—1865.

Dispute with Ashanti — The Protectorate invaded — Engagements at Essikuma and Bobikuma—Military mismanagement—Native feeling —Mr. Pine's proposals—Expedition to the Prah—The Home Government puts an end to the operations—Effects of the campaign—Delusive proclamation—War with the Awunas—Ashanti intrigue in Awuna—Governor Blackall's treaty.

AT the close of the year 1862 the Gold Coast was in a condition of prosperity such as it had never before reached. Interior disturbances had ended with the termination of the Krobo war, the Ashantis were on most friendly terms with the Government and the protected tribes, and every week dozens of their traders, laden with the commodities of the interior, arrived at the sea-coast towns. Never before had trade been so prosperous and the outlook so peaceable, when suddenly, without any warning, a misunderstanding with Ashanti arose and ultimately resulted in hostilities. The matter was as follows.

·An Ashanti chief, Kwaku Djanin, was charged with appropriating to his own use, contrary to the laws of the kingdom, certain nuggets of gold that he had found, and was summoned to Kumassi by Osai Kwaku Dua to answer the charge; but being, perhaps, conscious of guilt, he, after at first feigning compliance, fled from Ashanti with some eighty followers, subjects of the King, and took refuge in the protected territory. As soon as this escape was dis

covered an ambassador of high rank was despatched to
Cape Coast to inform the Governor, Mr. Richard Pine, of
all the circumstances of the case, and to request the extra-
dition of the runaways, and that of a slave boy who had
also escaped into the Protectorate. This embassy arrived
at Cape Coast in December, 1862, and a meeting, which
was attended by the Governor and Council, the naval and
military commanders on the station, the principal merchants
of the town, and the chief and head-men of Cape Coast,
was at once held in the Palaver Hall of the Castle. The
Ashanti ambassador, who had brought with him the golden
axe to show that the matter was important, set forth the
case for the King in a speech remarkable for its clearness,
and concluded by demanding the surrender of the fugitives
on the ground that there was an agreement between the
Government and the King of Ashanti that criminals should
be mutually given up. Kwaku Djanin had broken the
law of his country; he was therefore a criminal and should
be surrendered.

Although there is now no evidence of the existence
of any such agreement as that alleged, there is presumptive
proof that such a compact did exist. The demand was
evidently made in all sincerity as a demand that the King
was entitled to make; and it cannot be supposed that he
had the hardihood to invent an imaginary agreement to
suit a present need. It was generally believed on the Coast
that there was such an agreement. Mr. Brodie Cruickshank,
whose work on the Gold Coast was published in 1853,
that is, nine years before these events, refers to it in the
following terms: "It was stipulated in our treaties with
the King that his fugitive subjects should be re-delivered
to him in the same way that Fantis, flying into his
dominions, were to be restored to the Governor. This
arrangement was necessary to prevent malefactors escaping
punishment." In the case of the runaway being merely a
fugitive slave and not a criminal, he adds that the Governor,
before surrendering him, always required security that his
life should be spared. Colonel Nagtglas, Netherlands Com-

missioner on the Gold Coast in 1869-70, and who had served on the Gold Coast for many years prior to that date, also gives similar evidence. He says in a letter dated February, 1874: "There is an agreement in existence between the local British Government and the King of Ashanti, either oral or in writing, that on both sides runaway prisoners for crime should be delivered."

It seems, then, reasonably certain that there was such an agreement, and that the King of Ashanti, in demanding the surrender of Djanin, was making a demand he was entitled to make; but Governor Pine did not go into that question at all. It was well known that to surrender Djanin would be to consign him to certain death, and the question simply was whether, knowing what the consequences would be, they should surrender him. On this point the meeting was divided in opinion. Many of the merchants, with Commodore Wilmot, strongly supported the claim of the King, but the head-men of Cape Coast, who it was said had been bribed by Djanin, and others of the merchants, were against it. The Governor also was of opinion that the fugitives should not be surrendered, so, as a matter of course, the official members of the Council voted with him, and it was finally decided by a considerable majority to reject the King's demand. This decision met with the approval of the Home Government; and the Duke of Newcastle, in a despatch upon the subject, said: "I entirely approve of your having refused to surrender to the King of Ashanti the old man and the boy who had been brought into British territory. No person once brought within the limits of a British possession can be then seized and handed over to a foreign power except with the sanction of the law of the colony; and no law should authorise such delivery to the authorities of a country in which justice is not fairly administered, except in the case of heinous crimes."

It was well known on the Gold Coast that the result of this refusal would be war. It was true that Osai Kwaku Dua was the most pacific ruler that had ever sat on the stool of Ashanti, but even if he were disposed to overlook what must have appeared to him to be a breach of contract, the chiefs of Ashanti would not have suffered him to do so. In fact, if he did not declare war his throne would be endangered. Consequently, at a grand palaver held at Kumassi, the King asked the assembled chiefs if it was to be submitted to, that a subject, having violated the laws of his country, should find protection in a neighbouring state, and the King have no power to demand his surrender; and in a scene of the greatest excitement it was universally agreed that such an insult could only be avenged by war. The King, however, had not then a sufficient stock of gunpowder for such a struggle, so to gain time he sent a second message to Governor Pine complaining strongly of his action, and immediately began purchasing large quantities of arms and ammunition at Elmina. The dispute was soon further complicated by the action of the Fantis, who seeing that war was inevitable, and considering it the height of folly to quietly allow the Ashantis to complete their preparations, seized and put in log a large number of Ashantis who were returning with ammunition from Elmina. The reasoning of the Fantis was undoubtedly sound, but as war had not been yet declared with Ashanti the Government was supposed to be at peace with it, and the prisoners were ordered to be released and their goods restored to them.

The preparations for war being at last completed, an Ashanti army crossed the Prah early in 1864; one division of some two thousand men being despatched to the frontier of Wassaw, with orders to keep the Wassaws and Denkeras in check, but to avoid as much as possible any general engagement; and a second division, eight thousand strong, being sent, with similar orders, down the main road from Prahsu to push into the middle of the Protectorate. The main body, twenty thousand strong, under Awusu Kokkor, the King's uncle, soon followed and marched on the east of Fanti, through Akim. At this time almost the whole of the troops on the Gold Coast, consisting of the Gold Coast Corps and small detachments of the 2nd and 3rd West India Regiments, were stationed in the eastern districts of the Protectorate, at

Accra, Prampram, Kwantanan,* and Kpong,† to effect the settlement of the fine which had been imposed upon the Krobos for their rebellion of 1858. From these stations they were at once withdrawn as soon as the news of the invasion reached the Governor, and a detachment of the 2nd West India Regiment, which opportunely arrived in a transport from Lagos, was detained and landed at Cape Coast. The protected natives also came forward in considerable numbers to offer their services, and were formed into two bodies, the Agunas and Gomoas being encamped at Essikuma, and the Denkeras, Arbras, Assins, and people of Cape Coast and Anamabo at Mansu.

While these defensive measures were still being taken, the main Ashanti army under Awusu Kokkor traversed Western Akim, the inhabitants of which fled before it, and falling suddenly upon the native force at Essikuma, completely routed it after a six hours' engagement. The regular troops were now pushed to the front to check a further advance, and on April 19th, four hundred men under Major Cochrane, Gold Coast Corps, with seventy Cape Coast Volunteers, marched to Mankassim. Here they remained for ten days, and then proceeded to Bobikuma, where a large native force had been collected. Bobikuma is some fourteen miles to the south-east of Essikuma, where the Ashanti head-quarters still were; and this movement was designed to cover Winnebah, and prevent any advance of the enemy upon Accra. On May 10th the Ashantis advanced to within a quarter of a mile of the camp of the allies, and a slight skirmish took place between them and the native scouts, in which several of the latter were killed. A general engagement was now confidently expected for the next day, and there was a reasonable prospect of victory, as the native contingent at Bobikuma numbered nearly twenty thousand men; but to the astonishment and indignation of the entire force, both regular and native, Major Cochrane issued orders for the whole of the former and the greater portion of the latter to retire to the village of

* Kwantanan—literally "Four roads," *i.e.*, Cross-roads.
† Kpong—Island.

Adijuma; and this retrograde movement was carried out on the day following, while the gallant commander himself proceeded to the sea-coast town of Mumford. On May 12th the remnant of the native contingent left at Bobikuma was attacked in force by the Ashantis at two o'clock in the afternoon, and by five o'clock the allied natives were completely routed, losing very heavily. The town of Bobikuma was destroyed, and had Awusu Kokkor pushed on to Adijuma the disorganised force there waiting, without orders and without a commander, would no doubt have been swept away before him. Fortunately, however, he did not follow up his success, but after destroying upwards of thirty towns and villages in the neighbourhood, retired unmolested on May 24th to Akim Swaidru, a town on the southern frontier of Ashanti-Akim, and close to the River Birrim, the eastern tributary of the Prah. From this town he sent a Fanti prisoner to the Governor with two sticks, one long and one short, and requested him to make a choice. If he took the short one he was to give up the refugees and the war would be at an end; but if he chose the long one the war would be continued. The Ashanti general also demanded the surrender of the King of Western Akim, on the grounds that he had, on some former occasion, insulted Kwaku Dua's father. Governor Pine chose the long stick, and sent a reply that he was prepared to continue the struggle till the Ashanti kingdom was overthrown.

While these operations had been going on in the east, the large native force that had been collected at Mansu had remained quite inactive, though if properly handled it might have cut off the retreat of the enemy. The Governor, who showed the greatest activity, soon succeeded in collecting a second native force at Adjumako, and having inspired Major Cochrane with some of his own spirit, at last prevailed upon that officer to agree to a simultaneous movement being made by both forces upon the Ashantis at Akim Swaidru. Major Cochrane, however, was so very dilatory, that before the preparations for the advance were completed, intelligence was received that the Ashantis had retired into their own country. In fact, after having received the Governor's message, Awusu Kokkor had decided to defer further operations till the next dry season; for the rains were now approaching, and being fully aware of the disastrous effects of keeping the field at such a time, he sent most of his men back to their homes, leaving only a few detachments quartered in the towns on the main road to Kumassi. Thus disgracefully terminated the campaign of 1863. Through mismanagement, to use no harsher term, the Ashantis had been allowed to attack the allies in detail and win two battles, and to remain for over eighty days in one of the most fertile districts of the Protectorate, burning, ravaging, and slaying. The disappointment and shock to Governor Pine were so great that he was taken seriously ill in the camp at Denkari, near Adjumako, where he had gone to inspire and encourage the natives, and he was brought down to Cape Coast almost lifeless. The regular troops returned to the forts for the rainy season, and the native levies dispersed.

This abortive expedition was followed by a great outbreak of feeling amongst the protected tribes, the chiefs and influential members of which, by petitions and indignation meetings, clamoured for the removal of Major Cochrane. Numerous petitions were forwarded to the Governor praying him to urge upon the Home Government the necessity for adopting prompt and adequate measures for relieving the Protectorate of all future apprehension of an Ashanti invasion; and at the various meetings that were held very strong language was used concerning the action of the Dutch authorities, who had freely allowed the Elminas to supply the Ashantis with arms and gunpowder while they were actually in occupation of a portion of the territory of a friendly power. The Dutch Governor, Colonel Elias, it seems, had even been in direct communication with Awusu Kokkor while the Ashanti army was in the Protectorate, for one of his letters had been intercepted.

This political agitation soon bore fruit. Governor Pine made strong representations to the Government of Lord Palmerston, and the 4th West India Regiment was ordered from the West Indies to the Gold Coast, where it arrived, some eight hundred and fifty strong, under Lieut.-Colonel Conran, on August 13th, 1863. The Gold Coast Corps, which had proved to be thoroughly useless and unreliable, was disbanded, and preparations for taking the field were recommenced. The Imperial Government in sending this reinforcement had in view the clearing of the Protectorate of all hostile bodies of Ashantis, but Governor Pine wanted far more than this. With a clear-sightedness and a perfect appreciation of the necessities of the case which the lapse of a few years proved to be perfectly just, he urged upon the Government the necessity of invading Ashanti territory, and striking a final blow at the Ashanti power. He wrote: "It is with the deepest regret that I find myself involved, in spite of all my precautions, in a serious and, I fear, lingering war; but such being the case, I will not conceal from your Grace the earnest desire that I entertain that a final blow shall be struck at Ashanti power, and the question set at rest for ever, as to whether an arbitrary, cruel, and sanguinary monarch shall be for ever permitted to insult the British flag, and outrage the laws of civilisation. This desirable object can be attained only by the possession of such a force as I fear the Governor of these settlements can never hope to command, unless your Grace should be pleased to urge upon Her Majesty's Government the policy, the economy, and even the mercy, of transporting to these shores an army of such strength as would, combined with the allied native forces, enable us to march to Kumassi, and there plant the British flag. To a stranger the course I point out may appear a visionary one; but I am convinced that, even with all the disadvantages of climate, the expedition would not be so dangerous, so fatal, or accompanied by such loss of life as have attended expeditions in other and apparently more genial climes; and with 2,000 disciplined soldiers, followed by upwards of 50,000 native forces, who require only to be led and inspired with confidence by the presence of organised troops, I would undertake (driving the hordes of Ashanti before me) to march to Kumassi."

The soundness of Mr. Pine's views were fully vindicated by the Ashanti War of 1873-4, but the Ministry, either because they considered the project too hazardous, or because they did not wish to engage in operations of such magnitude, withheld their assent, though at the same time they sent orders to the West Indies for a further reinforcement of three hundred men of the 1st West India Regiment to be despatched to the Gold Coast.

Although the Ashanti forces had entirely evacuated the Protectorate, the protected tribes had so nearly lost all belief in British protection, that the Governor found it necessary to undertake some defensive measures in order to restore confidence. A supply depôt was accordingly formed at Mansu, and on February 5th, 1864, an advance to Prahsu was made by the troops from Cape Coast under Colonel Conran. Simultaneously with this movement the detachment from Accra moved to Akim Swaidru. While these movements of troops were taking place the Governor, in reply to his protestations, received from the Home Government a conditional sanction of the scheme he had proposed. If he found that he could not make a lasting peace without invading Ashanti territory, he might march to Kumassi.

At first sight it seemed as if there was now nothing to hinder an immediate advance across the Prah, but when seriously considered, such a movement was found to be impossible. The entire force of regular troops on the Gold Coast consisted only of 1,200 West India soldiers, and deducting from this number the sick, and such detachments as it would be necessary to leave at Mansu and Prahsu, there would not be more than 1,000 men left for the forward movement. This number was far too small to force its way to Kumassi, and as the native levies were not yet ready, it was decided to await the arrival of the reinforcements which were daily expected from the West Indies. In the meantime the troops at Prahsu were to be employed in fortifying that post, in convoying supplies, and in clearing the forest round their camp and on the further bank of the river.

Week after week passed by without the arrival of the promised reinforcements, and the unhealthy climate at last began to tell upon the men at Prahsu, who were encamped under shelter tents on wet ground. Still, the novelty of the situation kept them in health and spirits, and, being continuously employed, they remained in fairly good health till the commencement of March, when the rains set in, and all work was necessarily suspended. Then the troops, planted under an incessant downfall of rain in the midst of a tropical forest, on the banks of a swollen and miasmatic stream, and without occupation of any kind, rapidly succumbed to fever and dysentery, and by March 31st twenty-five per cent. of the force was in hospital. In consequence, three out of the six companies at Prahsu were withdrawn to Cape Coast, and when, on April 9th, H.M.S. *Tamar* arrived with the long-expected reinforcements, it was decided to send the new-comers to the front, and withdraw the detachment which had been so long exposed to all the evil influences of the bush.

Unfortunately, this measure, which at first sight appeared well-advised, was really the worst that could have been adopted. The native of the West Indies, on first arriving in West Africa, is affected by the climate in the same way as is the European, though much less seriously; and it is only after a residence of a few months that he becomes acclimatised. The new comers, then, from the West Indies were much more likely to suffer from exposure to the rains in the bush, than were those West India soldiers who had already been eight months in the country, and so the sequel proved. Towards the end of April the detachment at Prahsu was relieved by two companies of the 1st West India Regiment, who marched to their destination through torrents of rain; and before they had been encamped a month, 4 officers and 102 men were sick out of a total of 7 officers and 214 men. The hospital accommodation was so insufficient that the sick had to lie on the wet ground, surrounded by pools of water; the rains were unusually severe, the camp speedily became a swamp, and the troops had food of a poorer quality than they were accustomed to. The rain was so continuous that it was impossible to light fires for cooking except under sheds made of branches; and night after night the men turned into their dripping tents, hungry and wet to the skin. Not any enemy had been seen since the formation of the camp in February, and news there was none, for communication with Cape Coast was slow and uncertain. Under these circumstances it is not surprising that a general despondency set in, and as the sickness continued to increase, it was decided to reduce the force at Prahsu to one hundred men, the remainder marching for Cape Coast on June 6th.

In the meantime the Home Government, alarmed at the great loss of officers and men, somewhat hastily decided that all operations against Ashanti should cease, and that the troops should be withdrawn. This intelligence reached the Gold Coast in the middle of June, and was received with the greatest consternation. It was hard upon Governor Pine, whose theory as to the practicability of invading Ashanti was now generally held to have been proved to be incorrect, and whom many people did not hesitate to charge with the responsibility of the loss of life that had taken place ; it was hard upon the troops, who after months of weary waiting saw the reward of patience close at hand, only to be deprived of it ; and it was particularly hard upon the protected tribes, who saw themselves about to be once more abandoned to their foes. In truth the failure of the expedition was due to the vacillation of the Home Government, and that alone. Firs it would not sanction an advance into Ashanti territory, anc then it accorded a conditional sanction. Troops were sen over in driblets, so that the first arrivals had to wait, doing nothing, for those who were still to come. Then, having by its lack of decision made an expedition before the com mencement of the rains impossible, it impatiently put a; end to the operations because sickness prevailed during th rains. There was no reason why the original scheme shoul not have been adhered to. As the rains ceased the troop would have recovered in health and spirit ; the hardest part c the work, the collection of supplies and munitions of war at Prahsu, was already done ; at the commencement of the dry season an immediate advance to Kumassi could have been made ; and had it been made, all the miseries suffered by the inhabitants of the Gold Coast during the invasion of 1873 would in all human probability have been spared.

The transport of the stores which had been collected at Prahsu had cost the Government so much, that it was considered better to destroy them than to incur further expense in their removal. The detachment at Prahsu was therefore engaged for several days in destroying munitions and supplies of all kinds; the guns were buried secretly, so that no information as to their place of sepulture might reach the Ashantis, and on July 12th the troops finally turned their backs on the Prah. On the 27th the detachments of the 1st, 2nd, and 3rd West India Regiments embarked for the West Indies, and the 4th West India Regiment was left to garrison the forts. Thus terminated the campaign of 1864, in which not a shot had been fired, and which left the question in a worse state than ever, since Kwaku Dua had really gained a moral victory. The Ashantis, in fact, lost almost all respect for the British power, and there grew up a belief that the white man ceased to be formidable as soon as he left the shelter of his forts. Kwaku Dua said : " The white men bring many cannon to the bush, but the bush is stronger than the cannon." Fortunate was it that that King was of an eminently peaceful disposition, otherwise the year 1865 would probably have witnessed another Ashanti invasion, and the Protectorate would have been once more deluged with blood.

This abortive expedition provoked so much discussion in England that Parliament found it necessary to appoint a committee to investigate thoroughly the condition of the British Protectorate. Many persons recommended the entire abandonment of the Gold Coast, while others strongly advocated a more enlightened and energetic management of it. A middle course was eventually adopted. It was recommended that the government should be gradually left more and more in the hands of the natives, and that the

British should carefully avoid any further increase of territory, and make no more treaties with the native tribes; so that the protecting power might, as soon as it was possible without breach of honour, withdraw entirely. In the meantime the governments of the Gold Coast, Lagos, and Gambia were placed under a Governor-in-Chief, who resided at Sierra Leone; the local Governors were termed Administrators, and could only communicate with the Colonial Office through the Governor-in-Chief, who visited his dependencies once a year.

This was the effect of the expedition as far as England was concerned; its local effects were worse. The apparent proof of the utter incapacity of the Government to conduct military operations in the bush weakened British prestige to an enormous extent, and an official announcement which soon followed, to the effect that in the event of a future invasion the inhabitants were not to expect any assistance from the Government, caused it to be regarded almost with a feeling of contempt. This announcement, which amounted to a renunciation of the obligations that had been voluntarily assumed by the treaty of 1852, caused intense dissatisfaction, and several chiefs of the Protectorate showed signs of disaffection. They could scarcely be blamed for this, for they had only submitted to British control on the understanding that they would enjoy British protection; and if they were now to be deprived of the latter they had certainly a claim to be relieved of the former; but the Government evidently did not take this view, for they for once acted with vigour, and the insubordinate chiefs were soon called to order. Later on, Aggri, chief of Cape Coast, came into conflict with the Government concerning the ownership of some land within a few yards of the Castle, and became insulting and offensive. The Government consequently refused any longer to recognise him as chief of Cape Coast, and Colonel Conran, who had succeeded Mr. Pine, had him removed to Sierra Leone. The Home Government approved of Aggri's deposition, and since 1865 there has been no chief of Cape Coast.

During the year 1865 several abortive attempts were made by the Government to arrive at some understanding with Ashanti ; but at the close of the year, in response to overtures made on behalf of the Government by Mr. Blankson, a native merchant of Anamabo, who was on friendly terms with several influential Ashantis, messengers were sent down from Kumassi to consider terms of peace. No peace was definitely concluded, but, on the strength of the arrival of these messengers, Colonel Conran, on January 16th, 1866, issued a proclamation setting forth that the Ashanti King having solicited peace between his kingdom and the British Protectorate, peace was therefore declared and proclaimed. The King was very indignant when he heard of this proclamation, and at once repudiated it, declaring that it was not he who commenced negotiations, but the Governor, through his agent ; and he now refused to hold any further communication with the Government till Djanin was given up.

During the Ashanti invasion the Eastern Districts of the Gold Coast had remained perfectly tranquil, but a few days after the publication of Colonel Conran's peace proclamation, the Awunas, a tribe who inhabit the country to the east of the Volta, made war upon the Addahs. This outbreak was caused by the machinations of a native slave-trader, commonly known as Geraldo de Lema, and as we shall hear more of this man later on, it will be as well to here give some account of him, if only for the purpose of showing the complications which persons, who in a civilised land would be totally insignificant, are able to create in a country like the Gold Coast.

Geraldo de Lema, whose real name was Geraldo de Vasconcellos, was one of the domestic slaves of Cosar Cerquira Lema, a Brasilian slave-dealer who lived at Voji, a village about three miles to the east of Kittah, and who died in 1862, leaving a large fortune. The bulk of his wealth was in London and Bahia, but he had considerable sums of money at Voji, and also at Addah, at which place Geraldo was his agent for the purchase of slaves ; and these sums, when Lema died, Geraldo contrived to seize, together with his master's native wives, and, adopting the late slave-trader's name, continued the same business. In 1865, being still at Addah, he grossly ill-treated one of the principal chiefs of the town, and the Addahs in revenge drove him out of the place and plundered his property. He then went to Voji, where he induced the Awunas to adopt his quarrel, and, led by Geraldo, an Awuna force of four thousand appeared suddenly on the banks of the Volta opposite Addah. Being frustrated in an attempt to cross the river by the boats of H.M. ships *Dart* and *Lee*, he proceeded further up the river, where he sacked and burned Kpong, the great emporium for trade, and completely put a stop to the navigation of the Volta.

The trade of Accra greatly suffered by these acts, and strong representations were made by the merchants to Colonel Conran to interfere and to demand the surrender of Geraldo de Lema, who was the cause of all the disturbance. Colonel Conran accordingly tried to open negotiations with the Awunas, but without success, and the Accras, who were closely allied to the Addahs, were then allowed to declare war against the Awunas, and were supplied with arms and ammunition by the Government. The men of Accra, Christiansborg, and the neighbouring villages, who were placed under the command of Lieutenant Herbert, 4th West India Regiment, marched to the Volta and formed a camp at Kanar,* a village about fifteen miles higher up the river than Addah, and some two hours' journey from the town of Mlantfi,† opposite to which, on the left bank, was the Awuna encampment. Here, by March 12th, a force of some 9,000 men was gathered, including a fairly well disciplined volunteer force of 200 men, that had been raised by two English merchants, Messrs. Irvine and Clayton, and two native gentlemen of the name of Bannerman.

On 17th March, Lieutenant Herbert marched to Mlantfi, the inhabitants of which crossed the river, here only four hundred yards broad, to join the Awunas as he approached ;

---

* Kanar - Corner.   † Mlantfi—Leopard.

and the camp of the latter being plainly visible on the opposite bank, the guns and rockets opened fire and destroyed a great part of it. Up to this point the expedition had been conducted strictly in accordance with the new policy of the Government, viz., that the natives were to manage their own wars and look for no assistance from the troops quartered in the colony; but, on the 18th, Captain Humphrey arrived with a detachment of the 4th West India Regiment, and, by virtue of his seniority, assumed the command. Next day, under cover of a fire from the guns, a force of Accras was sent across the river to seize the canoes of the enemy, which were drawn up on the bank. They crossed without much loss, but, instead of carrying out their orders, followed up the retreating Awunas, and were drawn into an ambuscade, where they were thrown into confusion; and, being driven back to the river, lost more than sixty men, among them the chief of Addah, while recrossing it.

On the 21st, Kwow Dadi, King of Akwapim, and Tacki, chief of Dutch Accra, having arrived with a reinforcement of seven thousand men, the Volta was crossed in force, and the Awuna camp being found to be abandoned, a pursuit was ordered by Captain Humphrey. But now a conflict of authority arose. Tacki was the recognised King of all the eastern littoral, and the natives, regarding him as their leader rather than Captain Humphrey, refused to obey the latter's orders; so he, not wishing to jeopardise the existence of a force which had been brought together with so much difficulty, gave up the notion of a pursuit, but urged the chiefs at least to remain on the spot abandoned by the enemy, so that no opposition might be offered to the passage of the river by the main body of the allies, which still remained on the right bank. This proposition all the assembled chiefs, except Dawuna, chief of Christiansborg, also refused to agree to; and as they compelled the Christiansborg contingent to return, Captain Humphrey withdrew from the camp, and proceeded with his detachment to Addah, leaving Lieutenant Herbert in charge of the force.

As it was impossible that the expedition could succeed so long as authority was divided, Lieutenant Herbert called a meeting of all the chiefs, and declared that if they hesitated to obey his orders, and chose to regard Tacki as their leader, he and the volunteers would return to Accra, and leave them to their own devices; and the chiefs, afraid to act alone, finally submitted. The 23rd and days following were then occupied in moving the main body across the Volta, and on April 3rd it moved to attack the Awunas, who were supposed to be within a day's march. On the 4th it crossed the Tojeh River, a tributary of the Volta, and encamped in a forest of palms till the 12th, when it again advanced, and after a few miles was suddenly surprised by a body of about eight thousand Awunas, who had ambushed themselves in front and on both flanks. Such was the want of organisation, that the head of the column consisted of the women, carrying baggage and supplies, and these, being driven back upon the men, threw everything into confusion. Numbers of the allies were shot down or captured, the baggage was abandoned, and the whole army would soon have been in full flight, had not the King of Akwapim moved his contingent through the bush at some distance from the scene of conflict, and fallen upon the enemy in rear. This checked the advance of the Awunas, and gave the Accras time to rally, and a severely contested engagement raged for some time. A gun which the allies had brought up was captured and recaptured half-a-dozen times, and for two hours the result of the battle was doubtful; but at last the enemy began to retreat, and being followed up vigorously, were pursued with great slaughter for several miles. The defeat of the enemy was so complete that had the allies followed up their success by marching upon the Awuna chief towns, the war would have been finished at one blow; but the hard fighting of that day had been quite enough for the ill-disciplined natives, and, disregarding alike Lieutenant Herbert's orders and expostulations, they retreated to the Volta, and, crossing it on the 14th, disbanded themselves and returned to their homes.

The Awunas had lost so heavily that for some months they remained perfectly quiet; but the Government also remained inactive, and it was not until October, when Colonel Conran, with two influential merchants of Accra, went to Jella Koffi, an Awuna town on the sea-coast, that any attempt was made to arrive at a settlement. Colonel Conran's terms were that Geraldo de Lema should be surrendered, and the Awunas pay two thousand dollars to the Accras for expenses incurred in the war. Had these proposals been made immediately after the defeat of the Awunas, they might have been accepted; but now they were at once rejected, for while the Government had allowed valuable time to slip away, Ashanti, ever on the look-out for opportunities of recovering its lost sway over the coast tribes, had made an alliance with the Awunas. In fact, directly the news of the Awuna reverse was known in Kumassi, Kwaku Dua had sent messengers to the Awunas, and the Akwamus, who were also threatened by the Accras, offering them assistance; and the offer being accepted by both tribes, an Ashanti army was, as a first step, sent against the Krepis, who were in alliance with Accra, with instructions to enter the Protectorate as soon as a favourable occasion offered.

Affairs remained in this unsettled state until April, 1867, when Major Blackall, Governor-in-Chief, arrived at Accra and at once proceeded to Jella Koffi to endeavour to come to some understanding with the Awunas. No real representative of the Awuna nation met him, but the chief of the insignificant hamlet of Srongbi, and a native trader of Jella Koffi, went on board the Governor's vessel, and after some discussion agreed to sign a treaty of peace on behalf of the Awunas, which was not worth the paper on which it was written. Indeed, at the very time at which it was signed, the Awunas, with their Ashanti allies, were engaged in pillaging the Krobo villages near the Volta, had again entirely stopped the navigation of that river, and were blockading all the roads leading to Krepi. The treaty did not produce the slightest effect, and was immediately repudiated by the Awunas, who declined to be bound by the promises of two persons who were not authorised to act for them. Thus, curiously enough, the Government of the Gold Coast had at this time two so-called treaties which were absolutely valueless; namely, the treaty of peace with the Ashantis which had been proclaimed by Colonel Conran, and the treaty just entered into by Governor Blackall.

CHAPTER XIX.

1868—1869.

Exchange of territory with the Dutch—Native protests—Bombardment of Kommenda—The Fanti Confederation—Investment of Elmina—Fruitless negotiations—Condition of affairs in Ashanti—Palaver at Elmina—Dutch prisoners at Kommenda—Bombardment of Dixcove.

THE incessant petty squabbles which took place between the natives subject to Dutch control and those subject to the British, and the difficulties which were continually arising from the difference in the customs duties levied by the two Governments, induced the Home Government about this time to endeavour to arrange some mutual cession of territory on the Gold Coast, by which these might be obviated. The question of the customs duties was the more important of the two, as the Dutch duties on imports were merely nominal; and this not only seriously affected the British revenue in those places where each nation had a fort, but was a cause of continual conflict between the authorities and the natives, who naturally smuggled their goods through the Dutch possessions. The British Government at first proposed that the duties should be equalised, but the Dutch objected to increase theirs, and the result of a diplomatic exchange of views was that in March, 1867, a convention was concluded between the two Governments, by which the Dutch ceded to the British all their possessions to the east of the Sweet River, and received in return all the possessions of the latter to the west of that river. The treaty was signed by the plenipotentiaries of both countries on March 6th, 1867, and ratified on July 6th. It came into effect on January 1st, 1868, and by it the British handed over Appollonia, Dixcove, Sekondi, and Kommenda, and received Mori, Cormantine, Appam, and Dutch Accra. The British also relinquished to the Dutch the protectorate over Wassaw, Denkera, and Appollonia.

Although the interests of the natives were materially concerned in this exchange of territory, it does not appear that any of the tribes affected by it were consulted, nor was it thought necessary to obtain their consent to what was really a transfer of allegiance. As far as that portion which now came under British rule was concerned, there was no difficulty, for the Dutch natives had for many years been on friendly terms with the British; but the case was very different with the western half of the Gold Coast, which had now entirely become Dutch territory. As will have been seen from the preceding chapters, the bitterest animosities prevailed between the British and Dutch protected natives on the sea-coast between Elmina and Appollonia. The Elminas were the deadly foes of the Kommendas, and were also hostile to the Denkeras and Wassaws; while Sekondi had an hereditary feud with Chama, Dixcove with Butri, and Appollonia with Axim. Moreover, the Dutch natives of the western half of the Gold Coast were on the most friendly terms with the Ashantis, the people of Elmina being even regarded as Ashanti subjects; while the British natives had repeatedly been in arms with the Government against Ashanti. By this partition of the Gold Coast the natives of Appollonia, Dixcove, Sekondi, and Kommenda were now required to effect a complete change of front in their politics. As Dutch subjects they were required not only to live on peaceable terms with those neighbours with whom they had quarrelled for years, but also to extend the hand of friendship and alliance to Ashanti, to that power from which, for more than half a century, they had suffered the greatest cruelties and oppressions. For the Wassaws and Denkeras it meant more than this. The inhabitants of the sea-coast towns might be guaranteed from Ashanti extortion and violence by the Dutch authorities, but the latter were too weak to afford protection to these inland tribes, who now had before them the alternative of becoming tributary to Ashanti or of withstanding another Ashanti invasion. It is not surprising, therefore, that all the natives now about to be transferred to the Dutch made indignant protests against that measure, and it certainly does seem a most extraordinary proceeding to have transferred a number of people, who were not British subjects but were only living under British protection, to another power, without even going through the form of asking them if they were willing to accept the control of that power. In fact, the natives could not have been treated more unceremoniously if they had been the absolute property—the slaves of the British Government. The matter was further complicated by the fact that, no treaty of peace having been concluded with Ashanti since the invasion of 1863, the British and their native allies were to be considered as being still at war with Ashanti, to whose indirect rule, through the Dutch, a portion of those very native allies was now to be transferred.

In December, 1867, a few days before the actual transfer took place, Mr. H. T. Ussher, Administrator of the Gold Coast, issued a proclamation setting forth the convention between the British and Dutch Governments; and at the same time a circular letter was sent to the Kings and chiefs of the Protectorate who were about to be transferred to the Dutch, informing them that, in order to facilitate trade and civilisation, the British protectorate over them would be abandoned, and they would be handed over to the Government of the King of the Netherlands. The letter concluded with the hope that their relations with their new rulers would be as satisfactory as those they had maintained with their old ones.

Dutch Accra was the principal town to be transferred to British rule, and on January 4th, 1868, the Dutch Governor, Colonel Boers, there met Major Blackall, who, as Governor-in-

Chief, had come from Sierra Leone to effect the transfer. The Dutch flag was lowered on Fort Crève Cœur, and the British flag hoisted, under salutes from the vessels of war and the forts, without any opposition. Appam, Mori, and Cormantine were also handed over to the British without trouble; and this part of the business, which was simple enough, having been concluded, Major Blackall then returned to Sierra Leone, leaving Mr. Ussher to hand over the British protected towns to the Dutch. This, however, proved to be a very different affair. The inhabitants of those towns, always having been strong supporters of the British, determined, should that Government decide to withdraw its protection, to decline to accept Dutch rule; and they drew up a petition against the transfer, praying the British not to desert them. The Kings of Wassaw and Denkera flatly refused to accept either the convention or proclamation, but the inhabitants of the towns on the sea-coast, with one exception, were compelled to temporise. That exception was the people of Kommenda. They refused positively to allow a British flag that they had hoisted to be lowered, and attacked the crew of a boat from the Dutch man-of-war *Metalen Kruis*, which had landed for this purpose on January 30th. In return the Dutch bombarded Kommenda and next day landed a force from their corvette which burned the town, destroyed the fishing canoes, killed many of the inhabitants, and drove the remainder into the bush.

The Elminas rejoiced over the calamity which had befallen their ancient enemies, but the bombardment of Kommenda acted like an electric shock throughout the Protectorate, and the passive resistance of the various Kings and chiefs was now turned into armed opposition. The Kings and chiefs of Wassaw, Denkera, Assin, Arbra Anamabo, Mankassim, Winnebah, and Gomoa assembled at Mankassim, and, after a council of war, decided to resist to their utmost the Dutch occupation of those towns which had hitherto been under British protection. As they expressed it—their father had no right to enslave them, his children, to another master. They had been brought up from childhood under the British flag, and they would not submit to the Dutch. Appollonia, which consisted of two districts, namely Atwaambu* and Bayin†, was divided in opinion as to what should be done. Atwaambu, being near the Dutch fort at Axim, accepted the Dutch flag, but the Bayins refused to accept it; and when their chief town was bombarded retired to the bush towns, and sent to the Administrator at Cape Coast for munitions of war to enable them to fight the Dutch. This was of course refused, but the Fanti chiefs supplied them with powder and lead and several ounces of gold-dust. The inhabitants of Dixcove, being under the guns of Dixcove Fort, were obliged to submit, as, for a similar reason, were those of Sekondi; but the people of the bush villages of both districts refused to recognise Dutch authority. The transfer was particularly obnoxious to the people of Cape Coast, as by it most of their important villages and plantations—such as Effutu and Mampon,‡ from which they derived the greater part of their food supply—being situated to the west of the Sweet River, were transferred to the Dutch. The Dutch also levied certain taxes on staple articles of food, a species of impost which the British had never imposed; so that the people of Cape Coast, though living under British rule, now found themselves under the necessity of paying taxes to the Dutch, or of abandoning their plantations. Being, however, under the guns of the Castle, they did not join the confederation of the chiefs, which was soon known as the Fanti Confederation.

Not long after the bombardment of Kommenda, the Kommendas killed a native of Elmina, and forwarded his jawbone to the Kings and chiefs assembled at Mankassim, as a token that they had commenced hostilities. A few days after this the Elminas, in retaliation, suddenly fell upon some British protected natives who had for several years lived peaceably in a village belonging to Elmina, killed several of them, and paraded the remainder through Elmina as prisoners. The chiefs at Mankassim at once ordered the

---

* Atwaambu—Doom.   † Bayin—Witchcraft.
‡ Mampon is probably a corruption of Mampam—the iguana.

Arbras, under their King, to move to Effutu; the King of Arbra being the traditional leader of the Fantis, whose business it was to be the first to take the field. At Effutu he was soon joined by the King of Denkera, and the combined forces marched to Semu, where they were shortly reinforced by the chief of Mankassim and the other chiefs of the Confederation, and Elmina was closely invested.

The British and Dutch authorities on the Gold Coast viewed with consternation this result of an exchange of territory which had been effected with the best intentions, but which, so far from producing that era of peace and quietness that had been expected, had caused a general conflagration. It was but another example of the profound ignorance of the natives and their political sympathies and antipathies which seems always to have been conspicuous in the British authorities on the Gold Coast. The scheme had been conceived and carried out without the smallest consideration for native interests or prejudices, and perhaps no example better serves to show the ignorance of its designers than the selection of a boundary by which the town of Cape Coast was placed under one power, and its principal dependent villages under another. Any native, or indeed any European who knew anything of the natives, could have foretold what would be the result of this ill-advised measure, and the local officials were probably the only persons who had not foreseen it.

To endeavour to cripple the resources of the confederated Kings and chiefs, Mr. Ussher issued a proclamation suspending for an indefinite period under heavy penalties the sale of powder, lead, and firearms, and the people of Cape Coast and its neighbourhood were warned against taking any part in the disturbances. He also wrote to the King of Arbra demanding an explanation of his conduct, and warning him not to compel the Government to use extreme measures against him. The King of Arbra had, it appears, despatched a considerable force to attack the Dutch at Kommenda, and he excused this action to the Administrator by saying that the Elminas had sent three of their town companies to

Kommenda to assist the Dutch. The other Kings and chiefs, however, took a higher standpoint. They declared that they could not understand how the people of Kommenda, who were not the slaves of either Government, could be bartered; and they reminded the Administrator that the very ground on which the deserted fort of Kommenda stood was the property of the people, and that, when the fort was inhabited, the Royal African and other Companies had paid a ground rent for it.

The people of Cape Coast had up to this time remained neutral, but on April 4th a party of Elminas suddenly attacked and burned the village of Abina, which belongs to Cape Coast, killing four of the inhabitants and taking several prisoners. It was not to be expected that the people of Cape Coast would tamely submit to this, and they marched out under their head-man, Kwasi Attah, drove the Elminas out of Abina, and then joined the confederate force. Mr. Ussher viewed this action with great severity. He issued a proclamation in which he charged Kwasi Attah with a breach of his oath of allegiance, proclaimed him an outlaw, and confiscated his property to the Crown; and further decreed, which decree was carried out to the letter, that his house should be razed to the ground as a warning to all seditious persons.

The confederate force now disposed around Elmina consisted of between twenty and thirty thousand men. On the right were the Kommendas, Denkeras, Anamabos, and Tufels; in the centre, at the village of Frampun, were the Arbras, Adjumakos, and people of Mankassim; and on the left, near Abina, were the people of Cape Coast, Mori, and Cormantine, with a contingent from Gomoa. At his wits' end, Mr. Ussher sent Mr. T. B. Freeman to the camp to endeavour to persuade the chiefs to disperse their forces, but he entirely failed in his mission, and an attack on Elmina was arranged for May 27th. The Kommendas were to commence the action, which was then to be taken up on the left; and while the Elminas were thus engaged on both flanks the centre was to force its way into the town. A traitor, however, in the camp of the confederates betrayed the plan to the Elminas, who anticipated events by making a vigorous onslaught on the left at daybreak on the 26th. The Cape Coast people, though taken by surprise, fought well, and the centre coming to their assistance, the Elminas, who were supported by the Dutch troops, were driven back to the town after some five hours' fighting; a destructive fire which was opened from Fort Conraadsburgh alone preventing the victorious confederates from entering Elmina itself. The suburbs fell into their hands and were burned, as were the Dutch camps, where a number of breech-loading rifles were captured; but several attempts to fire the town failed, and about 3 p.m. the confederated chiefs, having decided to recommence operations next day, returned to their various camps.

In this engagement the greater part of the confederates had taken no part, the King of Arbra, either through jealousy or through the influence of Mr. Freeman, who was still in his camp, having withheld his men; while the Kommendas, and the others on the right, had remained in complete ignorance of what was taking place. During the remainder of the day Mr. Freeman redoubled his efforts to arrange matters, and the chiefs, suspecting that the King of Arbra was about to desert them, at last agreed to leave to the Administrator the settlement of the quarrel between themselves and the Elminas. Next morning the King of Arbra struck his camp and retired some ten miles further from Elmina; towards evening his example was followed by several other chiefs, and the blockade terminated with the retreat of the whole force on the day following.

A commission, consisting of the Collector of Customs (Mr. Simpson), Mr. Freeman, and a native named Dawson, who was styled Secretary to the Confederated Kings and Chiefs, was now sent by Mr. Ussher to Elmina to discuss the terms of peace, and the following were agreed upon: (1) That hostilities between the two parties should cease. (2) That the alliance between the Elminas and Ashantis should be suspended for six months. (3) That the Elminas should be allowed free intercourse with and through every part of the districts of the confederates. When these terms, however, were communicated to the confederated chiefs they declined to accept them, and demanded, very reasonably, that the Elminas should altogether put an end to their connection with Ashanti, and join them in a defensive alliance against that power. This the Elminas refused to do, and the negotiations therefore came to an end, but the allied forces which had thus been dispersed to no purpose were not reassembled. A semi-blockade of Elmina was, however, maintained by the inhabitants of the surrounding villages, and the Elminas, who were often reduced to great straits for food, made occasional sorties upon unprotected hamlets, slaying the occupants, and parading their heads through the streets of Elmina as proofs of their prowess. The struggle was also carried on by sea, the canoes from the Dutch ports being waylaid and attacked; and sometimes battles in which hundreds of men were engaged were waged upon the water. In these sea-fights the Elminas and Dutch natives were nearly always worsted, and the supply of fish, one of their staple articles of food, was almost entirely cut off.

Fortunately the condition of affairs in Ashanti had been such that that people, who would never have allowed so good an opportunity for interfering in the affairs of the coast tribes to have escaped them, had been fully employed at home. Osai Kwaku Dua had died at Kumassi on April 27th, 1867, before any exchange of territory between the British and Dutch had taken place, and the events which followed his death prevented his successor from taking advantage of the anarchy in which that transfer plunged the Protectorate. On the death of a King of Ashanti, any prince is allowed by custom to take the life of any subject, and on such occasions frenzied members of the royal family rush into the streets and highways and fire their muskets indiscriminately; but they usually preserve sufficient self-control to distinguish individuals, and are careful only to kill such as have no near relatives of sufficiently high rank to become dangerous enemies. But when Kwaku Dua died, a nephew of Asamoa

Kwanta, the Ashanti general, was slain by Prince Buakji Asu, who seized this opportunity for gratifying his private malice; and the aged general, furious at the murder, took up arms, and raised a formidable insurrection which threatened to destroy Kumassi. For some months it seemed as if the Ashanti kingdom was about to be torn to pieces by a civil war, but after a variety of negotiations Asamoa Kwanta consented to lay down his arms, on condition that Buakji Asu and two of his sisters were handed over to him to be sacrificed; and these conditions being complied with, the insurrection came to an end, but henceforth Asamoa Kwanta kept aloof from the palace. This serious affair had delayed the election of the new King, Kwoffi Kari-kari, and, after he had been elected, the latent disaffection of the general's party rendered a policy of adventure inadvisable. According to custom, Kwoffi Kari-kari sent a messenger to each ally and tributary to inform them of the death of his predecessor and his own accession; and these messengers, on arriving at their destinations, were, as is the rule, at once put to death. Amongst others a messenger was sent to Elmina, and was there publicly sacrificed without the Dutch authorities taking any notice of the act. The King of Elmina sent in return one of his chiefs, named Andor, to Kumassi, with a considerable retinue, to convey his expressions of condolence and to assist at the funeral obsequies of the late King.

The Ashantis, who were kept thoroughly well informed of all that took place on the seaboard by the Elminas, had received with delight the news of the transfer of territory between the British and Dutch, by which their old foes, the Wassaws, Denkeras, and Kommendas, were brought under the rule of the Dutch; and the news of the investment of Elmina by the confederated chiefs so roused them to action that, though affairs in Ashanti were still in a tentative condition, the King sent messengers to the Dutch Governor, offering to send an army to his assistance. This offer Colonel Boers was obliged to decline, and so for the moment an invasion was postponed; but the Ashantis were firmly resolved again to try conclusions with the protected tribes as soon as a favourable opportunity offered. It is worthy of note that at the time of his death Kwaku Dua was projecting a second invasion of the Protectorate to revenge the refusal to surrender Djanin, which matter was still unforgotten and unforgiven. The chiefs even asserted that he had died of grief because he was unavenged, and when they assembled round his body they declared that he should not be buried till the insult was wiped out. The young King, Kwoffi Kari-kari, however, would not consent to this; but he promised that Djanin's affair should not be forgotten, and when he was placed on the stool he swore: " My business shall be war."

Matters were in this condition when, on October 27th, 1868, Sir Arthur Kennedy, the Governor-in-Chief, arrived at Cape Coast on a tour of inspection. He was much moved by the deplorable condition of the country, and shocked at the dreadful atrocities which took place almost daily; and shortly after arrival proceeded to Elmina, where, with Colonel Boers, he met the Elmina chiefs to endeavour to arrange a peace. He pointed out that the exchange of territory between the British and Dutch had changed the relative political position of Ashanti, and endeavoured to show the advantages which were to be derived from a combination of all the people on the sea-coast for mutual support. The Elmina chiefs seem to have been convinced by his arguments; at all events, when they retired to consult together, the majority had made up their minds to follow his advice; but to the surprise of every one, when they returned to the Palaver Hall, they emphatically refused to enter into any alliance with the Fantis, Wassaws, or Denkeras, and declared that they intended to continue the payment of tribute to Ashanti, whose friendship they greatly preferred. This unexpected change of opinion is said to have been effected by Colonel Boers, who, having observed the effect of Sir Arthur Kennedy's appeal, secretly sent one of his officers to join the chiefs in their consultation, and remonstrate against any renunciation of Ashanti. The fact was that for years the Dutch Government had been in the habit of purchasing slaves from the King of Ashanti, whom they then sent to Java to serve as soldiers; and as this was a very economical way of obtaining recruits (for now that there was no export trade, slaves were exceedingly cheap), the Dutch local authorities, who no doubt profited personally by it, did not at all wish it to be brought to an end by a cessation of intercourse with Ashanti. Sir Arthur Kennedy was much disappointed at this unexpected frustration of his hopes, and on returning to Cape Coast, informed the confederated chiefs that they were now at liberty to undertake any expedition they pleased against the Dutch natives; so that in November it became lawful to do that for which in April Kwasi Attah had been outlawed and his property confiscated and destroyed.

The people of Elmina, being of opinion that Colonel Boers had not afforded them proper assistance during the attack on the town in 1868, had, shortly after the dispersion of the confederated natives, sent a deputation to Holland to petition for his removal; and early in May, 1869, Colonel Nagtglas, who had previously served many years on the Gold Coast in a military capacity, was sent out as a Royal Commissioner, with extensive powers, to replace him. Immediately after his arrival an unfortunate occurrence took place which much embittered the already sufficiently hostile feeling between the Dutch and those British-protected natives who had been transferred to them. A Dutch man-of-war, the *Amstel*, when off Kommenda, sent a boat manned by two officers and nine seamen, to take soundings near the shore, and to endeavour to discover the mouth of a river that was shown in an old chart in the possession of the captain; but through some mismanagement the boat got into the surf and was capsized, one officer and five of the crew being drowned, and the remainder being able to reach the shore only with great difficulty. The Kommendas who, since the arrival of the *Amstel*, had been lying in wait in the bush ready to repel any attempt to land a force, rushed down upon the survivors as they struggled ashore to make them prisoners, and in the scuffle that ensued one of the sailors was killed. The prisoners were taken into the bush, where one of them died, and the others were not surrendered until a ransom of three hundred ounces of gold-dust had been paid by the Dutch authorities.

About the middle of June, 1869, the Dutch bombarded Dixcove, the inhabitants of which had made no secret of their antipathy to Dutch rule, and had foolishly exulted over the boat disaster at Kommenda. To render their destruction complete, the Dutch Commandant, Captain Alvarez, supplied the hereditary foes of the Dixcove people at Butri with ammunition, and instructed them to attack the town from the land side, while the fort bombarded it. But though driven from the town by the fire of the fort, the Dixcoves completely defeated the Butris, and then retired to their bush villages, where the Commandant was unable to reach them. The chief sufferers by this affair were the European traders, whose shops were plundered by the Dutch garrison, and who were never able to obtain any compensation.

CHAPTER XX.

1868—1869.

An Ashanti force sent to Elmina—Bloody march of Atjiempon—Affair at Elmina—Treaty with the Awunas—Ashanti invasion of Krepi—Mr. Simpson's adventure—Capture of German missionaries by the Ashantis—Hostages sent for their safety—Policy of the Government.

THE funeral customs for Osai Kwaku Dua were prolonged in Kumassi till the end of 1868, and at their conclusion chief Andor and the deputation from Elmina requested permission to return home. The internal affairs of the kingdom had now recovered from the effect of Asamoa Kwanta's insurrection, and the occasion being a suitable one for introducing a force to the coast, the King, in dismissing the Elminas, sent with them his uncle, Atjiempon, accompanied by several hundred armed men. The roads through Fanti, Denkera, and Wassaw being still closed by the Fanti Confederation, this force was obliged to proceed through Awuin and Assini to reach the Dutch seaboard. The King of Awuin, who was on the most friendly terms with Ashanti, freely permitted its passage through his territory; but one of the chiefs of the Amantifu territory detained Atjiempon at Kinjabo for nearly four months, and it was only after the exchange of several messages with Kumassi that he and his following were allowed to proceed. The French authorities at Assini offered no obstacle to the passage of the force, which crossed the Assini River, and, traversing Appollonia, arrived at Axim.

At Axim Atjiempon commenced a series of atrocious acts which marked his march along the coast to Elmina with a trail of blood. At the instigation of chief Andor, he cut out the tongue and then struck off the head of a Fanti who had been living at Axim for some time; and this, although done in the market-place openly, and within three hundred yards of Fort St. Anthony, provoked no remonstrance from the Dutch Commandant. This murder was committed early in November, 1869, and on the 14th of that month, encouraged by the apathy of the Dutch Commandant, Atjiempon seized two Englishmen, Mr. Cleaver, agent of Messrs. F. & A. Swanzy, and the master of the brig *Alligator*, who had both landed at Axim in the usual course of their business; and declared his intention of putting these two to death also, giving as a reason that he had taken an oath before he left Kumassi to kill every Englishman he met. In this instance, however, the Commandant, alarmed at what might be the consequences to himself if he quietly allowed two Englishmen to be murdered in a town under Dutch rule, interfered, and after considerable difficulty and delay succeeded in persuading Atjiempon to release his prisoners.

From Axim Atjiempon next marched along the coast to the east, killing every Fanti, Wassaw, and Denkera he happened to meet. Two men were murdered at Takoradi, and at Sekondi he seized some Fantis who had claimed the protection of the Dutch flag, and put them to death in front of the fort. From Sekondi Atjiempon continued his bloody progress through Shamah and Kommenda to Elmina, where he was received with a perfect ovation, and several Fantis, who had thought themselves secure from molestation under the guns of the Castle, were beaten to death by the assembled mob. The day before entering Elmina he had beaten a woman to death and beheaded a man at Aduapehnin, a small village to the west of Elmina, and the head he now carried in front of his triumphal procession.

Complaints of all these atrocities were made to the Administrator, Mr. Ussher, who forwarded the declarations

s

to Colonel Nagtglas, with a letter expressing the hope that he would inflict upon Atjiempon such a punishment as would prevent the recurrence of such barbarities. But Colonel Nagtglas was not in a position to inflict punishment; he was really powerless, and though he might have destroyed the town from the Castle and forts, yet he was hardly likely to do so, considering that his predecessor had been removed by the Netherlands Government for not affording proper protection to the Elminas. Personally he felt the greatest detestation for Atjiempon, but he was the servant of his Government, and the most he was able to do was to refuse for some days, as a mark of displeasure, to give Atjiempon an audience.

In March, 1870, when Atjiempon was still at Elmina, an occurrence took place which so well illustrates the license enjoyed by natives under Dutch control that it is given in detail. On the 12th of the month Mr. Finlason, an Englishman who was engaged in trade at Cape Coast, landed at Elmina, and went to stay at a house in the town, where in the course of the evening he received a message that the King of Elmina wished to see him. To this he replied that he would come presently, and the messengers retired, but soon returned, saying that the King ordered him to come at once or take the consequences. Mr. Finlason thereupon said that he had intended going to see the King, as a matter of politeness; but now that the King sent him an order, he would have him to know that he was a British subject, and would only obey orders given by the Dutch officers, who were the only authorities he could recognise in Elmina. The messengers retired, vowing vengeance, and half an hour later the King of Elmina and Atjiempon, with a body of armed men forced their way into the house, charged Mr. Finlason with being the secretary to the Fanti Confederation and therefore an enemy, and declared that he should be put to death Atjiempon's death-drum was beaten, the executioner entered the room brandishing his knife, and all hope seemed gone when a Dutch officer suddenly appeared on the scene with a strong body of soldiers from the Castle, and rescued the prey, who next day had to be escorted on board his vessel by a guard of two hundred men to protect him from the mob.

While these events had been taking place in the western districts of the Gold Coast, the eastern districts had, owing chiefly to the machinations of Geraldo de Lema, remained in a disordered condition ever since Governor Blackall's proclamation of peace ; raids being so frequently made upon unprotected villages that some of the most fertile districts were rapidly becoming depopulated, and trade had almost ceased. Sir Arthur Kennedy, after his Elmina meeting, had proceeded to Accra, and he now, with Captain Glover, the Administrator of Lagos, concerted measures for the pacification of the countries bordering on the Volta. Rightly supposing that no permanent settlement could be effected as long as Geraldo de Lema was at large, he went to Kittah and offered two hundred pounds for his apprehension, and being unable to secure him, caused his house at Voji to be bombarded by H.M.S. *Pert*, and destroyed, after which he returned to the Volta. The dangerous bar which closes the mouth of that river had never been crossed, but Captain Glover thought that a channel for small vessels might be discovered; and as the presence of a steamer on the Volta would show the Awunas that they were liable to be attacked in the interior, it was decided to attempt the passage with the Colonial steamer *Eyo*. This was effected with great difficulty, but without accident, and the Awunas were so much alarmed by the appearance of this vessel in a stream hitherto supposed to be unnavigable, that they at once sent representatives to the Governor to make peace, and a treaty was finally concluded on November 30th, 1868. It stipulated that the Volta should be kept open for all lawful trade, and that all disputes should be referred to the Governor-in-Chief, whose decision should be final. The contending parties were at once to lay down their arms.

Unfortunately the allies of Awuna, the Ashantis and Akwamus, were not represented at this meeting, so that the treaty really accomplished no more than the detaching of the Awunas from the alliance ; and only a few days after it had been signed the Akwamus and Ashantis invaded Krepi, and again put a stop to the navigation of the Volta. The Ashanti army, thirty thousand strong, was commanded by Adu Boffo, the old general, Asamoa Kwanta, being still in retirement; and the invasion was prosecuted with vigour, for it was imagined in Kumassi that the Government would not pay any serious attention to matters beyond the frontier, and the Ashanti plan was to acquire territory on the east, so that with increased prestige and increased strength they might eventually invade the Protectorate from all sides. It was at this time that Atjiempon was sent to Elmina, partly in accordance with long-established custom to protect that town from the Fantis, and partly to watch for a favourable opportunity and prepare the way for an attack on the British; for it was intended that at the right moment the Protectorate should be attacked by Atjiempon and the Elminas on the west, and by Adu Boffo on the east, while the King himself crossed the Prah.

The Ashantis and Akwamus met with a most unexpected and obstinate resistance at the hands of the Krepis, who, led by a brave and skilful leader named Dompreh, returned again and again to the struggle as if invigorated by defeat. The war was characterised by all the worst horrors of such a conflict, and thousands of men, women, and children were slaughtered or driven into captivity. The Krepis, outnumbered but still struggling gallantly, sent appeal after appeal to the Kings of Akim, Akwapim, Krobo, and Accra to come to their assistance against the common enemy; and the excitement became so intense in the eastern districts of the Protectorate, that the Acting-Administrator, Mr. W. H. Simpson, being apprehensive that if something were not done to allay the general irritation he would find himself involved in a war, determined, towards the end of February, 1869, to visit the interior and ascertain the real state of affairs. On March 5th Mr. Simpson arrived at Odumassi,* in Krobo, from which place he sent an order to the King of

* Odum-assi—Under the odum tree.

Akwamu to come to him; but the King owed no allegiance to the British and declined to obey, upon which Mr. Simpson determined to visit him in his own territory. The object of the Administrator in undertaking this journey was to detach Akwamu from the alliance with Ashanti, and after several palavers had been held, he apparently succeeded, for the King and chiefs, converted by his arguments or moved by his eloquence, signed a treaty of peace that was drawn up on the spot. Almost immediately afterwards, however, they were persuaded by the Ashanti general, Adu Boffo, who, as soon as heard of the transaction, came to the spot, to reconsider their decision to abandon the Ashanti alliance; with the result that when Mr. Simpson, a few days after the signing of the treaty, declared his intention of returning to Accra, the King of Akwamu informed him that he was a prisoner. One can imagine the dismay of Mr. Simpson, who had been congratulating himself upon having brought a delicate mission to a successful termination, and now found himself in a position of great danger; for though some of the chiefs wished merely to detain him, others were in favour of sending him to Kumassi as a present to Kwoffi Kari-kari, and others again demanded his immediate death; and it was the arguments of these last that prevailed. Fortunately it was contrary to Ashanti policy at this time to take any action which might precipitate a quarrel with the English, they having not yet succeeded in crushing the Krepis, and the arrangements for the simultaneous invasion of the Protectorate from three sides not being yet perfected; consequently Adu Boffo strongly opposed and finally overruled the decision of the Akwamus. The Ashantis, he said, had at present no quarrel with the white men, and did not wish to create one. The time had not yet come, consequently Mr. Simpson must be allowed to depart, or the Akwamus be prepared to withstand the anger of Kwoffi Kari-kari. This argument, backed by the presence of five thousand men, had the desired effect, and Mr. Simpson was allowed to return to the coast.

The invasion of Krepi was now continued with renewed

vigour by the Ashantis, and in June, 1869, the German mission stations at Anum* and Ho† were destroyed. The inhabitants of the latter were warned in time and effected their escape; but at Anum, which is situated on some high ground about eight miles to the east of the Volta, the Ashantis captured four Europeans, namely, the missionary, Mr. F. A. Ramseyer, his wife and infant son, and Mr. J. Kühne, who managed the mercantile affairs of the mission. On the 9th, of June, early in the morning, these peaceable people were taken away from their home by the Ashanti leader of the party which had captured Anum, and roughly driven on all day under a burning sun, and past blazing villages whose heat increased their terrible sufferings, until sunset, when they were confined in a village for the night. Next day they were again driven onward, without food or water; and, after passing the scene of an engagement in which the Ashantis had evidently suffered heavily, for the ground was cumbered with mangled corpses, were finally halted at an encampment full of armed men, where they were placed in irons by order of Adu Boffo, and exposed to the taunts and insults of the whole camp. They remained here for three days, expecting instant death, which, indeed, they would have regarded as a happy release from their inconceivable sufferings; but on the 14th they were driven on to another village, and again fettered. They stayed at this place, subjected to every privation and indignity, till the 24th, when the Ashanti general decided to send his white prisoners to Kumassi, and on that day they started on their long journey. An escort of soldiers accompanied them, under the command of a brutal confidential slave of Adu Boffo, named Ageana, who did much to increase their miseries, for he drove them on pitilessly day after day under a blazing sun, with scarcely sufficient food to support life. Mrs. Ramseyer was nearly barefooted; all were footsore, weary, and starving; and the poor child

---

* Anum—five or fifth; proper name of a fifth son, who probably founded the town.

† Ho—Saturday.

deprived of its proper food and exposed to the sun by day and to the rain and cold by night, was dying by inches under the very eyes of its agonised parents. On July 30th they halted at the village of Totorassi, in Ashanti proper, where they remained for ten days, and buried the child, who here succumbed to its barbarous treatment. From Totorassi they were taken onward through the town of Djuabin to the village of Abankoro,* where they were detained for the remainder of the year. Here they were joined by Monsieur Bonnat, a French trader from Ho, who, confident that the Ashantis would not molest him, had foolishly remained there while the missionaries made their escape. He also had been treated with the greatest brutality by his captors.

The Local Government was much exercised as to what steps should be taken to obtain the release of these European prisoners, but while they were considering what they should do, the missionaries at Odumassi in Krobo acted, and persuaded the King of Krobo to intervene in their behalf. He was at first put off with excuses; but the tide of battle unexpectedly turned against the Ashantis, upon whom the indefatigable Dompreh in October inflicted a serious defeat; and this, and a rumour that the eastern tribes of the Protectorate were preparing to assist the Krepis, seriously alarmed the King of Akwamu. He dared not break with the Ashantis, who were his too near neighbours, and on the other hand he did not wish to find himself embroiled with the tribes of the Protectorate, whom he must pacify at any cost. Adu Boffo also found himself in a difficult position; for with Dompreh and the Krepis in front, an attack in flank by an army of Krobos, Akwapims, and Akims would have utterly destroyed him. Hence he, too, thought it advisable to do something to calm the tribes within the Protectorate; and as both he and the King of Akwamu believed that the excitement was due to their fears for the safety of the white captives, they sent to the King of Krobo hostages who would answer for

---

* Aban-koro—One fine house.

their lives, among them being a son of the Ashanti general himself. A report of the difficult position of Adu Boffo also reached Kumassi, and to keep the protected tribes from rising, Kwoffi Kari-kari sent messengers to the Government to express his readiness to exchange the missionaries for Ashanti prisoners. These messengers arrived on November 2nd, 1869, and the artifice succeeded; for the eastern tribes of the Protectorate, believing that the missionaries would now certainly be released, desisted from any further preparations for war, and sent Adu Boffo's son (Kwami Opoku) with the other hostages to Cape Coast for safe keeping.

In the western half of the Protectorate affairs still remained unsettled, and frequent skirmishes between the inhabitants of Cape Coast and Elmina kept alive the blood feud between these two peoples. At this time also the Colonial Government took alarm at the action of the Fanti Confederation. This Confederation had been originally composed of all the Kings of the British protected tribes from Wassaw to Winnebah, and its objects were to resist, by force of arms if necessary, the attempts of the Dutch to bring under their rule the peoples who had been transferred to them, and to combine for offence and defence in time of war. Later on, although the ostensible leaders of the Confederation were still the Kings of Arbra and Mankassim, the management fell into the hands of a few semi-educated natives and malattos, who engaged in it as a political speculation, by which they might gain money or power, or both. According to their scheme the Confederation was to be used to procure self-government for the Fantis, and they justified their action by the third resolution of the Committee of the House of Commons in 1865, which had laid down that the natives ought to be encouraged to exercise such qualities as might render it possible for the administration of the government to be transferred to them. Possibly, but for the resolution of the House of Commons the idea of self-government would never have occurred to the natives; but now that they declared their intention of making a step in that direction, the

Government cried out that they were endeavouring to usurp its functions. The policy, however, embodied in this and other resolutions had never been followed by the Local Government, with the solitary exception that fresh treaties had been avoided; and no attempt had ever been made to train the natives to self-government.

Indeed the policy of the Home Government with regard to the Gold Coast had undergone a great change; for though in 1865 it had been resolved that no more territory should be acquired, in 1868 they had taken over part of the Dutch possessions, and in 1869 a purchase of the remainder was talked of as probable. From this it was clear that Great Britain had abandoned the notion of withdrawing from the Gold Coast, and leaving the natives to govern themselves; but the latter had never been informed of this change, and so ought not to have been blamed for endeavouring to prepare themselves for the duties and responsibilities which they expected would soon be imposed on them. The Local Government, however, not only blamed them but treated them as quasi-rebels, for when the Fanti Confederation issued an appeal to all the natives so unite for self-government, the Administrator, Mr. H. T. Ussher, wrote: "Your conduct has been such that I can no longer have any relation with you. . . . As you voluntarily throw off your allegiance, you must not be surprised that I accept your act, and treat you, until you come to your senses, as apart from Great Britain. . . . In case of war with the Ashantis, you will bear the brunt thereof without help from the Government."

CHAPTER XXI.

1870—1872.

Condition of affairs—Negotiations for the transfer of the Dutch possessions—Ashanti claim to Elmina—Affairs in Krepi—Negotiations for the release of the Europeans—Alleged renunciation of the Ashanti claim to Elmina—Further negotiations.

AT the commencement of the year 1870, the following was the condition of affairs on the Gold Coast. There had been no peace with Ashanti since 1863, and the Ashantis were only awaiting a favourable opportunity for a fresh invasion of the Protectorate; but their plan for an attack in front and on both flanks being for the present frustrated by the unexpected reverses met with by Adu Boffo in Krepi, they were dissimulating to enable the latter to escape from his critical position. The King of Ashanti's uncle, Atjiempon, was actually in Elmina with a body of armed men, and an additional force of five thousand Ashantis was on the borders of Assini, waiting permission from the French authorities to pass through French territory and join him. In Appollonia there was war between the Wassaws and Bayin and the Atwaambus. There was also war between Cape Coast and Elmina; and in the east the Awunas had again joined the Ashantis and Akwamus, and stopped the navigation of the Volta. The Ashantis had four European prisoners in Kumassi, but the Colonial Government had in their keeping as hostages for them, a son of Adu Boffo, and some influential personages sent by the King of Akwamu.

It was while affairs were in this state of confusion that negotiations commenced for the transfer to the British of the Dutch possessions on the Gold Coast ; but the Government was determined not to take them over if the cession was likely to cause any disturbance among the natives, and instructions to report fully and carefully on this point were sent out to the local authorities. Now it was almost certain that the cession would give rise to fresh outbreaks, but the Dutch, as the correspondence between Sir Arthur Kennedy and Colonel Nagtglas shows, were most anxious to effect the transfer, and the local British officials were equally desirous of the change ; so that, between them, they persuaded Sir Arthur Kennedy, who had no great local knowledge, that the risks were merely nominal, and he consequently reported that the Dutch possessions could be taken over without danger. Sir Arthur Kennedy appears to have had some suspicion about Elmina, but Nagtglas assured him that if the Elminas were subsidised they would offer no opposition, and solemnly declared that the King of Ashanti had no treaty with Elmina, and no claim to its people or territory. These assurances, however, were directly at variance with the truth, for there was an alliance between Elmina and Ashanti, and the latter had some claim to Elmina territory ; but the British Government was satisfied with the report of the Governor and the negotiations for the transfer continued.

As the nature of the connection between Elmina and Ashanti became before long a question of the highest importance, it will perhaps be convenient to here see what it really was. The alliance between the two was an historical fact that could not be controverted. In 1811 an army had been sent from Kumassi to relieve Elmina, which was then besieged by the Fantis ; in 1817, Mr. James, the leader of the embassy sent to Kumassi, was instructed to request the King to prevent the Elminas, who were " presuming on their connection with the Ashantis," from attacking the people of Cape Coast ; and in the treaty of 1817 the King of Ashanti guaranteed the security of the people of Cape Coast from the hostilities threatened by the people of Elmina. During the peace negotiations in 1827, the Ashanti King declared that the Elminas, being his subjects, must be included in any treaty that might be made; in 1868, when Elmina was blockaded by the confederate tribes, the Elminas sent to claim assistance from Kumassi, and the ambassador was living in the Ashanti capital as the accredited agent of the Elminas, when the captive missionaries arrived there. That an Ashanti army was not sent on this occasion to raise the blockade of Elmina, was simply due to the representations made by the Dutch Governor. In the same year when Sir Arthur Kennedy endeavoured to persuade the Elminas to renounce their alliance with Ashanti, the chiefs in their official reply declared their intention of continuing "to pay tribute" to that power, whose protection and friendship they highly valued; and in 1869 Atjiempon was sent with an armed force to protect Elmina, and was still in the place in 1870. From all this it is evident that there had been at least an alliance between Elmina and Ashanti for more than half a century; and since Sir Arthur Kennedy must have been aware that it existed in 1868, it is difficult to conceive how he was persuaded to believe that in 1870 the connection had come to an end.

From the native point of view there was much more than an alliance between them, for by native law and custom the Elminas had become Ashanti subjects and Elmina an integral portion of the Ashanti kingdom; a fact which was universally recognised by the natives of the Gold Coast, and certainly had been by the Local Government in 1817, since they engaged the Ashanti King by treaty stipulations to restrain the Elminas. The Ashantis thus had some claim to the people of Elmina, and that they had a claim to at least a portion of its territory, the Dutch themselves had acknowledged by paying to them without demur, since 1702, the ground-rent for the Castle promised in the "note," which in that year passed into the hands of Ashanti. After paying ground-rent for one hundred and sixty-eight years, it was a little late to say that Ashanti had no claim to any of the territory of Elmina.

While the negotiations for the transfer of the Dutch possessions were still going on, it became known to the Imperial Government that the Ashanti, Atjiempon, was in Elmina with a body of Ashanti soldiers, and the Dutch Government was informed that the transfer could not be concluded until this chief and his men had left the territory about to be ceded. This took place towards the close of the year 1870, and about the same time the Administrator, Mr. Ussher, received a letter from King Kwoffi Kari-kari, written on November 24th, in which a direct claim to the town and castle of Elmina was advanced. The letter was as follows: "I beg to bring before your Excellency's kind consideration regarding the Elmina, if it is included in the change. The fort of that place have from time immemorial paid annual tribute to my ancestors to the present time by right of arms, when we conquered Intim Gackidi (Dakari), King of Denkera. Intim Gackidi, having purchased goods to the amount of £9,000 from the Dutch, and not paying for them before we conquered Intim Gackidi, the Dutch demanded of my father, Osai Tutu I., for the payment, who, Osai Tutu, paid it, the full £9,000, and the Dutch delivered Elmina to him as his own, and from that time tribute has been paid to us to this present time. I hope, therefore, your Excellency will not include Elmina in the change, for it is mine by right."

The King's version of the circumstances under which the "note" for Elmina Castle had been issued was not quite correct, but a long time had elapsed since it passed into Ashanti hands, and the actual facts might well become distorted by a people who had only oral tradition to rely upon. In any case the letter made a clear claim to the ownership of Elmina, and Mr. Ussher at once informed Colonel Nagtglas that the British Government "could not and would no purchase forts from the Netherlands Government which lay under the suspicion of being feudatory to a powerful native prince, the traditional enemy of its protected tribes." Colonel Nagtglas in reply reiterated his former denial of the Ashanti claims, and said that the twenty-five ounces of gold that had been paid annually by the Dutch West India Company to the King of Denkera was not a tribute, but a gift to promote trade, and had, on this understanding alone, been continued to Ashanti. Possibly Colonel Nagtglas had never heard that the sum was originally paid as ground-rent, for he did not allude to that point at all, and simply affirmed that neither the present King of Ashanti nor any of his ancestors had ever had any claim to the forts, territory, or people of Elmina. Notwithstanding this denial, the Government would not conclude the agreement till the Dutch had proved their title beyond doubt. It was pointed out to them that the presence of Atjiempon and his soldiers in Elmina supported, to some extent, the Ashanti claim, and, as a first step, their expulsion was demanded. After some delay, the Dutch, on April 14th, 1871, arrested Atjiempon, in order to prove their case, but released him in May, upon his taking an oath to return to Kumassi within twenty days; and, something further being still required to put an end to the hesitation of the British Government, they, in the same month, despatched to Kumassi a native in their employ named Plange, to endeavour to obtain from the King a withdrawal of the claim advanced in his letter to Mr. Ussher; for though the convention for the transfer of the Dutch forts had been signed at the Hague on February 25th, the ratification of the treaty was still delayed on this account.

It is from the narrative of the captive missionaries that we derive our information of Mr. Plange's doings in Kumassi, and it will therefore be convenient to return to them. We left them in the Ashanti village of Abankoro, and there they remained till the end of the year 1869, when they were removed to one of the villages of Kumassi, all the negotiations that had been carried on for their release having been unsuccessful.

In the autumn of 1870, however, exaggerated reports

reached Kumassi of an engagement which had taken place at Duffo Island, in the Volta, where a body of Ashantis and Akwamus, who had stopped the navigation of the river, had been defeated and driven away by a small detachment of the 2nd West India Regiment and a contingent of Accras; and Kwoffi Kari-kari, anxious for the safety of Adu Boffo, who with his army was still engaged with the Krepis, agreed to exchange the captive missionaries at Prahsu, on December 20th, for the hostages that were in the hands of the Government. These latter were accordingly sent to Prahsu in change of Major Brownell; but before they arrived there the King learned that Adu Boffo, so far from being in difficulties, had defeated and slain the gallant Dompreh, and shattered the Krepi army; and in consequence he refused to carry out the agreed-upon exchange. The missionaries were thus still in Kumassi when Mr. Plange arrived there in June, and they watched his proceedings with some interest. He declared to the King that if he did not withdraw his claim the annual payment of twenty-five ounces would be stopped; but Kwoffi Kari-kari said that his ancestors had paid nine hundred ounces for Elmina, and he would never abandon it; and on September 2nd Mr. Plange left Kumassi, having completely failed to obtain any renunciation from the King. Nevertheless, immediately on his return to Elmina, he produced a document which purported to be a withdrawal of the Ashanti claim, and which was as follows:

"CERTIFICATE OF APOLOGY.

"1. These are to certify that the letter addressed to his Excellency H. T. Ussher, the Administrator of her Britannic Majesty's Settlements on the Gold Coast, dated Kumassi, 24th November, 1870, by me, Kwoffi Kari-kari,[*] King of Ashanti, residing at Kumassi Kingdom, was totally misrepresented on the part of the parties intrusted with the writing and dictating.

[*] The orthography of this and other native names in this document has been altered to agree with that already adopted.

"2. I, therefore, do solemnly declare in the presence of your Excellency's Ambassador, Mr. H. Plange, profession writer of the Government Office at St. George d'Elmina, and my chiefs, that I only meant board wages or salary, and not tribute by right of arms from the Dutch Government.

"3. On account of circumstances relative to my ancestor, Osai Tutu the First, having conquered Intim Dakari, the then King of Denkera, a friend or a kind of commission, agent of some transactions for his Netherland Majesty's Government on the Gold Coast, to the amount of £9,000, my said ancestor was caused to make it good by the said Dutch Government; and in virtue of which the custom pay-note of the said Intim Dakari was transferred to my said ancestor, who enjoyed it in times immemorial, and became heritable to his heirs the King of Ashanti, who now hold the said custom pay-note in possession to this present moment.

"4. The said £9,000 was paid to insure friendship and goodwill or feeling towards the Dutch Government on the Gold Coast Settlement in Elmina Fort, castle or fort.

"5. Tradition tells us that Ashanti and Elmina are relatives; offspring of one mother; they are brethren; also, they are not to have hostilities against each other by oath of allegiance.

"6. In conclusion, I must acknowledge that the aforementioned letter, dated Kumassi, 24th November, 1870, about my commission to his Excellency H. T. Ussher, concerning Elmina Fort, is a vague, formal, or nominal expression, the sentiments of which I therefore must now write that the whole is a mistake.

"Signed in the presence of the ambassador and the chiefs, Kumassi, 19th August, 1871.

"KWOFFI KARI-KARI X (his mark),
"King of Ashanti.
"Reside at Kumassi Kingdom.
"H. PLANGE, Ambassador.
"Chiefs: TUSUASI POKU X (his mark).
"BUAKJI TINTIN X (his mark).
"TORNO NYCHWI X (his mark)."

Although this "Certificate of Apology" was acknowledged at Elmina by the King and chiefs of that town, and by Ansa, the Ashanti prince who had been delivered to Mr. Maclean as a hostage, and who had been living at Cape Coast since his return from England in 1841, there is no doubt that it was a forgery. It was in the handwriting of Mr. Plange, and the missionaries, whom the King always asked to read and translate any document before he affixed his mark to it, had never seen or even heard of this particular one. On the contrary, they believed and said that Plange had altogether failed to obtain any renunciation. It is scarcely to be supposed that the Dutch officials were privy to the fraud, but they had no doubt impressed upon their agent the absolute necessity for some such withdrawal of claim being obtained, and he had thought it to the advantage of his own interests not to disappoint them. We cannot even suppose that they had any suspicion of the genuineness of the certificate, which certainly deceived the Elmina chiefs, who had every interest in procuring its rejection. The Certificate of Apology was at once transmitted by Colonel Nagtglas to Mr. Salmon, who was now administering the government, Mr. Ussher having proceeded to England; and on the faith of it being genuine, the British Government concluded the agreement with the Dutch, the ratifications of the treaty being exchanged on February 17th, 1872. By it the Dutch ceded the whole of their possessions on the Gold Coast to the British, who paid £3,790 for certain stores that were in the forts.

While this matter was being transacted at a distance, the King of Ashanti had shown that he knew nothing of the existence of the "Certificate of Apology," by writing to Mr. Salmon to support certain claims made by the Elminas upon the Fantis; and to demand that some Elminas, who had been made prisoners by the Fantis, should be delivered to him. As this claim was utterly irreconcilable with the alleged renunciation, it ought to have aroused some suspicion of the true facts; but it seems to have failed to do so, and Mr. Salmon merely replied that the King must not interfere

T

in the affairs of the Protectorate, and that until peace was proclaimed between Great Britain and Ashanti the subjects of the latter would not be allowed to pass through the Protectorate. He added that, as a preliminary to peace, the European captives must be returned.

The King had, on a former occasion, said that he would exchange the missionaries for the hostages as soon as Adu Boffo came back from Krepi; but when the general returned he refused to allow them to be released except for a ransom of eight peredwins of gold—£6,480. A very stormy meeting was held, which the missionaries regarded as a farce played to amuse the Colonial Government; for in their opinion the council of chiefs, called the Kotoko,* which decides all matters of importance, had already determined to make war on the Protectorate. In fact, on February 20th, 1872, the King wrote to Mr. Salmon, saying: "I and my great chiefs have decided this: after the ransom is paid to Adu Boffo then peace between us shall be finally settled, and not before;" and his object really was to obtain the ransom without releasing the captives.

* Kotoko—porcupine; meaning that the council could not be molested without hurt.

CHAPTER XXII.

1872.

Transfer of the Dutch forts—Mr. Hennessey's policy—Riot at Elmina—Question of a ransom for the Europeans—Palaver in Kumassi—War decided upon—Various messages—The captives sent to Fomana—Despatch of an Ashanti army—Causes of the war.

ON April 2nd, 1872, Mr. Pope Hennessey, who had been sent out from England to effect the transfer of the Dutch forts, arrived on the Gold Coast; and in the instructions given him occur the following passages, which show the intentions of the Imperial Government at this time:

"The objects which Her Majesty's Government have throughout had in view in negotiating this treaty, are not the acquisition of territory or the extension of British power, but the maintenance of tranquillity and the promotion of peaceful commerce on the coast; and nothing could be further from their wish than that a treaty made with these objects should be carried into effect by violent measures. At the same time, they trust that by judicious and cautious management, the excitement which may possibly arise upon an event of so much importance as the retirement of the Dutch from the coast may not lead to any serious difficulties; and I need not say that they would greatly regret that arrangements which they believe are calculated to be of much benefit to the whole population, by putting an end to old feuds and difficulties, inseparable from the division of authority which has hitherto prevailed on the coast, should be frustrated by the jealousies of the native tribes.

"But you will on no account employ force to compel the natives to acquiesce in the transfer of the forts; and if you find that the attempt to assume possession of the forts on the part of the British authorities would probably be followed by resistance on the part of the surrounding native tribes, you will not accept the transfer of the forts, but will report the circumstances to Her Majesty's Government, and await further instructions."

On April 4th Mr. Hennessey held a palaver with the chiefs of Elmina, and on the 6th the transfer took place. The King of Elmina, and the chiefs of the districts under the other forts that were to be transferred, were asked in turn if there was any objection to the transfer, and each chief declared that there was none. A detachment of the 2nd West India Regiment was landed at Elmina to relieve the Dutch troops, and by April 10th, Sekondi, Dixcove, and Axim were garrisoned by men of the same corps.

On April 20th the Dutch Commissioner, Colonel de Haes, wrote to the Ashanti King, informing him of the transfer, sending some presents, and asking him to deliver the white captives to the English. Mr. Hennessey also wrote, announcing the transfer and sending some presents; but in addition he informed the King that, as a token of friendship, he had ordered the trade with Ashanti to be reopened, and the embargo on munitions of war, which had been maintained for some months, to be removed; and offered to pay double the sum that had been paid yearly by the Dutch for Elmina. He said nothing about the ransom of the European captives or the settlement of a peace; and, in fact, ignored all the matters in dispute, while he went out of his way to remove the prohibition upon the importation of munitions of war, and make war easier for the Ashantis. Nothing had conduced more to the maintenance of peace than this prohibition, for the Ashantis had expended vast quantities of ammunition in the war with Krepi; and, while the embargo remained, could only ob tain fresh supplies by the long and circuitous route through Assini. Although Mr. Hennessey was a total stranger to the Gold Coast and native affairs, he acted in this matter directly counter to the advice of the experienced officials; and, further, selected Mr. Plange to convey his letter and presents, although Mr. Salmon had strongly complained of that agent's behaviour when in Kumassi, where he had brought various local matters between the Elminas and Fantis before the King, who had in consequence made the demands already mentioned. Mr. Hennessey was, in fact, full of self-confidence; and Prince Ansa, who throughout these negotiations appears to have acted with the most perfect good faith, deplored, in a letter to the captive missionaries, that new-comers unacquainted with the country declined to take advice from experienced natives. He specially complained that, without reference to him, the way to the coast had been declared open to every Ashanti.

On April 22nd Mr. Hennessey left Elmina to visit the dependency of Lagos, but before leaving he contrived to do some further mischief by appointing, in defiance of the expressed opinion of the local officials, a native named Emissang to the position of Civil Commandant. All the important places on the Gold Coast always had European commandants, and it was well understood that natives were only appointed to the smaller towns; so that the Elminas regarded the appointment of Mr. Emissang as an indication that Elmina was to be reduced to a position very inferior to that which it had hitherto held, and were consequently much offended. In their eyes a white man was a very superior being to a native, and being of opinion that an important town like Elmina ought to have a superior commandant, they informed Mr. Hennessey that they would never accept one of their own colour for that office. As the Elminas had already suffered some loss of position by the departure of the Dutch Governor and staff, and had only just come under British rule, it was most important to avoid wounding their susceptibilities; but Mr. Hennessey persevered in his design, without paying the least attention to the advice of his officers or the protests of the natives. The result was that a riot took place on the 25th and 26th, which at one time assumed so serious an aspect that the garrison of the Castle was kept under arms to resist any attack that might be made by the large bodies of armed men that paraded in front of it; and the natives, in endeavouring to kill Mr. Emissang—who, however, escaped—so severely wounded Lieutenant De Joost, of the Dutch Navy, that he expired from his wounds next day.

On returning from Lagos, Mr. Hennessey received, through Prince Ansa, a communication from the King to the effect that the only matter now requiring settlement was the ransom of the missionaries. To this he replied, on June 4th, that he could not even speak of exchanging men for money, but at the same time he suggested that the Basel Mission, to which Messrs. Ramseyer and Kühne belonged, might very properly be asked to pay the actual expenses incurred by Adu Boffo on their behalf. Shortly after writing this, he actually released Adu Boffo's son, Kwami Opoku, the principal hostage for the white captives, and paid his expenses back to Kumassi; upon which the superintendent of the Basel Mission very properly said that it was unjust for the Governor to call upon the Mission to pay the ransom, while he himself was releasing the hostage free. However, after some negotiation, the Mission undertook to pay a sum not exceeding one thousand pounds, and Mr. Hennessey duly informed the King, saying that the money would be paid, and the captives received, at Prahsu. He now conceived that every outstanding difficulty was settled, and wrote home, on June 8th, that "the anticipation of hostilities with Ashanti no longer exists."

In Kumassi, however, affairs wore quite another aspect. Mr. Plange, who had left the coast with the letters and presents in April, did not arrive at the Ashanti capital till the beginning of July, being delayed by the difficulty in transporting along the narrow bush paths a large mirror, which was among the presents sent by the Dutch Government; and three or four weeks were allowed to elapse after his arrival before he was summoned to a palaver. This delay was in itself of sinister augury, and on July 29th, when Mr. Plange was at last sent for, the King, after having the letters read to him, broke up the meeting without having vouchsafed any reply. After this nothing more was again done for some weeks, during which appearances daily grew more warlike, powder, lead, and arms being brought into the capital in large quantities.

On September 2nd the Kotoko council met, and Mr. Plange and the missionaries were called before it. After some discussion about the amount of the ransom, the King suggested that it should be reduced from the sum originally asked to £2,000, to which, after a long argument, the chiefs agreed. Mr. Plange was then called upon to give his opinion, and, utterly unable to conceal his annoyance, said abruptly that the Government would not pay one farthing more than the £1,000 offered; and that if he returned to the coast without the missionaries, the roads would be immediately closed. The chiefs first laughed at this, then they murmured their dissatisfaction, and finally broke out into a storm of curses and threats.

"A few days ago," said the King, "I thought you were joking. If you are in earnest you may come. We are ready. Your Governor cannot leave his fort without an umbrella, so afraid is he of sun and rain. Let him try to come to us. For a long time the Ashantis have been going up to Fanti, and then the white men hid themselves in their forts; it would be something new if the Fantis were to come here."

This was spoken amid thundering applause. The chief of Bantama then shook his fist in Mr. Plange's face, and in the most insulting and offensive language threatened war; while the queen mother said:

"I am only a woman, but I would fight the Governor with my left hand."

"I am but a small chief," said another, "yet shall the Governor pale before me"; and several voices cried, "Whoever sells fixes the price. We had trouble enough to get these goods here; if the Governor will not buy them, he may leave them." At last there was a frantic and united cry of, "We will not give them up; let him fetch them with fire and sword, we will kill them"; while the King turned angrily to Plange, and said: "If you wish, I can show you my supply of powder." Only one man preserved silence during the uproar, the chief of Mampon, and to him Mr. Plange turned, asking him to pacify the council. The King thereupon exclaimed, "That is a good word, we will now break up"; for he felt he had gone too far, and in a moment of excitement had shown his hand. The preparations for war, a lengthy process involving many religious ceremonies, were not yet completed, and it would be folly to arouse the suspicions of the Government. The linguists, therefore, told Mr. Plange that he need not report to the Governor what he had just heard, and he actually did not report; but Mr. Kühne wrote, telling him that the chiefs had gained the upper hand and would gladly draw the King into another war.

A new cause of trouble now arose out of Mr. Hennessey's ill-judged action in reopening the trade with Ashanti. Some Ashantis returning to Kumassi with munitions of war had been stopped by the Assins, for all the protected tribes were fully aware that war was imminent; and the King demanded redress. In every direction preparations were made for war the King of Elmina sent his brother to Kumassi, asking for assistance; the chief of Kwantiabo sent to beg help for himself and chief Amiki of Appollonia against chief Blay; and the chiefs of Ashanti-Akim warned their relatives in Akim to be on their guard, as the King thought of making war on them. Everybody seemed to be aware of the critical condition of affairs except the Colonial Government. On October 22nd, the Kotoko council again had a meeting, at which it was decided to send a force to Appollonia to assist chief Amiki, and at the same time the chiefs, with the concurrence of the King, took an oath to march against the Protectorate.

In the meantime Mr. Pope Hennessey had left the Gold

Coast for Sierra Leone, and Mr. Salmon was once more administering the government. As Atjiempon, who had been removed by the Dutch to Half Assini, was found to be in Appollonia in October, fomenting strife between chief Blay and chief Amiki, and inciting the inhabitants of the old Dutch settlements to rebel against the British, Mr. Salmon ordered his arrest, which was effected unexpectedly by Colonel Foster, the Inspector-General of the Armed Constabulary, and Atjiempon was lodged in prison at Cape Coast. Soon after this a letter was received from the Ashanti King, accepting the offer of £1,000 as ransom for the captives, and asking that the money should be sent to Kumassi; but Mr. Salmon knew the Ashantis too well to trust them, and therefore replied that the money was lodged in the hands of Mr. Grant, a native merchant of Cape Coast, as agent for the King, and would be paid to his messengers as soon as the prisoners arrived at Cape Coast. The King on November 9th acknowledged the receipt of this letter, and said that he was sending the Europeans to Fomana, whence they would be sent on, when the money was paid to his messengers at Cape Coast.

By this time Colonel Harley had arrived on the Gold Coast and had relieved Mr. Salmon of the government, a most unfortunate change to have taken place at such a critical moment. On November 26th a legislative council was held to consider the King's last letter, and it being decided not to pay the money till the captives had arrived at Cape Coast, a letter to this effect was written and forwarded by a Mr. Dawson, a native interpreter. For some inscrutable reason it was decided at the same time to release Atjiempon, who, as the uncle of the King, might very properly have been made use of to effect the release of the Europeans. He left Cape Coast on December 12th with an escort of armed police, but was stopped at Da-man* by the Arbras, and again at Yan-Kumassi Assin by the Assins, neither of whom could understand why so important a

---

* Da-man—"Grave Town."

personage was allowed to return to Ashanti while the missionaries still remained unreleased; but on the representations of the Governor they suffered him to proceed, and on December 25th he crossed the Prah.

The course of events now compels us to return to Kumassi, where on November 8th the King gave audience to the missionaries and Mr. Plange; and, after telling them that he would accept £1,000 as a ransom, said they were to leave for Fomana next day. They expressed their gratitude, Mr. Plange thanking the King on his knees; and two days later they did quit the capital, but though they were hurried on as fast as possible, Mr. Ramseyer's illness prevented them from reaching Fomana before the evening of the 15th. From that place messengers were sent on to inform the Administrator of their arrival so far, and to receive the money; but a few days later some of Mr. Plange's people, who had been left behind to finish their preparations, joined them, and brought the news that everybody in Kumassi was preparing for a campaign. Since they had been in Fomana, the missionaries had noticed a continual stream of men passing through with loads of ammunition, rum, and salt; and they now understood that they had been sent there to induce the Government to pay the £1,000 whilst they still remained in the hands of the Ashantis, and also to keep them in ignorance of the preparations for war against the Protectorate, which had been decided on for months, but were only now made openly. On December 7th the two messengers, who had been sent to Cape Coast for the money, passed through Fomana on their way back to the capital, accompanied by Mr. Dawson. Next day some excitement was noticeable, and in the evening, when the captives were told that they were to go back to Kumassi, a mob plundered the missionaries of their property, and beat and fettered Mr. Plange, whom the Ashantis accused of having advised the Administrator not to pay the money till the captives were in his hands. On the 11th they commenced their return journey, and on the 14th reached Kumassi, which they found almost deserted and unusually quiet, for the Ashanti army had quitted it on the 9th.

In considering the causes which led to this new invasion of the Protectorate, the failure of the expedition of 1863 to recover the fugitive Djanin must not be lost sight of, for that was the remote and original cause, though later occurrences had somewhat forced it into the background. It was this unredressed grievance which had led to the plan of invasion from three sides in 1868, a plan which had failed from the unexpected opposition and losses experienced by Adu Boffo in Krepi, for one hundred and thirty-six important chiefs fell in that campaign, and of his army of 30,000 scarcely half returned to Kumassi. Owing to these prodigious losses the invasion of the Protectorate would no doubt have been postponed for some time had not the transfer of the Dutch forts to the British brought matters to a crisis, for the Ashantis fully believed that Elmina belonged to them, and they could not tamely submit to its surrender. The chiefs therefore determined on war, but owing to the great scarcity of gunpowder, lead, and salt, which could only be obtained from the sea-coast, they were compelled to resort to the various devices we have mentioned, to quiet the suspicions of the Colonial Government, and have the roads to the coast declared open. Thus they made no protest when the news of the transfer of Elmina was communicated to them, and the missionaries say that a hint was conveyed to the King of Elmina to accept the British flag and wait events. The game was continued till the removal of the embargo by Mr. Hennessey enabled them to complete their preparations; and then, at the last moment, when all was ready, the captives were sent to Fomana, with the double object of keeping them from seeing too much, and of endeavouring to obtain the amount offered for their ransom. The missionaries say: "Every one knew that this campaign was very different from that against Krepi. It was to decide once for all whether the Fantis were to be subject to the Ashantis, or the Ashantis to them."

It has often been charged as a crime against the King that he made no declaration of war before invading the Protectorate; but, without entering into the question of whether we can reasonably expect a barbarous power to observe the usages of civilised nations, the charge is in this case ill-founded, since the war of 1863 had never been terminated by any peace. It is also worthy of note that both in 1863 and in 1872 the Ashanti King had a fair *casus belli*; for in the former year the Colonial Government failed to comply with the terms of an agreement, of the existence of which there is presumptive proof, and in the latter it took possession of Elmina, which the King declared to be a part of his kingdom.

CHAPTER XXIII.

1873.

Invasion of the Protectorate—Helpless condition of the Government—Defeat of the Assins—Actions at Dunkwa—Break up of the allied force—Adu Boffo and Atjiempon—Distress of the Ashantis—Defeat at Jukwa—Arrival of Colonel Festing—Bombardment of Elmina—Action at Elmina—Condition of Cape Coast—Arrival of reinforcements—Unfortunate affair at Shamah—Cape Coast covered.

THE Ashanti army marched from Kumassi on December 9th, 1872, in three divisions, one of which was to march against Denkera, another against Akim, and the third against the despised Fantis. This last body, which was to advance down the road from Prahsu, consisted of but few troops, many a chief who had formerly commanded twenty or thirty men being now only followed by three or four, so heavy had been the losses in Krepi. The whole army was under the command of Amankwa Tia,* but Adu Boffo had charge of the division which was to operate on the west. Amankwa Tia's appointment was really against the law, which confided to him, as chief of Bantama, the defence of the capital; but he envied Adu Boffo the large numbers of slaves he had obtained in the campaign in Krepi, and had consequently intrigued for the command, the real general, Asamoa Kwanta, being still in retirement. His appointment, however, much offended the army, which despised him as an habitual drunkard; and complaints

* Amankwa Tia means Little, or Short, Amankwa.

against him were sent to Kumassi even before Mansu was reached.

On January 22nd, 1873, the invading army crossed the Prah at Prahsu and Attassi, losing some twenty or thirty men by drowning in the passage; and the Assins, who had been duly alarmed, after firing a few shots at those who crossed first, retreated to Faisowa. The news of the invasion first reached Colonel Harley from the King of Arbra, who wrote a letter saying that messengers had reached him from the King of Assin, bearing the head of an Ashanti, and bringing word that the Ashantis had crossed the Prah and taken possession of seven towns. The Legislative Council was at once assembled, and a proclamation issued and sent to the chiefs of Fanti by special messengers, while the Houssa police, fifty in number, were ordered to Dunkwa. The movement of these police was only, it was said, to be regarded as a demonstration in favour of the Protectorate; for they were not to fight unless attacked; and if attacked they were to fall back on Cape Coast. Colonel Harley urged upon the native chiefs the necessity of co-operation in this emergency, and the Kings of Arbra, Denkera, Assin, and Mankassim applied to him for assistance in arms and ammunition; but as he had only 381 flint muskets and 190 Enfield rifles available for issue, he was unable to do much. He reported the invasion to Mr. Pope Hennessey at Sierra Leone, and asked for a reinforcement from that place, there being only about 160 officers and men of the regular troops, all told, on the Gold Coast, and these scattered between posts one hundred and sixty miles apart; for the Government had been taken completely by surprise. He wrote: "I need scarcely convey the profound astonishment with which I have received these tidings, as nothing but the most amicable relations have existed between this Government and Ashant for some time; and assurances of lasting peace and goodwill have been sent down by the King ever since my assumption of the government." Mr. Hennessey, even after receiving this letter, still declined to believe in the hostility of Ashanti and the failure of his own policy, and wrote: "I do not believe that this is an Ashanti invasion, or the prelude to an Ashanti war." What else he conceived it to be he did not say.

On February 1st, 1873, information was received at Cape Coast that the Ashantis had advanced one day's journey from the Prah, the inhabitants flying before them; and from the report of an Assin scout it was conjectured that about 12,000 men had invaded the Protectorate. The Assins had mustered their forces at Yan-Kumassi-Assin, but it was evident that, unaided, they would be unable to stem the advance of the enemy. The King of Arbra also had collected a small force at Dunkwa, but none of the other Fanti chiefs had moved, notwithstanding every effort made on the part of the Government; and they openly said that they would fight the Ashantis when they came, but would not go to meet them. It was the old story of former invasions; namely, an entire absence of co-operation between native chiefs, by which the enemy would be able to destroy each tribe in succession. On February 9th the Ashantis advanced to Yan-Kumassi-Assin, where a battle took place, and the Assins, who were totally unsupported, were completely defeated.

Early in February Mr. Keate arrived at Sierra Leone from England as Governor-in-Chief, and, having relieved Mr. Pope Hennessey of his duties, at once proceeded to Cape Coast, where he arrived on March 7th, and on the 17th died of fever, another victim to the terrible climate. Mr. Keate held the opinion that wars in which the chiefs of the Protectorate might be engaged were matters in which the Colonial Government had no direct concern; and during his few days at Cape Coast he issued two or three notices to this effect, saying that the English could only defend their forts, and that the natives must look after themselves; which, of course, created a great deal of dissatisfaction. Mr. Keate seems to have formed this opinion from a despatch of the Secretary of State, in which the principle was laid down with respect to the chiefs of the Protectorate that "the wars in which they are engaged are their wars, and not the wars of Great Britain; that they must rely upon themselves for success in their wars and that the British Government is unable to make itself responsible for their defence in case they should prove themselves unable to defend themselves." In this case however, the war was due to the action of the Government in having taken possession of Elmina, and it was ridiculous to describe it as a purely native war, and cowardly to endeavour to shirk the responsibility of defending the protected tribes; but, as usual, the merits of the question were not in the least understood in England.

The King of Arbra had advanced with his small force from Dunkwa to Mansu, to which place the Assins had retired after their defeat; but on the nearer approach of the Ashantis the whole of the allies fell back to Yan-Kumassi Fanti. A volunteer company, which had been embodied at Cape Coast, was now sent to this place, and, together with a force of one hundred Houssas which had arrived from Lagos, was placed under the command of Lieutenant Hopkins, 2nd West India Regiment, who was instructed to act so as to give every *moral* aid to the Assins and Fantis and, if he should find himself in a position to do so, help them to drive back the enemy beyond Mansu. Later on, however, he was informed that his chief duty was to cover Cape Coast from any sudden attack, and he was enjoined to make no movement endangering his safe concentration on that town. The Fantis were now coming forward in some number, and an extensive camp was formed on the right and left of the road in advance of Yan-Kumassi Fanti.

On March 10th the allies marched from their camp to attack the enemy, but, after advancing about a mile, returned, saying they were unable to find them; and were then setting about preparing their morning meal when the Ashantis suddenly fell upon them. The contingent from Mankassim, under their chief, Adu, at once hastily retired, and thus enabled the Ashantis to get in rear of the Cape

Coast people, who thereupon retreated in great confusion, as did the Arbras. The Assins and Denkeras at first stood firm, but upon finding themselves deserted by the greater portion of the allies, also retreated. During this action the Houssa and volunteer force under Lieutenant Hopkins, consisting of some 350 men armed with Sniders, had not been engaged; and that officer, considering that his first duty was to cover Cape Coast, fell back upon that town when the allies retreated. Great complaint was made by the Fanti chiefs at the inaction of this force, and with reason, for the result of the battle might have been quite different had it taken part in it; but it was now sent back to Dunkwa, where the chiefs were ordered to assemble their men and make another stand.

By March 31st 25,000 men were assembled at Dunkwa, but nothing could induce the chiefs to attack, and every day they demanded three or four days' further delay. While they were still delaying, Amankwa Tia, who had now been joined by the division originally detached against Denkera, and had with him from 15,000 to 18,000 men, took the initiative, and about seven in the morning of April 8th, attacked the allied camp along its whole front, which extended for a length of six miles; but the allies contrived to hold their position at every point, and after five hours' fighting the Ashantis fell back. In this action the Houssas had some 17 killed and wounded, and the allies lost 221 killed and 643 wounded; an exceedingly insignificant loss considering the numbers engaged, and from which it may be inferred that the fighting was not very close. Next day Lieutenant Hopkins urged the chiefs to take the offensive, but they excused themselves on various pleas, and decided to await another attack from the enemy; who, however, astonished at the unexpected resistance they had met with, also remained quiet.

On April 13th great excitement was caused in the allied camp by a charge which was made against a Mr. G. Blankson of supplying the enemy with gunpowder and furnishing them with information. This Mr. Blankson, who was now a member of the Legislative Council of the Colony, was the same native merchant of Anamabo who, in 1865, in consequence of his friendly relations with Ashanti chiefs, had served as a channel of communication between Colonel Conran and the King, and the case against him looked suspicious. The chiefs demanded his arrest and imprisonment, and he was sent to Cape Coast, where it was decided that the investigation of the charges against him should be postponed till the war was over, with the result that they were never really investigated at all. It appears that the accusation was well-founded, for a letter from the King, dated March 12th, was found on him, and in Kumassi it was said that he had sent consignments of powder in bottles, so as to avoid detection.

On April 14th the Ashantis again attacked the allies along the whole line, and the action continued from eight in the morning till seven in the evening without any decisive result. The fighting principally took place in a deep and thickly-wooded valley, into which the Ashantis poured in swarms, the allies advancing to meet them over the cleared ground in front of their camp. A rocket battery in the centre of the position did excellent service, and but for the allied force, estimated at 56,000, would probably have been cut in two. Immense quantities of ammunition were expended, but with a most disproportionate result, for after eleven hours' fighting the loss was only trifling. At nightfall the chiefs announced their intention of sleeping on the ground they occupied and renewing the fight on the following morning; but next day they retreated *en masse*, declaring, with reference to Mr. Blankson, that they could not fight while there was treachery in their midst; but the truth was that they had had enough fighting. The retreat to Cape Coast was covered by the Houssas and volunteers. It afterwards transpired that the Ashantis had been so disheartened by the unexpected resistance they had met with that they also had commenced to retreat, and had destroyed much of their baggage, when the news was brought them that their foes were running away.

The break up of the allied army caused the greatest consternation, and an attack on Cape Coast and Elmina was considered imminent. It was found impossible to persuade the various chiefs to reunite their forces again, and measures were therefore adopted for the concentration of the men in their own districts, to prevent the country from being overrun by small bands of Ashanti plunderers. Some Houssas were sent to Anamabo to form a nucleus for a force from the neighbouring villages; the Assins, Arbras, and Akims collected at Assi-bo; and some minor chiefs promised to cover Elmina.

In the meantime the western division of the invading army, under Adu Boffo, had entered Wassaw, defeating the inhabitants in a great engagement, and on April 13th the entry of the Wassaw prisoners into Kumassi was witnessed by the missionaries. The men, who were tied together in gangs of ten or fifteen by ropes round the neck, and presented a pitiable spectacle, were followed by the women, young and old, some with infants on their backs, and others leading little children by the hand, who crouched in terror at their mothers' sides, and were threatened and struck by the cruel spectators. On the day after their arrival fourteen Wassaw men were sacrificed at Bantama to the *manes* of the former Kings of Ashanti. In the west, Atjiempon, who had been so unwisely released, had penetrated with a force of 3,000 men into Appollonia, where he was assisting chief Amiki against the faithful chief Blay; and the former Dutch subjects at Takoradi, Sekondi, and Shamah were only awaiting the approach of the Ashantis to rebel. The Elminas were also ripe for rebellion, and on March 12th the King refused to take the oath of allegiance to the British Government, saying that he had taken a "fetish" oath to oppose the English coming to Elmina; for which he was arrested and deported to Sierra Leone.

The main Ashanti army, instead of advancing on Cape Coast or Elmina, after the dispersion of the allies, had concentrated at Dunkwa, and prisoners captured by the Fanti scouts reported the camp to be in a most wretched condition.

Small-pox had broken out, provisions were scarce, and the camp was full of wounded, while its surroundings were foul in the extreme, and the air poisoned by the stench from dead bodies which lay scattered through the bush in all stages of decomposition. Small parties of Ashantis were discovered foraging for food at long distances from their camp, and several slaves deserted from it in the hope of getting food. As Colonel Harley wrote on May 15th, in any other country the position of the Ashanti force would have been very critical. They were a long way from their base of supplies, in a hostile country, with no provisions left, a swollen river in their rear, and the rainy season just commenced; yet the chiefs of the Protectorate would not take advantage of these favourable conditions.

About the middle of May the Ashantis broke up their camp at Dunkwa, and commenced to move in a westerly direction towards Jukwa, the capital of New Denkera. The Denkeras at once applied for assistance in arms and ammunition, and requested that the Arbras and Cape Coast people might be sent to Jukwa to assist in its defence but the King of Arbra refused to go on the ground that his own town, Arbrakampa, was threatened, and the chief of Anamabo advanced the same plea. The fact was that general dissatisfaction prevailed, for the native chiefs, with some reason, thought the assistance lent by the Government was inadequate, as did the traders, both native and European ; and the latter, moreover, charged Colonel Harley with concealing the critical condition of affairs from the Imperial Government. However, better counsels prevailed and by May 24th most of the Fanti chiefs had concentrated at Arbrakampa, and commenced to move to Jukwa, which town it was considered most important to hold. On the 3rd and 4th of June there was some desultory fighting around Jukwa, and on the 5th the Ashantis attacked it in force completely routing the Fantis and their allies, who scarcely offered any resistance. Kwasi Keh, King of Denkera, a unworthy successor of old Kwadjo Tchibbu, was one of the first to take to flight; and when the tribes who had come t his aid asked for him, he was nowhere to be found. The routed army and the inhabitants of the bush villages poured into Cape Coast, and all through the evening and night of June 5th the roads to it were crowded with fugitive men, women, and children. At daybreak on the 6th a rumour was circulated that the Ashantis were at the Sweet River, and the panic reached its height when the letter-carriers, sent from Cape Coast to Elmina, returned reporting the road stopped.

Affairs were in this condition when, on June 7th, H.M.S. *Barracouta* arrived at Cape Coast with a detachment of 110 marines, under Lieutenant-Colonel Festing, R.M.A., who had been sent from England on the receipt of Colonel Harley's despatches reporting the battle of April 14th and its results. It was now decided that martial law should be proclaimed in Elmina and the surrounding districts, and that the Elminas should be called upon to give up their arms; it having been proved beyond doubt that the inhabitants of what was called the "King's town" of Elmina were in daily communication with the Ashantis, and supplied them with provisions of all kinds. The River Beyah at Elmina runs for a short distance in a westerly direction nearly parallel with the sea, and on the sandy plain between it and the sea stood the King's town, which was thus situated in the old kingdom of Commani, while the mercantile quarter of Elmina, where the traders had their dwellings and stores, lay on the eastern side of the river, and consequently in Fetu.

The marines were marched over to Elmina from Cape Coast on June 12th, and by daybreak next morning the King's town was surrounded. A line of boats from the *Druid, Seagull, Argus,* and *Barracouta* was stationed in the river, to prevent any escape across it; the ships guarded the sea front; the Castle, garrisoned by marines, closed the eastern side; and a cordon of marines, Houssas, and soldiers of the 2nd West India Regiment was formed on the western side, in front of a dense thicket of prickly pear. Martial law was then proclaimed, and a proclamation issued requiring the surrender of arms within two hours; but though many armed men were seen in the town, and some of the chiefs came with excuses to gain time, no arms were given up; and at half-past ten a second proclamation had to be issued, granting one hour's respite for the removal of women and children, after which should the arms not have been surrendered, the town would be bombarded. At a little past noon, no submission having been made, the bombardment commenced from the Castle and the boats in the river, and in twenty minutes the town was completely destroyed. A number of armed Elmina succeeded in breaking through the cordon on the west and, assembling in the bush, where they were joined by some Ashantis, fired on the boats; but they were soon put to rout and chased along the beach, and about 3 p.m. the troops returned to the Castle. The enemy were supposed to have lost some thirty men; the British loss was one killed and three wounded.

At about 5 p.m. the boats of the squadron were on their way back to their ships, when a Dutch pensioner ran into the town and informed Mr. Von Hamel, the Dutch Vice-Consul, that the Ashantis were advancing towards the loyal quarter of Elmina across the grassy plain which lies to the north, their intention being to revenge the destruction of the King's town by that of the loyal quarter. The troops hastened out to meet the enemy, whom they found, to the number of some 3,000, advancing in good order in a long line, that was covered by a cloud of skirmishers. The Ashantis pressed on very boldly, and were beginning to outflank the small force, when an unexpected fire was opened on them in flank from the wall of the Government Garden by the seamen and marines of the *Barracouta*, whom Mr. Von Hamel had informed of the situation, just as they were pushing off in their boats from the beach. This fire was so destructive that the enemy, after a little hesitation, began to fall back; and an advance being ordered by Colonel Festing, a runing fight was continued across the plain; the Ashantis, however, retiring in good order till they reached the bush, into which they were not followed. The British loss was only one killed and four wounded, but the Ashantis left more than two hundred dead on the field, and this lesson was quite sufficient to prevent the renewal of any attempt upon the loyal quarter.

The Ashantis, who after their victory at Jukwa had moved to the south and encamped at Mampon and Effutu, now remained quiet for some time, but repeated alarms occurred in Cape Coast, the condition of which was most deplorable. The rains had set in with unusual severity, and the streets were crowded with fugitives who had no shelter, while the mud roofs of numbers of houses fell in, burying many people in the ruins. The natives dared not venture into the bush for provisions or fuel, and famine raged in the town, where hundreds of gaunt and emaciated wretches were encamped in the streets, under the flimsy shelter of a cotton cloth supported on sticks, shuddering in the incessant downpour. Night alarms were frequent, and the Ashantis were on several occasions reported to be rushing into the town. One night a party of them advanced to within three miles and burned a village, the glare of the flames of which was plainly seen, and the greatest terror prevailed, an immediate attack being expected. The Ashantis might have made an easy prize of the town had they been acquainted with its weakness, for the Government had made no preparations for its defence, and the merchants had been obliged to fortify their houses and arm their servants. The natives seemed to have abandoned all hope of defending themselves, and every time an alarm occurred there was a rush for the Castle. Universal panic and confusion reigned, and it is impossible to imagine a state of affairs more discreditable to a civilised Government.

The Ashantis at Mampon and Effutu were now much better off for food than they had been when encamped at Dunkwa, as they drew supplies regularly from the outlying villages of Elmina; but on the other hand they suffered severely from the rains, and small-pox and dysentery carried off many. The chiefs, too, were tired of the campaign, and dissatisfied with the general, Amankwa Tia, who was now rarely sober; so they brought pressure to bear on him, and compelled him early in July to send to Kumassi for permission to return, without which no Ashanti army may go back to the capital.

On July 6th the troopship *Himalaya* arrived at Cape Coast with 13 officers and 360 men of the 2nd West India Regiment, which had been ordered from the West Indies at the same time that Colonel Festing's detachment of marines had been sent from England. Every movement of the troops was at once known in the Ashanti camp, and the arrival of this reinforcement was made known to the enemy even before the men landed; but no information could be gained concerning the movements of the Ashantis, the native scouts being utterly worthless. Indeed, the majority of them never went near the enemy, but lay down in the bush all day and returned to Cape Coast in the evening with such information as they thought would best suit. In July and August reconnaissances were made to the northward of Elmina, and a redoubt was thrown up on the Sweet River at Napoleon, about five miles to the north-west of Cape Coast. From this point it was ascertained that the Ashantis were still at Mampon and Effutu, that a body of them held the village of Simeo, some miles in advance of the main body, and that it was from Simeo that they communicated with Elmina. In the meantime reinforcements had to be sent to Axim, Dixcove, and Sekondi, which were threatened by Adu Boffo and the natives who had joined him; while two of chief Blay's towns had been destroyed by Amiki and Atjiempon in Appollonia.

In consequence of a rumour that the Ashantis were trying to cross the Prah to the west, to effect a junction with Adu Boffo, Commodore Commerell, R.N., proceeded on August 13th to Sekondi, and next morning left that place with a number of armed boats to hold a palaver with the chiefs of Shamah, who, it was believed, were supplying the Ashantis with provisions. He was accompanied by Captain Helden, Civil Commandant of Sekondi, and Commander Luxmore of the *Argus*; and it was intended, if all went well, to ascend the Prah a short distance, and learn something of the nature of the river. At the palaver which took place the Shamah chiefs denied that they had rendered any assistance to the Ashantis. They expressed their intention of remaining neutral during the war, and, on learning that the commodore was going up the Prah, advised him to keep close to the right bank, or Shamah side of the river, for safety. The commodore unfortunately took their advice and fell into their trap, for he had not proceeded more than a mile and a half up the stream when, without warning and without a single native being seen, a volley was suddenly poured into the boats from the bush on the right bank, and he, Captain Helden, and Commander Luxmore were severely wounded. The boats put off into mid-stream, and the small-arm men opened fire; but so many of the seamen were disabled that they could not continue the engagement, and it was all they could do to get the boats out of the river. While this had been taking place up the river another affair had occurred on the beach in front of Shamah, where a party of ten Fanti policemen, who were being landed to garrison the deserted fort, were fired upon by the natives, one European sailor, two of the police, and a Kruman being killed. In these two unfortunate affairs four men were killed, and sixteen wounded, including four officers. On Commodore Commerell's return to his ship it was cleared for action, the town of Shamah was bombarded, and in about two hours completely destroyed.

Towards the end of August a second redoubt was completed at Abbeh*, in the Sirwi valley, and garrisoned by fifty men of the 2nd West India Regiment; the volunteer company, composed of native clerks and shopkeepers from

---

* Abbeh—Palms.

Cape Coast, having, with one or two honourable exceptions, shown itself quite unworthy of trust. Cape Coast being now covered from attack on the north-west, the labourers who had been employed in the construction of the redoubts were removed to Akrufu, to improve the road between that place and Cape Coast, and a detachment of fifty men of the 2nd West India Regiment was posted there for their protection.

CHAPTER XXIV.

1873.

Arrival of Sir Garnet Wolseley—Captain Glover's command—Sir Garnet's instructions—Palaver at Cape Coast—Expedition to the Elmina villages—The Ashantis break up their camps—Reconnaissances from Dunkwa—Defence of Arbrakampa—Amankwa Tia's retreat—Skirmish at Faisowa—Return of the army to Kumassi.

THE Ashantis were still quietly encamped at Mampon and Effutu, awaiting the long asked for permission to return to Kumassi, when, on October 2nd, Major-General Sir Garnet Wolseley arrived at Cape Coast. In spite of the efforts made by the local authorities to minimise the serious state of affairs, the Imperial Government had at length gained some inkling of the true facts, and a policy more worthy of a great nation than that which had hitherto been pursued was now to be inaugurated. Sir Garnet Wolseley had instructions to take the civil and military command upon the Gold Coast, to organise a native army, to drive the Ashantis out of the Protectorate, and, should he deem it necessary, to march to Kumassi. Two British regiments were held in readiness, but it was hoped he might be able to defeat the enemy, and establish an enduring peace, without requiring their aid.

While Sir Garnet Wolseley was thus to clear the Protectorate of the enemy and establish a lasting peace, Captain Glover, R.N., the Administrator of Lagos, was to operate against them from the Volta with a native force, and make a diversion in favour of the Protectorate by threatening the rear of the Ashanti army. Captain Glover's dealings were to be confined to the eastern tribes of the Protectorate, and the Houssa police, increased to a thousand strong, was to form the nucleus of his force. He had thus, supposing no European troops were sent out, by far the best of the arrangement, for the eastern tribes were the only ones who, from a military point of view, were worth anything. When Sir Garnet Wolseley, arrived at Cape Coast, the whole of the Houssas had, under this plan, already been sent to Captain Glover at Accra, so that the disciplined force he found at his disposal consisted only of the 2nd West India Regiment and a small body of Fanti police; and as the former was garrisoning Axim, Dixcove, and Sekondi, the entire force available for the defence of Elmina, Cape Coast, and the outposts was less than 400 men. It was under these unsatisfactory conditions that he commenced his administration, and the superiority of Captain Glover's position was so generally admitted, that it was expected by everybody that he would be in Kumassi long before the General could cross the Prah.

In Sir Garnet Wolseley's instructions he was directed to summon the Ashanti King to withdraw his forces, and to threaten, in the event of non-compliance, that he would be compelled to; but if he withdrew his army, negotiations for a treaty of peace might be commenced forthwith. The notion that the Ashanti King might be influenced by threats, showed how little the authorities in England understood the situation. At this time the natives of the Gold Coast had no idea that Great Britain was a military power, and an army of white men would have appeared to them impossible; for in their eyes all white men were chiefs, men of rank, who rode in hammocks and ruled the blacks. Consequently threats would have appeared ridiculous to the King, since he would have believed that they could only be backed up by the native levies, and these his troops had already defeated in three general engagements. The manifesto, however, summoning him to withdraw his army, never reached the King, it being taken by Amankwa Tia, who replied by a counter manifesto, to the effect that the King had no quarrel with the white men, and that they could have peace by surrendering Denkera, Wassaw, Assin, and Akim to Ashanti.

On October 4th, Sir Garnet Wolseley held a palaver with the Kings and chiefs of the Protectorate, at which the old fallacy that the war was not an English war, but a native war, was repeated, and the chiefs were informed that they would receive no assistance unless they were prepared to help themselves; but if they united to fight the Ashantis, the General promised to drive the enemy out of the Protectorate, and to inflict such a punishment upon them that they would never again return. The chiefs were promised ten pounds a month for every thousand fighting men furnished by them, and the men themselves would receive sevenpence halfpenny per diem if they were warriors, and one shilling per diem if they were employed as carriers. The chiefs reserved their reply till the 6th, and when they reassembled it was evident that they were not at all eager for war. The fact was they knew the invasion was at an end, and that the Ashanti army was about to return to its own country; and they thought it better to allow it to go away unmolested, than to engage in fresh operations which might only have the effect of making it stay longer. They were also profoundly dissatisfied with the conduct of Colonel Harley, who had not supported them with such regular troops as he had at hand, and who, by not bringing the Accras and other eastern tribes to the assistance of the western, had allowed the latter to be defeated in detail. The rates of pay offered to fighting men and carriers also gave dissatisfaction. From their point of view it was unjust that the men who would have to incur the risks of war should only receive sevenpence halfpenny a day, while those who would be engaged in the comparatively safe duties of the commissariat should receive one shilling. However, not daring to express their real feelings, they said they were willing to accept the terms offered, and ready to proceed at once and collect their men, all, probably, secretly intending to do nothing at all as soon as they had got clear of Cape Coast. A number of officers were sent to the bush with the different Kings and chiefs; and, as it was intended to raise, if possible, some native irregular regiments, other officers were sent along the coast between the Gambia and the Niger. These efforts did not meet with much success, and in the end, all that were obtained were a few men from Sierra Leone, 120 Kossus from the Sherbro, 100 men from the Gambia, and 53 Opobos and 104 Bonnys from the Niger Delta.

In October the Ashantis were still in their camps about Mampon and Effutu, where small-pox and dysentery were very prevalent, but they had now received permission to return to Kumassi, and were preparing food for the march. They drew their supplies from the outlying villages of Elmina, chiefly from Ampeni and Amkwana, the line of communication lying through Essaman; and in order to put a stop to this traffic the headmen of these villages were summoned to Elmina. Instead of coming, they sent insulting messages, being confident that the white men would not dare to advance into the bush, and the destruction of their villages was consequently determined on. As Cape Coast and Elmina were said to be full of Ashanti spies, the expedition was kept secret, and a mixed force of marines, Houssas, and West India soldiers, amounting in the aggregate to some 500 men,* was landed unexpectedly at Elmina on October 14th. A short distance from Essaman the force was attacked, but after a slight skirmish the natives were routed and the village burned; and the column then marched for Amkwana, which it reached after midday. This village was found deserted, and was also burned; but the marines and seamen were now so thoroughly exhausted that they could go no further, and the West Indians and Houssas alone continued the march to Akimfu and Ampeni, both of

* The actual composition of this force was 149 marines, 205 2nd West India Regiment, 126 Houssas, and 29 seamen, with 1 rocket-tube, and 1 7lb. gun.

which they destroyed. The troops had that day marched twenty-one miles, and the moral effect of this proof of ability to cope with the natives in the bush was excellent; but it had been purchased at some loss, as Colonel McNeil, the chief of the staff, was seriously wounded, and had ultimately to be sent to England, and two other officers were also wounded.

It was now evident that the Kings and chiefs either could not or would not induce their men to turn out, for out of the whole of the tribes of Fanti, Assin, and Denkera, only a sufficient force was forthcoming to form, in conjunction with the men brought from other parts of West Africa, two native regiments and an irregular contingent of some 1,500 men; and Sir Garnet Wolseley, therefore, wrote home to urge the despatch of two British regiments, without which nothing could be done. One of the newly-formed native regiments was placed under the command of Lieutenant-Colonel H. E. Wood, and the other under Major B. C. Russell; they were called Wood's and Russell's Regiments, and about half the strength of each consisted of natives of the Protectorate.

About the middle of October the Ashantis broke up their camps at Mampon and Effutu, and commenced to move in their usual leisurely manner towards the main road to the Prah; one body moving from Mampon through Jukwa, Ainsa, and Assanchi, to strike the main road at Dunkwa, and another through Effutu and Ahonton, to strike the main road at Akrufu.* By this time the main road had been occupied as far as Dunkwa, where Colonel Festing was in command with 50 2nd West India Regiment, and about 1,000 natives; and strong posts existed at Akrufu and Arbrakampa. The column which moved by the Jukwa-Assanchi road, with which were the sick and prisoners, marched on October 16th, and the commander, on finding the road closed by the British occupation of Dunkwa, halted and encamped at Iscabio, a village some three miles to the west of Dunkwa. On October 25th the remainder of the

* Akrufu—Village folk.

Ashanti army, under Amankwa Tia, left Effutu, moving slowly along the road towards Arbrakampa, and it was commonly supposed that he intended to strike the main road at Akrufu, and so retire to the Prah; but the Fantis asserted that he had sworn the King's oath to destroy Arbrakampa, on account of the resistance which had been offered by the Arbras during the early part of the campaign. According to the Ashantis, both of these notions were incorrect. Their version is that the whole army was intended to move *viâ* Jukwa and Assanchi to Dunkwa, which was the shortest and best route; but when the commander of the leading column reported that the exit of this road was closed by the British at Dunkwa, Amankwa Tia determined to attack one of the posts lower down the road, in the expectation that the force at Dunkwa, afraid of being cut off, would retire and leave the road open. It is perhaps needless to say that all this was discovered after the war, for in October, 1873, nobody knew for certain what the Ashantis were doing.

It being reported at Cape Coast that the Ashantis were at Assanchi and Iscabio, Colonel Festing received orders to march his force along the road to the latter place, and find out what he could regarding the enemy's movements. On October 27th he accordingly marched out with 13 officers and 701 men, 73 of whom were West Indians, and advancing undetected during a drenching thunderstorm, succeeded in surprising a camp on the summit of a hill about a mile from Iscabio. The enemy, who were completely taken by surprise, were at first thrown into some confusion but they soon recovered themselves and opened a heavy fire from the bush, to which the West Indians replied with spirit; but the native levies had to be thrashed into action and numbers of them disappeared altogether. After an hour and a half the force was marched back to Dunkwa having burned a portion of the camp; but the enemy had not abandoned their position. Next day Sir Garnet Wolseley advanced, with a force which he had collected at Arbrakampa, to Assanchi, hoping that Colonel Festing of whose affair of the previous day he was ignorant, would advance from Dunkwa, and that the Ashantis in and around Iscabio might thus be attacked in front and in rear. But Colonel Festing was unable to move because the native levies absolutely refused to turn out; and Sir Garnet, finding no enemy at Assanchi, rested his men a couple of hours, and then returned to Arbrakampa. On this day Amankwa Tia was actually moving along the road from Effutu towards Arbrakampa, and might, had he known of the Major-General's movement, have taken him in flank.

On November 3rd Colonel Festing made a second reconnaissance in the direction of Iscabio, with a force of eighty men of the 2nd West India Regiment and about one thousand natives. This time the Ashantis were not surprised, and made a stubborn resistance, while the native levies behaved even worse than usual. Whole tribes deserted and rushed pell-mell into Dunkwa, and even beyond it; and but for the staunch behaviour of the West Indians, who stood their ground well and engaged the Ashantis for two hours, there would have been a serious disaster. Lieutenant Eardley Wilmot, R.A., was severely wounded early in the action, but would not fall to the rear, and about an hour later was shot through the heart. Colonel Festing brought in his body from where it was lying in the extreme front of the action, and after two hours' fighting, withdrew his men to Dunkwa. No appreciable impression had been made upon the enemy, while out of nine officers who had gone into action, one had been killed and five wounded.

On the afternoon of November 5th Amankwa Tia, in accordance with his alleged plan for clearing the road at Dunkwa, attacked Arbrakampa, which had been put in a thorough state of defence, and was garrisoned by 60 of the Naval Brigade, under Lieutenant Wells, a small party of West Indians, 100 Houssas, 200 of Russell's Regiment, and about 500 native allies. The attack commenced about 4 p.m. to the west of the village, by the Ashantis driving in the picquets and firing upon the advanced skirmishers. They then lined the bush and kept up a hot fire until 5 p.m., when a most furious attack was made on the west and south-west of the village, the Ashantis suddenly rushing out into the open, but being driven back by the West Indians and Houssas, who lined the shelter trenches on that side. After this an incessant fire was kept up with great violence for about two hours, when it slackened, but was again repeated and continued till midnight, after which occasional shots only were fired, and at 4 a.m. on the 6th these ceased. At 11 a.m., however, the Ashantis again attacked the village, on three sides at once, but they did not show the same spirit as on the previous afternoon, and never came beyond the edge of the bush, whence they kept up a continuous fusillade, which only ceased at dusk. At sunset a reinforcement of 141 seamen and marines arrived, who had been landed at Cape Coast the previous evening, when the news of the attack on Arbrakampa reached there. A total force of 22 officers and 303 men had been put ashore from the men-of-war, and had marched from Cape Coast that morning; but owing to their not being supplied with helmets or any covering to protect the head from the sun, only the number above-mentioned succeeded in reaching Arbrakampa, more than ten per cent. of the whole force failing even to reach Assibo,* less than ten miles from Cape Coast.

It was fully expected that the Ashantis would renew the attack next day, but the morning passed without anything being seen of the enemy, and at 2 p.m. Colonel Wood was sent out with about one thousand natives, who had arrived with him from Cape Coast, to endeavour to ascertain their position and intention. The natives advanced to the edge of the bush, but when ordered to enter it and search for the enemy, lay down on the ground and refused to stir. The Kossus, however, went in and presently returned with two or three heads, which they had obtained from the bodies of Ashantis who had been killed in the fighting of the previous day. When the Arbras saw that the Kossus were not fired upon, they suspected the truth, namely, that the Ashanti army

* Assi-bo—" Under the rock."

had already decamped; and they at once rushed in search of plunder down the road towards Anasmadi, where they came upon a small bivouac, with a few Ashantis who had been left to clear out the remaining baggage. These were soon driven off, and a number of Fanti prisoners, who had been kept back to carry the baggage, were released. Among these was a young woman whose throat her master, seeing that he would not be able to carry her off, was actually in the act of cutting, when he was shot by the Arbras; and she was brought into Arbrakampa with a broad cut on her neck, from which the blood was still flowing. The loss suffered by the garrison of Arbrakampa during the attack was very trifling. One officer and one private of the 2nd West India Regiment were slightly wounded, one seaman severely, and about sixteen natives slightly. This small loss was partly due to the garrison having acted purely on the defensive and being under cover, but chiefly to the fact that, as the bush had been cleared for some distance round the village, and the Ashantis would not leave its cover, the range was too great for their muskets. An escaped prisoner said that the Ashantis complained that the defenders shot at them through holes in the houses, and that when they fired back they only struck the houses.

On withdrawing from before Arbrakampa the Ashantis proceeded to the north-west, to Ainsa and Assanchi, and thence to Iscabio; where Amankwa Tia, instead of finding, as he had hoped, that the garrison of Dunkwa had marched to the assistance of Arbrakampa, learned that the road to the Prah was not only still closed at Dunkwa, but that posts had been established as far as Mansu. He accordingly ordered paths to be cut through the bush, parallel with the main road, and some three or four miles to the west of it; but this was a work that required several days to complete, and it would then take some time to pass the army, encumbered with sick, wounded, and prisoners, and a large quantity of baggage, along it. Hence, when on the 8th the native levies were ordered out to follow up the retreating Ashantis, they came up with them, with the result that ought to have been foreseen, for the rear is the post of honour in an Ashanti army, and the best troops are placed there. The Ashantis were first felt at Ainsa, where they turned upon their pursuers, and the levies were ordered to retire ; but they were followed up so closely by the Ashantis, who began to surround them, that they were seized with a sudden panic, and, rushing headlong down the path, knocked down a party of Houssas who were in the way. The stampede was continued till Arbrakampa was reached, where the bulk of the men quietly disbanded themselves and returned to Cape Coast. Fifty of their number were said to have been killed in this affair, which was called by the natives "a sacrifice to Amankwa Tia," and was considered by them to quite compensate him for his failure at Arbrakampa.

After this, touch of the enemy was lost completely until, on November 16th, a small party of Ashantis fired upon Surgeon-Major Gore between Dunkwa and Mansu, killing one of his escort, and wounding him and four others. It was then supposed that Amankwa Tia intended to strike into the main road at Adda Warra, a mile and a half north of Mansu, where a road branches off in a south-westerly direction; and the garrison of Mansu was increased, and the native allies echeloned along the road for some miles north and south of that post. However, reconnaissances made from Mansu on November 20th and 21st, established the fact that the Ashantis had already passed to the north of it, and on the 25th it was ascertained that Amankwa Tia, with the bulk of the army, was at Sutah, a village on the main road. The army had, it appeared, moved through the bush to the west of Mansu in three columns, marching at the rate of four o five miles a day ; and the column nearest the main road, with which was Amankwa Tia, had debouched upon the main road at Sutah on the night of the 24th. The centre column struck the road at Faisowa, the third still farther to the north and the whole retreat had been conducted in a manner tha would be creditable to a civilised power.

On the 26th, Colonel Wood, who now had charge of th

advance, moved his force, some 1,100 strong,* to Sutah, which was found deserted, though fires were still burning in a camp in its neighbourhood ; and later on in the day a party which was sent to reconnoitre along the road saw fires lighted near Faisowa. Next morning Colonel Wood received orders to harass the enemy in his retreat, and he accordingly marched out towards Faisowa, with 23 West Indians, 93 Houssas, 104 Kossus, and 53 natives, the Elmina Company of Wood's Regiment. About noon they reached Adubiassi, where an Ashanti prisoner advised Colonel Wood not to continue his march, as Amankwa Tia and other chiefs were at Faisowa, and, it being an Adae day, they would not retire. South of Faisowa the Ashantis opened fire, and, upon the Houssas and Kossus being extended through the bush, retired across the open ground at Faisowa into the bush beyond. The Elminas and Kossus were then sent in after them, but the enemy's fire soon increased, and Colonel Wood, finding his force was being outflanked, ordered the Elminas and Kossus to retire through the Houssas. The retreat was carried on in an orderly manner till a sudden panic seized the Houssas, who rushed in upon the Kossus, who in their turn ran into a company of Wood's Regiment which, in defiance of orders, was coming up, each man with his bundle on his head. The men, crowded up in the narrow path, became an unruly mob, and when the Ashantis, who were pressing on closely, fired a few shots, the disorder became complete, and the whole party took to their heels. A considerable quantity of baggage was lost as well as a box of ammunition, and the flight was only stopped at Adubiassi, where Colonel Wood was joined by seventy-seven West Indians.

The Ashantis now continued their retreat without further molestation, and crossed the Prah at Prahsu, Attassi, and Kohea. The greater portion of the army crossed in canoes,

* This force was composed as follows : 134 2nd West India Regiment, 93 Houssas, 207 Wood's Regiment, 110 Kossus, and 620 native allies.

of which they had thirteen; but the river was much swollen, and to expedite the passage an attempt was made to bridge it by felling on each bank an enormous silk-cotton tree, in the hope that their branches would interlace in mid-stream and form a kind of bridge. The trees however did not quite meet, and many men who tried to pass the chasm were swept away by the current and drowned.

On December 22nd the army re-entered Kumassi, having lost about half its number, for the captive missionaries estimated that 40,000 men had marched to the coast, of whom only 20,000 returned. These enormous losses must be attributed to the epidemics of small-pox and dysentery which had devastated the Ashanti camps, for their losses in action were comparatively small, and, judging from those suffered by the natives of the Protectorate in the early part of the war, probably did not exceed 3,000 men. The capital was filled with lamentation when the army returned, and nearly every one appeared painted red, the sign of mourning. Two hundred and eighty chiefs had fallen in battle or succumbed to disease; and captains who went out in command of twenty men returned alone with their baggage on their heads.

The affair at Faisowa had so terrified the scouts that they could not be induced to advance, and the whole Ashanti army had crossed the Prah before any news was brought to Colonel Wood which would justify a fresh move beyond Sutah. The first reliable information was furnished by two soldiers of the 2nd West India Regiment, who, having volunteered to go on to the Prah and reconnoitre, came back and announced that all was clear to the river, on the bank of which they had posted their names on a tree. Colonel Wood's force now pushed on, and found the road and the bush on each side of it strewn with dead and dying Ashantis, the victims of small-pox and dysentery. At Prahsu sixteen dead bodies were seen, and as the river went down, other corpses were found caught in the branches of the trees with which the Ashantis had tried to bridge the stream. Now that the enemy had withdrawn, the camp at Mampon was examined. It was nearly a mile square, cleared and covered with huts; and the whole area was so dotted with graves, skulls, and human bones, that thousands of men must have perished of disease while they were here encamped.

This closed the first phase of the war, so far as the main army under Amankwa Tia was concerned, and in England it was not properly appreciated. No European regiments with well-known names had been employed, and the public thought little of operations in which only a West India Regiment and a few marines and sailors had been employed; but it may unhesitatingly be said that the difficulties subsequently experienced north of the Prah were as nothing in comparison with those that had already been met and overcome.

CHAPTER XXV.

1873—1874.

Affairs in the West—Arrival of the European troops—Difficulties with the commissariat—The plan of operations—Captain Glover's proceedings — His trans-Volta campaign — Ultimatum sent to the King — Alarm in Kumassi — Release of the Europeans — Further correspondence with the King—Movements of the auxiliary columns.

WHILE the events narrated in the last chapter had been taking place in the centre of the Protectorate, chief Blay had in Appollonia still been fighting chief Amiki and the Ashantis; and as the whole of Ahanta, except Dixcove, had joined the enemy, Axim, Appoassi, Aboadi, and Takoradi had been bombarded by the ships of war. At the last-named place a detachment had been landed in August to destroy some canoes, and three officers and twelve seamen of the *Argus* had been wounded. Chief Amiki's town in Appollonia had been bombarded in September, and constant skirmishing had continued near the forts till the close of the year, when the Ashantis withdrew.

A little affair was now undertaken for the punishment of the people of Shamah, who, since the bombardment of their town, had been living in the bush villages a few miles inland. The Kommendas, whose town had been destroyed by the Elminas and Shamahs early in the war, and who had been taken off in ships to Cape Coast for safety, had now returned home, and they were directed to attack the Shamahs. The *Active*, *Encounter*, and *Merlin* sailed for the mouth of the Prah, and on the morning of December 24th about 700 Kommendas, who appeared on the left bank of the river, were taken across in the boats. They set fire to the ruins of Shamah, and had a slight skirmish with the enemy; but next day they asked to be ferried back to the safe side of the river, declaring that they had neither food nor ammunition left, and when this was done they at once returned to their homes, so that the expedition effected nothing of importance.

On December 9th H.M.S. *Himalaya* arrived at Cape Coast with the 2nd Battalion of the Rifle Brigade, and on the 11th H.M.S. *Tamar*, with the 23rd Fusiliers; while on the 17th the hired transport *Sarmatian* also arrived with the 42nd Highlanders, which regiment had been sent out in compliance with a request made by Sir G. Wolseley for a third European battalion. These troops arrived either too late or too soon; they were too late to take part in the operations south of the Prah, and too early for those which were to be undertaken north of that river; for it was imperatively necesssary, having in view the deadly nature of the climate, that the Europeans should not be landed until all was ready for a forward movement. At present this was far from being the case, for, in spite of every effort, the road to Prahsu had not yet been made suitable for the passage of troops, and the eight camps, which it had been decided to make for the accommodation of the troops during the march from Cape Coast to Prahsu, had not yet been formed; but it was hoped that all would be ready by the first week in January, and the transports were accordingly ordered to sea till the end of the year.

Great difficulties were now experienced in the transport of supplies and munitions of war, for the carriers deserted by thousands. This was chiefly due to the faulty arrangements of the commissariat officers, who, instead of forming the men into gangs under their own chiefs and headmen, mixed natives from all parts of the Protectorate indiscriminately, and then selected for the charge of parties men who could speak a little English, who generally were not natives of the Gold Coast, and in no case had any authority over those they were supposed to control. There was no one to attend to the complaints of the carriers, who were not paid with regularity, or fed, and it is certain that hundreds deserted through hunger. The ordinary plan of giving subsistence money to carriers in lieu of rations answers well enough in ordinary times, provided that the number is not large, in which case the villages cannot supply the food required; but it was absurd to adhere to it now when thousands of men were concerned, and provisions were unusually scarce through the destruction of the plantations by the Ashantis. Large numbers deserted from this cause alone, and in addition the men were often overworked; for there was no general system and men were directed to take loads without any inquiry being made as to whence they had come or what was to become of them after the loads were delivered. There became such an absolute dead-lock, that the whole of the native levies had to be disarmed and turned into carriers; but it was not until the transport was taken from the commissariat and placed under Colonel Colley and a body of combatant officers, that any real improvement was effected.

The plan of campaign now was to invade Ashanti territory on January 15th, 1874, from as many points as possible. The main body, consisting of the three European battalions, the Naval Brigade and Wood's and Russell's Regiments, was to advance from Prahsu directly upon Kumassi; while, on the extreme right, Captain Glover's force was to move from the Volta upon Djuabin. Between these two, a column composed of Western Akims, under Captain Butler, 69th Regiment, was to enter Ashanti-Akim; and on the extreme left, a diversion was to be created by a column of Wassaws, Denkeras, and Kommendas under Captain Dalrymple, 88th Regiment. During the advance of the main body, the 1st and 2nd West India Regiments, the former of which had arrived from the West Indies on December 27th, were to guard the line of communication.

In the meantime various occurrences had taken place in

the eastern districts in connection with the force that Captain Glover had to raise. In September he interviewed the principal chiefs, and successfully defeated an attempt made by chiefs Tacki and Solomon of Accra to act as middlemen, through whose hands all presents and communications should pass, by giving an assurance that he would deal directly with each chief. The chief of Addah, however, was unable to attend the meeting, as the Awunas were again up in arms and had seized some of his people; and the King of Eastern Krobo not only refused to take the oath of allegiance, but used rebellious and insulting language, for which he was lodged in Accra gaol. A difficulty then arose in connection with the raising of the Houssa force similar to that which had occurred when the Gold Coast Corps was formed, in 1852. The nucleus of the Houssa force consisted of men brought from Lagos, who really belonged to the Houssa tribes, and it was intended to complete the force with Odonkos, who were erroneously supposed to be something akin to Houssas, and of whom there were many thousands in the Protectorate. All these Odonkos were slaves, and such as presented themselves for enlistment were enrolled without any reference being made to their owners. Indeed, the officers of Captain Glover's force, knowing nothing of the peculiar relations that were supposed to exist between the Colonial Government and the natives, used to reply, when persons came to them to claim their slaves, that slavery could not exist under the British Government. On this account a serious disturbance took place in Accra on October 1st, in which two men of Ussher Town were wounded; and a large number of armed men who assembled under their chiefs were only persuaded to disperse upon a promise being given that no more Odonkos should be enlisted without the consent of their owners, who would in that case receive five pounds for each slave.

Early in October the Awunas, who were well informed of the preparations that were being made, plundered and burned some stores at Kittah, and the Accras, Addahs, and Krepis stipulated that that tribe should be dealt with first before any advance was made on Kumassi. Captain Glover readily agreed to this, for he was himself disinclined to leave an untouched enemy in his rear, even at a distance; and on November 7th he went to Addah with a semi-disciplined body of about 900 Houssas and Odonkos, hoping that the native levies would follow; but these came in so slowly that even by December 14th there was not a sufficient force to undertake the punishment of the Awunas. He now found himsel unable to fulfil an engagement he had made with Sir Garne Wolseley to be on the Prah with 15,000 men on January 15th to join in the combined advance on Kumassi, and on December 22nd he wrote to ask for a delay of forty days To have permitted this would have been to abandon the idea of all assistance from Captain Glover, who would have been conducting his operations against the Awunas while the other columns were marching on Kumassi. Sir Garnet Wolseley therefore ordered him to move all his disciplined force, and such natives as he could persuade to follow him, to the Prah at once, and to abandon all projected operations on the east bank of the Volta. It was essential, ran the despatch, that his force should co-operate with the main column, and cross the Prah on January 15th.

After writing to say that he could not be on the Prah for forty days, Captain Glover commenced his trans-Volta campaign on December 24th. The native levies crossed the river near Sofi, a skirmish ensued and an Awuna village was burned; on the 25th some more skirmishing took place and some more villages were burned; but on the 27th while preparations were being made for another advance Sir G. Wolseley's letter arrived, ordering Captain Glover to march at once for the Prah. He summoned the Kings and chiefs, read them the despatch, said that the General's order must be obeyed, and called upon them to follow him to the Prah, to which they replied that they would do so after they had subdued the Awunas. The truth was that they cared very little about making war on Ashanti—which had not troubled them during the late invasion—and a great deal about making war upon the Awunas, upon whom they had many injuries to avenge, and they had simply made use of Captain Glover. They had received his money, arms, and powder, and the assistance of his steamers and Houssas, not to carry out his wishes but their own. Finally, finding that the natives would not abandon the trans-Volta campaign, Captain Glover started on December 29th, with his Houssas and Odonkos, for the Prah; leaving Mr. Goldsworthy and Lieutenant Moore, R.N., with 11,780 native allies, to proceed against the Awunas.

The disembarkation of the European regiments commenced at Cape Coast on January 1st, 1874, in the following order: Rifle Brigade, 42nd, 23rd. The Rifle Brigade drew its transport from Cape Coast, and that of the 42nd, chiefly consisting of Gomoas, was brought down from Mansu, so these two battalions marched off without difficulty; but before the disembarkation of the 23rd was completed, reports were received from Colonel Colley that such numbers of carriers had deserted, that only a sufficient number remained to keep up the flow of supplies to the front; and in default of transport, the men of the 23rd who had landed had to be re-embarked. By this time a bridge had been completed over the Prah, and by January 7th the advanced party of native troops, consisting of Lord Gifford's scouts and Russell's Regiment, occupied Essaman, a village north of the Prah.

On January 6th Sir Garnet Wolseley sent to the King from the camp at Prahsu an ultimatum, to the effect that he would be prepared to make peace upon the following terms: (1) All prisoners, both European and African, to be at once delivered up; (2) An indemnity of 50,000 ounces of gold to be paid; (3) A treaty of peace to be signed at Kumassi, to which place the Major-General would proceed with a sufficient force of Europeans, hostages for their safety being first given. This document was sent to Kumassi by two messengers, who had come down with two letters from the

King; one saying that he had forbidden Amankwa Tia to attack the forts, and the other, dated a month later, complaining of the attack made at Faisowa, when, he alleged, he was only withdrawing his army from the Protectorate, as requested by the English.

When they reached Kumassi, the messengers reported that the advanced party of the army was already at Essaman, and the Adansi chiefs were at once ordered to Fomana to bar the approach to the capital. But though this precautionary measure was taken, the King, now thoroughly alarmed, wished for peace, as did most of the chiefs; and the queen-mother, who is the most influential person in the kingdom, had already appealed to the Kotoko Council to release the European captives and make peace. The missionaries say that the ultimatum was quietly heard, and if an exclamation escaped a chief the King at once commanded attention; there were none of those furious outbursts to which they were accustomed, for this time the matter was too serious. The army, disheartened by its great losses, and disgusted with its commander, had been disbanded, and could not be reassembled for some weeks, and here was the white man already north of the Prah. The King, therefore, wrote to Sir Garnet Wolseley, on January 9th, that he accepted the terms of peace, and in proof of his friendship sent one of the Europeans, Mr. Kühne. He said that Amankwa Tia had disobeyed orders in attacking Elmina, and he begged, to prevent any misunderstanding, that the British force might not proceed any further, "for fear of meeting some of my captains as to cause fighting." This last was the pith of the matter, and the King was willing to promise anything if the invading force would only stop. He would certainly have complied with the first, and probably with the second demand of the ultimatum to effect that object; but the third would never have been agreed to, for the presence of a European force in Kumassi would have been regarded by all the surrounding tribes as proof of the downfall of Ashanti, and their haughty spirit would never submit to it without a struggle. To the King's letter Sir Garnet replied, on January 13th, that he could not halt his force till the terms he had mentioned were complied with, and he urged the King to send the other prisoners as a proof of his sincerity.

It had been supposed that, if the Ashantis intended to fight, they would commence to resist as soon as the troops crossed the Prah; but the territory of Adansi, then the most southerly province of Ashanti on this road, only began on the north side of the Adansi Hills, and the country between these and the Prah was the old Assin kingdom, whence the Assins had long been driven, and which was now only inhabited by a few hunters. Hence the troops were able to push on rapidly, and by January 17th the summit of the Adansi Hills had been occupied and fortified by Russell's regiment, with the 2nd West India Regiment in support at Akrufumu.* On the 18th the scouts pushed on to Kwisa, the first Adansi town, which, being deserted, was occupied next morning by Major Russell, and a further advance made to Fomana, which was also found deserted. Lying on the road near the south side of the town was found a gun, roughly carved out of wood, which had a number of knives stuck into it; and close by was a dead man impaled on a stake, and horribly mutilated, with the dissevered parts of the body hung round the neck. This was a sacrifice offered to the chief war-god of the tribe, to induce him to prevent the English from advancing further into Adansi.

On January 20th the passage of the Prah was commenced by the European troops, upon whom the climate was now beginning to tell, the Naval Brigade having sent back 40 men out of 250 who had left Cape Coast, and the Rifle Brigade 57 out of 650, and this in a little less than three weeks. In consequence of this loss, and the probability of the number of sick daily increasing, a detachment of 200 men of the 23rd was ordered to be landed and marched

---

* Akru-fumu—Place of village folk.

to Prahsu. On January 23rd another letter was received from the King, in which he urgently entreated that the advance of the troops should be suspended, and in proof of friendship he released all the European captives. He said that he had no quarrel of any kind with the white men, and that he would make Amankwa Tia, whom he charged with having disobeyed his instructions, pay the indemnity, if only the further advance of the force would be stopped. The released captives said that the King was thoroughly frightened, and was most anxious to have peace proclaimed Yet, when it had been pointed out to him, and the chiefs, that all the prisoners, native as well as European, were required to be surrendered, and that the payment of 50,000 ounces wa one of the conditions of peace, a violent outburst of passion had taken place. Even the queen-mother became greatly excited, and all the chiefs sprang to their feet, swearing and shouting in the wildest confusion, for the Ashantis conside it the greatest disgrace to be coerced by threats. In the end the counsel of the King, who foresaw defeat and his own ruin in the near future if any fighting took place, prevailed and he sent the Europeans "to speak a good word fo him," hoping they might persuade the Major-General to stop It appeared that the Kotoko Council had really agreed t release all the European and native prisoners on the occasio when Mr. Kühne was sent down; but while it was sti sitting, Obeng, chief of Adansi, the "boundary guard of Ashanti," sent a message to say that he would fire upon th enemy, and that if the people in Kumassi had no powde he at least had some; which so wounded the pride of th chiefs that they recanted their former decision, and sen Mr. Kühne alone. This chief, Obeng, it may here b observed, was afterwards the first to desert the Ashan kingdom. On their way to the British camp the captive saw him at Dompoassi, which swarmed with soldiers; an now that his own towns were threatened, he had at la discovered that war was a bad thing. "Look at this village he said, "it is quite deserted. Does it not make one's hea ache?" It was refreshing to find that the Ashantis, after having burned so many scores of peaceful villages, were at last forced to tremble for their own.

On January 24th, Sir Garnet Wolseley, at Fomana, replied to the King's letter, saying that he intended to go to Kumassi, and that it was for the King to decide whether he went there as friend or foe. If the King wished him to come as a friend, all the native prisoners must be released at once, and 25,000 ounces of gold must be sent with the following six hostages—Prince Mensa, heir to the stool, the queen-mother, and the heirs of the chiefs of Djuabin, Mampon,* Bekweh, and Kokofu.† These conditions being complied with, he would proceed to Kumassi, with an escort of 500 European soldiers, to make a treaty of peace. Although the General was not aware of it, these terms were such as it was impossible for the King to fulfil, for the six hostages demanded were the principal people in the kingdom, and, united, were much more powerful than he; while under no circumstances, as long as Ashanti remained a kingdom, could the queen-mother and the heir apparent be given up.

On the 25th Dompoassi was occupied, and next day reconnaissances were made to Adubiassi, to the left of the road, and to Essia-Kwanta,‡ in front; there was a slight skirmish at Adubiassi, and the village was burned. As some prisoners taken at this place reported the presence of a force of 1,000 men at Borborassi, a reconnaissance against that village was made on the 29th, and the Ashantis driven out into the bush; but unfortunately this was not done without loss, Captain Nicol being killed, and four of the Naval Brigade wounded. The troops were all now well up to the front, but out of a force of 1,800 Europeans, 218 had already become non-effective through sickness. On the 30th the advanced

* Mampon is probably a corruption of Mampam, the iguana.
† Koko-fu probably means People of the Hill (Koko), there being a well-marked range of hills in the Kokofu District.
‡ Essia-Kwanta—Six Roads.

guard was at Kwaman, the European troops at Insarfu, and the 1st West India Regiment, which had been ordered up, between Fomana and Essia-Kwanta. The scouts had found the Ashantis in force just beyond the village of Egginassi, and it was evident that the following day would bring about a battle.

It will now be as well to inquire what the auxiliary columns to the right and left of the main body had been doing. Captain Glover crossed the Prah on January 15th with about 800 Houssas and Odonkos, and on the 16th a slight skirmish took place at Abogu, where the Houssas expended so much ammunition that the force had to remain halted till the 26th to allow a further supply to come up; but this delay enabled the King of Eastern Akim, and the chief of Assum, who were not much interested in a campaign against the Awunas, to join with some 500 men. Captain Butler had crossed the Prah at Beronassi on January 15th, in compliance with orders, but without one man of the force he was to have raised from the Western Akims. A few days later, however, some men came in, and by the 20th about 900 had arrived, with whom Captain Butler advanced, intending to strike into the main road at Amoafu.* He reached Yankoma on the 24th, and on the 25th an advanced part of his force occupied the deserted village of Enun-su. On this day Captain Glover, whose column was gradually converging on that of Captain Butler, detached a party of Eastern Akims to attack this very village, which he believed to be occupied by the enemy; and each party mistaking the other for Ashantis, a skirmish took place, which resulted in the Eastern Akims being driven off with three killed and several wounded. Although the two columns were only some eight miles apart, each was ignorant of the presence of the other, and these facts were only discovered after the war. It seems however, that the Eastern Akims had some suspicion of the truth, for on returning to Captain Glover they said they

---

* Amoa—mine, or pit ; fu, or fo—people.

thought Enun-su was occupied by Western Akims; but the report was attributed to cowardice, and no attention was paid to it. The Western Akims were much elated at their supposed victory over the Ashantis, but they could not be induced to advance any further till the 27th, when they moved to Akina, about ten miles south-east of Amoafu. Akina was found to have been hastily abandoned, and here Captain Butler halted, till, on January 30th, his whole force, seized with a sudden panic, retreated across the Enun River, and thence to the Prah, where the men dispersed to their homes, so that Captain Butler's column ceased to exist. Captain Glover, after his attack on the other column at Enun-su, pushed on to Odumassi, where a slight skirmish took place; but was obliged to halt at Conomo, three miles to the east of Odumassi, to wait for further supplies of ammunition. Captain Dalrymple's mission to raise a column from the Wassaws had failed so completely that up to January 24th he had only succeeded in raising fifty men from the seven Kings and chiefs to whom he had been commissioned; and as nothing could induce these men to cross the Offim River and enter Ashanti territory, Captain Dalrymple abandoned his task as hopeless, and rejoined the main column at Fomana.

These were all the movements of the auxiliary columns up to January 30th, the eve of a great battle. Of the three projected auxiliary columns one only remained; but insignificant as these operations were from a military point of view, they were not without some effect upon the Ashantis. On January 14th messengers had reached Kumassi with exaggerated reports of Captain Glover's doings, and, in consequence of his reported advance, Kokofu, which is regarded by the Ashantis as a holy town, was abandoned by its inhabitants on the 20th. Appeals for assistance were also made by the inhabitants of the villages threatened by Captain Butler's column, and the King had been constrained to send a few barrels of powder from his scanty stock. Captain Glover's movements also prevented the Djuabin contingent from joining the Ashanti army that barred the way to the capital, and thus drew off some 12,000 men. It was commonly supposed at the time that the rumour of Captain Dalrymple's advance had similarly drawn off the Bekweh contingent; but this was proved to be entirely without foundation, and it was the men of that province who offered the most obstinate resistance at Amoafu.

CHAPTER XXVI.

.1874.

Battle of Amoafu—Attack of Kwaman and Fomana—Battle of Ordahsu —Kumassi entered—Incendiary fires—The King's palace—Messages from the King—Burning of Kumassi.

AT daybreak on 31st January, 1874, the troops advanced in three columns, the centre one, under Sir Archibald Alison, consisting of the 42nd Highlanders and the scouts; the left under Colonel McLeod, of half the Naval Brigade and Russell's Regiment; and the right, under Lieutenant-Colonel Wood, of the other half of the Naval Brigade and Wood's Regiment. The Rifle Brigade and a company of the 23rd Welsh Fusiliers were held in reserve. Wood's and Russell's Regiments consisted now of but few men, so many having been left to assist in garrisoning the various posts along the road, and the total force, including engineer labourers, amounted to no more than 1,609 Europeans and 708 natives.

Touch of the enemy was first obtained about three-quarters of a mile from Kwaman, at the village of Egginassi, which was taken without serious resistance; but just beyond it he was found in considerable force. After leaving Egginassi the path turned to the right, and descended into a swampy hollow, where flowed a sluggish stream, after crossing which it again turned slightly to the right and ascended a ridge. This ridge, which projected forward on the left so as to take in flank the path descending to the hollow and the hollow itself, was the enemy's main position, and his camp extended along it for a great distance.

As the 42nd commenced descending to the hollow the enemy opened fire, and a hundred yards in advance the forest was obscured with smoke, from which shot forth countless tongues of flame without a single foe being visible. The fire was so heavy that the branches of the trees overhanging the path were almost stripped of their leaves; but the enemy were firing at a range too great for their weapons, and though many men were struck, the hail of lead was almost harmless. As company after company went down the path they were lost to sight in the forest, but their position could be told by the sharp reports of their rifles, so different to the loud dull roar of the Ashanti musketry, and their advance to the stream was rapid. Here, however, the affair became more serious, for the Ashantis were close up, and the men began to fall fast, and the wounded to stream to the rear. By half past nine, although seven out of eight companies of the 42nd were engaged, they were making but little way; the company of the 23rd was accordingly brought up from Egginassi, and a little later, this reinforcement being found insufficient, the two guns under Captain Rait, R.A., were ordered into action in front. With some difficulty they were got across the stream and a little way up the path beyond, when they fired up the ascent into the dense masses of the enemy crowded together for its defence; and fourteen or fifteen rounds fired in quick succession so shook the Ashantis, that the 42nd were able to carry the ridge with a rush. On the summit was found a large camp, and when this was traversed a determined opposition was offered from a ridge beyond; but the same tactics were repeated, the guns again brought into play, a fresh charge made, and this position also carried. This was the last serious stand offered by the enemy to the advance of the 42nd, and after a few rounds from the guns the village of Amoafu was rushed, the enemy flying from it in great disorder.

While the centre column had been thus engaged, the left column had moved to the left from Egginassi, and come menced cutting a path parallel to the main road; but so heavy a fire was brought to bear by the enemy that its progress was much impeded, and Captain Buckle, R.E., fell mortally wounded while encouraging his labourers. At last, however, a path was cut to the crest of a hill, and, a clearing being made there, some rockets were brought into play, under cover of which Russell's Regiment drove the Ashantis from the bush in front. The right column had commenced cutting a path to the right a little beyond Egginassi, but the fire from both flanks was so heavy that Colonel Wood was unable to advance, and, a clearing being made, the men lay down and engaged the Ashantis.

While the 42nd had been employed in the hollow, persistent attacks had been made on both flanks at Egginassi; and after Amoafu had been carried, the Ashantis reoccupied the ridge commanding the hollow, and even came into the road in rear of the village. The opposition in front and to the left, however, gradually ceased after midday, and the left column then cut its way into the main road a little to the south of the hollow; but about 1 p.m. a furious attack was made on Egginassi, and on the right side of the road as far as Amoafu, which was lined with troops the whole way, and was not repulsed till the Rifle Brigade advanced into the bush and took Egginassi hill.

The Ashantis, who were in very superior numbers, had endeavoured to follow their usual outflanking tactics, and the battle was really won by the piercing of their centre by the 42nd while the columns to the right and left prevented the Ashantis from enveloping it. The 42nd owed much of their success to the fact that they kept moving on; for the Ashantis, wonderfully adroit at taking cover, could face the fire of the breech-loaders, but could not stand the continual advance, which did not give them time to reload. The British casualties were Major Baird, 2 privates of the 42nd, and 1 native, killed: 21 officers, 139 Europeans, and 34 natives, wounded. The 42nd had suffered the most, having 2 killed, and 9 officers and 104 men wounded. The Ashantis had been commanded by the old general, Asamoa Kwanta, who had chosen his position with much skill. Among the slain were Amankwa Tia, who fell on the left, and the chief of Mampon, who was killed on the right. The Ashanti losses were alleged to be very heavy; but only about 130 dead Ashantis were found and buried by the troops, and it is not the custom of that people to carry off their slain, unless they are chiefs. The only trophy secured by the enemy was the head of a soldier of the 42nd, who had been surrounded when in advance of his company, shot down, and instantly decapitated.

It was now determined to send the wounded back to Insarfu, and to bring the baggage on from that place to Amoafu; but shots were soon heard in the direction o Kwaman, and a company of the Rifle Brigade was sent down to reinforce its garrison. The left of the Ashanti army had after attacking Egginassi, moved off to the south, and was now attacking the line of communications; but the garrison o Kwaman, consisting of fifty-three of the 2nd West Indi Regiment and thirty natives, held their own until the arriva of the Rifle Brigade, and at four o'clock all firing ceased. About five o'clock, however, the Ashantis again opened fir upon Kwaman, both from the north and south, just as large convoy of baggage and ammunition, nearly five mile long, which had started from Insarfu for Kwaman unde an escort of the 2nd West India Regiment, was approaching As it drew near, the Ashantis attacking on the south turne upon it, and the carriers, abandoning a number of load rushed back to Insarfu, leaving the road strewn with baggag Captain Dugdale, Rifle Brigade, then in command at Kw man, having some inkling of what was going on, endeavoure to clear a way for the convoy by sending out a party, whic found the enemy in great numbers in the bush at the edge the road, and engaged him till about half-past six, whe owing to the darkness and the increasing numbers of tl enemy, it returned to Kwaman. A great many loads f into the hands of the Ashantis, but during the night all th could be found were packed in the road and left under a guard of the 2nd West India Regiment.

In order to pass the baggage on from Insarfu to Amoafu, it was necessary next morning to line the whole of the road between these two places with troops; and after the convoy had arrived at its destination orders were issued for the attack of Bekweh, the chief town of the province of the same name. It was situated off the main road, about a mile to the west of Amoafu, and as the chief of Bekweh commanded a considerable force, it was considered dangerous to leave this large town on the flank. It was surprised and burned, and the force returned to Amoafu unmolested.

At daybreak on February 2nd the whole force advanced from Amoafu, which had been entrenched on the previous day, and was now left in charge of a garrison of the 2nd West India Regiment. Russell's Regiment led the advance, and was more or less opposed at each village on the road; but, without meeting with any serious opposition, it reached Agemmamu, about six miles from Amoafu, shortly before 1 p.m. The main body arrived soon after, and it was decided to move no further that day, as it would be late before the baggage, which had been left at Amoafu, could arrive. The difficulties connected with the advance of large convoys of baggage had now become so serious, that a change of plan was made at Agemmamu. The convoy from Insarfu to Amoafu had only been passed on by lining the whole road with troops on February 1st, and now, on February 2nd, many of the European troops had to be kept out till after dark to protect the carriers, who were still coming in, though the column had only made a march of six miles. If this slow rate of progress was to be continued, it would be necessary to make a protracted halt till more supplies were brought up. The alternative was to make a dash at Kumassi, only fifteen miles distant, and return; and as the force now concentrated at Agemmamu had with it four days' supplies, Sir Garnet Wolseley decided to adopt it.

On this day the post of Fomana was hotly attacked by the Adansis. It was garrisoned by an officer and 38 men, of the 1st West India Regiment, and 102 men of Russell's Regiment, while in the chief's house, situated in the main street of the long, straggling town, were 24 European soldiers and sailors, convalescents. The attack, which was somewhat of a surprise, commenced about 8.30 a.m., and the enemy, penetrating into all the southern side of the town, which was far too large to be defended by so small a garrison, fired the houses. The convalescents were hastily moved to a stockade which had been made at the northern end, the neighbouring houses being pulled down as rapidly as possible, and the struggle continued till 1 p.m., when the firing ceased, though a party which went down for water an hour later was fired upon. The British casualties were two officers and ten men wounded.

On the morning of February 3rd the advance to Kumass commenced, Agemmamu being garrisoned by all the weakly men of Russell's Regiment, and prepared for defence. Three quarters of an hour after starting the enemy was met a a stream, beyond which, on some rising ground, he had taken a position; but he was driven away after a smar skirmish, in which one scout was killed and seven European and ten natives wounded. From this point the advance wa continued more slowly, as the enemy formed numerou ambuscades, from which they fired and retreated, inflictin some loss at every discharge. Shortly before noon mes sengers arrived from Kumassi with a flag of truce an . a letter from the King, in which he begged for some delay, and said he was willing to meet all demands. Mr. Dawso also wrote to beg that the advance might be stopped, othe wise, he said, he and all the Fanti prisoners would be kille . Sir Garnet replied that he could not halt till the hostage were in his keeping, and, as time pressed, he would accept such the queen-mother and Prince Mensa. From the bear of the letter it was learned that the army which had fought . t Amoafu was encamped on the north side of the Ordah Rive to bar the approach to the capital.

About three in the afternoon the troops arrived at the

Ordah River, where it was resolved to bivouac. The stream was about fifty feet wide and waist-deep, and the engineers at once set to work to construct a bridge, Russell's Regiment being passed across the river as a covering party. A clearing was made on the south bank, and rough shelter-huts of palm-branches and plantain-leaves were soon made by the troops. Just as it was growing dark an Ashanti was captured in the act of loading his gun close to the bivouac, and on being examined, he declared that there were still 10,000 men on the south bank of the river, who only did not attack because they had received the King's orders not to do so. At dark the camp and picquet fires were lighted and the bivouac presented a gay appearance, which, however, was not doomed to last; for soon after sunset the sky became overcast, thunder was heard in the distance, and before long that cold gust of wind which is always the precursor of rain swept through the camp. The rain fell in a steady downpour all night, much to the discomfort of the men, who were soon drenched, a plantain-leaf hut affording but little shelter from tropical rain; and it was peculiarly unfortunate that the troops should have been subjected to this trial on the first night on which they had to bivouac.

By daybreak next morning the bridge was completed, and the advance from the Ordah took place shortly before six o'clock. The Opobo company of Wood's Regiment, and three companies of the Rifle Brigade, with a seven-pounder gun, formed the advanced guard, under Colonel M'Leod; while the remainder of the Rifle Brigade, the company of the 23rd, and the 42nd Highlanders, formed the main body, under Sir A. Alison. The Naval Brigade was ordered to wait till the baggage was across the river, and then to bring up the rear. Almost immediately the advance began the enemy opened fire on the head of the column, and as the Opobos fired wildly, and delayed the advance by lying down every few yards, a company of the Rifle Brigade was passed to the front; but a more vigorous resistance was then at once offered, and though the advanced guard was reinforced by three more companies of the Rifle Brigade, no progress could be made till after two hours' fighting. For the first half-mile from the river the path rose gradually, then after a rapid ascent it passed along a narrow ridge with a ravine on each side, after which it dipped again deeply, and finally rose to the village of Ordahsu. As the enemy's fire began to slacken a few rounds were fired from the gun, and the Rifles made a short rush; then the gun was again brought up and another advance made, and in this manner the village was at last reached and carried; but the enemy still held the bush round it, and kept up a hot fire.

While the advanced guard was thus engaged in front, a strong flank attack was made on the right of the main body, and the beating of drums was heard away in the right rear. The main body, however, pushed on till it reached the ridge along which the path ran, when a tremendous fire was suddenly opened by the enemy on both flanks; but, though very heavy, it was not nearly so destructive as at Amoafu, and the enemy did not close with the same vigour that they had there displayed. The road was now lined from Ordahsu to the river, which the baggage and the Naval Brigade had not yet crossed, and a halt was ordered so that they might come up. As the convoy passed on, the troops were drawn in and the enemy allowed to close round the rear. This they did with loud shouts and war songs, believing that they had cut off the retreat of the force, and a number of them at once entered the camp and destroyed it.

About 11 a.m. the Ashantis made a determined attack on Ordahsu, and the whole circle round the village was for the next hour one sheet of flame and one roar of musketry. The enemy at times pressed boldly up, cheering and shouting before they advanced; and on one occasion they came up in as close line as they could form in the bush and fired a regular volley, but were at once mown down by the fire o the Sniders. About noon it was decided to advance, and as the Rifle Brigade was engaged all round the village the 42nd was ordered to break through the enemy in fron and push straight on to Kumassi, disregarding all flank attack; the Rifle Brigade being directed to follow as soon as the cessation of the flank attacks on the village would permit it.

On first debouching from the village a heavy fire was opened on the 42nd by a body of Ashantis concealed behind an immense silk-cotton tree, which had fallen almost across the path, and six men fell at the first discharge; but the flank companies pressed steadily on through the bush, the men in the path sprang forward with a cheer, and the ambuscade was carried. "Then followed," says Sir A. Alison, "one of the finest spectacles I have ever seen in war. Without stop or stay the 42nd rushed on cheering, their pipes playing, their officers to the front; ambuscade after ambuscade was successfully carried, village after village won in succession, till the whole Ashantis broke and fled in the wildest disorder down the pathway on their front to Kumassi. The ground was covered with traces of their flight. Umbrellas and war-chairs of their chiefs, drums, muskets, killed and wounded covered the whole way, and the bush on each side was trampled as if a torrent had flowed through it. No pause took place till a village about four miles from Kumassi was reached, when the absolute exhaustion of the men rendered a short halt necessary." While the 42nd had thus been carrying all before them, the attack on Ordahsu had been continued with just the same vigour as before; but when, shortly before two o'clock, a despatch from Sir A. Alison, saying that he would be in Kumassi that night, was communicated to the troops, such a ringing cheer was raised that the enemy's fire immediately ceased, as if by magic, and not another shot was fired, the Ashantis knowing instinctively that the day was lost.

The arrangements for this battle had been made by Asamoa Kwanta, but the King himself had been present during the seven hours' fighting, looking on, seated on a golden stool, under his red umbrella. When defeat was certain he fled to Amanghyia, a suburb of Kumassi. The plan of action was ingenious. It was intended to make Ordahsu the main position, but a large clearing was made to the south-west of that village, with the design of collecting there a force sufficient to cut the only road of communication, and hold it, should Ordahsu be forced. This plan was fully carried out, and as the troops occupied Ordahsu a very considerable body of the enemy seized the road; but the irruption of the 42nd from the village, which had not been foreseen and provided for, neutralised its effect. The Ashantis could not understand how a force could push on, disregarding all attack in flank, and even leaving the foe behind; for to their ideas an army was lost as soon as it was outflanked. It must also be said that they had lost their former self-confidence, and did not stand against attack as they did at Amoafu. The strength of the British force engaged at Ordahsu was 118 officers, 1,044 European soldiers, and 449 natives; and the casualties were Lieutenant Eyre and 1 native killed, 6 officers and 60 men wounded.

When the 42nd reached Karsi, the last village before Kumassi, a messenger arrived with a flag of truce and a letter from Mr. Dawson, who wrote under the influence of great terror, begging the Major-General to stop, "since the destruction of the whole blessed kingdom after we are killed would not bring us back"; but no notice was taken of this and the 42nd pushed on. After leaving Karsi, the fores' dwindled to jungle, and numerous paths joined the mai1 road from the right and left. At a cross road, a numbe of executioners armed with knives were found on the poin of killing a man, who was to be offered as a sacrifice t stop the advance, and a little further on a second flag c truce was met with a letter. This messenger was mos anxious that the march of the troops should be arrested, an Sir A. Alison forwarded the letter to Sir Garnet, saying h would wait half an hour. A short distance from where th 42nd were halted was a group of armed men, who stood res lessly moving their guns in their hands and looking savagel at the white men; but when the messenger went an remonstrated with them, they shouldered their muskets and walked away.

As soon as the half-hour had elapsed the 42nd pushed on, and crossing the Suban swamp, entered Kumassi, without opposition, about half-past five. At the top of the first street, which was a broad road of rising ground, with here and there a detached house on either side, they turned to the left and entered the main street, which commands both the town and the palace. In the main street hundreds of armed men were collected to observe the entry, but not a shot was fired; and many men even came up to the soldiers and shook hands. The spectators seemed to have no feeling but that of wonder and pleasure, laughing and uttering cries of amazement and delight, as if the presence of the troops was a pleasant spectacle that had been arranged for their gratification, and bringing them water to drink. Among the crowd were numbers of men who had been engaged at Ordahsu, powder-stained and naked, with shot-belts round their waists and guns upon their shoulders. All this time there was a constant stream of people going by, with guns, and barrels, or kegs of powder upon their heads. They were taking these things to the bush, perhaps to use on another occasion, but they were not disarmed, nor was any one interfered with. Perhaps never before had an invading force entered a hostile town under similar circumstances.

About six o'clock Sir Garnet Wolseley arrived, followed by the remainder of the troops, and strong outlying picquets were placed at all the main entrances to the town, with one great inlying picquet in the market-place. Mr. Dawson, who was found at liberty in the street, had the effrontery to declare that he did not know the way to the palace, and could not point it out; but a building, which was believed to be the palace, was discovered, and a party at once sent down to it. The King, however, was nowhere to be found; he, the queen-mother, and all the persons of distinction having disappeared. Mr. Dawson also vowed that he had no idea where the King could be, and that he could not possibly find out; but after a little pressure had been applied he brought up a nephew of the King, named Awusu Kokor, and another Ashanti, who promised they would deliver any message or letter to the King, though of course they would not say where he had gone. A letter was accordingly written to the effect that as the King did not wish to give up the queen-mother and Prince Mensa, other hostages of rank would be accepted, and peace could be made next day upon the terms originally proposed. If the King, the queen-mother, or Prince Mensa would come to see the Major-General next day, they would be treated with all honour, and allowed to return in safety. At the same time the messengers were warned that all precautions had been taken against treachery, and that if during the stay of the troops in Kumassi, a single shot was fired against them, the town should be destroyed, and every living person in it put to death. On the other hand, if the King would come in to treat, the town would be untouched and the troops would leave it as they found it.

Sir Garnet Wolseley did not interfere with the remova of property, but an embargo was placed on the remova of arms and ammunition, and a proclamation was issued threatening with death any one caught plundering; whil at the same time an Ashanti crier went round and pro claimed, in the name of the King, that no one was t attack or molest the troops. After dark fires, evidentl the work of incendiaries, sprang up all over the town, an throughout the night the troops were employed in puttin them out, and in pulling down houses to prevent th spread of the conflagration. One lurid blaze after anothe sprang up in various quarters, followed by explosions of tl powder stored in nearly every house, and the men had t work hard, and deprive themselves of the night's rest, so muc needed after the exertions of the day, to save the town fro destruction. These incendiary fires were the work of tl Fanti prisoners who had been released from "log"; and whe they and Mr. Dawson left Kumassi, they took with them suspicious amount of property. Every effort was made check plunder, and a Fanti policeman, caught in the act, was hanged, while several of the carriers were flogged. The destruction caused by these fires, the glow of which could be seen for miles, must, to the King's mind, have harmonised ill with the promise made to protect the town ; and would naturally tend to prevent him from coming in to treat, or sending the queen-mother or Prince Mensa.

By daybreak next morning the Ashantis had all gone away, and the entire town was deserted. It has been said that a party had been sent down to the palace, but it does not appear that any guard had been placed over it, for Mr. Winwood Reade, *The Times* correspondent, tells us that he visited it at eight o'clock in the morning, and that there were no sentries. He says: "Any one might enter, and any one whose conscience allowed him could take whatever he pleased. As I passed through the courtyard at the foot of the stairs I met some natives passing in. I supposed them to be Fantis, and told them they could not go up to the private apartments. But it turned out that they were Ashantis, people of the King, and they said with a charming candour that they had come to fetch things away. I presume that this sort of thing had been going on all night. Some golden treasure was still left in the palace; how much, then, must have been taken away?" The palace consisted of many courtyards, surrounded with verandahs and alcoves, and having two gates or doors, so that each court was a thoroughfare. There were ten or twelve such courts, and in addition there was, fronting the street, a stone house, Moorish in style, with a flat roof and a parapet, and suites of apartments on the first floor. On the southern side the palace merged into an irregularly built cluster of houses. There were thus many entrances to the building, and as it was past six o'clock and nearly dark before its situation was discovered, it could not be expected that it would be carefully guarded that night. When Sir Garnet Wolseley visited the palace, one hundred men of the Rifle Brigade were at once ordered down, and sentries were so posted as to render it impossible to enter it or leave it without being observed; but thirteen sentries were found necessary to watch all the entrances. The supporting pillars of the roofs of the recesses of the great court, which would have held two hundred men, were highly ornamented with scroll-work in glazed red clay, and the floor of the recess at the southern end, in which the King received embassies, was ornamented with various devices in the same material. The heavy door of the King's bed-chamber was covered with stamped plaques of gold and silver, and the room itself contained a large four-post bed, covered with silk, and a brass basin containing some preparation made by the priests. In one place was found a number of litters covered with silks and velvets, or the skins of animals, and a quantity of umbrella canopies, amongst them the one afterwards brought to England. The rooms on the first floor of the stone building were filled with articles of all kinds—books in many languages, clocks, silver plate, Bohemian glass, pictures, rugs, carpets, silks, gold-studded sandals, gold ornaments, and heaps of chests and coffers. Other things also were seen—the great death-drum, on which three peculiar beats were given whenever a human victim was sacrificed, and country stools, which had belonged to the former Kings of Ashanti, and were clotted thick with the blood of the hundreds of human beings who had been sacrificed to their *manes*.

Early in the morning a messenger from the King was received, who said that his master would come in during the morning; and after a time another arrived, who said that he would come later in the day. The King, however, did not appear, and his messengers, being discovered taking of powder and arms from the town, were arrested. All this day, the only one which the troops could pass in the capital was spent in inaction, waiting for the King, and many have expressed an opinion that it ought to have been employed in destroying the mausoleum of the former Kings at Bantama The destruction of that building would undoubtedly have had a prodigious effect both upon the Ashantis and the surrounding tribes, and the spoil would probably have been great, as all the wealth accumulated by former Kings, and which could only be used in cases of national emergency, was kept there; but it was really impossible to undertake any operations which might involve another battle, and the Ashantis would certainly have defended Bantama. There were only enough hammocks and bearers to carry back to Agemmamu the present sick and wounded, and as the number of these would certainly have been increased by another battle, any advance to Bantama was put out of the question.

Early in the morning of this day all the wounded who were unable to march were sent off, escorted by Wood's and Russell's Regiments and a company of the Rifle Brigade; and about eleven o'clock news was returned that the Ordah had risen so that the water was about eighteen inches over the bridge. This report caused some anxiety, which was increased when, in the afternoon, a succession of furious tornadoes swept over Kumassi, and converted the market-place into a pool of water. In the meantime the day passed, and evening began to close in without the King having appeared, and as it was impossible to wait longer, there was nothing to be done but to destroy Kumassi and return to Agemmamu. Prize agents were appointed to collect from the palace such valuables as could be transported by thirty carriers, and orders were given for the engineers to make preparations for blowing up that building and firing the town on the following morning. During the night it rained heavily for many hours, an unusual occurrence for the time of year.

At six next morning the troops were formed up in the market-place, and soon afterwards commenced to march off. The rain had ceased, but the water in the Suban swamp had much risen, and the passage of the Ordah occupied all thoughts. The preparation of the mines for the destruction of the palace took longer than had been expected, and the last of the main body had left Kumassi a full hour before they were ready. Then the town was set on fire. Commencing on the north of the town the houses were fired down to the south side, the thick thatched roofs, as dry as tinder except just on the surface, blazing furiously. At nine o'clock the mines in the palace were fired, and the 42nd, who formed the rear-guard, quitted Kumassi.

CHAPTER XXVII.

1874.

Return march to the coast—Movements of Captain Glover's column—March of Captain Sartorius—Envoys from the King—The Treaty of Fomana—Adansi becomes independent—The trade in arms at Assini—The climate—Embassy from Kumassi—The Treaty signed—Treaty concluded with the Awunas—The Gold Coast made a colony—Abolition of slavery.

THE commencement of the return march was not without difficulties, as all the streams were much swollen by the rains of the preceding days. Fortunately the Ashantis had not thought of destroying the bridge over the Ordah, but the water was over it nearly two feet when the main body crossed; and by the evening, when the 42nd reached it, it had given way, so that the men had to swim the river. The troops bivouacked for the night on the site of their former camp, and next morning the Naval Brigade and the company of the 23rd were ordered on to Cape Coast, where they at once re-embarked; but the Rifle Brigade and the 42nd moved down more leisurely, waiting till the stores were cleared out of Agemmamu. So far the success of the expedition was not quite complete, for though Kumassi had been burned, a fact which would probably put a curb upon Ashanti ambition for a good many years, the King had not capitulated, had signed no treaty, and had not paid an ounce of gold; but on February 9th a messenger from him overtook the army, expressing his desire to make peace, and offering to agree to all the terms. This anxiety to conciliate a foe who had already done his worst, and was now evacuating his territory, was due to the advance of Captain Glover's column, and to the movements of that force we must now return.

We left Captain Glover, at the end of January, halted at Conomo, awaiting further supplies of ammunition, and on February 8th, four days after Kumassi had been entered by the main column, he was still there. In the meantime the Djuabin contingent of the Ashanti army had taken up a strong position on the north side of the Enun River, to dispute the passage, and a slight skirmish with them had taken place on the 1st, in which they had the advantage. On the 8th Captain Glover was reinforced by a body of Western Akims, which brought up the total strength of his force to about 7,000 natives and 923 Houssas and Odonkos, and on the same day he advanced to attack the Djuabin position, which, to his surprise, he found abandoned. The withdrawal of the Djuabins from the line of the Enun River was in consequence of the news of the capture of Kumassi having reached them, and next day the King of Djuabin sent to Captain Glover to make submission. The column now advanced without meeting with any opposition, and on February 10th Captain Glover sent Captain Sartorius to open communications with the General, whom he supposed still to be in Kumassi.

It was the near approach of Captain Glover's force that now alarmed the King, who had no sooner got rid of one invading army than he found another advancing. In ordinary times the approach of such a rabble as that commanded by Captain Glover would have caused very little concern for it would have been easily swept away or annihilated by an overpowering force of Ashantis; but the case was now very different. The burning of Kumassi had shaken the Ashanti kingdom to its very foundations, and the feudatory princes were showing signs of a desire to regain their independence; while the chief feudatory, the King of Djuabin, had actually made submission and ceased hostilities without any reference to his sovereign. The Kumassi men alone would doubtless have been fully capable of settling accounts with Captain Glover's force, but then there was the uncertainty whether the European troops might not return, a contingency which must be averted; so the messenger, who overtook Sir Garnet Wolseley on February 9th, begged that he would order Captain Glover's forces to halt. In reply he was informed that the Major-General would remain at Fomana till the 13th, and that if by the night of the 12th the King would send 5,000 ounces of gold, peace would be made, and Captain Glover ordered to return across the Prah.

In the meantime Captain Sartorius, with an escort of twenty Houssas, had started from the village of Essiam Impon, which was supposed to be about seven miles east of Kumassi, but was really eighteen. He passed through many villages, the inhabitants of which fled as he approached, and was fired at once from the bush, but once only. On the 11th he entered Kumassi, which was absolutely deserted, except by one or two stragglers, pushed on to Amoafu the same night, and surprised every one by appearing at Fomana next day, after having marched fifty miles through the heart of the enemy's country with only twenty men.

On the night of the 12th the envoys from the King returned, and halted at Dompoassi, sending on word that he had fulfilled the conditions, and on the 13th they were received at Fomana. They at first stated that they had brought only 1,000 ounces of gold, and declared that the King could not at present produce any more. They said he had never before been required to pay so large a sum, and that even Governor Maclean had only demanded 600 ounces as a temporary security. They were told to produce what gold they had, and they took from a heavy leathern bag ornaments of every description, and nuggets, weighing altogether about 1,040 ounces. The question of the amount of payment was, however, of little importance, so long as the King made submission, and the envoys were given the following draft treaty to take back for the King's signature:

Article 1. There shall be hereafter perpetual peace between the Queen of England and her Allies on the coast on the one part, and the King of Ashanti and all his people on the other part.

Article 2. The King of Ashanti promises to pay the sum of 50,000 ounces of approved gold as an indemnity for the expenses he has occasioned to Her Majesty the Queen of England by the late war; and undertakes to pay 1,000 ounces of gold forthwith, and the remainder by such instalments as Her Majesty's Government may from time to time demand.

Article 3. The King of Ashanti, on the part of himself and his successors, renounces all right or title to any tribute or homage from the Kings of Denkera, Assin, Akim, Adansi, and the other allies of Her Majesty, formerly subject to the King of Ashanti.

Article 4. The King, on the other part of himself and of his heirs and successors, does hereby further renounce for ever all pretensions to supremacy over Elmina, or over any of the tribes formerly connected with the Dutch Government, and to any tribute or homage from such tribes, as well as to any payment or acknowledgment of any kind by the British Government in respect of Elmina, or any other of the British forts and possessions on the Coast.

Article 5. The King will at once withdraw all his troops from Appollonia and its vicinity, and from the neighbourhood of Dixcove, Sekondi, and the adjoining coast-line.

Article 6. There shall be freedom of trade between Ashanti and Her Majesty's forts on the Coast, all persons being at liberty to carry their merchandise from the Coast to Kumassi, or from that place to any of Her Majesty's possessions on the Coast.

Article 7. The King of Ashanti guarantees that the road from Kumassi to the River Prah shall always be kept open and free from bush to a width of fifteen feet.

Article 8. As Her Majesty's subjects and the people o Ashanti are henceforth to be friends for ever, the King, ir order to prove the sincerity of his friendship for Queer

Victoria, promises to use his best endeavours to check the practice of human sacrifice, with a view to hereafter putting an end to it altogether, as the practice is repugnant to the feeling of all Christian nations.

Article 9. One copy of this Treaty shall be signed by the King of Ashanti and sent to the Administrator of Her Majesty's Government at Cape Coast Castle within fourteen days from this date.

Article 10. This Treaty shall be known as the Treaty of Fomana.

The treaty was explained to the envoys, paragraph by paragraph, and they objected to two clauses. They professed not to have understood that the sum of money demanded was so large as 50,000 ounces; but it was explained that the King had already given a written promise to pay that amount. They also objected to the Adansis being included in the list of those tribes to which the King was to renounce all claim. The Adansi tribe had been placed in this list at the request of the King of Adansi, who, accompanied by a number of his chiefs, and by some chiefs of Wassaw and Denkera, had come to Fomana, and expressed his desire to secede from the Ashanti kingdom, and to settle with his people south of the Prah, under British protection. He told the officer sent to see him that his people were regarded by the Ashantis more as enemies than friends, and that he had been unwilling, and had even refused, to fight against the invading force. This was an utter fabrication, for we know, from the evidence of the captive missionaries, that he was one of the foremost of the war party, and that it was through his conduct that the other Europeans were not released when Mr. Kühne was sent down. It was the Adansis, moreover, who had made the attack on Fomana, and who had, on several occasions, interfered with the transport by firing upon convoys. However, this was not known at the time, and, his statements being believed, when the Ashanti envoys arrived to conclude a treaty, Sir Garnet Wolseley himself saw the Adansi King to hear what he had to urge. He asked to be placed under British protection, and declared that, whether it were granted or not, he must now emigrate, because his negotiations would bring upon him the vengeance of the King. This seemed true enough, and he was therefore told that no hindrance would be offered to his migration, and the name of his tribe would be included in the treaty. It is to be regretted that it was not made clear that the protection of the Adansis would be conditional upon their removal, for, as will be seen later on, after having succeeded in getting his tribe included in the treaty, the King of Adansi did not emigrate, but, conceiving himself to be under British protection, interfered with the Ashantis in many ways, and thus caused serious complications.

In the meantime, Captain Glover, who had had no intelligence from the main column since January 23rd, crossed the Ordah near Apragmassi on February 11th, and entered Kumassi next day. He there learned that messengers had gone down from the King, accepting the terms and carrying a first instalment of the indemnity; and accordingly marched down the road to Prahsu by easy stages. Just south of the Adansi Hills he was overtaken by a messenger from the King, requesting that he would order the King of Eastern Akim, who had gone to Djuabin to endeavour to detach the King of that province from the Ashanti kingdom, to return at once to his own country. This request was supported by a present of fourteen ounces of gold and a gold dish, which was returned; but, in accordance with Sir Garnet's instructions, the King of Eastern Akim was ordered to return across the Prah.

Captain Glover arrived at Prahsu on February 17th with about 4,450 men, who were at once made use of to remove the stores which had been accumulated at Essaman, and whose removal had been a matter of grave consideration. The village was now cleared out by the 20th, and on the 23rd the last troops were withdrawn across the Prah and the bridge over the river destroyed. On February 19th Sir Garnet Wolseley entered Cape Coast, where he was received by thousands of Fanti women, who were painted white, the sign of rejoicing, and waved green branches and sang pæans of praise. By the 27th all the European regiments had embarked, Wood's and Russell's Regiments were soon after paid off, and the 2nd West India Regiment sailed for the West Indies, the 1st West India Regiment remaining to garrison the Gold Coast, and being distributed between Prahsu, Mansu, Cape Coast, and Elmina.

It having been decided that the Government was to remain on the same footing as during Sir Garnet's tenure of office, with the military and civil command united in the senior military officer, the governorship of the Colony was in turn offered to Sir A. Alison, Colonel M'Leod, Colonel Greaves, and Lieutenant-Colonel Colley, and by them all refused on account of the climate. And this is the chief difficulty which even now stands in the way of progress and prosperity on the Gold Coast, for no really capable and first-rate man will accept the governorship, no matter what addition may be made to the salary. Much of the confusion and mismanagement that had occurred in the past was due to the fact that the Administrators were usually men whose abilities were below mediocrity, and who had been thrust into the appointment because no one better could be found to accept it; and there seems every probability of this state of things being continued. Finding none of the officers with him disposed to accept the governorship, Sir Garnet Wolseley summoned from Prahsu Colonel Maxwell, 1st West India Regiment, who had to remain on the Gold Coast with his regiment, and handing over the government of the Colony to him, sailed for England on March 4th. Before quitting the Gold Coast he sent Mr. Goldsworthy to make a treaty of peace with the Awunas and Akwamus, and Dr. Gouldsbury was despatched to the Ahanta coast to receive the submission of the different tribes. A number of Wassaw messengers had also come in, complaining that the King of Adansi had not fulfilled his promise to move to the south of the Prah, and requesting that an armed force might be sent to compel him to come into the Protectorate; but they were informed that nothing of the kind could be done.

During the war, the importation into the Protectorate of arms, ammunition, and warlike stores had been prohibited, but it had been found impossible to prevent the Ashantis from obtaining all they required from the French settlement of Assini, or from Kittah, to the east of the Volta; and to their discredit be it said, it was principally British traders who thus supplied the enemy, at a time when British soldiers were fighting him. In March, 1873, the commander of the French ship of war *Curieuse* told Colonel Harley at Cape Coast that large quantities of arms and ammunition were being landed at Assini, for sale to the Ashantis, from British vessels, and that one ship alone had landed 150 cases of muskets, and 2,000 barrels of powder. The officers of the French navy did all in their power to stop this traffic, and Captain Mathieu, of the sloop of war *Bregant*, gave Mons. Verdier, the French agent at Assini, orders not to sell munitions of war. Mons. Verdier, however, disputed his right to give any such orders, no blockade having been declared by the French Government, and explained that if his stores were full of munitions of war, it was only because he was unable to sell on account of the enormous quantities that had been imported and sold by the English before, but more especially after, the declaration of war. Messrs. F. & A. Swanzy, then the chief British traders on the Gold Coast, were believed to have landed most of these munitions at Assini; and although they denied this, and altogether repudiated having dealt directly or indirectly in the supply of arms or ammunition to the Ashantis, their ships continued to arrive on the coast with arms and ammunition on board, and they did not endeavour to prove their sincerity by ceasing to export such articles while the war continued. The naval officers, however, who knew that, whatever the intentions of the partners of the firm might be, most of the local agents could not be trusted, acted with vigour, and several of their vessels were detained during the course of the blockade.

The unhealthiness of the climate of the Gold Coast was strikingly illustrated during the campaign of 1874. Seventy-one per cent. of sickness occurred amongst the white troops landed, and forty-three per cent. were invalided to England; while ninety-five per cent. of sickness took place in the Naval Brigade, and thirty-nine per cent. were invalided to England. And this, it must be remembered, occurred in a body of men full of health and vigour, who were subjected to a searching medical examination before being landed, and only remained some seven weeks in the country, during the healthiest time of the year. The mortality amongst the men was small, as invalids were sent away promptly; but more than forty officers died, only six of them from wounds.

On March 13th an Ashanti embassy arrived at Cape Coast, consisting of a son of the King, Kwoffi Intin by name, representatives from the various provinces of Ashanti, and a number of court officials. They presented the treaty, which had been sent from Fomana by Sir Garnet Wolseley, marked at the foot by the King with two crosses, in token of assent; but as they stated that the King believed the amount of the indemnity to be 5,000 bendas (10,000 ounces), it was explained to them that it was 50,000 ounces, and Colonel Maxwell desired them to withdraw and consult, so that there might be no possibility of mistake. On the third day they were again received, and the treaty was then signed by them in token of its full acceptance by the King, after which they asked, on behalf of the King, that the ground rent formerly paid by the Dutch for Elmina might be continued by the Colonial Government, and that the King of Adansi might be compelled to return to his allegiance to Ashanti. They complained that the King of Eastern Akim had taken by force a number of hostages from towns belonging to Ashanti-Akim, and was endeavouring to force the inhabitants of that district to throw off their allegiance; and requested that he might be directed to give up these men and cease from further interference. With regard to human sacrifices, the King promised to do what was required of him, but hoped he might be allowed to sacrifice two or three lives when any great chief died, otherwise the people would think the nation was declining. Lastly, the embassy, in the King's name, presented Kwoffi

Intin to the British Government, in token of confidence, and asked that he might be educated in England. Later on, another message was received through a fresh embassy, to the effect that the Kings of Eastern and Western Akim had compelled the inhabitants of certain towns in Ashanti-Akim to throw off their allegiance and emigrate; and that the King of Eastern Akim had taken hostages from the King of Djuabin to ensure his secession from the Ashanti kingdom. The King begged the Governor to put a stop to these intrigues, and Colonel Maxwell wrote forbidding the Kings of Akim to interfere with Ashanti affairs.

Dr. Gouldsbury's mission to the Ahanta coast was completely successful. The chiefs who had joined the Ashantis and whose towns had in consequence been bombarded, expressed their contrition; fines were imposed upon some of them, and the mutual release of all prisoners that had been taken was promised. Mr. Goldsworthy, however, was not equally successful, for though he proceeded to the Volta, he did not succeed in communicating with the Awunas and Akwamus.

Colonel Maxwell's health soon breaking down, he sailed for England early in April, and died on the passage home. He was temporarily succeeded by Lieutenant-Colonel Johnston, but only for a few days, as a commission arrived almost at once appointing Mr. Charles Cameron Lees Administrator. On June 22nd Mr. Lees concluded a treaty of peace with the Awunas at Jella Koffi, in which it was stipulated that the Volta should be kept open for all lawful trade, and the Awunas acknowledged the right of the British Government to occupy Jella Koffi, Kittah, or any other place deemed necessary, in order to place Awuna country under the same jurisdiction as the Gold Coast This was an important concession, as the jurisdiction of the Danes, which the British had acquired by the purchase of Kittah Fort, had been limited to Kittah and Jella Koffi but now there was no obstacle to the incorporation of the whole of the Awuna territory with the Gold Coast Colony.

On the 24th of July a new charter was issued, in which

the Gold Coast and Lagos were separated from the Government of Sierra Leone, and formed into a separate Colony, styled the Gold Coast Colony. Captain George Cumine Strahan, R.A., was appointed Governor.

The Ashanti War, which had brought temporarily to the Gold Coast so many Europeans, and amongst them newspaper correspondents, had made the British public acquainted with a fact of which it was before in ignorance, namely, that slavery was a recognised institution in the Protectorate, and that English Courts of Law could be invoked to compel a fugitive slave to return to or be restored to his owner. The public was very indignant, and the Home Government was compelled to take the matter in hand, for it was everywhere felt that the recognition of slavery by the nation which had taken the first steps for the suppression of the slave trade, and had been the first, even at the cost of the ruin of its West India possessions, to abolish slavery, was an anomaly that must at once cease. The Government had, however, no treaty right to take any such measure, and all the old fallacies concerning the conditions of our jurisdiction on the Gold Coast were again brought forward to show that they ought not to take it. It was once more reasserted that British territory on the Gold Coast consisted only of the ground upon which the forts actually stood, although, by usage and sufferance, the Coast towns had for years been British possessions, in which policemen, who were paid by the Colonial Government, patrolled the streets, and arrested persons who committed offences against English law, who were then tried by English magistrates, and imprisoned in Colonial gaols. Now it was said that these towns were foreign territory, in which the British had no jurisdiction, and where, consequently, they could not abolish slavery; but this quibble was brushed aside, with many others, and the ordinances disposing of the question of slavery were sent out from England to be passed by the Legislative Council of the Colony. And, indeed, it was quite time that something was done, for Colonial officials had not hesitated to accept slaves in payment of debts contracted by natives, and several officers of the Government had, when Captain Glover was enlisting recruits at Accra, flatly refused to allow their Odonko slaves to be enrolled.

On the 3rd of November, 1874, a meeting of all the Kings and chiefs of the western and central portions of the Gold Coast was held in the Castle at Cape Coast, and Captain Strahan informed them in a lengthy address that slavery, whether domestic or other, and the custom of pawning, were to be at an end. Pawning was a custom under which the head of a family could give any subordinate member of it to a creditor, to be retained by the latter as a temporary slave, until the debt and interest, which continued to run, were paid. A father could likewise, with the consent of the mother, pawn his children, and a mother could pawn them without the consent of the father, provided that he refused to give her the sum she required. As the debts for which pawns were given as security were rarely, if ever, paid, numbers of people were thus given into perpetual bondage, which was transmitted from generation to generation, for if a pawn died without being redeemed, another, usually one of his children, had to be substituted.

The chiefs consulted together, and, after a short interval, Adu, chief of Mankassim, asked permission for them to be allowed to retire till next day, in order that they might deliberate as to the answer to be returned; but this was refused, and the Governor withdrew to allow them full freedom of debate. In an hour he returned, and the Kings and chiefs then said they were willing to cease buying and selling slaves, but objected to those slaves they now had being permitted to go free without payment, or any cause being shown. They also objected to the custom of pawning being prohibited. After some discussion, however, the question of pawning was settled by the debtor being held responsible for the amount for which the pawn had been pledged; and when it was explained to the chiefs that it was not intended to compel slaves to leave their owners, but only to give any slave who wished to leave his owner liberty to do so, the expressed themselves as satisfied. To have endeavoured to force every slave, willing or unwilling, to leave his owner would have been an unwarrantable interference with individual freedom of action, and would besides have been a severe blow to the chiefs and influential natives, whose property largely consisted of slaves. The chiefs were perfectly satisfied when the conditions of the abolition of slavery were explained, because they knew that most slaves would rather remain with their owners, who fed them and supplied their daily wants, than go out into the world to seek the means of existence ; and in the end it was only the idle and disorderly slaves who availed themselves of their freedom, and, it may be said, thus added seriously to the criminal population. Slavery as it existed on the Gold Coast had none of the degrading characteristics of slavery in the West Indies or America, for a slave was always regarded as one of the family, and not unfrequently married into it. Sometimes even the social position of the slave was superior to that of his owner, and as the slave had the right to acquire and hold property, it was possible to see a master swelling the retinue of a slave who had amassed wealth.

On December 17th, 1874, a proclamation was issued forbidding slavery and the dealing in slaves, and declaring that all children born after November 5th, 1874, were free. The proclamation concluded thus : " But it is not intended by any of the aforesaid laws or otherwise to offer inducement to any persons to leave any master in whose service they may be desirous of remaining, or to forsake the *kru'm* where they have been accustomed to inhabit, and that it is intended to permit the family and tribal relations to continue in all respects according as used and wont, except only that of slavery, and such customs as arise therefrom, and are thereon necessarily dependent."

CHAPTER XXVIII.

1875—1881.

Affairs in Ashanti—Secession of Djuabin—Conquest of Djuabin by Ashanti—Fresh troubles in Awuna—Ashanti intrigues in Adansi—The Golden Axe—An invasion of Assin threatened—Protracted negotiations.

SHORTLY after the termination of the Ashanti War, the Kotoko Council of Kumassi dethroned Kwoffi Kari-kari, placing his brother, Mensa, on the stool in his stead, and about the same time Asafu Agai, King of Djuabin, definitely seceded from the Ashanti kingdom, and with the chiefs of Assuri, Affidguassi, and Nsuta formed an independent kingdom. This example was soon followed by others, the distant province of Kwao first declaring its independence, and the chiefs of Bekweh and Kokofu shortly after. All these former feudatories of Ashanti made overtures to the Colonial Government, being desirous of having British protection extended to them, but the Imperial Government, anxious not to increase its responsibilities on the Gold Coast, rejected the offers. This was a great mistake if it was the policy of the Government to put it out of the power of Ashanti to ever again make aggressions on the Protectorate, for though the Ashanti kingdom had now fallen to pieces, yet it was certain that the Ashantis would by diplomacy, intrigue, or force do everything in their power to reconstruct it, and probably with success. It would therefore have been politic to have taken at least Djuabin under British protection, for that kingdom was

now as powerful as what remained of Ashanti, and would
have proved a useful ally in the event of any future disturbance, while our recognition of its independence would have
guaranteed it against attack from Ashanti. However, in
accordance with the rule that had been laid down of strict
non-intervention in the affairs of the tribes beyond the
Protectorate, nothing was done, with the result that Mensa
very soon endeavoured to win back to their allegiance the
seceded districts. At first, apparently, he met with little
success, but about July, 1875, the chief of Mampon, acting
under Mensa's instructions, commenced negotiations with one
of the principal chiefs of Djuabin, who for some reason was
dissatisfied with his position. This chief promised to assist
the Ashantis should they invade Djuabin, but Asafu Agai
discovered his treachery and put him to death, and then, in
revenge for Mensa's intrigues, kidnapped and plundered a
number of Ashantis. Upon this Mensa demanded of the
Colonial Government that the King of Djuabin should be
called upon to pay a fair proportion of the indemnity which
had been claimed from the whole kingdom; and in July,
1875, he addressed a letter to the European merchants of
Cape Coast, complaining of the action of the King of Djuabin,
whom he accused of kidnapping Ashantis who lived near the
Djuabin frontier, and of closing the roads to trade. He
further complained that Asafu Agai had boasted that several
of the tribes of the Protectorate, especially the Eastern and
Western Akims, had promised to support him in a war with
Ashanti, and stated that he had patiently borne a number of
insults without retaliating, in order to prove to the Government his good faith and his desire for peace. He therefore
appealed to the merchants to use their influence with the
Government to restrain the King of Djuabin, and declared
that, if the Government would not do this, war would ensue,
as the Ashantis could no longer submit to such outrages.
This important letter was duly forwarded by the merchants
to the Governor, but only drew from him the reply that he
would act in reference to the affairs of the interior as seemed
to him advisable.

In making this declaration Mensa acted in good faith, and it is much to be regretted that the Government did not send a message to restrain Asafu Agai, for, though there were faults on both sides, he was chiefly to blame. It is probable that his head had been turned by his sudden accession to power, for he sent insulting messages to Mensa, and invited the protected tribes to come and share the spoils of Kumassi with him; with the result that by August, 1875, the tension had become so great that war was inevitable. In view o[f] the approaching conflict, some of the former feudatories o[f] Ashanti found themselves obliged to take one side or th[e] other, and the chiefs of Bekweh and Kokofu returned t[o] their allegiance. The first step towards the reconstructio[n] of the Ashanti kingdom was thus directly caused by th[e] inaction of the Colonial Government.

Matters were now further complicated by M. Bonnat, wh[o] was engaged in a scheme for opening a trade route wit[h] Salagha, a large and populous Mohammedan town, said to b[e] situated eight days' journey to the north-east of Kumassi. [It] had formerly been to some extent subject to Ashanti, but [in] 1873 all the Ashantis had been killed or driven out of t[he] country. In pursuance of his scheme, M. Bonnat visite[d] the Ashanti capital in company with Prince Ansa, a[nd] apparently forgetting all he had suffered at the hands of t[he] Ashantis during his captivity, was won over to their interes[t] and became a strong partisan. In this capacity he went [to] Djuabin and tried to induce Asafu Agai to go to Kuma[ssi] and make submission, but failed, and was regarded with [so] much suspicion that his own life was in some danger, wh[ile] about sixty Ashantis who were in his following were actua[lly] put to death. In extenuation of this massacre Asafu A[gai] afterwards explained that he had no voice in the matter, [as] the slaughter of these men was ordered by the Keratchi g[od] the chief deity of Djuabin; but the priests had really o[nly] issued the order after consultation with him, and it [is] probable that he suggested it. Notwithstanding this outr[age] Mensa was so afraid that the Colonial Government wo[uld] interpose if he invaded Djuabin, that he still delayed act[ion] but towards the end of September a fresh cause of quarrel arose. In that month the inhabitants of five villages on the borders of Djuabin notified their desire to become subject to Ashanti, and Mensa accordingly sent some court officials to them; but the Djuabins strove to prevent the secession, and a skirmish ensued, which resulted in the defeat of the Djuabins and the emigration of the people of the villages to Ashanti.

When the news of this affair reached Cape Coast, the Colonial Government at last awoke to the fact that something ought to be done, and they sent Dr. Gouldsbury on a mission to the interior, with instructions, first, to proceed to Eastern Akim and warn the King of that tribe, who had been tampered with by the Djuabins, not to take part in the impending hostilities; and, secondly, to proceed from Akim to Djuabin and Kumassi and forbid the war. Dr. Gouldsbury left Accra on October 23rd, 1875, but his mission had been kept so little secret that his approaching departure had been known for some time, and, long before he started, Prince Ansa had sent warning to Mensa that if he intended to fight he must do so at once before the white man arrived "to palaver." Mensa acted upon this advice, and on October 30th Djuabin messengers reached Dr. Gouldsbury at Kibbi, in Eastern Akim, with the news that the Ashantis had invaded their country in two armies, one of which was, when they left, encamped within a few miles of the capital. On October 31st the town of Djuabin was attacked; the conflict raged during the two succeeding days, and on November 3rd the Djuabins fled in all directions, completely routed. Dr. Gouldsbury now proceeded to Djuabin, which he found in the hands of the Ashantis, and foreseeing that the prestige of this conquest would do much to restore Ashanti to its old position, and undo the work of Sir Garnet Wolseley's expedition, he wrote to the Governor strongly recommending that Djuabin should be occupied by a British force. This proposal was not entertained, and, unless the Government wanted a new Ashanti war on its hands, it would have been madness, with the handful of troops at its disposal, to have tried to snatch the fruits of victory from the Ashantis in their hour of triumph. The Governor had allowed the proper moment for intervention to escape him, and now it was too late to remedy it.

With the conquest of Djuabin, Assuri, Affidguassi, and Nsuta returned to their allegiance, and the results were soon perceptible in the altered tone adopted by Mensa; for when Dr. Gouldsbury went on from Djuabin to Kumassi, he was treated with scant courtesy and could effect nothing, while the constabulary officer who had been sent with an escort to receive an instalment of the war indemnity, was hustled by a Kumassi mob and his men pelted with mud. The officer marched out of the capital with his men in high dudgeon, and the King, thinking that he had perhaps gone too far, sent the gold after him; but this experience was so alarming that the Colonial Government never applied for the payment of another instalment, and out of the 50,000 ounces of gold promised by the treaty of Fomana not more than 4,000 were ever paid. Thus, within less than two years after the burning of Kumassi the Ashantis had, thanks to the Government policy of non-intervention, recovered the whole of their lost territory except Kwao and Adansi, and escaped the payment of the greater part of the indemnity.

As the Djuabins were driven across the Prah they were disarmed by a party of Houssa constabulary under Captain J. S. Hay, and settled in a tract of country to the north of Accra, where they founded a town called New Djuabin. In 1877, the ex-King of Djuabin was discovered plotting with some of the chiefs of the eastern districts to recover his lost kingdom, and on 16th July a meeting of chiefs was convened at Accra by the Governor, Mr. Sandford Freeling, at which they were told that they could not be allowed to use the Protectorate as a base for making attempts against Ashanti. Chief Tacki, of Accra, who was one of the principal offenders, was fined, and all were warned that any future offence would be punished with transportation.

In 1878 Geraldo de Lema was again the cause of an outbreak among the Awunas. When we last left the person, a reward of £200 had been offered by Sir Arthur Kennedy for his apprehension, but he was never taken, and owing to the rapid change of Governors and officials, the fact that he was a disturber of public peace whose arrest was necessary, seems to have been lost sight of, as, though he visited Cape Coast and Accra after 1874, he was not apprehended. Under the treaty of Jella Koffi the Gold Coast Colony had been extended to the east as far as the village of Adaffia, about eighteen miles beyond Kittah, and the usual import duties were levied on goods landed between the Volta and that place. The district, which was termed the Kittah district, was of peculiar formation. The sea-coast consisted of a ridge of sand, or rather a succession of ancient sea-beaches, varying in breadth from about three miles near the town of Awuna to about two hundred yards at Kittah, and behind it lay the broad sheet of water known as the Kittah Lagoon. This lagoon contained many islands, of which the most important was Anyako, and extended on the east to within a few miles of Adaffia; so that persons desirous of avoiding payment of customs dues could land goods just beyond the boundary of the Colony, and transport them a short distance by land to the lagoon, which afforded every facility for their concealment and distribution. The Awunas of the sea-coast, equally with those of the islands and northern shores of the lagoon, were not slow to avail themselves of this easy mode of smuggling, and the European merchants also connived at it, for they established stores and factories at Danu, about a mile beyond the frontier, and gave the native traders orders for goods to be delivered at this place, in return for the palm oil and palm kernels delivered at Kittah. By this arrangement, while continuing to enjoy the protection of the Colonial Government at Kittah for the storage of native produce, they evaded the payment of dues on imported goods, and at the same time left all the risks of smuggling to their native correspondents. Geraldo de Lema, who, now that there was no longer any market for slaves, had abandoned slave dealing, and engaged in the profitable business of supplying the Awunas with spirits, tobacco, gunpowder, and muskets, was one of the chief offenders against the revenue laws, and had stores on the north side of the lagoon, to which goods were regularly smuggled from Danu.

In consequence of these practices the revenue of the district was not sufficient to meet the expenditure, and this condition lasted till 1878, when Lieutenant A. B. Ellis, 1st West India Regiment, was appointed District Commissioner. That officer, seeing that there was no prospect of improvement as long as the natives were suffered to smuggle with impunity, took vigorous measures, and organised and led by night surprise parties of Houssa Constabulary, who made so many seizures between the end of the lagoon and Adaffia that the trade of Danu was virtually ruined, the natives finding the risks of smuggling too great to be incurred. The revenue of Kittah at once became trebled, but, however satisfactory this might be to the Government, the natives did not at all appreciate the change, and rumours of disaffection were soon heard from various quarters. Geraldo de Lema, who was one of the chief sufferers by the suppression of smuggling, incited the Awunas to rebel, and at his instigation a meeting of the chiefs was held at the town of Awuna, about the middle of October, 1878, to discuss the advisability of making war upon the Government. The feeling of hostility, however, was directed more against the District Commissioner personally, than against the Government, and on the 23rd October, an attempt was made to murder him, the Awunas hoping that if he were removed, matters would drift back into their old course. He had crossed the lagoon in company with another European, and was just about to land near a village on the northern shore, when a number of men armed with swords, who had been concealed in a dense growth of reeds, rushed upon the boat. A hand-to-hand struggle ensued, in which in the course of two or three minutes both Europeans and one of the boat's crew were wounded, but four or five of the Awunas were shot down, and the remainder, cowed by this unexpected resistance, paused. The boat was at once pushed off into deep water, and although it was pursued by several canoes filled with armed men, succeeded in reaching Kittah in safety. This incident precipitated matters; the different Constabulary detachments were called in, and the whole force of the district, amounting only to 120 men, was concentrated at Kittah, which next day was blockaded by the Awunas. On the night of the 26th an attempt to surprise the place was made by a flotilla of canoes, but every precaution against surprise had been taken, and the enemy were driven off by the discharge of a few rockets. On the 29th a reinforcement of some ninety Houssa Constabulary, that had been asked for from Accra, arrived, and with them the acting Colonial Secretary, Captain J. S. Hay, who at once sent messages to the Awuna chiefs to come to a meeting. The next night, however, a desultory fire was opened on the fort during a heavy tornado, and on the night of 6th November, the outposts on the western side of the town were attacked, and several houses, the property of the Government, or occupied by the civil police, were fired by disaffected natives in the town itself. On the 8th, Mr. Jackson, the Chief Justice of the Colony, arrived to hold an inquiry into the cause of the disturbances, and through the exertions of one or two chiefs, who were engaged in trade, and had a good deal to lose by war, the Awuna forces were induced to withdraw from the sea-board; but though an inquiry was held, nothing was done, and the affair died a natural death. In consequence of the outbreak, however, and in order to render smuggling less easy, the boundary of the Colony was moved to Aflao, about eight miles beyond Adaffia, the sea-board of Agbosomi and Aflao being incorporated with the Colony by proclamation on December 2nd, 1879.

No sooner had the Ashantis firmly re-established their rule in Djuabin, than they turned their attention to Adansi, and commenced intrigues with some of the chiefs to persuade them to return to their allegiance to Kumassi. As the Adansi tribe was numerically weak, King Mensa could easily have compelled it to submit to his rule, but he thought that the British Government was, if called upon, bound by the Treaty of Fomana to guarantee its independence, and therefore, instead of proceeding openly against the Adansis by force of arms, strove to attain his end by bribes and promises. By the spring of 1879 these methods had so far prevailed that a considerable section of the Adansi tribe had been won over to Ashanti interests, and the King of Adansi, who was not by any means desirous of resigning his lately gained independence, sent messengers to the Colonial Government, complaining of Mensa's conduct. At this time the administration of the Government was in the hands of Mr. C. C. Lees, who had had the advantage of many years' experience of native affairs and he saw clearly that however well a policy of non-intervention beyond the Protectorate might look in theory, it was practically impossible, when dealing with barbarous tribes, to say that south of an imaginary line we had certain duties and interests, but that north of it we had neither. The Ashantis had so far repaired the disastrous effects of the campaign of 1874 that the independence of Adansi was now almost the only remaining evidence of their defeat, and he saw that to allow them to erase it would have the worst possible effect upon the protected tribes. He therefore, in response to the complaint of the King of Adansi, sent Captain J. S. Hay to Kumassi, to demand that the Ashantis should respect the third article of the Treaty of Fomana, with respect to Adansi, and withdraw their emissaries to their own country. This straightforward course had the desired effect, and Mensa's agents were recalled from Adansi, but so wedded was the Colonial Office to its policy of non-intervention, that though this mission was the only political success that had been secured since the Ashanti War, the Secretary of State found fault with Mr. Lees. He declared that the question of requiring the observance of the third article of the treaty was one of external policy, and that the Government of the Gold Coast ought not to have taken action without consulting the Home Government.

Though the Ashantis were checked for the moment they did not abandon all hope of reducing Adansi to the condition of a tributary state, and when, in 1880, Mr. Ussher, according to the established usage, sent presents to the Ashanti King on taking up his appointment of Governor, Mensa availed himself of the opportunity to send messengers down to the coast, ostensibly to thank Governor Ussher for his presents, but really to ascertain secretly the views and position of the Government with regard to Adansi. These messengers, after being received at Accra, returned to Cape Coast, and remained there collecting information and watching events, explaining their delay in returning to their own country by a number of frivolous excuses. There was at this time an influential war party in Kumassi, which included, among other powerful chiefs, Opoku, chief of Bekweh, and the Ashanti General, Awua, chief of Bantama, who were desirous of removing the last important trace of the national defeat by annexing Adansi. They knew that they could easily drive the Adansis across the Prah, and they hoped that the Colonial Government would not interfere; but they were willing to take the risk, for they had for some three or four years been purchasing breech-loading rifles, and in the confidence which these new weapons inspired, they thought they could hold their own even against another British expedition. Mensa, who had most to lose by a reverse, was opposed to the war party, whose hands were greatly strengthened by the intrigues which the ex-King of Djuabin and chief Tacki, of Accra, were notoriously carrying on for an invasion of Ashanti by the eastern tribes of the Protectorate; and though the former was banished to Lagos and the latter arrested and sent to Elmina, the rankling effects of their actions still remained. In December, 1880, matters looked so threatening that Mr. Buhl, Secretary of the Basel Mission Society, reported to the Colonial Government that there were rumours in Ashanti that the country was going to war; and in the same month chief Tabu, of Adansi, informed the District Commissioner of Cape Coast that the chief of Bekweh had publicly sworn in Kumassi that he would force Adansi to become subject to Ashanti. On December 1st, 1880, Governor Ussher died at Accra, and Mr. W. B. Griffith, the Lieutenant-Governor, assumed the administration of the government of the Colony.

This was the condition of affairs when, on the 18th of January, 1881, a fugitive from Kumassi presented himself at Elmina Castle to claim protection, stating that he was a Gaman prince, named Awusu, and that, having incurred King Mensa's displeasure, he had sought safety in flight. His grandmother was a Gaman princess who had married in Kumassi and borne a daughter, who, in her turn, had married Prince Kwadjo, of Ashanti. Awusu was the fruit of this union, and according to European notions, he would be an Ashanti, but as by native custom descent is traced solely and exclusively through mothers, he was, in the eyes of the natives, a Gaman, and was, in Kumassi, considered an important personage, as a possible heir to the stool of Gaman.

The day after the arrival of the fugitive at Elmina, an embassy from Kumassi, bearing the golden axe, arrived at Cape Coast to request his surrender. After the usual compliments, the messenger told the Lieutenant-Governor, Mr. W. B. Griffith, that Awusu had been persuaded by an Assin trader, named Amankra, to run away from Kumassi, and that the King had sent to ask that he might be given up. The envoy further asked that Amankra might be surrendered, because, although he had resided for many years in Kumassi, and had been regarded as a friend by the King, he had received bribes from the King of Gaman to induce Awusu to go to that country. To this Mr. Griffith said that as Awusu had not committed any crime, and was now under British protection, it was not in his power to give him up to the King. The messenger then asked if Awusu would be prevented from going to Gaman, and was told in reply that the refugee was free to go from British protection, or remain under it, no one having any right to control his movements. The messengers seemed much annoyed at this refusal, and, according to one version, Engui, one of the messengers who had been sent down to Mr. Ussher, and who had remained at Cape Coast ever since, then said that the Assins were a tribe who always caused trouble between Ashanti and the Protectorate, and that if Awusu were not given up the King would invade Assin; but, according to another version, this statement was made to the Government interpreter, in his own house, before the meeting with the Lieutenant-Governor. In any case, the threat of invasion was made in the one place or the other, so Mr. Griffith caused the treaty of 1874 to be shown and explained to the messenger.

The critical condition of affairs in Ashanti being well known, this menace was naturally regarded as alarming, and the alarm was accentuated by the belief that the golden axe signified that if the demands made were not complied with, war would ensue. This belief was altogether ill-founded, as the emblem only indicated that the matter was one of great importance; but, the existence of a powerful war party in Kumassi being well established, the Government at once asked for reinforcements from Sierra Leone and from England. Then a panic seems to have broken out. Nothing being known of the history of former invasions, and the leisurely movements of Ashanti armies, it was supposed that in a few days an overwhelming hostile force would arrive at the Coast; and it was decided to abandon the whole of the Protectorate to the enemy and only attempt the defence of Elmina, Cape Coast, Anamabo, and Axim. The walls of Elmina Castle were heightened with sand-bags, and earthworks thrown up in the Government Garden and on Java Hill, Elmina; while the detachments of Houssa Constabulary, which had been maintained at Prahsu and Mansu since 1875, were withdrawn in such haste, that several thousand rounds of Snider ammunition were left behind for want of carriers to transport them. On the night of 1st February an Ashanti army was reported to be within a few miles of Cape Coast, and the detachment of West India troops at Connor's Hill, which covers the approach to the town, was hastily reinforced from the Castle. This state of alarm was not shared by the natives, who remained in their villages quietly engaged in their usual avocations, and it ought to have been known that any invasion would have been heralded by the flight of the inhabitants of the towns along the Prah road to seek the protection of the forts; but public confidence was only restored when two hundred men of the 1st West India Regiment arrived at Cape Coast on 2nd February.

The rumour of the defensive preparations undertaken by the Government soon reached Kumassi, and the King, whatever his former intentions might have been, being alarmed thereby, sent messengers, who arrived at Cape Coast on the 8th, to assure the Lieutenant-Governor that he had no hostile designs upon the Protectorate; and on the 17th a third embassy arrived from Kumassi, repudiating on the part of the King any hostile intention, and declaring that, if Engui had said he would invade Assin, the statement was altogether unauthorised. The King protested that his only desire was to live in peace with the English, and that he would never bring a single gun across the Prah. Whether Mensa had really meditated an invasion has never been decided, but what seems most probable is that the unexpected flight of Awusu had caused great excitement in Kumassi, and the Kotoko Council, which was largely composed of members of the war party, had, in an ebullition of anger, caused the threatening message to be sent. That the Ashantis wished to invade Adansi is certain, but it is extremely doubtful if the threat to invade Assin was ever more than a petulant exhibition of annoyance.

The newly-appointed Governor, Sir Samuel Rowe, being expected to arrive in a few days, no answer was sent in reply to the messages of the 8th and 17th of February; nor was any notice taken of them after his arrival, which took place on the 4th March. On the contrary, warlike measures became more in the ascendant than ever, and nothing was talked of but meetings of friendly chiefs, and the raising of native levies. All this was, of course, duly communicated to the King by his agents in Cape Coast, and, not unnaturally concluding that the Colonial Government had some aggressive action in contemplation, he sent a fourth embassy to Cape Coast, instructed, as further appeal to the Government appeared useless, to solicit the good offices of the merchants both European and native, to place matters on a friendly footing. This embassy, which was received by the merchants on 18th March, was very humble and apologetic. It declared that the King wanted peace, and that if he had done anything wrong in the message with the axe, he asked pardon for it. It said that he was willing to do anything to maintain peace, and suggested that a European officer should be sent to Kumassi so that it might be seen that no preparations for war were in progress.

After being interviewed by the merchants the messengers were received by Sir Samuel Rowe, who had an unfortunate habit of making ambiguous speeches, a very dangerous practice when dealing with uncivilised peoples, with whom nothing answers so well as plain and straightforward dealing. On this occasion, instead of saying he was pleased to hear the King had no hostile intentions, he told the messengers he had nothing to do with the message they brought, and what the merchants might have said was their own affair ; and dismissed them with the remark that the difficulty between the King and the Government had not in any way been cleared up. The Ashantis regarded this as a thinly-veiled threat, and the arrival of the 2nd West India Regiment on 20th March from the West Indies, confirmed in their minds the impression that, for some reason of his own, the Governor was bent upon making war. The difficulty, which had hitherto been easy of solution, was thus made serious, for there was a limit to the self-abasement to which a proud nation like Ashanti would submit, and the danger of it being driven into war through fear of aggression. These dangers, and the advisability of at once settling the matter, were urged upon the Governor by Colonel W. C. Justice, Commanding the Troops, Captain Hope, Senior Naval Officer, and the Chief Justice of the Colony, at a meeting held at Elmina on 21st March ; but he overruled this sensible advice, and two days later held a public conference with the chiefs of Appollonia, Axim, Ahanta, Akim, Assin, Anamabo, and Elmina, to ascertain what contingent of fighting men each could furnish. Next, an expedition to Prahsu was talked of, and daily, after 26th March, quantities of stores and detachments of constabulary were sent up country.

In the meantime King Mensa had made one more attempt to obtain peace, and had despatched an embassy, under the leadership of Buakji Tintin, the husband of the queen-mother, to endeavour to effect a settlement. This embassy left Kumassi on 3rd April, but on arriving at Akankuassi learned that an expeditionary force was encamped at Prahsu. Imagining this to be the prelude to an invasion, Buakji halted and sent word back to Kumassi, where the mobilisation of the warriors at once took place, and to Bekweh, the chief of which province immediately called out his men to defend the approach to the capital. Thus the very danger which had been pointed out to the Governor now actually occurred, and in all human probability an unnecessary war with Ashanti would have ensued, had not Sir Samuel Rowe, who had himself gone to Prahsu, fortunately received intelligence of what was taking place, and then done that which he ought to have done long before, namely, send a message to the Ashantis to come down and put an end to the situation Upon receiving this invitation Buakji Tintin came on at once, and arrived in the camp at Prahsu on the 16th. Or the 19th the camp was broken up, and the stores which had been brought up country at so great an expense to the Colony were reconveyed to Elmina, where a palaver was held on the 29th. At this meeting each member of the embassy rose in turn and assured the Governor that the King and the nation had never contemplated war with the Protectorate. They declared that the sending of the golden ax could not be construed as a declaration of war, and mentioned several occasions on which it had been sent before with peaceful result; but as they had been privately informed that the Government would not make peace unless some money was paid, 2,000 ounces of gold were promised as an indemnity for the expenses incurred. The Ashantis, and, indeed, all the tribes of the Gold Coast, regarded the payment of this sum as a kind of black-mail, extorted in accordance with native practices. The Ashantis had, in bygone days, been accustomed to foment quarrels with the tribes on the coast, threaten war, and then demand gold as the condition of peace; but now, in the eyes of the natives, the parts were changed, and it was the Government that kept a dispute open and then asked for money as the price of a settlement. On the 17th of July, Awusu, the Gaman fugitive, committed suicide at Elmina.

CHAPTER XXIX.

1882—1886.

Gold Mining Companies in Wassaw—Human sacrifices in Kumassi—
Quarrel between Ashanti and Gaman—Dethronement of Mensa—
Rival factions in Ashanti—Election and death of Kwaku Dua II.—
Renewed disturbances in Awuna—Disorganisation of Ashanti—War
between Bekweh and Adansi—The Adansis driven across the Prah—
Boundary Commissions.

DURING the three or four years immediately preceding the Golden Axe scare, the gold-producing districts of Wassaw, which had been neglected for nearly two centuries, were explored and opened up on a large scale by various mining companies. The African Gold Coast Company had, in April, 1877, been the first to arrive, and had, in February 1878, obtained a concession at Tarkwa, a village situated in a densely-wooded valley at the foot of the Tarkwa Mountains, in the Apinto district of Wassaw. The gold field was distant about six hours' journey from the limit of boat navigation on the Bonsa River, a tributary of the Ancobra, and twelve hours from the latter, and was surrounded by fetid swamps, which caused it to be very unhealthy for Europeans. The first assay of the ore was so promising that the African Gold Coast Company was soon followed by the Swanzy, Effuenta, and Gold Coast Mining Companies, while a French company, termed the Abosso Gold Mining Company, established itself at Abosso, about twelve miles from Tarkwa. These mines, however, did not prove remunerative in consequence of the enormous cost of transport, which amounted to about £30 a ton. All the machinery, as it arrived from England, had to be taken to pieces, so that no section weighed more than four men could carry; it was then taken up the River Ancobra to Tomento in boats, and thence carried by men through an extensive swamp, and over several steep hills and ravines, to the Tarkwa valley. In 1882, two new companies appeared, and, to avoid the cost of transport, obtained concessions nearer to the coast: the first, the Akanko Gold Mining Company, commencing operations at Akanko, about twenty-six miles up the Ancobra River; and the second, the Guinea Coast Mining Company, at Izrah, about six miles from the sea, and to the west of the Ancobra.

The whole 2,000 ounces of the indemnity demanded from Ashanti having been paid, the embassy of Buakji Tintin started on its return journey to Kumassi on 15th October, 1881, and was accompanied by Captain R. La Touche Lonsdale, who had orders to remain in the Ashanti capital for a few weeks, and then proceed to Salagha, to endeavour to open a trade route between that inland market and the Colony. In September of the same year a report reached Cape Coast that King Mensa had put two hundred young girls to death, in order to use their blood for kneading the clay required for the repairs of his palace, and this aroused some attention in England, as by Article 8 of the Treaty of Fomana, the King had promised to do all in his power to check human sacrifices. The truth of the report was denied; but though the particulars were inexact, there is no doubt that human sacrifices on a large scale had taken place, the occasion being the death of Yah Affileh, sister of the queen-mother. She was buried at Bantama, and for four weeks, girls and women, in parties of ten or twelve, were put to death; while at the termination of the funeral ceremonies, her tomb was built up of clay kneaded with human blood. Up to this time the 8th Article of the Treaty of Fomana had really been a dead letter, and Captain Lonsdale reported that human sacrifices frequently took place in Kumassi, though generally in secret. The necessity of putting a stop to these practices had been impressed upon Buakji Tintin, who was entrusted with a message to that effect to the King; but it afterwards transpired that he falsely rendered it, and told Mensa that persons who had spoken disrespectfully of the King and the royal family, or had broken the great oath, or committed adultery, might be reserved for sacrifice.

In February, 1882, King Mensa sent to the Governor to complain that the Gamans had invaded the Ashanti province of Banna, and, the non-intervention policy of the Government being now quite abandoned, instructions were sent to Captain Lonsdale to proceed to Buntuku, the Gaman capital, and report on the situation. He found that the Kumassi war party was responsible for the friction between the two nations, and that the disturbances had been commenced by the chiefs of Banna and Inkrusima, who, acting under orders from Kumassi, had robbed and killed several Gaman traders. In revenge for this, the Gamans attacked and destroyed the Ashanti town of Wonki, taking about fifty prisoners, and Mensa thereupon sent two armies to the Gaman frontier. These forces had marched from Kumassi before the messenger to the Governor had left that town, but owing to native dilatoriness no conflict had taken place when Captain Lonsdale arrived, and he succeeded in inducing the two Kings to refrain from hostilities on the understanding that the Government would, at some convenient time in the future, make a settlement of the dispute between them. The chief contention was about Inkrusima, which had formerly belonged to Gaman, but had seceded and joined Ashanti when that power was dominant.

Mensa, who had lost a great deal of prestige by his submissive attitude towards the Colonial Government in 1881, and was already regarded with a feeling of contempt by the leaders of the war party, now sank further in the public estimation on account of the peaceful compact made with Gaman. It appears that great deeds had been expected of Mensa, because when he was placed on the stool of Ashanti, he had adopted the "strong name" of Bonsu, or Whale. This epithet had also been taken by Tutu Kwamina, the conqueror of Fanti, and by a confusion of connection common amongst uncivilised peoples, it had been anticipated that the conquests of the new holder of the name would rival those of the old. In this the Ashantis had been disappointed, and Mensa had also rendered himself very unpopular by his tyrannical conduct in imposing the most exorbitant fines for very trivial offences; by the new impulse he had given to human sacrifices, which were much more frequent than had been the case under his predecessor; and by his unrestrained licentiousness, the wife of no subject being secure from his advances. The young men complained that the King took their wives, and that if they made objections they lost their heads also. The wives of chiefs could not be taken thus openly, but he intrigued with all who took his fancy, and it was this propensity which led to the incident which ultimately caused his downfall. The brother of Awua, chief of Bantama, discovered that his wife was guilty of adultery; without, however, discovering her paramour, who was no other than Mensa himself. As the woman would not divulge his name, her husband brought her before the King's Court, in order to compel her to confess; but when there she completely discomfited him by swearing the King's oath that he and his brother were plotting to join the Gamans and deliver Mensa to the white men. Probably some conspiracy was on foot, but in any case Mensa appears to have had no doubt that there was a design to dethrone him, and he seized the Queen of Mampon and her son, together with some forty members of the royal family of Ashanti, and put to death about seventy of his councillors and officials. Among those who suffered death was the injured husband, whose brother, Awua, Mensa also sought to slay, but he managed to escape to Inkwanta.*

* Inkwanta means a cross-road, or crossing. It is the name of a district.

This massacre, which took place in September, 1882, terrorised for a time the malcontents, though it added to the general discontent, and nothing but a leader was required to produce an insurrection. In January, 1883, the first step was taken by Amuofa, chief of Dadiassi,* a sub-province of Kokofu, who rebelled against Assaya, chief of Kokofu and brother to Mensa, on account of an exorbitant fine of 1,800 dollars, which the King had inflicted on his son. The rebellion was at once joined by the chief of Daniassi, and adherents came in so rapidly that on 24th February, 1883, messengers arrived at the coast, representing thirty-three chiefs who had revolted against Mensa, and who wished, together with 6,000 fighting men, to be admitted to British territory. All the sub-chiefs of Bekweh next joined the movement, and in March Kumassi itself rose in rebellion and Mensa took to flight. On 31st March the Governor despatched Captain Barrow, with an escort of forty Houssa Constabulary under Assistant-Inspector Kirby, to Kumassi to report upon the situation, and it was found that Mensa who was living in the village of Abrodi,† near Kumassi, and was afraid to return to the capital, was only supported by the chiefs of Kokofu and Bekweh, the latter of whom had been deserted by all his people. The revolt was not against the dynasty, but against Mensa, and the chiefs desired to place Kwaku Dua, a nephew of Mensa, on the stool.‡

Kwoffi Kari-kari, who since his dethronement had been living in the village of Akrapon, thought the present a favourable opportunity for regaining the kingdom, and sent towards Kumassi a small force, which Captain Barrow, however, succeeded in turning back. In June, 1883, when Captain Barrow left Kumassi, Kwaku Dua had not yet been placed on the stool, some of the provincial chiefs thinking he was too young, and in August, Kwoffi Kari-kari renewed his attempt. He advanced with a force to the village of Dadiem,§ where he encountered an armed party from

---

* Dadiassi—"Under Iron."   † Abrodi—"Plantain Tree."
‡ See Genealogical Table.   § Dadiem—"Place of Iron."

GENEALOGICAL TABLE OF THE KINGS OF ASHANTI.

```
                                    PRINCESS (name unknown)
                                              |
        ┌──────────────┬──────────────────┬──────────────────┬──────────────┐
   KING TUTU      KING APOKO I.     PRINCESS (name    PRINCESS (name    KING AKWASI
  (1700–1731)     (1731–1741)         unknown)          unknown)       (1741–1752)
                       |                                  |
                  KING KWADJO                       PRINCESS KUN ADUA*
                  (1753–1781)
                       |
        ┌──────────────┼──────────────────┐
   KING KWAMINA   KING APOKO II.    KING TUTU KWAMINA†    PRINCESS AMA SAWAH    KING OKOTO‡
   (1781–1797)   (1797–1799)         (1799–1824)                              (1824–1838)
        |                                  |                      |                   |
                                  KING KWAKU DUA I.§      PRINCESS EFFUA SAPONG    PRINCESS YAH FREH
                                    (1838–1867)
        |                                  |                      |                   |
   ┌────┴────┐                   ┌─────────┼─────────┐      PRINCESS ODEH      PRINCE ARCHIRIBOANDA
KING KWOFFI  KING MENSA     PRINCESS   PRINCESS  PRINCE AKWASI TCHISSI
KARI-KARI    (1875–1883)    EFFUA KOBRI  YAH KIA  EKUA AFIRIA
(1867–1874)                              |
                                    KING KWAKU DUA III.
                                      or PREMPEH
        |
   KING KWAKU DUA II.
       (1884)
```

* Kun Adua married her cousin, the son of King Kwadjo. At her death in 1811 upwards of 3,000 human victims were sacrificed, 2,000 being Fanti prisoners.

† Prince Ansa, sent to Governor Maclean when the Treaty of 1831 was made, was a son of King Tutu Kwamina. This King had a daughter, Tacheow, who married her cousin, King Kwaku Dua I.

‡ Prince Kwanta Bisa, sent to Governor Maclean with Prince Ansa, was the son of King Okoto.

§ King Kwaku Dua I. had, by his cousin Tacheow, a son, Kwasi Afiria, who married his second cousin, Princess Yah Kia. Thus, on the male side, of which the Ashantis take no account, Kwaku Dua II. was the grandson of Kwaku Dua I.

Kumassi and was driven back to Boreman,* losing some eighty killed and sixty wounded, among the former being the chief of the town of Aguna. His following, which had never been large, now dispersed, and Kwoffi Kari-kari, being pursued by a force from Kumassi, was eventually captured near the village of Bekem, about six days' journey to the west of Kumassi. Being of the royal blood his opponents dared not put him to death, and he remained a prisoner at large in one of the villages near Kumassi.

These events were duly reported to the Governor, Sir Samuel Rowe, on 5th of September by a messenger from Kwaku Dua and the Kumassi chiefs, who asked that an officer might be sent to Kumassi to place the young King on the stool. No direct reply was given to this message, and in November Kwaku Dua was elected King by the Kumassi chiefs, but not formally placed upon the golden stool, which ceremony answers to a coronation. This fact was reported in December to the Governor, who had in the meanwhile been authorised by the Secretary of State to ratify the election of Kwaku Dua, provided he was able to satisfy himself that he was likely to establish himself firmly in power, and to be acknowledged by the Ashanti tribes. To have ratified the election would now have put an end to all further differences, for Assistant-Inspector Kirby, who was sent to Kumassi in December, reported that the Kari-kari faction could never have been a source of danger to Kwaku Dua, the number of its supporters being insignificant, and that the Kumassi chiefs only refrained from stamping it out altogether because they believed the Colonial Government to be favourable to Kwoffi Kari-kari's re-election, a belief which was chiefly due to the machinations of Prince Ansa at Cape Coast, but had been supported by some ambiguous expressions used by the Governor to the messengers of the 5th of September. Unfortunately, Sir Samuel Rowe was always loth to accept the responsibility of decisive action, and on the 2nd of January, 1884, he dismissed the messengers from

---

* Boreman—" Poison Town."

Kumassi with a number of vague expressions, and a few words upon the desirability of peace.

This inaction prolonged the unsettled condition of Ashanti, and the chiefs of Dadiassi and Inkwanta declared their intention of remaining independent of Kumassi. The chief of Bekweh also adopted this course, but was speedily dethroned by his sub-chiefs and people, who were favourable to Kwaku Dua. Shortly after his secession from the kingdom, the chief of Dadiassi, pretending a friendly visit to his feudal lord, the chief of Kokofu, seized him, together with his mother and many influential persons, destroyed the town of Kokofu, and carried off his captives to Dadiassi. No steps were taken to avenge this, for Kari-kari's party was too weak, and Kwaku Dua was afraid to commit himself to any adventures until his installation was complete. He appears to have known that the Governor had been authorised to ratify his election, and at all state meetings he sat by the side of the royal stool, as keeper of it, waiting for the sanction of the Government, before taking his seat on it. At last, on the 24th of April, 1884, tired of waiting for the expected ratification, the provincial chiefs and those of Kumassi formally placed him on the stool, and the kingdom would no doubt have speedily quieted down, and Dadiassi and Inkwanta have been reduced to obedience, had not the young King died of small-pox on the 10th of June. A few days after his decease, the chiefs brought to Kumassi Kwoffi Kari-kari, who was lying ill of dysentery in the village in which he had been interned, but he succumbed to the disease on the 24th of June. The two rival candidates thus expired within fifteen days, and by the death of Prince Ansa at Cape Coast on the 13th of November, the three principal actors in these events were removed from the scene in the same year.

Towards the end of the year 1884, Geraldo de Lema, who had returned to Voji in 1882, and had been living there unmolested ever since, once more caused disturbances in the Kittah district, by inducing the inhabitants of the island of Anyako to blockade Kittah ; and as the people of Kittah are entirely dependent upon the productions of the islands and northern shores of the lagoon for food, for the sea-coast produces nothing but cocoanuts, the Governor, Mr. W. A. G. Young, who had been appointed in the spring of 1884, ordered his arrest. Captain Campbell, the District Commissioner, with the aid of two friendly Awuna chiefs named Támaklo and Akolatsi, succeeded in seizing Geraldo at night in his house at Voji; but then, most imprudently, considering the great local influence of the man, instead of sending him to Accra by sea, he placed him in charge of five men of the Houssa Constabulary to be conveyed there by land. The escort passed through the town of Awuna with their prisoner in safety, the inhabitants being taken by surprise, but swift messengers were sent on ahead of the party and when it reached the village of Huteh it was stopped and detained. The news of this reached Kittah on the morning of 17th January, 1885, and Captain Campbell, with the very inadequate force of thirty-eight Houssas, immediately proceeded to Huteh, in company with chiefs Tamaklo an Akolatsi. On arriving at the village, where he found tw Anyako chiefs with a large number of armed followers, h released the Houssa escort and sent them on their journey t Accra with their prisoner ; and, remaining at Huteh for th night, commenced next morning his return march to Kittal taking with him the two Anyako chiefs to answer for the conduct. About a mile and a half out of the village the part was fired upon by a force of Awunas, estimated at three thousand, and a conflict ensued in which the District Commi sioner was severely wounded, and ten Houssas killed ar several wounded. Most unwisely only twenty rounds ammunition per man had been provided, and when the were exhausted the constabulary was compelled to retre towards Kittah, closely pursued by the Awunas, now led the two Anyako chiefs who had escaped from custody du ing the confusion of the fight. Time after time the Hous had to turn upon their pursuers and charge with the bayon but fortunately the Awunas had not the courage to pr s their attacks home, and after about an hour the pursuit d away. Captain Campbell had received five wounds, a chief Akolatsi was wounded, while two of Tamaklo's sons, and several of the followers of the two chiefs, had been killed. Geraldo de Lema was conveyed to Accra in safety and lodged in the gaol.

As soon as the news of this affair reached the Government, H.M.S. *Frolic*, and reinforcements of Houssa Constabulary from Elmina and Accra, under Inspector C. Dudley, were sent down to Kittah. The Governor demanded the surrender of the rebellious chiefs, and the payment of a fine of £1,000, but no attention was paid to these demands, and it was accordingly determined to destroy the town of Anyako, and also that of Awuna, as its inhabitants had joined in the attack upon the Constabulary. On 31st January, Commander Parr of the *Frolic*, with a small party of seamen, and about one hundred Houssas under Inspector Dudley, proceeded in boats across the lagoon to Anyako, and burned the town, which had been abandoned by the enemy. On 2nd February the Houssas marched to Awuna, which was also found deserted, and was similarly destroyed without any resistance being met with.

A few months after the deaths of Kwaku Dua II. and Kwoffi Kari-kari, the Kumassi chiefs, who, when there was no King, considered themselves entitled to represent the nation, commenced negotiations with certain of the Inkwantas, to induce that people to return to their allegiance. This being discovered by the King of Inkwanta, he forbade his people to resort to Kumassi to trade, as they had been in the habit of doing, and the Kumassi chiefs thereupon marched with a force to the district, where they suffered a serious defeat, eleven chiefs being killed, and several, among them Buakji Tintin, made prisoners. This defeat had the effect of completing the disorganisation of Ashanti, each provincial chief now maintaining his own authority and being virtually independent, and many of the inhabitants abandoned Kumassi, which fell into a poor condition. In order to prevent the complete disintegration of the kingdom the queen-mother sent to ask the provincial chiefs to assemble in Kumassi and elect a new King, which they agreed to do, provided that a

European officer was sent up by the Government to be present at the election. She accordingly sent messengers to the Governor asking him to send an officer, and stating that it was proposed to place Akwasi Tchissi, a grandson of Effua Sapong, and cousin of the late King Mensa, on the stool.* The messengers were received by Mr. Young at Accra on 16th October, 1884, and he promised to send Assistant-Inspector Kirby, who was shortly expected to return from England; but that officer retired from the service of the Colony, then the outbreak at Kittah diverted attention from Ashanti affairs, and on 24th April, 1885, Mr. Young died at Accra. He was succeeded by Mr. W. B. Griffith, who was now appointed Governor, but no European officer was sent to Kumassi during the whole of the year 1885, and the Ashanti messengers were still waiting at Accra in February, 1886, when war broke out between Bekweh and Adansi.

The Adansis, taking advantage of the disorganisation of Ashanti, had for some months been plundering and kidnapping Ashanti traders passing to and from the coast and the King of Adansi, Kwaku Inkansa, had treated with contempt the complaints made by the chief of Bekweh, who appears to have been regarded by the Ashanti chiefs as the guardian of the trade route. In December, 1885, four traders from Nsuta were murdered by an Adansi chief but the immediate cause of the war was the seizure and execution by the King of Adansi of one hundred and fifty Ashantis, who were returning from the coast, and were murdered for the sake of the goods they were carrying Failing to obtain any redress for this massacre, Kari-kari chief of Bekweh, called out his men, and the King of Adansi thereupon sent to ask the Governor for assistance, he being still under the impression that Adansi was under British protection. In consequence of this application Mr. Griffith sent Inspector Firminger, of the Constabulary, to Prahsu to ascertain the exact condition of affairs, and to mak

* See Genealogical Table.

arrangements, should the Adansis be driven across the Prah, for locating the fugitives "in those portions of the Protectorate bordering on Prahsu." This, it may be remarked, was a most injudicious arrangement, as it was certain that the Adansis, if driven across the Prah, would, if possible, use the Protectorate as a base from which to make incursions into Ashanti; and orders ought consequently to have been given for their internment in districts of the Colony as remote as possible from Prahsu.

On February 1st, 1886, before any collision between the opposing tribes had occurred, Kari-kari of Bekweh died; but Yow Janfi was elected to the vacant stool the same day, and soon after, two skirmishes, the result of reconnaissances made by the Bekwehs, took place. Mr. Firminger arrived at Prahsu early in March, and found that the Bekwehs, who had been joined by a contingent from Kumassi, and were about 6,000 strong, were concentrated at Donkuassi, near Amoafu, and that the Adansis expected to be attacked almost immediately. The Adansi King fully expected to be driven from his country, a punishment which he richly deserved, and he was most eager in his appeals to Mr. Firminger, who, in the interests of peace, sent a messenger with a letter to the chief of Bekweh, informing him that the Governor wished to prevent bloodshed, and requesting him to state his grievances against Adansi, and refrain from hostilities till he received a reply thereto. The chief of Bekweh replied, with great moderation, that he had for a very long time had to complain of the Adansis; that more than two years ago he had sent messengers to Sir Samuel Rowe to complain of their conduct, but had received no satisfactory answer; that he had to revenge the murder of many of his people, and was now in a position to drive the Adansis out of the country; but that, as a mark of respect for the Governor, he would take no action till 20th March, by which time a reply ought to be received from Accra.

The Adansis, who had induced the Inkwantas to join them, were, to the number of some 3,000, encamped at

Dompoassi, near the Bekweh frontier, the women and children being all distributed among the villages near the Prah, ready to cross that river in the event of a reverse. The 20th March having passed without any reply being received from Mr. Griffith, the Bekwehs, on the 23rd, pushed forward a force of about 2,000 men, who attacked the Adansi village of Akrocheh early in the morning, and a desultory skirmish lasted till late in the afternoon, when the Bekwehs retired, leaving five heads, one of them that of a chief, in the hands of the Adansis. The latter were so elated by this trifling success, which they regarded as a great victory that their King, Kwaku Inkansa, completely changed his tone, and now, instead of humbly begging the Government to protect him, forcibly detained an accredited messenger sent by Mr. Firminger to the chief of Bekweh, an act which according to native etiquette was a deliberate insult. The Adansis declared their intention of at once invading Bekweh, but as several days passed without any movement being made, Mr. Firminger crossed the Prah and proceeded to Fomana, to see what could be effected by negotiation. The exultation of the Adansis having by this time died away, the King was able to take a more accurate view of the situation, and at a meeting held at Fomana on the 7th and 8th of April, he and his chiefs promised to leave the settlement of the quarrel with Bekweh in Mr. Firminger's hands. From Fomana he accordingly went to Begroassi, where the Bekweh army was now encamped, and had a conference with Yow Janfi and his chiefs, who at first promised to make peace if the Adansis would cede certain villages, but ultimately declared their resolution to drive the Adansis across the Prah. This decision could surprise no one, for the Adansis had only owed their long immunity from punishment to the belief, carefully promulgated by themselves, that the Government was bound to protect them, and the Bekwehs had now learned that this was not the case. The Bekweh army numbered about 7,000 men, and while Mr. Firminger was with it, a reinforcement of 200 men, a large number of whom were armed with Snider rifles, marched in from Kumassi. Finding nothing could be done, Mr. Firminger returned to Prahsu, and on his way there effected the release of forty women and children, who had fallen into the hands of the Adansis, and were about to be sacrificed.

The destruction of Adansi now seemed imminent, when the situation was suddenly changed by an alliance which Kwaku Inkansa succeeded in making with Dadiassi, the chiefs of which district were probably afraid that if Adansi were destroyed, they would soon lose the independence they had enjoyed since the early part of the year 1884. Dadiassi was now more powerful than either Bekweh or Adansi alone, and could put some 5,000 men into the field. The frontier tribes of the Protectorate now began to be drawn into the quarrel, the Akims making an agreement with the Dadiassis to allow them to enter their territory, and promising to close the roads to all Ashanti traders, while the Upper Denkeras offered to assist the Adansis. The active co-operation of these tribes was only stopped by the despatch of officers of the Colony to their respective Kings, but several Ashanti traders had already been plundered and seized by the Akims.

On 23rd April the Adansi army, with a strong force from Dadiassi, advanced against the Bekwehs, and reached their outposts at the village of Ahiman, shortly after noon. The outposts fell back upon a detachment about one thousand strong at Pampassu, which then advanced and engaged the Adansis at Ahiman till nightfall, when both sides returned to their camps. During the night the Bekwehs were reinforced from Begroassi, and on the 25th they renewed the conflict at Ahiman, but unsuccessfully, the Adansis holding the place after fighting all day, while next day they made a forward movement and drove the Bekwehs back beyond Pampassu, which was burned. The greater part of the Bekweh army had taken no part in these affairs, it having been engaged in watching the main Dadiassi army, which had taken up a position threatening the Bekweh left flank. On the 13th April and 14th May other battles took place, in which the Adansis and Dadiassis captured and destroyed the camp at Begroassi, and threatened the town of Amoafu.

From some unknown cause the Kumassi forces had all been withdrawn from the Bekweh camp, and the Bekwehs had, so far, fought single-handed; but now the chiefs of the capital and the northern provinces, alarmed at the success of the Adansis, sent messengers and state officials to Attobiassi, the principal town of Dadiassi, to induce the chief to withdraw from his alliance with Adansi. Partly by threats of invasion and partly by bribes, they succeeded in persuading him to suspend hostilities, and join with them in electing a King at Kumassi; and they then sent a message to the King of Adansi that he must stop the advance of his army, and submit his dispute with Bekweh to them for arbitration. At the same time, Amuofa, chief of Dadiassi, sent to inform his ally of the step he had taken, and to advise him to go to Kumassi and take part in the forthcoming election, as a large Kumassi army had joined the Bekwehs The King of Adansi rejected this advice, and being defeated in a general engagement, began to take measures for retiring into the Protectorate. On 13th June he abandoned Fomana, and retired to within six miles o the Prah, which he crossed three days later with som(3,500 followers. In all, 12,411 Adansis came into th(Protectorate, and, as the Governor had directed, wer· distributed in the neighbourhood, the King, with his imme diate following, filling up the Assin villages on the Pra road, chief Kotiko, with about 600 men, going to Uppe Denkera, and chief Affakwa, with about 7,000 mer, women, and children, settling in Akim. The Bekweh destroyed Fomana and all the Adansi villages, and the turned their attention to the Inkwantas, whom they drov out of their country; after which they sent messenge: to the Governor to report what had taken place, and to sa that the road from Prahsu to Kumassi would now be ke t open by them. They also announced that the chiefs f Ashanti were about to assemble at Kumassi to place a Kir on the stool.

The German Government having in 1885 declared a Protectorate over Togoland and Beh Beach, and thus made their territory conterminous with the colonial frontier at Aflao, a Commission was appointed to delimit the boundary, and in 1886 it was laid out for a distance of two and a half miles inland, beyond which it was not defined. The German Government was therefore at liberty to acquire territory beyond that limit, and in March, 1886, it announced that it had taken over the districts of Agotine, Toveh, and Keveh, which lay behind the sea-board of the Colony; whereupon the British Government, to protect itself from any further extension of German territory in that direction, annexed the Krikor country, which lies north and east of the Kittah lagoon. In the same year, and for the same reason, the Kings of Krepi 'and Akwamu were informed that, as their territories had been included in the Danish Protectorate when the Danes ceded their possessions, they must now be considered to be under British protection.

The western boundary of the Colony was not yet defined. In a convention between the Dutch and French it had been fixed at a point three miles to the west of Newtown, but the convention had never been ratified, and in 1880 the Colonial Government requested that the matter might be settled. A joint Commission, appointed in 1882, met in November, 1883, and it was decided that the boundary line should separate the districts of Western Appollonia and Awuin, which were under British protection, from the kingdom of Kinjabo, which was under French protection; but the limits of these states were not defined, and the Commission separated without any boundary having been actually traced.

CHAPTER XXX.

1886—1888.

Rival candidates for the stool of Ashanti—Raids made on Ashanti from the Protectorate—Effect of the unsettled condition of affairs upon British trade—War between Bekweh and Kokofu—The Colony intervenes to restore peace—Prempeh placed on the stool—Murder of Mr. Dalrymple in Tavievi—Expedition to Tavievi—Rebellion and defeat of Kokofu.

IN August, 1886, the Government of the Gold Coast at last determined to send an officer to Kumassi, in accordance with the request delivered on October 16th, 1884, by the queen-mother's messengers, who were still at Accra awaiting a reply; but, instead of sending a European officer, as had been asked, they entrusted the mission to a native interpreter, named Badger. Mr. Badger, who took with him a letter from the Governor to the queen-mother and chiefs of Ashanti, asking if they still wished a white officer to be sent, and promising, if they did, to send one within two months, visited Bekweh, Kokofu, and Kumassi, and was well received. He learned that there were two candidates for election to the royal stool of Ashanti, namely, Prince Prempeh, brother of the late Kwaku Dua II., and Prince Archiriboanda, son of the Princess Yah Freh,* and that consequently the nation was divided into two parties. The Kumassi chiefs had referred the decision to the chief of Bekweh, but he, declaring that it must be settled by the majority, had sent to the different

* See Genealogical Table.

provincial chiefs to ascertain their wishes, and he now said that as soon as a selection had been made he would send to the Governor for a white officer to be present at the installation. Mr. Badger reported that the destruction of Adansi was so complete that no house remained in which a traveller could find shelter for the night.

Nothing more was heard from Ashanti till December 17th, when a message was received from the chief of Bekweh to the effect that a decision as to the person to be chosen as King of Ashanti had been delayed by Atjiempon, who was threatening to attack Bekweh. This chief, who was the same who had been released by Colonel Harley in 1872, was, it appeared, a supporter of Archiriboanda, while the chief of Bekweh and the Kumassi party supported Prince Prempeh. What, however, concerned the Colony more nearly was that the Adansi and Inkwanta refugees, just as ought to have been foreseen, were making raids from the Protectorate into Ashanti, and had induced the people of Upper Denkera to join them. A party had recently formed an ambuscade on the main road, a mile or two north of the Prah, and had attacked some Bekweh traders who were returning from Cape Coast, killing three, wounding four, and carrying off all the goods. The chief of Bekweh very naturally complained of the Protectorate being used as a base for such forays, and asked that the Denkeras, and the Adansi and Inkwanta refugees, might be restrained, otherwise the result might be serious. Inspector Dudley, who had lately returned from England, was accordingly sent to Upper Denkera, and an arrangement was made by which, every tenth day, traders were to be escorted by a guard of Houssa Constabulary from Prahsu to the frontier of Bekweh, where they were to be received by an escort of Bekwehs, who would transfer to the safe custody of the Houssas such Ashanti traders as wished to go down. This was the best arrangement that could be made under the circumstances, but the necessity for it would never have arisen had the Adansis been interned in parts of the Colony remote from the frontier, when they were driven across the Prah. During the last week in December, however, and before the plan had been put in force, an Adansi chief, named Karsang, made an incursion from Upper Denkera at the head of a considerable force, with which he destroyed two Bekweh villages, killed several men, and carried off about one hundred prisoners of both sexes. A few days later, a party of Ashanti traders were attacked on the road between Bekweh and Prahsu, and about the same time it was discovered that the Adansis in Akim had entered into a league with the chief of Akim Swaidru to make war upon Bekweh. Even now the Government did not seem to see that the only way to put a stop to these occurrences was to remove the Adansis and Inkwantas from the frontier, and it was not until the necessity of this course was urged by Inspector Dudley that it seems to have been thought of; but even then it was not acted upon. Inspector Dudley found that the whole of the people of Upper Denkera were implicated in the raids, and that the King of Lower Denkera had accepted bribes to assist the Adansis against Bekweh. He was unable to recover any of the Bekwehs who had been carried off by Karsang, most of them having been slaughtered, and the survivors, a few women and children, sold as slaves in Sefwhi to any chance purchaser.

The unsettled condition of affairs that had so long prevailed in Ashanti, and the persistent attacks made on native traders, were naturally detrimental to commerce; and the imports of British cottons, which in 1884 amounted to £591,000, fell in 1885 to £388,000, and in 1886 to £318,000 The revenue of the Colony had been fully maintained during this period, but this was due to the large duties levied on spirits, which, being chiefly of foreign manufacture, and the trade in them in foreign hands, benefited in no way British manufactures. In February, 1887, this serious diminution was brought to the notice of the Secretary of State for the Colonies by the Manchester Chamber of Commerce, which complained of the apathy shown by the Gold Coast Government in regard to the commercial interests of the Colony. More especially it pointed out the neglect shown to the affairs of the interior, calling attention to the fact that a letter from the Secretary of State to the Governor, written in July, 1885, asking for information as to the condition of Ashanti, and on the future policy of the Government in regard to that country, was not acknowledged and answered till April, 1886, and even then no opinion as to the future policy was given.

The Chamber of Commerce was undoubtedly right in its contention that the affairs of the interior had been neglected, and that the decrease in the value of British imports was due to that neglect. The great falling-off was in 1885. Kwaku Dua II. had, as we have seen, died in June, 1884, and, on the 16th of October of that year, Mr. Young had received messengers from the queen-mother asking that a European officer might be sent to Kumassi, to meet the provincial chiefs, and assist at the election of a new King. As we have also seen, no officer was sent up till August, 1886, and then only a native; and, at the commencement of the year 1887, the election of a King seemed as far off as ever. Had a European officer been sent up when first asked for, a King would have been elected; the presence of an officer of the Government at his installation would have given him a prestige which would have enabled him to reduce to obedience any provincial chiefs who might show a disposition to be unruly, and peace and quietness would have been restored to the country.

In January, 1887, no settlement having been arrived at, the ill-feeling between the rival factions in Ashanti broke out into hostilities. The supporters of Prempeh were the Kumassi chiefs, the chief of Bekweh, and the King of Djuabin, while Archiriboanda was supported by the chiefs of Kokofu, Mampon, and Nsuta. The leader, and most active member of the latter party, was Atjiempon, whose support was said to have been purchased by the promise that he should not be asked to restore 3,200 ounces of gold that had been entrusted to him for safe keeping by the late King Mensa, payment of which the Princess Yah Kia had demanded on behalf of her son Prempeh. Towards the end of January the chiefs of the two factions had a conference at Siwah, at which it was agreed that the candidate who secured the most votes should be elected; but as the various representatives were returning to their homes, the chief of Bekweh attacked and killed Atjiempon and the head linguist of the chief of Kokofu. The Bekwehs then attacked the Kokofus near the town of Kokofu, which they burned, driving their opponents back to the village of Tupraitu.

About the same time the Bekwehs were engaged on their south-western frontier with the Inkwanta refugees, who, aided by the Denkeras, openly invaded Bekweh territory in large bodies; and, Inspector Dudley having returned to Elmina from Upper Denkera in February, Captain Lonsdale, the Commissioner of Native Affairs, was sent there to restrain them. He found that the Denkeras had assisted the Inkwantas with men and guns, that the Denkera chiefs had received gold and pawns in return for the assistance lent, and that some Kumassi messengers had been put to death in the village of Akwabosu,* in the Protectorate. He also learned that a battle had taken place on the 27th of January, in which the Bekwehs had been worsted, and, like Inspector Dudley, he recommended that Karsang and the other Adansi chiefs should, with their followers, be removed to the coast, or to any district where they could not foment border troubles. Mr. Griffith had by this time proceeded to England, and Colonel F. B. P. White, who had been appointed Acting Governor of the Colony, at once made arrangements for the removal of the Adansis, who were finally located near Insabang, in the Aguna district.

In April the Kokofus took the field to revenge the death of Atjiempon, and, on the 26th of the month, a battle was fought at Ehuren, near the town of Bekweh, in which the Kokofus were completely routed. Six days later the Bekwehs were equally successful in the south-west, and repulsed an inroad of the Inkwantas, whom they drew into

---

* Akwabo-su—" Welcome water."

an ambush, and caused to lose some three hundred men. After this event, Captain Lonsdale, who was still in Upper Denkera, arrested the King and ex-King of Inkwanta, who were chiefly responsible for the raid, and had them removed to the coast. On the 14th of May a second battle took place between the Bekwehs and Kokofus, in which the former were driven from the camps they had formed on the main road, and forced to retire towards Kumassi; but being joined by the Ashanti general, Awua, chief of Bantama, with a large number of men from the south-west of Kumassi, were able to take the field again almost at once. The Prempeh party had at this time in their hands the opposing claimant, Archiriboanda, but dared not kill him because he was of the royal blood.

So far the struggle for the supremacy had been confined to Bekweh and Kokofu, neither Kumassi or Djuabin on the one side, nor Mampon or Nsuta on the other, having taken any part in it. The reinforcement of the Bekwehs by the chief of Bantama again equalised the opposing forces, and as each side appeared to be doubtful of the result of a further appeal to arms, Colonel White determined to make an effort to put an end to the hostilities and to establish a central government for the country. He accordingly instructed Captain Lonsdale to proceed to Ashanti, and on August 10th that officer, who had been joined by a party of Houssa Constabulary under Assistant-Inspector Barnett, crossed the Prah.

Between the Prah and the village of Adjaman, three days' journey from the river, no sign of human life was seen, every town and village having been completely destroyed, and the very trees growing in them cut down. The chief of Kokofu was encamped at Adjaman with some 6,000 Kokofus, Dadiassis, and Adansis, and he endeavoured to persuade the embassy to stop there, but Captain Lonsdale continued his journey to Adwabin, four hours south of Kumassi, passing numbers of dead, and several deserted villages, on the road. The Bekwehs, like the Kokofus, were encamped and ready to recommence hostilities. Some skirmishing had taken place on the 8th of

August, and a general engagement had been expected on the 15th, but this Captain Lonsdale was able to prevent, as well as an attempt of the Bekweh party on the 18th to march through the Kokofu camp at Adjaman on the pretence of coming to see him, which would certainly have caused a conflict. The first thing to be done towards the restoration of peace was to persuade the hostile chiefs to return to their own districts, and on 24th August Captain Lonsdale visited the Bekweh camp and requested Awua, and some Kumassi chiefs who were with him, to return to their homes, as he could not discuss Ashanti questions in the Bekweh camp. They objected to do this, but finally promised compliance if Captain Lonsdale would dethrone the chief of Kokofu, whom they declared to be the cause of there being no King of Ashanti; and this proposition being refused, the meeting terminated without anything being settled. Next day, however, Awua and the Kumassis left the Bekweh camp for the capital, and shortly afterwards the Kokofus were persuaded to withdraw from their camps; which disbandment restored confidence to such an extent that the women and children at once commenced returning to and rebuilding their villages.

On 28th August, having heard that the opposing factions in the districts to the north of Kumassi, who had hitherto remained quiet, had now taken the field, Captain Lonsdale sent Mr. Barnett to persuade them to disperse and return to their homes. That officer found Mampon and Nsuta arrayed against the people of the Offin River district (Offinsu), but managed affairs so well that when he returned to Adwabin on the 18th of October, he was able to report that the armies had been disbanded and peace restored. In the interim, after overcoming great difficulties, Captain Lonsdale had succeeded in making the chiefs of Bekweh and Kokofu "drink fetish" together by proxy, in the persons of their respective princesses, and swear to keep the peace. It afterwards became known that, immediately after this ceremony, the chief of Kokofu put to death all the Bekweh prisoners who were in his hands; but, fortunately, this murder did not transpire at the time, or the war would at once have been renewed.

Captain Lonsdale remained at Adwabin till the 18th of November, when, as everything was quiet, and the different chiefs were preparing for the forthcoming election, he returned to the coast to confer with the Governor as to the policy to be followed in the future, leaving Mr. Barnett in charge at Adwabin. On arriving at Accra, however, his health broke down, and in January he had to be invalided to England, where he died on the 28th of the month, immediately after his arrival at Liverpool.

Shortly after Captain Lonsdale's departure from Adwabin, Archiriboanda escaped from the custody of the Prempeh party and fled to the chief of Kokofu, who then ordered all his people to join him in the camp he had formerly occupied. Next, the chief of Kokofu "drank fetish" with the King of Inkwanta, who, without any intimation to Captain Lonsdale or Mr. Barnett, had been sent by Mr. Griffith to reoccupy with his people the territory from which he had been driven by the Bekwehs. As a police sergeant had been sent with the King, this resumption of territory by the Inkwantas was considered by the surrounding tribes to have the official sanction of the Government. By great exertions Mr. Barnett succeeded in preventing the Inkwantas from taking any active part with the Kokofus, whose chief was now the only obstacle to a settlement. He had gathered all the unruly members of the different Ashanti tribes into his camp, every criminal being sure of an asylum with him, and he had between six and seven thousand men under arms, with whom he threatened to renew the war with Bekweh.

On the 18th of January, 1888, all the representatives of the Ashanti tribes, except Kokofu, sent to Mr. Barnett to know when steps would be taken to place a King on the stool; saying that nearly three months had elapsed since they "drank fetish" together, and nothing had yet been done. Mr. Barnett had been waiting for the return of Captain Lonsdale, who was the person charged with this business, but when on the 23rd of January he learned that that officer had been invalided to England, he sent to urge the chiefs not to delay. The election of a King, however, was still hindered by the supporters of Archiriboanda, in the hope that time would give them some advantage over the other party, for their candidate had recently greatly damaged his cause, while in the Kokofu camp, by his notorious intrigues with married women. It was, however, acknowledged by all that Prempeh, as the brother of the late King, was the legitimate successor, the order of succession being from brother to brother, and then to sister's son.

At last, in March, Awua of Bantama and the Kumassi chiefs, impatient of further delay, placed Prempeh on the Odum stool, a ceremony of nomination preliminary to being placed on the golden stool; and the chief of Mampon, afraid that the King would be installed without any European officer being present, sent to ask Mr. Barnett to come at once to Kumassi, which he did, arriving there on March 15th. On the 17th he sent to all the provincial chiefs, asking them to come to Kumassi and hold the election on the 27th, which was the only day suitable for an occasion of such importance before the Great Adae* of April 27th; and all promised to attend, except the King of Inkwanta, who declared that he was now no longer subject to Ashanti, but to the British Government. Everything was now prepared for the ceremony, but on the 26th of March the chief of Kokofu sent to say he could not come to Kumassi unless pardon was promised to all who had committed the crimes of rebellion, murder, rape, adultery, and theft, a stipulation which showed clearly of what kind of men his following was composed. After a long conference, these terms were agreed to, and the Princess Ya Kia, with Awua, chief of Bantama, and Asafu Buaki, principal chief of Kumassi, agreed to meet the chief of Kokofu outside Kumassi, and "drink fetish" with him to that effect. The Kokofu messengers thereupon departed, apparently highly pleased, but in the afternoon others returned together with messengers from Mampon, saying that their respective chiefs could not arrive in time, and asking that the election might be postponed till the next Great Adae

---

* The Ashantis usually reckon time by periods of forty or forty-two days, every fortieth or forty-second day being a festival, termed the Great Adae; eighteen or twenty days after which is the Little Adae.

As Mr. Barnett had just received orders from the Governor to leave Ashanti on the 10th of April, whether a King was elected or not, this was impossible, and Prempeh was placed on the stool of Ashanti at midnight on the 26th of March, without the chiefs of Mampon and Kokofu being present; but representatives of these chiefs, who were present, said they had no objection to offer to Prempeh, and that there would be no further trouble. Thus, at last, through the exertions of Captain Lonsdale and Mr. Barnett, who had shown great tact and unwearied patience, there was a prospect of a termination being put to the state of anarchy that had prevailed in Ashanti since 1885. The new King, on being placed on the stool, took the name of Kwaku Dua III.

In April, 1887, a quarrel broke out between Kwabina Archiri, chief of Wanki, in Eastern Akim, and Attah Fua, King of Western Akim, the former claiming the ferry over the River Birrim* at Insuaim,† and also that town itself, which was the capital of Western Akim; and affairs looked so threatening that Assistant-Inspector Brennan was sent with a party of Houssa Constabulary to the scene of disturbance. In the same month, Kwadjo Deh, King of Krepi, sent down to inform the Governor that the Tavievis, between whom and the Krepis there had been a long-standing quarrel, had attacked the Krepi town of Zavi, and killed seventeen of its inhabitants. The King of Krepi likewise announced that he was about to attack the Tavievis, and as such a step would probably entail very serious consequences, Assistant-Inspector Dalrymple was sent with sixty-three men of the Houssa Constabulary to restrain the King, and settle the quarrel peaceably. On arriving at Zavi he found Kwadjo Deh with about 3,000 men under arms, and preparing to attack the Tavievis, who were ambuscading the roads, and murdering all passers-by indiscriminately. It was with great difficulty that Mr. Dalrymple stopped the projected attack, for the Krepis were greatly excited by the shocking atrocities committed by the Tavievis, who, after capturing a number of Krepi children, had pounded some to death in the wooden mortars used for pounding yams, had dashed out the

* Birrim—Dark, or black.   † Water-place.

brains of others against trees, and had lopped off the hands of the remainder, whom they had then sent back to their friends. The native war, however, was prevented, and then, in accordance with later instructions received from the Governor, Mr. Dalrymple went to Tavievi, to arrest and bring to trial those who had been most prominent in the attack on Zavi, and in the committal of the atrocities. Mr. Bennett, the District Commissioner of the Volta district, accompanied the party.

Mr. Dalrymple discovered that Belli Kwabina, the chief of Tavievi, had himself been present with several of his captains at the attack of Zavi, and he accordingly told them that they would have to accompany him to Accra. To this they made no open objection, but they secretly instructed their men to form an ambuscade on the road, and to fire upon the Constabulary if they should be in their custody. At a meeting on the 11th of May, Mr. Dalrymple formally arrested Belli Kwabina and his captains, and, after having sent on Mr. Bennett in advance with the carriers and baggage, left Tavievi for Ho at two p.m. with his men and his prisoners. About two miles out of Tavievi the Houssas discovered the ambush that had been prepared, and warned their officer, but he, thinking that the natives would not dare to fire ordered his men to push on. Suddenly a man sprang out of the bush, and pointed his musket at Mr. Dalrymple, who waved him off; but Belli Kwabina called to him to shoot, saying the white man was taking him away, and he thereupon fired killing Mr. Dalrymple on the spot. A general discharge of musketry from the ambushed natives then followed, and the Houssas, who behaved exceedingly well, fought their way through them to Ho, carrying with them the body of the officer, and losing six of their number killed, and two wounded. Belli Kwabina escaped during the confusion, but the Houssas killed ten of their prisoners who endeavoured to break away, and brought five with them to Ho.

The death of Mr. Dalrymple created a profound sensation on the Gold Coast, for never before, as far as was known, had a European been killed except in open warfare; and the life of a white man had always been respected, even in the most troublous times. Unless this immunity was now to be at an end, a severe example would have to be made of the Tavievis, and, with this object, Assistant-Inspector Brennan was ordered to march from Insuaim, with the Constabulary he had with him there, to Kpong, on the Volta; to which place Assistant-Inspector Akers was directed to proceed without delay from Kittah, with all the Houssas that could be spared from that district.

The Tavievi district was a difficult one to operate in, it being an oval-shaped valley, about eight miles long from north to south, and two miles broad at its widest part, shut in on the east and west by densely forested mountain ranges, 2,000 feet high. Ho, the town from which an attacking force would advance, was situated about a mile and a half to the east of the eastern range of mountains, and from it two roads led into the Tavievi valley, one, which was very steep and difficult, over the mountains, and the other through a gorge at the southern end of the valley, near which the town of Zavi was situated. There were known to be other paths by which the valley could be reached, but their exact position was kept secret by the Tavievis, who only used them in time of war, to take an enemy unexpectedly in flank or rear. The chief of Ho was friendly. He had, indeed, on the 11th of May, when the news of Mr. Dalrymple's death reached him, called out his men to go and attack the Tavievis, but had been persuaded by Mr. Bennett to await instructions from the Government.

On the 20th of May Assistant-Inspector Akers, with one hundred and twenty-two Houssas from Kittah, arrived at Kpong, where he found twenty-seven more who had been sent up from Accra, and, Assistant-Inspector Brennan not having arrived, he pushed on to Ho, where he was joined by the men who had been with Mr. Dalrymple. In the meantime, in consequence of the alarming reports sent from Insuaim by Mr. Brennan, who declared that war was imminent and that he required immediate reinforcement, orders were sent to Mr. Akers on 24th of May to leave fifty Houssas at Ho with Mr. Bennett, and proceed with the remainder to Insuaim, viâ Accra, it being intended to defer the punishment of the Tavievis until Akim had been pacified. Before these orders reached him, however, Mr. Akers marched out of Ho at one in the morning of the 29th of May, crossed the summit of the mountains at three a.m., and arrived within two miles of the town of Tavievi before his approach was discovered. At this point his advance guard was fired upon, and a little further on fire was again opened from the bush, and a Houssa killed; after which the Tavievis kept up a desultory fire till the town was taken, but without inflicting any further loss. The supplies and the remainder of the Constabulary were now ordered up from Ho, and with them came 1,500 men under the chief of Ho, who were set to work to clear the bush surrounding the town.

On the night of the 31st Mr. Akers received the order to return to Accra, so, leaving the Krepis from Ho and fifty Houssas to hold Tavievi, he quitted that place on the morning of the 2nd of June, and, proceeding by forced marches, reached Aburi, which was in telegraphic communication with Accra, on the 5th. By this time it was known that there was no probability of an outbreak at Insuaim, where the state of affairs had been much exaggerated, and the force with Mr. Akers was consequently halted at Aburi, and was still there when, on the night of the 10th of June, news was received that the Krepis and Houssas left in Tavievi had been driven out of the valley. The return march was commenced next day, and on the 17th Mr. Akers reached Zavi, where he found the party he had left in charge. It appeared that the chief of Ho, instead of remaining quietly in Tavievi and acting only on the defensive, as he had been told to do, had marched out on the 6th of June and attacked the Tavievis in the mountains. Almost at the outset of the engagement ten of his men were killed and several wounded, whereupon a panic seized the remainder, and they fled in haste through Tavievi to Zavi, sweeping along with them a few of the Houssas, all of whom had remained quietly in the town. Mr. Bennett, upon hearing of this, ordered the remainder of the Houssas to evacuate the valley and retreat to Ho, with the intention of retiring still further to Kpong, and they had reached Zavi in compliance with these orders when they were stopped by Mr. Akers. On the morning of the 18th the force left Zavi, advancing by the road which led up the Tavievi valley; and a camp which the enemy had formed on the hillside above the town was attacked and carried, with a loss to the natives of about one hundred killed and wounded, and all their state umbrellas and paraphernalia. From this date the Tavievis were harassed daily by parties sent up and down the valley, till on the 23rd they hoisted a white flag on a hill, and sued for peace. They surrendered Belli Kwabina and their principal war-chief, Bochukeri, and a fine of £300 was imposed on the tribe.

In Ashanti it was soon evident that the chief of Kokofu did not intend to recognise Kwaku Dua III. as King, for before Mr. Barnett had crossed the Prah on his way back to the coast, he commenced raiding the villages and plantations of all those who would not take an oath to serve him, and blocked the main road by encamping at Adjaman. The result of this conduct was a renewal, in June, of the war between Bekweh and Kokofu, in which the Kokofus lost the first battle; but being strongly reinforced by Dadiassis and Adansis from across the border, completely defeated the Bekwehs in a second engagement. A Kumassi detachment under Awua of Bantama came up too late to assist the Bekwehs in this battle, but had a skirmish with the Kokofus and retired to Akkassi, in which village Awua was treacherously seized by night, and conveyed to the chief of Kokofu, who at once put him to death. Kwaku Dua III. sent to report these events to the Governor, adding that the Kokofus were advancing on Kumassi, and asking that they might be ordered to keep the peace; but before his messenger reached Accra he was compelled to take action, and, with a combined force of Kumassis, Bekwehs, and Djuabins, completely routed the Kokofus in a two days' battle, on the 26th and 27th of June, at Agemmamu.

The Kokofus, and a number of Adansis who had been assisting them, fled across the Prah on July 1st, and orders were sent to them to settle near Insabang; but as no one was at hand to enforce these orders the fugitives remained where they were, and the chief of Kokofu, who had with him Archiriboanda and some 4,000 armed men, at Kotoko, near the Prah, commenced making incursions along the main road to the north of that river. On the 9th of August a deputation from Kwaku Dua arrived at Accra to complain of this, and Assistant-Inspector Akers was then sent to effect the removal of the refugees. He found that Attah Fua, the King of Western Akim, had suppressed the orders that should have been given to the Kokofus, and, in direct opposition to the wishes of the Government, was endeavouring to induce them to settle in the neighbourhood of Insuaim. The women and children of the Kokofus, to the number of some 10,000, were distributed in the villages between Insuaim and Essikuma, while the chief and the men were at Kotoko. Great difficulties were experienced in effecting their removal, for the fugitives were desirous of remaining near the frontier in order to be able to take immediate advantage of any favourable occasion for renewing the struggle with Ashanti, and the King of Western Akim threw every obstacle in the way; but by the exercise of great firmness Mr. Akers at last succeeded in removing them to the borders of Aguna.

The overthrow of Kokofu removed the last discordant element from Ashanti, and peace being restored, the country rapidly regained its prosperity. This happy result can only be attributed to the prestige which the presence of a European officer lent to the election of Kwaku Dua, for in the eyes of the chiefs of the different Ashanti tribes it amounted to an acknowledgment that he would have the support of the Government. But for this the chief of Kokofu would probably have been able, by bribery or other insidious means, to engage the Mampons and Nsutas to act with him in support of Archiriboanda; in which case the country would have been torn to pieces in a protracted struggle for the supremacy, and thousands would have suffered.

THE END.

CHARLES DICKENS AND EVANS, CRYSTAL PALACE PRESS.

www.ingramcontent.com/pod-product-compliance
Lightning Source LLC
Chambersburg PA
CBHW022117290426
44112CB00008B/702